THE FENIAN IDEAL AND IRISH NATIONALISM, 1882–1916

This book analyses Fenian influences on Irish nationalism between the Phoenix Park murders of 1882 and the Easter Rising of 1916. It challenges the convention that Irish separatist politics before the First World War were marginal and irrelevant, showing instead that clear boundaries between home rule and separatist nationalism did not exist. Kelly examines how leading home rule M.P.s argued that Parnellism was Fenianism by other means, and how Fenian politics were influenced by Irish cultural nationalism, which reinforced separatist orthodoxies, serving to clarify the ideological distance between Fenians and home rulers. The book discusses how early Sinn Féin gave voice to these new orthodoxies, and concludes by examining the ideological complexities of the Irish Volunteers, and exploring Irish politics between 1914 and 1916.

M. J. KELLY is Lecturer in Modern History at the University of Southampton.

Irish Historical Monograph Series

ISSN 1740–1097

Series editors
Marie Therese Flanagan, Queen's University, Belfast
Eunan O'Halphin, Trinity College, Dublin
David Hayton, Queen's University, Belfast

Previous titles in this series

I. Ruling Ireland 1685–1742: Politics, Politicians and Parties, *D. W. Hayton*, 2004

II. Lord Broghill and the Cromwellian Union with Ireland and Scotland, *Patrick Little*, 2004

III. Irish Migrants in New Zealand, 1840–1937: 'The Desired Haven', *Angela McCarthy*, 2005

The Fenian Ideal
and Irish Nationalism,
1882–1916

M. J. Kelly

THE BOYDELL PRESS

First published 2006
The Boydell Press, Woodbridge

Transferred to digital printing

Reprinted in paperback 2008

Hardback ISBN 978-1-84383-204-1
Paperback ISBN 978-1-84383-445-8

The Boydell Press is an imprint of Boydell & Brewer Ltd
PO Box 9, Woodbridge, Suffolk IP12 3DF, UK
and of Boydell & Brewer Inc.
668 Mt Hope Avenue, Rochester, NY 14620, USA
website: www.boydellandbrewer.com

A CiP catalogue record for this book is available
from the British Library

This publication is printed on acid-free paper

When I was a boy public opinion in Ireland was contemptible. The country was dead. The Fenians breathed the breath of life into it. Fenianism was crushed and the country went to the D. again. And Fenianism though morally changed saved the country again. The country is going to the D. now. Can Fenianism save it again? That is the question we have to face. We are again going the round of the circle.

R. Barry O'Brien to John O'Leary, 31 March 1891

Mr Parnell and his political friends have substituted constitutional agitation for lawless and revolutionary agitation. He has only succeeded in this by persuading his countrymen that his actions will result in success. If he be doomed to failure, the Fenians will once more gain the upper hand in Ireland.

Letter to *The Times* from Henry Labouchere M.P., 26 December 1885

Committees of insurrection sat constantly in the secret societies, and in the offices of the republican journals. We are ignorant of what passed there. They were probably rather engaged in observation than in action. The limited power of a conspirator, who has but scanty numbers at his disposal, only possesses influence as it ministers to a sentiment generally entertained, or a pre-existing passion.

Alphonse de Lamartine, *Histoire de la révolution de 1848*

To my parents

Contents

Acknowledgements

My principal debt of thanks is owed to Professor Roy Foster. He taught me Irish history as an undergraduate and supervised the D.Phil. thesis this book is based upon. Without his unstinting support, encouragement, and friendship this project would not have reached completion. Dr Martin Conway and Dr Simon Skinner were brilliant undergraduate tutors at Balliol and since then they've supplied me with a great deal of patient advice. I hope this book goes some way towards repaying the tremendous debt I owe all three.

I was the beneficiary of excellent history teaching at school and it is a pleasure to be able to recognise in print Jean Mace of St Luke's High School, Exeter and Jeremy Cushing of Exeter College, Exeter.

Professor Vincent Comerford of the National University of Ireland, Maynooth and Dr Senia Pašeta of St Hugh's College, Oxford were kind examiners of my thesis. I am grateful to the general editors of this series, especially Professor David Hayton of Queen's University, Belfast, for the particular interest he took in the book and the close reading he made of the text at a late stage. Few authors can have benefited from such professorial attention to their work – few, perhaps, so needed it. Peter Sowden at Boydell & Brewer has been an encouraging and patient editor. Sarah Pearsall smoothly took the book through to production, and Sarah Cahill did an excellent job as copy-editor. Any mistakes are my own.

In these straitened times I have been very lucky. I would like to acknowledge the A.H.R.B. for awarding me a Postgraduate Studentship and the British Academy for electing me to a Postdoctoral Research Fellowship.

Thanks to the librarians and staff of the Bodleian Library and the History Faculty Library in Oxford, the British Library and its newspaper archive at Colindale in London, the National Archive at Kew, the National Library and National Archive in Dublin, the archives of University College, Dublin, the Cork Archives Institute, and the Central Library, Belfast.

Versions of Chapters 1 and 3 have been previously published, respectively in the *Historical Journal* and *Irish Historical Studies*. Parts of Chapters 5 and 6 have appeared in essays written for volumes edited by D. George Boyce and Alan O'Day. I have benefited from the advice of the editors and readers of all. Further details can be found in the bibliography.

I was Lecturer in Modern History at Lady Margaret Hall, Oxford for a year after finishing my D.Phil. and Dr Clive Holmes, whose energy and enthusiasm are the stuff of legend, was a wonderful senior colleague. The Principal and Fellows of Hertford College, Oxford have made me feel welcome first as

Lecturer in Modern British History and more recently as a British Academy Postdoctoral Research Fellow. Dr Toby Barnard, Dr Geoffrey Ellis, and Dr Christopher Tyerman have been great to work with, sustaining those prized Oxford traditions of scholarship and conviviality.

I have enjoyed endlessly stimulating conversations on all things historical (as well as trips to the gym) with William Whyte. James McConnel has been an excellent friend in Irish history and Ian McBride has provided a great deal of wise advice. Sarah Best did much more than help me tidy up a messy D.Phil. text; Richard Bourke commented on parts of Chapter 5. Sarah Foster made research trips to Dublin fun and I am indebted to her for her unfailing hospitality. David Anderson generously provided some leads early on in my research. More generally, it is hard to exaggerate how privileged I feel to have been part of the Oxford Irish history gang, which in my time has been very lively, variously including Ciara Boylan, Jack Dunn, Ultán Gillen, Peter Leppard, Richard Mann, Marc Mulholland, Ben Novick, Tadgh O'Sullivan, Senia Pašeta, Rory Rapple, Ian Sheehy, Robert Tobin, Fran Yeoman, and others. Genuine and lasting friendships have emerged from our shared intellectual interests and we owe Roy a great deal for helping to nurture this vocational fraternity.

Love to all my friends and family, to Granny, Nana and Arfer, Mum and Tom, Dad and Rita, and to my sisters and brother, Hannah, Laura, and Sam. My greatest debt is recorded in the dedication.

M.K.
November 2005

Abbreviations

A.F.I.L.	All-for-Ireland League
A.O.H.	Ancient Order of Hibernians
C.B.S.	Crime Branch Special Papers
C.L.S.	Celtic Literary Society
C.O.	Colonial Office Papers
C.S.O.R.P.	Chief Secretary's Office Registered Papers
D.E.T.	*Dublin Evening Telegraph*
D.I.	*Irish Daily Independent*
D.M.P.	Dublin Metropolitan Police
D.P.B.	William O'Brien and Desmond Ryan (eds), *Devoy's Postbag*, (Dublin, 1948), i & ii
D.U.R.	*Dublin University Review*
F.J.	*Freeman's Journal*
G.A.A.	Gaelic Athletic Association
I.F.	*Irish Freedom*
I.H.S.	*Irish Historical Studies*
I.N.A.	Irish National Association
I.N.F.	Irish National Federation
I.N.L.	Irish National League
I.P.P.	Irish parliamentary party
I.R.	*Irish Republic*
I.R.B.	Irish Republican Brotherhood
I.T.C.	Irish Transvaal Committee
I.V.	Irish Volunteers
N.A.	National Archives, Dublin
N.L.I.	National Library of Ireland
P.R.O.	Public Record Office, London
R.I.C.	Royal Irish Constabulary
S.F.	Sinn Féin
S.V.V.	*Shan Van Vocht*
T.N.A. (P.R.O.)	The Public Record Office at the National Archives, Kew
U.I.	*United Irishman*
U.I.L.	United Irish League
W.F.	*Weekly Freeman*
W.I.	[*Irish*] *Weekly Independent*
Y.I.L.	Young Ireland League
Y.I.S.	Young Ireland Society

Introduction

Mr Casey's tears

I

Fenianism was the name, sometimes celebrated sometimes excoriated, given to the Irish revolutionary and republican movement active in Ireland and Britain from the late 1850s through to the First World War. It had sister organisations in the U.S.A. and elsewhere, the most important being the Irish-American Clan na Gael which bankrolled the organisation. Fenianism was organised through the Irish Republican Brotherhood (I.R.B.), under the leadership of the Supreme Council, and hierarchically structured around circles under the direction of a series of county centres. The Supreme Council consisted of a representative of each of the four provinces of Ireland, as well as one each from England, Wales, and Scotland. At various points in its history, provision was made for further nominees to join its highest deliberations. The membership was bound by an oath, committing it to secrecy and a readiness to fight to achieve an Irish republic when so instructed. Fenian orthodoxy demanded that Irish independence be achieved before attempts were made to address other Irish problems because only an independent Irish government could do so legitimately. The I.R.B. was also a secular organisation, strongly opposed to 'priests in politics', believing the clergy's role should be confined to the spiritual realm. The catholic hierarchy in Ireland responded in kind, condemning Fenianism and threatening known members with excommunication. From the mid-1860s Cardinal Cullen sought a papal denunciation of the movement by name, which he got in 1870.

After a decade of organisation, and under increasing pressure from Clan na Gael, the I.R.B. attempted a revolution through insurrection in 1867. As a military exercise it was an abject disaster, but it scored a major publicity coup, renewing the revolutionary tradition in Irish nationalism and creating a new generation of nationalist martyrs (many of whom were exiled as treason-felons under emergency legislation). Sympathy for the Fenians was further generated by the imprisonment of suspects in the aftermath of the rising. This sympathy greatly increased in 1868 following the government's treatment of a group of twelve Fenians who attempted to free a comrade from a prison van in Manchester. The rescue failed, a policeman was mistakenly killed, and three

Fenians were hung. It was the government's most severe response during the crisis period and immediately created the 'Manchester Martyrs'. Nationalist opinion in Ireland was outraged and popular pressure ensured a series of high profile masses were said for the martyrs by Irish catholic bishops. William Ewart Gladstone, the British prime minister from 1868, having already announced that his 'mission was to pacify Ireland', told the house of commons in May 1869 that 'the Fenian conspiracy has been an important influence with respect to Irish policy'.[1] The disestablishment of the church of Ireland in 1869 and the Irish Land Act of 1870, rightly or wrongly, were generally understood in Ireland to have resulted from Fenian pressures.

This interpretation of the succession of events placed the Fenians in a complex ideological position. Although pledged to the achievement of an Irish republic and rejecting any engagement with the British political process, it seemed clear that their actions had generated British attempts to ameliorate the condition of the catholic majority in Ireland. The question now arose regarding how far Irish nationalists could legitimately engage with the British political process in order to influence these and future developments. Isaac Butt, an Irish protestant Tory barrister, was alarmed by Fenianism but also saw an opportunity to build on the rapid politicisation it represented, focusing these energies on more productive methods. He proposed home rule as an alternative to Fenian separatist republicanism, arguing that devolved government within the union would satisfy Irish nationalist dignity while allowing Ireland the benefits of imperial partnership with Britain, the strongest and richest nation in the world. Over the course of the 1870s home rule became popular in Ireland, partly because it was associated with the interests of the Irish catholics, most obviously through demands for further reform of the land system and the state endowment of denominational education. In this way, agrarian activists and catholic nationalists (including the catholic hierarchy) became closely associated with Butt's party and at the 1874 general election sixty nominally home rule M.P.s were returned to Westminster. As home rule became a popular and, structurally, a more democratic movement, Butt's early protestant supporters became alienated and by the mid-1870s this once significant presence had become near irrelevant to its counsels.

The I.R.B.'s responses to these developments were confused. From 1870 it worked closely with Butt through the amnesty movement, campaigning for the release of Fenian prisoners – Butt's presidency of this organisation was possible owing to the tacit approval of the Supreme Council. Prominent Fenians who had avoided exile in the late 1860s became leading home rulers in the early 1870s, establishing a common career pattern that saw an early Fenianism evolve into a later commitment to constitutionalism and home rule; their Fenian links strengthened their nationalist credentials. Indeed, some later home rule M.P.s concocted fallacious Fenian connexions; others were

---

[1] Quoted in Alvin Jackson, *Ireland 1798–1998* (Oxford, 1999), p. 106.

never quite taken seriously because they lacked the requisite heritage.[2] More immediately, prominent Fenians who aligned with home rule gave the movement an enormous boost in particular regions. Such relationships evolved into a shadowy commitment by the I.R.B. to support Butt's home rule organisation for a fixed period, after which it would revert to orthodox I.R.B. activity. Co-operation formally ended in August 1876 and four members of the Supreme Council, including two M.P.s, were expelled for refusing to obey this injunction. These developments reflected a more serious problem facing the Fenian leadership, which was the weakness of I.R.B. authority: short of expelling large numbers from the organisation, there was little the Supreme Council could do to prevent the rank-and-file from becoming involved in proscribed political activities. This became very clear with the onset of the agrarian crisis of the late 1870s, which culminated in the Land War of 1879–82. Historians have shown how important I.R.B. members were as organisers of the Land League,[3] while Clan na Gael, initially impressed by Charles Stewart Parnell and J. G. Biggar's campaign of parliamentary obstructionism in the late 1870s, soon advocated support for the emergent land agitation and home rule despite its apparent incompatibility with Fenian orthodoxy.

Under these pressures the Supreme Council had became more rather than less dogmatic, but it was clear the I.R.B. could ill afford to distance itself completely from all political movements that attracted mass support but were incompatible with its principles, particularly given the pressure it was coming under from Clan na Gael. Following a series of agonising debates in the Supreme Council initiated by the Clan's leader, John Devoy, the Fenians partially acquiesced in the New Departure. This compact allowed I.R.B. members to agitate on behalf of an independent home rule party and for land reform while retaining the commitment to the achievement of independence through insurrection. There is probably little to be gained from trying to establish the extent to which Parnell's leadership of the home rule party in the 1880s was shaped by the New Departure but it was significant that his famous insistence that 'no man had the right to set the boundary to the march of the nation' was consistent with its provisions. Above all, the New Departure meant that those Fenians who thought about these things felt able to engage in political activities that did not explicitly repudiate Fenianism's ultimate objectives. This important development helped shape the relationship between the home rule movement and Fenianism during the period covered by this book.

[2] James McConnel, '"The Fenians at Westminster": The Irish Parliamentary Party and the Legacy of the New Departure' in *Irish Historical Studies* (*I.H.S.*), xxxiv, no. 133 (2004), pp 41–64.
[3] Donald Jordan, *Land and Popular Politics in Ireland* (Cambridge, 1994) contains many references, especially pp 223–7; Paul Bew, *Land and the National Question in Ireland, 1858–82* (Dublin, 1978), pp 91, 110–11, 132–4.

II

Owing to the seditious content of the Fenian newspaper *The Irish People*, its editor John O'Leary was convicted of treason-felony in 1866 and exiled for nearly twenty years. Thirty years later O'Leary wrote a diffident and evasive memoir of Fenianism in which he meditated on the relationship between the origins of the Irish Republican Brotherhood and Irish nationalism in general: 'The Fenian spirit is ever present in Ireland and needs at any time but a little organisation to make it burst into renewed activity.'[4] By associating Fenianism with the timeless Irish nation rather than the specifics of the I.R.B., O'Leary gave classic expression to the notion of Fenianism as the embodiment of a fundamental and irreducible Irish nationality. As Mark Ryan (the dominant figure in London Fenian circles) argued in response to the ascendancy of the home rule demand, 'for the time being the Voice of Fenianism – the real Voice of Irish Nationalism – was drowned, as it had been before, and since, in the welter of party politics.'[5] The Fenian distinction between nationalism and politics is one that will recur throughout this book, but it will be undermined by an account that suggests that the development of Irish separatism in this period can only be understood as part of wider political, social, and cultural changes. A more emblematic starting point, therefore, comes not from a man associated with the orthodoxies of Fenianism, but from the Irish Republican Brotherhood's greatest apostate. Analysing the progress of Irish nationalism and the transformation in Irish social relations that brought about the 'fall of feudalism in Ireland', Michael Davitt, the founder of the Land League, wrote:

> There has always been an erroneous impression in English and often in some Irish minds as to the actual extent to which the total separation sentiment prevailed among Irishmen. The numerical strength of the strongest revolutionary organisation by no means measured the strength of the feeling for complete independence. Millions of Irishmen were and are separatists in conviction and aspiration who would on no account become members of a secret society – nationalists who could see a perfectly consistent course in supporting a strong moral-force policy like Mr Parnell's where the immediate object might be some subordinate issue or question.[6]

This extract points to one of the issues with which this book is concerned, namely the extent to which Irish nationalists were separatist between the Kilmainham treaty of 1882, which ended the Land War, and the 1916 Rising. The period begins with Parnell's repudiation of the insurgency of the Land War and the beginning of the long period when constitutionalism dominated Irish political debate and agitation. This phase ends with the Ulster crisis, the

---

[4] John O'Leary, *Recollections of Fenians and Fenianism* (London, 1896), p. 10.
[5] Mark Ryan, *Fenian Memories* (Dublin, 1945), p. 134.
[6] Michael Davitt, *The Fall of Feudalism in Ireland* (London, 1904), pp 119–20.

consequent undermining of constitutionalism, and the 1916 Rising. Shortly afterwards Irish politics was transformed, Irish nationalist demands intensified, Sinn Féin overwhelmingly won the 1918 general election, and a number of activists embarked on a guerrilla war intended to drive the British authorities from Ireland. This book examines some of the pre-conditions of this process. Although recognising that the events stimulating these developments were facilitated by the short-term pressures and opportunities afforded by the Great War, it will argue that the causes of this transformation can only be understood over the longer term; not that the Irish revolution would have occurred without the intervention of the war, but that the war generated a different crisis from the one which was previously developing as a result of the third home rule bill and the concomitant likelihood of some form of partition. In both processes separatists played prominent roles, moulding the political agenda to suit their ideological aspirations.

Davitt's observation that many separatists were not inclined to join secret societies is significant, for Irish separatism cannot be properly understood if the Irish Republican Brotherhood is considered the exclusive repository of separatist sentiment. Assuming that separatist sentiment was insignificant because the I.R.B. was organisationally weak is historically simplistic. Instead, it is useful to think about the tension between occurrent and dispositional attitudes. Many Irish nationalists inclined towards separatism, but supported home rule and a broadly constitutional approach for strongly pragmatic reasons. So complex were these sentiments that it is not absurd to believe Roger Casement's contention that John Redmond, leader of the home rule party after 1900, said privately to him on 8 May 1914: 'Well, Sir Roger, I don't mind you getting an Irish Republic if you can.'[7] Some held back from separatist activity because they were repelled by secret societies and their disreputable associations; others bowed to the authority of the proscribing authorities, especially the catholic church. As Frank Henderson recalled,

> Even though I had decided to take part in the Rising which I knew was to happen later and even though I did not know how such a Rising could be effective without some system such as the I.R.B., I could not reconcile the two viewpoints – the aim of the Brotherhood and the prohibition of the Church.
>
> Therefore when the Irish Volunteers were founded, the mental agony over this question which had disturbed me disappeared.[8]

Long before the Irish Volunteers were established in late 1913 a wide range of literary and cultural nationalist organisations provided an adjacent forum

---

[7] Undated manuscript by Roger Casement, 'Professor MacNeill's Connection With Me', Casement Papers (N.L.I., MS 36203/1).
[8] Statement to the Irish Bureau of Military History quoted in Michael Hopkinson (ed.), *Frank Henderson's Easter Rising: Recollections of a Dublin Volunteer* (Cork, 1998), p. 26.

to the I.R.B. for advanced nationalist activity. Notable were the Young Ireland Societies of the 1880s and the various circles associated with Arthur Griffith and William Rooney in the 1890s and 1900s. The cultural separatism of these groups formed part of a national debate that equally involved constitutional and separatist nationalists. More generally, however, the I.R.B. itself remained an important element in the texture of Irish society and politics. Fergus Campbell has drawn attention to their role as agrarian agitators in County Galway,[9] while, as suggested, the progress of the home rule party can be further illuminated by considering its interactions with the I.R.B. Although Parnell's catering to Fenian interests went into a minor key between the 'Kilmainham treaty' that ended the Land War in 1882 and the party split of December 1890, home rule politicians still tried to secure their separatist rivals as collaborators, protecting the ideological interests of advanced nationalism for strategic and ideological reasons. Other M.P.s felt the advantage of distancing themselves from the Fenian tradition. Redmond's failure to hold together a strong coalition of nationalist support during the protracted home rule crisis of 1912–18 partly stemmed from the growing ideological divergence between separatists and constitutionalists after the home rule party's reunification in 1900. Redmond's intensified imperial conception of home rule was paralleled with the development of a separatism strongly predicated on anti-imperialist ideas. Parnellism's notorious ambiguity had made home rule less vulnerable to radical, separatist critiques; Redmond's advocacy of imperial home rule left his ideological flanks exposed.[10]

A taxonomy of Irish nationalists out of sympathy with the Irish parliamentary party, however, is difficult to construct owing to the variety of political tendencies at work and the heavy reliance historians must place on police reports. Activists might be tagged as Fenians, I.R.B. men, 'suspects', 'advanced nationalists', 'physical force nationalists', 'Sinn Féiners', 'separatists', 'cultural separatists', or 'republicans'. To be fingered as an I.R.B. man in the police files suggests a precise act of political identification, to be labelled a Fenian was much more ambiguous. Despite such connotations, these appellations were often used interchangeably, although the latter three were rarely used by contemporaries. Labelling could also be deliberately misrepresentative. When reporting the general election results of 1895, the *Irish Times* provided an implicit political commentary by dividing the results between

---

[9] Fergus J. M. Campbell, 'Land and Politics in Connacht, 1898–1909' (University of Bristol, Ph.D., 1996), pp 222–262 and *idem*, 'The Social Dynamics of Nationalist Politics in the West of Ireland 1898–1918' in *Past and Present*, 182 (Feb. 2004), pp 175–211.

[10] For example, to the consternation of both separatists and constitutionalists Redmond reportedly described home rule to U.S. audiences in 1910 as a means to create a relationship between London and Ireland comparable to that between the federal and state authorities in the U.S. On his return to Ireland he denied making these statements and his fellow home rulers were keen to believe him. See Michael Wheatley, 'John Redmond and Federalism in 1910' in *I.H.S.*, xxxii, no. 127 (May 2001), pp 343–64.

Unionists (Conservatives and Liberal Unionists) and Separatists (Liberals, Parnellites, and Anti-Parnellites).[11] In general, however, 'advanced nationalist' provides a useful umbrella term for activists whose aspirations were more radical than the official aims of the Irish parliamentary party, and although the phrase suggests teleological assumptions, it is more satisfactory than the politically loaded 'extremist', which implies sympathy for political violence. For just an advanced nationalist need not be wholly separatist and/or republican, she could equally be wholly committed to peaceful means. Political affiliations in this period were riddled with such complexities, the most important stemming from the ambiguous status of agrarian agitations directed by organisations aligned with constitutional nationalism. As the great Indian nationalist Gopal Krishna Gokhale observed of his nationalist compatriots: 'There is at times a great deal of moderation among some of those who are called Extremists and, on the other hand, there is no small amount of what is the reverse of moderation among some who are called Moderates.'[12]

It is perhaps unnecessary to point out that all discussion of nationalist strategy was shaped by the central problem of how Ireland's nationhood could be restored; embedded in such arguments were more complex questions regarding the moral legitimacy of any approach. No political strategy was exempted from such assessment because it was understood that the end, Irish nationhood, would in some sense embody the means by which it was achieved. Indeed, the most violent advocate of dynamite 'outrages', Jeremiah O'Donovan Rossa, came up with a moral justification for the possible murder of civilians.[13]

A further complication raised by the phrase 'advanced nationalist' is that it suggests an a priori spectrum of correspondences between the possible constitutional settlements for Ireland and the extent to which an Irish nation would be achieved. Something of the confusion such questions raised was evident during the 1886 home rule parliamentary debates. Opinion divided on whether an Irish nation already existed, or whether the passage of the bill would create one. There was not a shared sense of the possible distinction between a nation and a nation-state. In this book, the use or not of the description 'advanced' does not imply a moral judgement regarding the extent to which the recipient was a nationalist; it is not intended to imply that some nationalists were more nationalist than others. For while many Fenians would have applauded such assumptions, developments in Irish cultural nationalism had greatly complicated the possible means by which nationalists might adduce their commitment. By some reckonings, for example, home rulers active in the Gaelic League and absorbed in the peasant culture of the west of Ireland might be considered more attuned to their Irishness than the I.R.B. man preoccupied by the politics of the Dublin corporation.

[11] *Irish Times*, 16 July 1895.
[12] G. A. Natesan (ed.), *Speeches of Gopal Krishna Gokhale* (Madras, 1920), p. 305.
[13] Seán McConville, *Irish Political Prisoners, 1848–1922: Theatres of War* (London, 2003), pp 338–9.

A further issue is raised by how recent histories of the Irish revolution have reinvigorated class-based analyses of that revolution. For instance, work by Senia Pašeta and Patrick Maume has done much to illuminate the sensibilities of the catholic middle class between Parnell and Pearse. Both writers argue strongly for the marginality of Irish separatism and, in particular, republicanism before 1916.[14] A more advanced nationalist *mentalité*, it will be argued, could be found in working-class political and social associations, a tendency reinforced by the marginality of working-class socio-economic interests to the home rule movement. It is important to be conscious of this political strata when considering Tom Garvin's account of the revolutionary elite as constituted of the 'men in the middle'. Garvin's marginal yet educated petit-bourgeoisie, positioned between the men of the labourers' organisations and Pašeta's university-educated putative civil servants, found in advanced nationalism an answer to their social and vocational frustrations.[15] Like R. V. Comerford's Fenians of the 1860s and '70s, these were (mainly) men 'trying to find a more significant place for themselves in the world'.[16]

Although the explanatory force of Comerford's mode of socio-economic analysis is made evident in his work – 1867 can be portrayed as a (failed) revolution of rising expectations – Irish separatists are generally approached in this book through what might be considered an ironic empathy rather than a detached scepticism. While acknowledging subconscious causal motivations, it seems useful to pursue an analysis rooted in how the separatists saw themselves and justified their actions.[17] Such an approach makes sense if Irish politics in this period are thought about in terms of the problem of legitimate authority. All collective actions of historical or political significance are sanctioned by some kind of authority, political or ideological, and among the primary tasks of the historian is the analysis of such authority, how it is achieved, sustained, and exercised. Historians of the modern period are chiefly concerned with the nature and legitimacy of state authority. Indissolubly linked to such study is the analysis of collective action that is not sanctioned by the state authority. In Ireland the authority of the British state was in

---

[14] Patrick Maume, *The Long Gestation: Irish Nationalist Life 1891–1918* (Dublin, 1999); Senia Pašeta, *Before the Revolution: Nationalism, Social Change and Ireland's Catholic Elite, 1879–1922* (Cork, 1999).
[15] Tom Garvin, *Nationalist Revolutionaries in Ireland, 1858–1928* (Oxford, 1987), and *idem*, 'Great Hatred, Little Room: Social Background and Political Sentiment Among Revolutionary Activists in Ireland, 1890–1922' in D. G. Boyce (ed.), *The Revolution in Ireland, 1879–1923* (London, 1988), pp 91–114.
[16] R. V. Comerford, *The Fenians in Context: Irish Politics and Society 1848–82* (Dublin, 1985, 1998), p. 249.
[17] To gauge how unhelpful overt hostility to the I.R.B. can be when actually trying to understand advanced nationalism see John O'Beirne Ranelagh, 'The Irish Republican Brotherhood in the Revolutionary Period, 1879–1923' in Boyce, *Revolution in Ireland*, pp 137–56.

permanent crisis, generating a relationship between the British government and Irish nationalists that L. P. Curtis has styled as torn between coercion and conciliation and Paul Bew conflict and conciliation.[18] Suppression of nationalist insurgency – in this period primarily agrarian – combined with legislative attempts to redress Irish grievances, usually in the face of powerfully entrenched interests. Great steps were taken, such as the succession of land acts after 1870 and the democratisation of local government in 1898. Home rule formed part of this evolving agenda because it was conceived by Gladstonian liberals as the means to render the state authority legitimate in order to secure the union. As an 1887 pamphlet by the Parnellite M.P. T. P. Gill demonstrated, even avowed home rulers were left uneasy by Gladstone's adoption of their demands:

> It is a strange, and one may be allowed to say a somewhat humiliating thing for all parties, that Ireland today, in pleading with England for home rule, should have need to assure her that home rule is not only a safe and vitally necessary policy for Ireland, but equally safe and equally necessary for the integrity of the British empire.[19]

This was a remarkable admission. To admit that it was 'humiliating' for Irish nationalists to 'plead' that home rule was good for the union and the empire served to emphasise the extent of the compromise over earlier Irish nationalist ideals that home rule represented. Moreover, as the 1886 home rule parliamentary debates demonstrated, rebellious home rule M.P.s were transformed by Gladstone's conversion into loyalists. Anti-home rulers quoted earlier speeches by Irish nationalist M.P.s which had stated that only complete separation could ultimately satisfy the Irish nation. Sometimes nationalist M.P.s responded by denying they had been quoted accurately, but in more honest responses they argued that Gladstone's conversion had transfigured Anglo-Irish relations, ending a centuries-long conflict. These highly emotional exchanges, in which home rulers literally avowed their love for the prime minister, were extraordinarily theatrical and moving moments of reconciliation. Ending a period of tentative courtship, this love blossomed into the 'union of hearts'. The pre-nuptial settlement demanded that home rulers provisionally acknowledge British state authority.

Observing from the wings, many nationalists were troubled by this rapprochement, especially adherents of Wolfe Tone's unambiguous republican

---

[18] L. P. Curtis, *Coercion and Conciliation in Ireland, 1800–1892: A Study in Conservative Unionism* (Princeton, 1963); Paul Bew, *Conflict and Conciliation in Ireland, 1890–1910: Parnellites and Radical Agrarians* (Oxford, 1987); also on this theme Andrew Gailey, *Ireland and the Death of Kindness: The Experience of Constructive Unionism 1890–1905* (Cork, 1987).
[19] T. P. Gill, 'The Home Rule Constitutions of the British Empire' in *The Irish Question*, no. 14 (London, 1887), p. 3.

separatism. For although the famous third clause of the 1873 I.R.B. constitution permitted support for 'every movement calculated to advance the cause of Irish independence', it emphasised that any such movement must be consistent 'with the preservation of its [the I.R.B.'s] own integrity'.[20] Advanced nationalists increasingly questioned whether the constitutionalist argument that home rule was Fenianism by other means could be justified. The New Departure needed continual reaffirmation, which, as this book seeks to demonstrate, became ever more difficult.

As suggested, denying the legitimacy of British state authority was funda-mental to the Fenian ideal. Consequently any form of political engagement with this authority had to be approached with great caution. As Joseph Chamberlain's famously over-blown description of the Irish government suggested, to live by these standards was very difficult:

> I do not believe that the great majority of Englishmen have the slightest conception of the systems under which this free nation attempts to rule a sister country. It is a system which is founded on the bayonets of 20,000 soldiers encamped permanently as in a hostile country. It is a system as completely centralised and bureaucratic as that with which Russia governs Poland, or as that which was common in Venice under Austrian rule. An Irishman at this moment cannot move a step, he cannot lift a finger, in any parochial, municipal, or educational work, without being confronted, interfered with, controlled by, an English official appointed by a foreign government, and without a shadow or shade of representative authority.[21]

Cultural nationalism provided separatists with a source of authority with which to contest this Foucaldian nightmare. By studying Irish history, literature, and the Gaelic language, and mingling this with the advocacy of economic ideas predicated on the ideal of Irish self-reliance, essentialist ideas of the Irish nation emerged that were by definition irreconcilable with British state authority. This revealed the disjunction between nation and state that characterised Ireland's existential status, a disjunction which home rule promised to sustain. Comprehending the status quo in this way configured the Irish nation as an alternative and unimpeachable source of authority that legitimised the actions of advanced nationalist initiates. This was the Fenian ideal. Tracing the evolution of this authority is one of the major purposes of this book. And although it is clear that the conclusions cultural nationalists reached were massaged by pre-existing sensibilities, an alertness to this should not obscure cultural nationalism's capacity for winning converts. Nor should sight be lost of how a sustained engagement with such ideas could intensify commitment:

---

[20] Quoted in Charles Townshend, *Political Violence in Ireland: Government and Resistance since 1848* (Oxford, 1983), p. 239.
[21] Quoted in John J. Clancy, 'The "Castle" System' in *The Irish Question*, no. 5 (London, 1886), p. 3.

as with all political convictions, emotional and intellectual passions combined. On the other hand, it is crucial that neither separatist evangelical zeal nor future political developments obscure the extent to which cultural nationalism was not exclusively tied to a separatist trajectory. Many nationalists were convinced that home rule was sufficiently compatible with this exalted version of Irish nationhood to be acceptable, just as a significant proportion of unionists embraced a version of Irish Ireland. In some cases, for example, the imperial-federation ideal of inter-dependent but culturally distinct nations was projected as an alternative political framework. Importantly, in these cases an Irish polity's legitimacy still stemmed from its compatibility with 'the nation'.

Through an analysis of the evolution of advanced nationalist versions of this *mentalité*, the lines of continuity with the post-1916 political transformation should become clearer. Although aiming to clarify the activities and significance of Irish separatists in this period, this book further complicates the overall anatomy of Irish nationalism. And by attending to the difficulties Irish separatists faced in maintaining their appeal while distinguishing themselves from constitutional nationalists, this account seeks to avoid reasserting the old binary distinction between separatist and constitutionalist. Advanced nationalism is examined as part of the texture of Irish society. It was neither the antiquated legacy of mid-Victorian Fenianism nor simply the descendant of urban/rural traditions of hostility to established authority. Instead, an ideologically sophisticated and strategically determined separatist vanguard emerged, and the analysis which follows to some extent affirms P. S. O'Hegarty's account of a small group of determined I.R.B. members sustaining separatist aspirations.[22] However, Irish separatism was a more complex and popular political and cultural presence in Irish nationalist society than it has appeared in previous accounts. This phenomenon can be best understood through a broadly chronological analysis of advanced nationalism in its strategic and contingent aspects, rather than through a simple chronicle of heroism (or 'terrorism').

III

With the other 'fellows' James Joyce's Stephen Dedalus was driven from Clongowes to Dublin, home for Christmas in 1891.[23] It was a lively, festive journey. The boys cheered and were cheered; greeted by the 'peasants' that lived on the roadside, they greeted them in their turn. All was suffused by the 'lovely smell' of 'rain and wintry air and turf smouldering and corduroy'. But this comforting return to the safety of family, so economically evoked, was not without political significance. 'The drivers pointed with their whips to

---

[22] P. S. O'Hegarty, *The Victory of Sinn Féin* (Dublin, 1924), pp 13–14.
[23] James Joyce, *A Portrait of the Artist as a Young Man* (Oxford, 2000), pp 16–33.

Bodenstown. They cheered.' To this day, Irish republicans gather at Bodenstown churchyard in November to stand by Wolfe Tone's grave and remember Ireland's 'republican' dead. In the late nineteenth and early twentieth centuries this day became known as Decoration Day, because the graves of United Irishmen, Young Irelanders, and Fenians were decorated with flowers. At Bodenstown itself, pieces of ivy were taken from the churchyard wall and kept as mementoes or good luck charms. As Joyce knew,[24] ivy was also worn as a memorial to Parnell, a symbolic blurring of the line between separatist and home ruler. The famous row during the Dedalus Christmas dinner that forms part of the opening of *Portrait* sustains the theme. Mr Casey and Simon Dedalus take Parnell's side against the clericalist Dante ('The bishops and the priests of Ireland have spoken, said Dante, and they must be obeyed'). Ostensibly, the dispute was over whether Parnell should have remained leader of the home rule party after he was named in Captain O'Shea's divorce proceedings. Things soon descended into a furious row concerning the role of the catholic church in Irish politics. Dante's defence of the authority of the catholic church against 'renegade catholics' saw Mr Casey and Simon push the classic Fenian line on the need to separate the spiritual and the political spheres. 'We go to the house of God, Mr Casey said, in all humility to pray to our Maker and not to hear election addresses.' Stephen is puzzled. Like his father, he is 'for Ireland and Parnell', but so must be Dante for she once hit a man on the head with her umbrella when he took his hat off when the band played *God Save the Queen*. Ever more provoked, Mr Casey and Dante abandon any pretence that they are having a reasonable discussion. Banging the table with his fist, Mr Casey gets to his feet:

> Didn't the bishops of Ireland betray us in the time of the union when bishop Lanigan presented an address of loyalty to the Marquess Cornwallis? Didn't the bishops and priests sell the aspirations of their country in 1829 in return for catholic emancipation? Didn't they denounce the Fenian movement from the pulpit and in the confession box? And didn't they dishonour the ashes of Terence Bellew MacManus?

In this brief outburst Mr Casey provides in skeleton outline a Fenian interpretation of modern Irish history. Every time Fenian sentiment became strong the catholic church used its spiritual authority to undermine it. The church supported the act of union following the United Irishmen rebellion, it fooled Irish nationalists into believing that catholic emancipation some-how answered their wider aspirations, it failed to get behind the I.R.B., and when the remains of the Young Irelander MacManus were returned from the United States to Dublin for burial in 1861, Paul Cullen, the archbishop

---

[24] James Joyce, 'Ivy Day in the Committee Room' in *Dubliners* (Harmondsworth, 1968), pp 116–33.

of Dublin, refused to say the funeral mass. This task was left to the renegade Fenian priest Father Patrick Lavelle. Although there is no simple identification to be made between the author and Stephen, it is clear where Joyce's sympathies lay. He ruthlessly skewers the anti-Parnellites for their sectarianism by having Stephen recall that Dante forbade him from playing with Eileen, a protestant girl. Mr Casey's outburst thrills Stephen and provokes Dante into leaving the house, raging 'Devil out of hell! We won! We crushed him to death! Fiend!'

Joyce was writing in the 1900s, looking back on his childhood and youth. For his father's generation, Irish history could be made sense of as a conflict between Britain (or, more likely, England), the catholic church, and a Fenianism which was understood in the general sense suggested by O'Leary and Ryan. There is much to be said for this reading, for one of the most important themes in nineteenth-century Irish history is the strengthening of the catholic church, both institutionally and as spiritual guardian to the majority of the Irish population. Part of this achievement stemmed from the hierarchy's capacity to convince a succession of British governments that a strong catholic church in Ireland was not a threat to the stability of the union. By the end of the century the church had, broadly speaking, achieved its aims and its anti-Parnellism was consistent with this overall trend. But for Joyce's generation things were rather more complicated. Whereas the catholic church, renegade priests aside, had opposed Fenianism, the home rule party's relationship with the separatists was rather more ambiguous. It was not that the catholic church's authority had been supplanted by the home rule party but that the effectiveness of the home rule–agrarian dynamic had left these other political forces trailing in its wake. Both the Fenians and the catholic hierarchy had to come to terms with the popular appeal of a political movement that was not so much opposed to the Fenian or catholic interests but had successfully redefined the most pressing questions in Irish politics. Much of what follows focuses on how advanced nationalists responded to this, attempting in turn to redefine the issues in line with evolving conceptions of the Fenian ideal.

The greatest shock in Joyce's scene is left for the end. Mr Casey sobs 'Poor Parnell! . . . My dead king!' and 'Stephen, raising his terrorstricken face, saw that his father's eyes were full of tears.' This moment of paternal fragility becomes ever more significant as the novel progresses. More pertinently, Mr Casey's 'sob of pain' recalls the visit made by the elderly James Stephens, the first I.R.B. president, to Parnell's grave where he too 'sobbed'.[25] These famous scenes, one fictional, the other true, reflected something of the ambiguous Fenian passions that animated the Dublin milieu Joyce knew as the child of lower middle-class catholics, and his works are filled with Fenian motifs, references, and commentary. Not one to stand dumb when confronted with Fenian xenophobia (most memorably in the 'Cyclops' episode of *Ulysses*), Joyce

[25] See above, p. 61.

nonetheless understood the highly emotional tribalism of Fenianism. For Fenianism met the authoritarianism of catholic and British Ireland with a credo of political liberation that had a strongly individualist bent. It was symptomatic of an adult need to defy inadequate authorities, be they British, Irish, or Roman. Mr Casey's rhetoric had carried him along, empowered by his certainty and the vigour of the argument; Dante's vicious triumphalism confronted Mr Casey with Irish realities, provoking tears of grief and a childlike frustration.

1

Dublin Fenianism in the 1880s

'The Irish culture of the future'?

I

Historians have largely neglected the activities of the Irish Republican Brotherhood in the 1880s, tending to focus on the two great flash-points of 1867 and 1916. R. V. Comerford, when concluding his brilliantly iconoclastic *The Fenians in Context*, dismissed Dublin Fenianism in 1882, claiming it had 'deteriorated into a miscellany of purposeless gangs'.[1] John Newsinger's critique of Comerford offers a cursory and Marxisant reading of Fenianism in the years following the excitement of 1867.[2] Even P. S. O'Hegarty, ever the advocate of the centrality of the I.R.B. in pre-1922 Irish politics, was muted on the subject of the 1880s. Writing in 1952, O'Hegarty argued that 'Parnell had crowded the I.R.B. out of public life, and out of the public mind, but it was there, underground, all the time, small in numbers, very often divided, without effective leadership, and without any current policy save that of keeping the separatist spirit alive and maintaining the framework of a separatist organisation.'[3] Against the ascendancy of Charles Stewart Parnell, a disciplined and highly organised home rule party, and the land war, the military stratagem of the Fenians appeared outmoded and irrelevant, consigned to the melancholic bar-room reminiscences of the increasingly aged men of '67.

Yet something more penetrating than merely political marginalisation had afflicted the Fenians. A number of violent and dramatic departures from the Fenian orthodoxy of Kickham, O'Leary, and Stephens seemed to have debased the creed. Desmond Ryan, the most eloquent of the post-1916 Fenian writers, encapsulated this redundancy with disarming logic, in a phrasing packed with resonance and implication. 'All the Invincibles had been Fenians. Fenianism was in decay.'[4]

---

[1] R. V. Comerford, *The Fenians in Context* (Dublin, 1985), p. 243.
[2] John Newsinger, *Fenianism in Mid-Victorian Britain* (London, 1994). See *Saothar*, xvii (1992), pp 46–56, for an antagonistic discussion between Newsinger and Comerford.
[3] P. S. O'Hegarty, *A History of Ireland under the Union* (London, 1952), p. 633.
[4] Desmond Ryan, *The Phoenix Flame* (London, 1937), p. 272.

As Parnell returned to London following his release from Kilmainham gaol, the brutal murder of the newly installed chief secretary Lord Frederick Cavendish and the under-secretary T. H. Burke by the Invincibles in Phoenix Park on 6 May 1882 shook political opinion throughout Britain and Ireland.[5] Parnell had to be dissuaded by Gladstone from resigning the leadership of the home rule party in response,[6] an action contrasting starkly with his notorious defence in parliament of the so-called Manchester Martyrs in 1878.[7] The Fenian paper *The Irishman* associated the crime with the 'soiling slough of Russian Nihilism', arguing that Ireland's proper response was '[a]nguish but not despair, for the crime is not Ireland's'.[8] It was 'not Ireland's' for the crime did not fit into a paradigm of Fenian revolution. A letter purportedly from the Leinster I.R.B. executive condemned the Invincibles for 'crime and outrages . . . as foreign to our organisation as is the enemy to our soil'; the Invincibles had 'set at naught the authority of the Supreme Council'.[9] In departing from the Fenian ideal, the assassins had forfeited their claim to the sympathies of the advanced vanguard, exculpating Fenianism of any responsibility for the stabbings. Nonetheless, in confluence with the associated dynamite campaign against political sites in England financed from America and inspired by O'Donovan Rossa,[10] Fenianism in – addition to proving politically inefficacious – had fallen into disrepute.

In response, during the 1880s elements within Fenianism underwent a process of reinvention, with the factionalism identified by Comerford superseded by a fresh cleavage of much greater long-term significance. A second generation of Fenians, qualitatively distinct from their fathers and uncles, responded to the ascendancy of constitutional nationalism by developing within Fenianism a fresh separatist dynamic based on the nurture of a distinctly Irish culture. John O'Leary was its charismatic centre. The major but not the only vehicle for this autodidacticism were the Young Ireland Societies. Originating in Dublin in 1881, but soon scattered throughout Ireland, England, and Scotland, they were arguably the organisational crucible of the literary revival and the cultural nationalism of the *fin de siècle*.[11] History, education,

---

[5] See Tom Corfe, *The Phoenix Park Murders* (London, 1968). Also, the ludicrously self-aggrandising P. J. P. Tynan, *The Irish National Invincibles and their Times* (London, 1894).

[6] F. S. L. Lyons, *Charles Stewart Parnell* (London, 1978), p. 209.

[7] Ibid., p. 54.

[8] *Irishman*, 13 May 1882, also 21 Apr. 1883, and 15 Mar. 1884 for Glasgow Y.I.S. view that in Russia people were 'goaded into Nihilism by the cruel acts of tyrants and despots'.

[9] T.N.A. (P.R.O), C.O. 904 10/200–4, 'Investigations regarding secret societies and individuals 1882–1884'. See bibliography for details of police reports.

[10] See K. R. M. Short, *The Dynamite War* (Dublin, 1979), and numerous references to Rossa in Terry Golway, *Irish Rebel: John Devoy and America's Fight for Ireland's Freedom* (New York, 1998).

[11] On the Scottish dimension see Máirtín ó Catháin, 'Fenian Dynamite: Dissident Irish Republicans in Late Nineteenth-century Scotland' in Oonagh Walsh (ed.), *Ireland Abroad: Politics and Profession in the Nineteenth Century* (Dublin, 2003), pp 164–5.

and commemoration became touchstones for the Y.I.S., prompting W. B. Yeats to write in 1891, before the full influence of the distorting lens of Parnell's death was felt:

> These new folk, limited though they be, are conscious. They have ideas. They understand the purpose of letters in the world. They may yet formulate the Irish culture of the future. To help them, is much obscure feeling for literature diffused throughout the country. The clerks, farmers' sons, and the like, that make the 'Young Ireland' Societies and kindred associations, showed an alertness to honour the words 'poet', 'writer', 'orator', not commonly found among their class.[12]

In this chapter an examination of traditional Dublin Fenianism in the 1880s, illustrating its paralysis, will provide a context and contrast for the activities of the Young Ireland Society, where Fenianism could be found at its most dynamic. Implicit to the approach taken is the sense that Parnellism, rather than achieving political hegemony after the Kilmainham Treaty, functioned in an atmosphere of uneasy compromise. This was heightened by the lack of formal barriers between advanced and constitutional nationalism. For Parnellite M.P.s, especially those with latent Fenian sympathies like William O'Brien, the public meetings of the Young Ireland Societies provided substantial Dublin and provincial forums. This interaction established a pattern that, in various forms, survived the length of the home rule party's existence: party patronage was provisionally extended to, and provisionally accepted by, organisations nominally hostile to constitutionalism. Rather than merely a glamorous accessory to Parnellism, Fenianism was integral to its articulation; clarification of Parnell's famed ambiguity, and Irish constitutional nationalism more generally, can be found by examining its rhetorical and organisational relationship with the separatists. Parnell's rhetorical strategy during the split, and, in particular, his request that constitutionalism be given one more chance to work, was continuous with the interactions between home rulers and the Young Ireland Societies in the 1880s.

II

Evidence for the day-to-day activity of the I.R.B. is sparse and rather anecdotal; little systematic intelligence was commissioned by the government. The Land War and home rule had diverted resources and attention away from Fenianism, with the organisation reported upon only when the authorities saw fit. But Dynamitard activity and the Invincible shock galvanised the home office into action and, notwithstanding departmental turf wars over the control of

---

[12] W. B. Yeats, *Representative Irish Tales* (Gerrards Cross, 1891, 1991), p. 32.

information, the government became better informed.[13] In Dublin, the metropolitan police gave Superintendent William Reddy a special responsibility to keep tabs on the movements and activities of the leading Fenians of the city. This was a task fraught with dead-ends and futile investigations, with numerous extant police reports containing little more information than the routes taken by suspects between their homes and various pubs and hotels. They were reliant on paid informers, who were notoriously unreliable, melodramatic, and expensive.[14] For example, 'Andrew' claimed in 1886 that Sullivan – discussed later in this chapter – had a well-organised band of 900 men and 150 revolvers. It is difficult to credit numbers of this magnitude, and such reports must be approached with the same slightly weary scepticism Reddy extended to them. Moreover, 'Andrew' claimed Sullivan would have no trouble getting money from the U.S. to commit outrages: 'If Sullivan says the thing must be done it must be done.'[15] Letters alleging the reorganisation of the Invincibles and the imminent assassination of members of the government – most especially Balfour – proliferated, the vast majority proving hoaxes, driven by vendetta or a transparent political agenda. The Dublin Metropolitan Police (D.M.P.), for example, received a gloriously lurid twelve-page letter written in thick red ink and signed 'A Loyal Informer'. Prompted by a supposed threat to Balfour's life, it advocated 'disfranchising the whole of Ireland' and putting Ireland under 'strict military control'; it concluded by praising Balfour's 'Cromwellianism'.[16] Memoranda from Dublin Castle urged continual vigilance, one of 1883 recommending that particular attention be paid to

> suspects from Dublin who may take excursions into the country during the summer. Many members of the secret societies avail of picnic parties and other large excursions for the purpose of meeting and making arrangements. . . . Excursions of members of the Antiquarian Society in particular should be carefully watched.[17]

---

[13] Bernard Porter, *The Origins of the Vigilant State: The London Metropolitan Police Special Branch before the First World War* (London, 1987); Richard Hawkins, 'Government versus Secret Societies: The Parnell Era' in T. Desmond Williams (ed.), *Secret Societies in Ireland* (Dublin, 1973), pp 100–12.

[14] The eastern division of the Royal Irish Constabulary requested permission to grant £12 a month to commercial traveller and informer 'Quentin' of County Carlow and Kilkenny. 'In order to do this [gain intelligence], he says, he will have to spend a great deal more money than heretofore both on traveling [sic] expenses and his living – and besides, he is obliged to frequent public houses, and spend a large sum on standing drink.' T.N.A. (P.R.O.), C.O. 904 10/551, 16 June 1884.

[15] D.M.P. 1887. The files of the Dublin Metropolitan Police are housed in the National Archive (N.A.) in Dublin. They are filed by year and are not systematically classified, hence the inconsistent references given.

[16] D.M.P. 1887.

[17] D.M.P. 1883 315 w/1716.

One policeman duly reported one Sunday in the summer of 1887 that groups were heading for the suburb of Dundrum, occasionally as many as 400, sometimes marching in a military style to Fenian songs and talking of oaths.[18] These men were probably members of the Gaelic Athletic Association (G.A.A.), the cultural nationalist organisation established by Michael Cusack (Joyce's 'The Citizen' in *Ulysses*) in 1884 to promote Gaelic games, and it is not hard to imagine them teasing the watchful policemen with exaggerated mutterings.

However, the severity with which the Fenians dealt with their own should not be underestimated. One informer's account of the murder of Bernard Bailey in October 1883 suggests the actions of a 'vigilance committee', an I.R.B. disciplinary body. Bailey had been employed by his brother-in-law Whelan, who kept a tailor's shop and was suspected of distributing arms among the Dublin Fenians. Bailey was sacked following a row over the shop's management and threatened to inform the authorities of Whelan's Fenian activities. Two days later he was ordered out of his bed by William Brophy and John Dunne. Having been brought to a vacant house in Temple Bar's Skipper's Alley, he was guarded day and night for three weeks by three armed men before being murdered. According to the informer, his wife was told he had been sent to safety in the United States. The decade was punctuated with occasional murders of this kind, and although it is difficult to confirm the veracity of this account, it is feasible.[19]

Fenianism also acted as a self-supporting network of contacts and assistance. John Clancy, a retired publican and highly influential sub-sheriff, later nicknamed the 'mayor-maker' on account of his influence in municipal politics, and the model for Joyce's Long John Fanning,[20] was suspected of using his influence to find work for known Fenians. Through Clancy, Pat Malloy, J. J. O'Brien, William Branton, and James Boland obtained employment in the service of the Dublin corporation in 1885,[21] Boland as an inspector of paving.[22] As a leading figure in the Paviour's Society, Boland became an influential Dublin Fenian. He is now principally remembered as Harry Boland's father.[23] Both Malloy and Boland had Invincible connections, Boland joining

---

[18] D.M.P. 1887 'Fenian doings in Dublin City 16th May to 7[*sic*] June 1887'.

[19] The report is wrongly filed among the D.M.P. papers of 1883.

[20] John Wyse Jackson and Peter Costello, *John Stanislaus Joyce* (London, 1997), pp 194–5. John Clancy was imprisoned in 1866, at the height of Fenianism, in Mountjoy prison for treasonable practices. Later a member of the Land League, he was arrested in 1882 under the Protection of Person and Property (Ireland) Act 1881, and imprisoned at Kilmainham. On release he was elected to Dublin city council for Inn's Quay Ward. On becoming sub-sheriff in 1885 he resigned his seat. T.N.A. (P.R.O.), C.O. 904 17/107, Fenian Suspects Vol.1.

[21] D.M.P. 1885.

[22] T.N.A. (P.R.O.), Balfour Papers 30/60/2 Intelligence Notes, 16–31 Mar. 1890.

[23] See David Fitzpatrick, *Harry Boland's Irish Revolution* (Cork, 2003), pp 18ff.

others making a temporary escape to the U.S.A. following the murders. Reddy noted in January 1888 that Michael Murphy, another Invincible, was making a new coat for Boland.[24] In March that year, William Brophy, another U.S. escapee, had a contract to repair a public house in Upper Exchange Street and had employed a number of men, all of whom were supposed Fenians.[25] Finally, there is the unnamed individual whom Reddy suspected of Fenianism on the grounds that Clancy got him a corporation job as a sanitary officer.[26] It is possible that this was James Cooke, a leading alumnus of 1867 suspected of involvement in the Clerkenwell prison explosion of that year which caused several fatalities.

Suspected Fenians worked and drank together, helping each other out as friends do, bringing business, providing jobs and, no doubt, protection in a rough city. There was a hint of the mafia or the freemasons in their activities, and for many members this aspect of the organisation increased its attraction in the 1880s. It was a complex web of association, allegiance, and intrigue. Filial and occupational ties bound together working men across the generations, allegedly in pursuit of the withdrawal of British government from Ireland through a military confrontation, but as concerned with interpersonal rivalry, vendetta, and an enjoyable social life. The more middle-class and puritanical separatists of the 1900s found this aspect of Fenianism distasteful. Although the police were alert to the possibility of a concerted reorganisation of the I.R.B., they tended to regard the Fenians more as a mildly criminal underworld to be kept in check than as a revolutionary threat.

In order to facilitate this necessary surveillance Superintendent Reddy drew up a list of the most dangerous Fenians in the Dublin area in 1886, with some additions in 1888.[27] This list consisted of seventy-seven names, and identified two main groupings in addition to the remaining Invincibles. The largest group was the Council Party – those loyal to the Supreme Council, the authoritarian governing body of the I.R.B. The second major grouping advertised their continued loyalty to the leadership of the exiled treason-felon James Stephens. It is unlikely that Stephens had much influence over these men – the coherency of the group stemmed primarily from their most dominant member, the aforementioned John Sullivan: they were Sullivanites rather than Stephensites.[28] A third group was made up of Invincibles and their associates, although this designation was especially vague, often arising from little more than an acquaintance with the murderers of 1882.

Each of the three groups was highly fluid and ill-defined and it is unlikely the clear demarcations imposed by Reddy would have been recognised by

---

[24] D.M.P. 1888/931.

[25] D.M.P. 1888/933.

[26] D.M.P. 1888/1128.

[27] D.M.P. 1886–1887, 3/974/3.

[28] Sullivan was 'stout' and 'walks very quickly with a very short pace, generally dresses in black clothes and square ferry hat'. D.M.P. 1888/1170.

contemporaries. Nonetheless, the report is suggestive of the nature of the divisions and hierarchies that existed within Fenianism. The men of '67 and the publicans were generally held in high esteem, the former for their revolutionary heritage, which could always be talked up over a jar, and the latter for providing an obvious focus for Fenian association. Of the seventy-seven, six are identified as having been of particular importance in 1867, nine had been investigated under the Protection of Persons and Property (Ireland) Act 1881, and several others had temporarily fled to the U.S.A. following the Phoenix Park murders, including Boland. There was a small collection of hangers-on. Of the 40-year-old marble-mason Mathew Comerford, Reddy's officers could agree that he was an alcoholic but not whether he was dangerous; while Michael Hickey would 'do anything for money', such as distributing arms.

As a group the Stephensites were socially typical and are a convenient size to examine more closely. They appear to have been among the more aggressive of the Dublin Fenians. The D.M.P. connected several of them to the Bailey murder, and believed Sullivan to be the president of an I.R.B. vigilance committee and the 'only man in Dublin' openly to advocate dynamite, although he was 'too cunning and cowardly to personally participate'. There were nineteen identified Sullivanites ranging in age from 27 to 53, with eight in their forties and seven in their thirties. It seems safe to assume that the foremost event in their teens and twenties was the 1867 rising, the zenith of I.R.B. influence and organisation. Indeed forty of the seventy-seven would have been 16 or over during the rising. Reddy seemed to have little respect for the seceders, describing one, Thomas Healy, as 'always associating for a number of years with debauched Fenians'.

In 1869 Lord Straithnarn, the commander of the forces in Ireland, had described the Fenians as that 'class above the masses',[29] a description borne out by Comerford's research and equally applicable to the 1880s. Among the Sullivanites there was a bookseller, a shoemaker, a rope maker, a butcher, a barber, a picture frame maker, a solicitor's clerk, a publican, two labourers, a carpenter, a coffin maker, a serviceman, two tailors, a gas fitter, and the assistant secretary to the public health committee.

The D.M.P. list as a whole gives some indication of the I.R.B.'s appeal across the generations. If the alleged membership was split into age groups of five years, the most populous cohort was that of the 26–30 year olds, with nineteen members. However, only five were 25 or under, the same number as were 51 or over. The relatively large number who came to prominence in their late twenties suggests that Fenianism had a reasonable appeal to those in the younger age group, as the growth of the G.A.A. and Y.I.S. over the course of the decade also suggested. Moreover, of the fourteen names added to the list

---

[29] Quoted in K. Theodore Hoppen, *Elections, Politics, and Society in Ireland 1832–1885* (Oxford, 1984), p. 359.

in 1888, six were between the ages of 28 and 35 and had come to the attention of the police through their work for the Y.I.S.

Coming to prominence under the aegis of literature, debate, and hurley, these younger men represented a departure from the first generation of Fenians. Chief among the six was Fred Allan, a 29-year-old journalist and member of the Supreme Council since 1883,[30] who was instrumental in ensuring that the Y.I.S. became identifiably Fenian. The other five were the clerk Michael J. Seery (joined the Y.I.S. in October 1883), the journalist P. J. Hoctor, the shop employee J. K. Shannon, and the two draper's assistants J. B. O'Reilly and John Bishop.[31] All identified with the Council Party and were involved in the Gaelic Athletic Association, particularly Hoctor, who was a close friend and colleague of P. N. Fitzgerald, a leading G.A.A. organiser.[32]

III

The history of the Young Ireland Society falls into three phases. From its inception in April 1881 until May 1883 the society had the approval of the Irish National League and epitomised a Dublin atmosphere of political exploration and cosmopolitanism. A destructive row of May 1883 facilitated the ascendancy of Fred Allan and friends, while the third phase began with the return to Dublin in January 1885 of the exiled treason-felon John O'Leary. Under his presidency the society became more intellectually ambitious, attracting the membership of a Trinity College clique seduced by O'Leary's erudite romantic nationalism. Increasingly alienated from the established leaders of Dublin Fenianism, the society's final phase is less distinct. Although surviving into the 1900s (notably in Cork), its Dublin branches were swallowed up by the Young Ireland League, a Yeatsian initiative, and the Y.I.S. lost its distinct identity. The support of O'Leary and other leading members for Parnell during the split saw attention diverted away from literary matters, while Parnell's death provided the opportunity for a rising generation of cultural separatists to assert their independence through a series of new literary organisations.

The analytic usefulness of this schema might initially be demonstrated by examining two brief statements of the aims of the society. Quoting their first president, John Dillon M.P., the first of the two surviving minute books opens

---

[30] T.N.A. (P.R.O.), C.O. 904 17/1.

[31] John Bishop was 'an exceedingly extreme man in his ideas and one of those who cannot tolerate anything short of total separation and is a strong believer in physical force or anything that could according to his ideas involve England in difficulties. He is I believe a rather intelligent fellow.' D.M.P. 1886–1887/899.

[32] See W. F. Mandle's exhaustive *The Gaelic Athletic Association and Irish Nationalist Politics 1884–1924* (Dublin, 1987).

with: 'It is almost if not absolutely essential to the greatness of the country that those who aim to be the leaven of the coming generation should know one another.'[33] The objects of the society are then listed in two bland statements of intent:

1 The advancement of the national cause.
2 The holding of a meeting once every week when some question will be discussed which may fasten amongst the youth of Ireland a taste for and interest in political debate.

Five years later, at the height of O'Leary's influence, the D.M.P. succinctly defined the aims of the Y.I.S.: 'To educate Irish youth in national Irish literature. To encourage debate and public speaking on national subjects, to foster resentment against English rule in Ireland, and to keep alive the agitation for separation.'[34]

The difference in tone evident in the quotations was not solely indicative of their varied provenance; it represented accurately the change the Y.I.S. had undergone. The 'national cause', suggestive of a whole range of nationalisms, had become 'separation', an ostensibly clear aim. A desire to politicise Ireland's youth through the passive medium of discussion had fed into political action – into 'agitation'.[35] In an echo of the development of the G.A.A., founded in 1884, and the subsequent history of the Gaelic League, the combination of I.R.B. organisation and an electric political atmosphere ensured that Y.I.S. literary and social activities were radically politicised.

In addition to the weekly lectures delivered at the meetings, the main activities of the Y.I.S. included educational initiatives aimed at the young, the drumming up of crowds during the annual November Manchester Martyrs commemorations, and the commissioning of memorials to dead heroes. A correspondent of the Fenian newspaper *The Irishman* was keen to emphasise the egalitarian ethos of the Y.I.S.: unlike many debating societies, argued Gadelus, the Y.I.S. did not presuppose knowledge of Irish history, but worked 'amongst the great body of the Irish people, amongst our farmers and shopkeepers'.[36] The society was run by a committee elected biannually consisting of a president, two vice-presidents, a secretary, a treasurer, and a number of ordinary committee members, usually from ten to twelve in

[33] Minute Book of the Young Ireland Society 1881–1884 (N.L.I., MS 16095). The secondary literature on the Y.I.S. suggests that this minute book has not been read before. Leon Ó Broin incorrectly dates the second minute book to 1884–5 in *Revolutionary Underground: The Story of the Irish Republican Brotherhood 1858–1924* (Dublin, 1976), p. 36. R. F. Foster, *W.B. Yeats: A Life. I: The Apprentice Mage* (Oxford, 1997), p. 640, dates the founding of the Y.I.S. to 1885.
[34] D.M.P. 1886 501/5801.
[35] Ironically, orthodox Fenians associated 'agitation' with supposedly apolitical agrarianism.
[36] *Irishman*, 1 Apr. 1882.

number.[37] Branches loosely affiliated to Dublin began to crop up across Ireland, as well as in Manchester, Liverpool, and Glasgow.

The society was launched on 3 April 1881 from rooms in York Street, Dublin. This was a significant location. Borrowed from the Workingmen's Club, but increasingly controlled by the Irish National League (I.N.L), the main home rule organisation, these rooms were an Irish nationalist palimpsest. I.N.L. growth depended on such pre-existing clubs affiliating to the national organisation and bringing their members with them. The class solidarities and communities established in such rooms often outlived such more immediate political allegiances. Mark Ryan's Chancery Lane medical practice, for example, famously hosted a succession of Fenian organisations, and in this it provided a typical illustration of the fragility of Irish nationalist organisation in this period. The nationalist working men shared York Street with an Orange Lodge and, from 1883, the Conservative Workingmen's Club, a venue for anti-papal working-class protestant conviviality. The street witnessed a series of violent confrontations provoked by the latter's determination to hang a large union flag from their upper windows and to decorate the building with bunting on special occasions. This conflict culminated in the 1886 general election riot when William Cruikshank fired on the crowd from these upper windows causing several injuries. The whole club was placed under arrest.[38] So, hardly an oasis of cerebral calm, York Street was a microcosm of the popular passions that animated Irish politics; this environment made the young protestant intellectuals who later attended Y.I.S. meetings all the more remarkable.

Robert Reilly, the Y.I.S. secretary, delivered the inaugural address on the life and times of Grattan to an audience composed primarily of medical students. Thereafter, a public address would generally be used to propagate the beginning of each of the society's two annual sessions. John Dillon, president of the society from 1881 to 1884,[39] urged that the rules promulgated by the organising committee be revised, allowing membership for those who did not adhere to the objects and principles of the society. Although the president felt it would be advantageous for the opposition to attend the meetings, Dillon's role as a symbolic figurehead – he rarely attended meetings – ensured that it was not until 30 March 1883 that poor attendance by members obliged the society to open its lectures and debates to the general public.[40]

The first committees of the society were broadly based.[41] Among the vice-presidents were Daniel Crilly, elected M.P. for Mayo North in 1888, and John

---

[37] Minute Book of the Young Ireland Society 1885–6 (N.L.I., MS 19158).

[38] Martin Maguire, 'The Organisation and Activism of Dublin's Protestant Working Class, 1883–1935' in *I.H.S.*, xxix, no. 113 (May 1994), pp 75–8.

[39] Dillon's presidency was overlooked in F. S. L. Lyons, *John Dillon* (London, 1968).

[40] N.L.I., MS 16095.

[41] Ibid.

Wyse Power, a journalist working for *United Ireland* and intermittently under police surveillance.[42] J. J. Clancy, Parnellite M.P. for Dublin County North, occasionally chaired meetings (as did Thomas Sexton M.P.) and briefly became the society's treasurer in December 1882,[43] while members of the Ladies' Land League were frequently in the audience. The pattern continued with the inaugural meeting for the first session of 1882; those attending included John and William Redmond, the Quaker intellectual and nationalist Alfred Webb, Daniel Crilly, and, of course, Fred Allan.[44] Week-to-week debates touched upon contemporary political concerns, while papers were regularly delivered on leading nationalist figures of the past. The attitudes expressed could imply the authoritarianism of Fenianism – a small majority voted against the motion that vote by ballot should prevail in a free country – or the enthusiasms of an urban intelligentsia touched by the latest political fashions: land nationalisation was deemed preferable to a peasant proprietary as the 'true solution to the land question', no doubt reflecting the ideas popularised by Michael Davitt under the influence of the Californian radical Henry George.[45] More conventionally, 'England's difficulty being Ireland's opportunity' was affirmed; democracy was considered more favourable than aristocracy for the furtherance of science and art; federation with the U.S.A. would be more favourable than with Britain; protection rather than free trade would benefit Irish industry (a Griffithite premonition); and Irish nationalists were not to think it necessary to conciliate English public opinion.[46] Predictably, papers were read on Thomas Davis, Mangan, Wolfe Tone, and Curran; and the opportunity was provided for the public pursuit of personal interests. Kenny spoke on 'Nooks and Corners of Ireland'; Alfred Webb presented his 'Notes on Foreign Travel'.[47]

Fenian designs on the society were suddenly and rapidly felt. The respectability of the society's debates was disturbed on 4 May 1883 when it was proposed that the Y.I.S. discuss whether the resolutions in support of constitutional nationalism and Parnell passed by the Philadelphia Convention

---

[42] For example see D.M.P. 315 w/884, 7 May 1883. J.W.P. was identified as a member of the Supreme Council in October 1892 by the D.M.P.; Major Gosselin was unconvinced, C.O. 904/16, 3. J.W.P.'s wife Jennie was to become a leading nationalist, suffragette and separatist agitator. Crilly lectured on 'Fanny Parnell, Poetess and Patriot', *Irishman*, 5 Apr. 1884.

[43] See N.L.I., MS 16095, 14 Oct. 1881, and *Irishman*, 22 Oct. 1881 (when Clancy proposed from the chair a motion condemning the arrests of Parnell and Thomas Sexton M.P.), 30 Sept. 1882 and 16 Sept. 1883.

[44] T.N.A. (P.R.O.), C.O. 904 17/1.

[45] N.L.I., MS 16095, 27 Oct. 1882 and 7 Oct. 1881; T. W. Moody, *Michael Davitt and Irish Revolution, 1846–1882* (Oxford, 1981), pp 413–14, 504–5, 527.

[46] N.L.I., MS 16095, 4 Nov. 1881, 2 Dec. 1881, 17 Feb. 1882, 31 Mar. 1882, 15 Sept. 1882.

[47] N.L.I., MS 16095, 10 Feb. 1882, 10 Mar. 1882, 24 Mar. 1882, 22 Sept. 1882, 25 Nov. 1881, 19 May 1882.

of Irish nationalists were worthy of Irish approval.[48] According to lengthy reports printed in *The Times*, extremist views had been effectively sidelined by the organisers in response to a public letter from Parnell. Similar tensions were evident at the Chicago Convention of 1886 when John Finerty, although a supporter of Parnell, questioned the promotion of home rule as 'the final settlement of all Ireland's troubles'. John Redmond, present at the convention, alongside Davitt, O'Brien, and John Deasy M.P., wrote a pamphlet playing down the controversy. The impression that Irish nationalism was unified behind the party was judged to be of paramount importance.[49] Having decided to pursue the issue at the next meeting, the Y.I.S. received a letter from the Irish National League forbidding the debate on their premises. The D.M.P. had considered Parnell's branch of the I.N.L. and the Y.I.S. 'one and the same society':[50] this was no longer the case.

The fallout was immediate. Three established and stalwart members of the society resigned their executive posts on 11 May. At the general meeting of 4 August a motion with an unmistakable Fenian tenor was proposed: the committee was empowered to prevent the discussion of religious and theological subjects.[51] The Fenian position was consolidated at the beginning of the second session of 1883 with the election of the new committee. Although F. D. F. O'Connor was re-elected vice-president, the Allan nominees R. J. O'Duffy and J. K. Shannon were elected vice-president and treasurer respectively, while Allan and his co-conspirator Bardon were re-elected as secretaries. Allan's instrumental manoeuvring ensured the society asserted its Fenian credentials and rejected the conclusions of the Philadelphia Convention by the narrow margin of three votes. It seems certain that the increased Fenian infiltration of the Y.I.S. was facilitated by the decision to open meetings to the general public in March.

Over the following year the society experienced a period of expansion, its activities taking on a focus and direction distinct from the discursive drift of its formative years. Committees were formed dedicated to encouraging 'national education' and financing graveside memorials to nationalist martyrs,[52] while meetings became more ambitious and better advertised. Mrs Ralph Varian, a now forgotten poet, was invited to give a lecture at the Rotunda

---

[48] N.L.I., MS 16095. The minute book does not report these resolutions, which can be followed in *The Times*, 26–30 Apr. 1883.

[49] J. E. Redmond, 'The Chicago Convention' in *The Irish Question*, no. 3 (London, 1886), pp 1–22.

[50] D.M.P. 1883 315w/2628.

[51] Cf. the small majority at Phibsborough branch against motion 'That Atheists should be permitted to take part in the legislation of a country'. Allan was among those in favour. Earlier that month they had decided Catholic emancipation was not of political benefit to Ireland, a decision that took Fenian hostility to O'Connell to its logical extreme. *Irishman*, 15 & 29 July 1882.

[52] *Irishman*, 17 Nov. 1883.

under the auspices of the society on 3 October. A thousand copies of one of her poems were printed for the occasion at her request and she received three guineas for her trouble.[53] Similar efforts were made in the organisation of the Manchester Martyr commemorations, with the cost of badges investigated. The minute book records that they were not to exceed ten shillings for twenty. The prohibition of the march by Dublin Castle reflected the tighter regime imposed by the government since the Phoenix Park murders and the increased profile and provocativeness of the I.R.B. It is tempting to see the huge influx of new members in November 1883 as illustrative of the increased notoriety of the society. Whereas it was more typical for members to trickle in in twos and threes, the meetings of 30 November and 18 January saw twenty-six and fifteen respectively proposed and elected to membership.[54] The D.M.P. estimated the society as having 200 members in 1886.[55] More significantly, the closer links Parnell had forged with the catholic church after the Kilmainham Treaty and the strict parliamentarianism of the home rule party must have left some of those attracted to Parnellism by the radicalism of the land agitation phase seeking a more advanced politics. The Fenian sympathies shared by the new membership were implied by a large majority affirming that the success of an agitation depended upon the impression that physical force lay behind it – the Phibsborough branch concurred.[56] No doubt perturbed by this unprecedented level of interest, the D.M.P. had an informer at the meeting of 7 December 1883.[57] The tone had been set for 1884: accusations of 'toadyism' met the corporation's vote of condolence to Queen Victoria in April; membership continued to rise, but gradually; and, in an act of comical self-aggrandisement, a copy of the society's resolution congratulating France and the U.S. for striking 'the first great blows at tyrannical institutions in the new and old worlds' was to be presented to the respective presidents of the two countries.[58]

There is, however, no reason to doubt the sincerity of the members. With the close of the Land War and the gradual emergence of a disciplined home rule party the political stakes in Ireland in the mid-1880s were high. The earnestness with which the Y.I.S. approached the teaching of nationalist history to children stemmed from the importance it placed on the nurture of a separatist generation for the future. The society extolled in the *Dublin Evening Telegraph*:

---

[53] N.L.I., MS 16095. This was probably Mary Varian who had a poem in the collection Ralph Varian edited *The Harp of Erin*. Varian's sister Hester was married to Dr George Sigerson, who combined science and revivalism, and they were close to the Yeats/O'Leary circle. See D. J. O'Donoghue, *The Poets of Ireland* (1912).
[54] N.L.I., MS 16095.
[55] D.M.P. 501/5801, 19 Nov. 1886, 'National Associations in Ireland'.
[56] *Irishman*, 17 June 1882.
[57] D.M.P. 1883.
[58] N.L.I., MS 16095.

The spirits of our dead heroes live in song and story, the study of whereof will transmit to those now living the love for the fatherland which filled the souls of our ancestors. It is not that the love is absent in the present day; but the machinations of the West Britons have to be contended against and knowledge of our country's history, our country's song, will help to buoy every Irishman in their march for political independence.[59]

Despite a successful prize-giving concert in the Rotunda in June 1884 for youngsters who had successfully demonstrated knowledge of Irish history,[60] the Education Committee of the Y.I.S. can hardly have been surprised to receive a letter from the Commissioners of National Education refusing to adopt their programme of history teaching in the national schools.[61]

In prescribing history the society reflected both the agenda of the original Young Irelanders and the current vogue for memoirs of the old Fenian and nationalist elite. Hundreds of newspaper column inches were covered by works such as James Stephens's *Reminiscences*, printed in the *Weekly Freemen* in 1883–4; Charles Gavan Duffy's *Four Years of Irish History 1845–1849* and *The League of the North and South* occupied significant space over the next two years. Ostensibly, Fenianism and rebellion were kept before the people as history rather than current affairs, but Stephens's work in particular can only have been interpreted as a timely comment on Parnellism. In one extract he had shown his contempt for the political pragmatism espoused by the home rule party. On reaching Tipperary during his mythologised walk through Ireland promoting Fenianism in the 1850s, Stephens came upon a man with whom he would not deign to sit down to dinner:

> It was the duty of every patriot . . . [the man] said, to have tact and prudence, and not to put himself in the noose we fell into in '48. This remark of his confirmed my first idea of the man. 'He has lost faith and become a soulless serf,' I muttered to myself, as I shook his hand with all due formality, and declined his pressing offer of dinner.[62]

Having shown himself servile to the English the man is then presented in the undignified position of imploring Stephens to sit down at his table. Stephens taught that history demonstrated that radicalism was synonymous with dignity, that freedom was in the first instance a state of mind, and that the Irish ought not to eat at the table of English constitutionalism with Mr Speaker looking on.

Coterminous with this increase in public access to history was a debate concerning the politics of public memorials. The Y.I.S. had founded the Y.I.S.

---

[59] *Dublin Evening Telegraph (D.E.T.)*, 7 Jan. 1884.
[60] *D.E.T.*, 21 June 1884.
[61] *D.E.T.*, 4 Oct. 1884.
[62] *Weekly Freeman (W.F.)*, 5 Jan. 1884.

National Monuments Committee in response to a suggestion by the *Freeman's Journal* in September 1883 that a monument be erected over the grave of the '48 poet James Clarence Mangan. The debate came into focus in September 1885 when Hogan's statue of Thomas Davis was removed from public view by the Mount Jerome Cemetery Company to protect it from the weather.[63] The controversy that followed pivoted on whether the statue belonged to the 'public' – it had been raised by public subscription – or the Cemetery Company. In an article in the *Dublin University Review* Charles Hubert Oldham outlined the necessity of having such memorials on public view. Having urged the Y.I.S. to mobilise support and the fund for its display, Oldham extolled:

> It is the indomitable, earnest, truthful, unselfish spirit that inspires us through admiration; the spotless life that humiliates us through contrast. It is in a word the man. It is for this we want this image in the midst of us, where our lives are lived: not hid away in a cemetery, where we go to be forgotten.[64]

The importance the authorities attached to this work was indicated by the controversy that arose in 1886 between the Y.I.S., the Catholic Cemeteries Committee, and the attorney-general. It had been a long-held ambition of the Y.I.S. to form out of the large plot in which the '67 heroes MacManus, MacCarthy, O'Mahony, and Reddin lay side by side a 'large vault in which others, who might express a desire to be buried where these soldiers of Ireland rest, could in future years be laid'.[65] Allan and Bardon had written to John Devoy, the president of the Clan na Gael, in November 1883 requesting the leader of U.S. Fenianism open a subscription list and ensure the project was given press attention. Evidently progress was made, for on 6 October 1886 permission was given by the Catholic Cemeteries Committee for construction to commence. An attempt by the Y.I.S. to have the statutory cemetery fee waived delayed the building and ensured that the project was brought to the attention of the attorney-general. A second letter from the Cemeteries Board in November reported that the attorney-general considered the proposed inscription seditious, instructing that it would have to be altered. The National Monuments Committee, furious with the 'Castle Catholics', insisted that it would adhere to the original agreement of October 1886.[66] Unfortunately, the exact outcome of this controversy is unknown, although during the 1888 Manchester Martyrs Commemoration a large black scroll was thrown across the MacManus plot inscribed with a verse of nationalist poetry, suggesting that the vault had not been built.[67]

---

[63] *Dublin University Review (D.U.R.)*, vol. 1, no. 8, Sept. 1885, p. 163 in the bound volumes.
[64] *D.U.R.*, vol.1, no. 9, Oct. 1885, p. 229.
[65] William O'Brien and Desmond Ryan (ed.), *Devoy's Postbag [D.P.B.1]* (Dublin, 1948), i, p. 221.
[66] *W.F.*, 1 Jan. 1887.
[67] *W.F.*, 1 Dec. 1888.

A year earlier the National Monuments Committee had experienced a notable success. P. N. Fitzgerald was invited to the Manchester Martyrs commemoration to unveil memorials to the Fenian poet J. K. Casey ('Leo') and to Stephen O'Donoghue, 'a young man who was shot during the insurrectionary proceedings at Tallaght on 4th March '67'. In a familiar trope, Fitzgerald invoked the dead of the past as witnesses to the present actions of the young, urging that 'they ought to vow over the graves of their martyred dead that they would never give up the struggle till the martyrs' hopes were realised and till they attained sovereign independence for their dear old land (cheers).'[68]

The monuments themselves successfully combined all the iconographic paraphernalia typical of Irish nationalism. Leo's 14ft 6in high Celtic cross of Ballinasloe limestone was festooned with shamrocks, its pedestal touched off with a wolf-dog, harp, and sunburst; the portal evoked the saints, scholars, and warriors of ancient Ireland via a round tower and ancient ruined abbey carved in bold relief. O'Donoghue's monument was augmented by the names of two further '67 men, Thomas Farrell and the exiled treason-felon Terence Byrne. In 1888, thanks to the Ladies Decoration Committee, the cross of the Martyrs was touched off by a 'large floral star with the choicest colours'.[69]

The raw material made available by the press provided a focus for the comradeship engendered by the literary groups, binding the generations in receipt of a shared heritage. Societies such as the Y.I.S. fostered a sense of collective empowerment that newspapers alone could not achieve. It is important to appreciate that the Y.I.S. was able to promote through memorials and the Manchester Martyrs commemorations a specifically Fenian agenda: its focus was primarily on the commemoration and legitimation of 1867. Against the instability and hope promoted by the Parnellite project, history helped provide a sense of certainty and a rationale for action: history provided an unfinished narrative into which current projects could slot and perhaps provide the culmination of a prestigious lineage.[70] Much of the discussion carried out under the auspices of the Y.I.S. was an attempt to create a mentality to suffuse a future Irish state.[71] Later separatists laid ever greater stress on this need to prepare the Irish people for independence, arguing that an authentic national independence could only be achieved with a mental transformation concomitant to the political.

For the society to maintain its prominence it was essential that its public face remained respectable, continuing to provide a venue for home rule M.P.s to meet with their constituents. Newspaper entries reporting the society's

---

[68] *Nation*, 28 Nov. 1885.
[69] *W.F.*, 1 Dec. 1888.
[70] For example, see R. F. Foster, *The Story of Ireland: An Inaugural Lecture delivered before the University of Oxford on 1 December 1994* (Oxford, 1995).
[71] Foster, *Apprentice Mage*, p. 41.

meetings were clearly submitted by the secretary and were bland, giving little indication of the style of debate or the rhetoric employed. The appointment diaries of Justin McCarthy M.P. provide ample evidence of the variety of concerns in which an Irish M.P. might show an interest. January 1881 saw the M.P. attending the Junior Liberal Association in Birmingham; an Irish concert at the Forresters' Hall in February 1883; and in 1885 anything from a Theosophist Society meeting in March (an interest he shared with other home rulers interested in Indian politics, and with Fred Allan), to a 'Colonial Institute Soiree' in June, and a women's suffrage meeting in July.[72] John Deasy M.P. presided at the establishment of the Cork Y.I.S., William O'Brien was elected its president, and McCarthy was to give the inaugural address in September 1884; Timothy Sexton M.P. committed himself to speak at some point.[73] Earlier in the year Dr Andrew Commins M.P. presided at a Liverpool Y.I.S. social.[74] These inaugural meetings and social events became a regular point of contact between the parliamentarians and the public; the inaugural lecture for the York Street branch session of January to April 1884 was particularly indicative of this symbiosis. Charles Dawson M.P., lord mayor for Dublin 1882–3, spoke on 'Young Ireland and the Future'.[75] The lord mayor, William Meagher, took the chair and William O'Brien M.P. gave thanks.[76]

Dawson took the opportunity to intervene in the ongoing debate concerning denominational education. He argued that the broad appeal of explicitly catholic schools would generate the skills necessary to encourage Ireland's industrialisation. In a comment informed by the pervasive rhetoric of temperance and the desire to put the Irish question into a non-colonial and hence constitutional context, Dawson asserted that 'Ireland had no enemy of a physical character – at least no enemy in the panoply of war trampling upon her soil, but her enemies were idleness, dissipation, and intemperance, which prevailed in this country to a terrible extent.' Aware of the need to placate the Fenian element in the audience, Dawson adopted the technique used by Parnell in his so-called 'appeal to the hillside men' during the split. In asserting the need for toleration, a recurrent theme at Y.I.S. public meetings, Dawson advocated non-peaceful means as a last resort. Dawson outlined his belief

---

[72] N.L.I., MS 3679–3714.
[73] *Irishman*, 6 Sept. 1884 and *D.E.T.*, 10 September 1884. Possible future speakers included the M.P.s Sexton, T. M. Healy, and T. P. O'Connor.
[74] *Irishman*, 3 May 1884.
[75] Dawson was an experienced local politician: he had been high sheriff for Limerick in 1876–7 and was elected to parliament for the Carlow borough in April 1880; although not particularly active, he was a loyal Parnellite. See Alan O'Day, *The English Face of Irish Nationalism* (Dublin, 1977), pp 14, 21, 25, 29 and *DOD's Parliamentary Companion 1885* (London, 1885), p. 212.
[76] *D.E.T.*, 11 Jan. 1884; *W.F.*, 19 Jan. 1884.

in no such thing as unconditional toleration any more than in unconditional loyalty (hear). Toleration meant that a person should bear towards others who differed from him a certain fashion and manner, but directly you found in place of toleration an ascendancy over the rights of others, then peaceful as he was, he would be prepared to abandon the path of toleration, and if necessary to assert with equal force to that arrayed against the rights he was entitled to enjoy (hear, hear).

Although clearly not advocating physical force under present conditions, in an era of intermittent coercion the ambiguity of these words could be construed as highly subversive.

William O'Brien was quick to dispel any note of rebellion that might have been inferred from Dawson's closing words. Just as Dawson had approved of the 'sound and rational' basis of the Y.I.S.'s aims, O'Brien praised the 'spirit of broadminded tolerance and sympathy and sincerity, in a serious sense of responsibility in all they did and said (hear, hear)'. In an astute move, O'Brien characterised current social conditions as largely meritocratic, placing the aims of the Y.I.S. into a context of personal development rather than national liberation. This was a direct appeal to the petit-bourgeois and working-class sentiments of the organisation's primary constituents, while suggesting that earlier rebellion might be understood and legitimised in a socio-political context that no longer existed. O'Brien avoided denigrating the past while clearly limiting legitimate action in the present, suggesting that the disaffection felt by the rebels of 1848 and 1867 no longer applied:[77]

> The young men of today [have] a wonderful advantage compared with those under of their grandfathers. The whole tendency of today was to exalt the lowly and reward intellect and pluck and industry, and not to honour a man according to the title deeds of his ancestors, but according to the good he did.[78]

In their attempt to impose limits on the legitimate ends of the Y.I.S., it is tempting to see the politicians as endeavouring to bring the society within their orbit, if not direct control. The pattern continued. At the inaugural meeting of the October–December session 1884, the M.P.s Dawson, Sexton, Nicolas Lynch, and Edward McMahon were present. It was an impressive meeting, comprising 400 people, 'principally young men of the clerk and draper

---

[77] See Sally Warwick-Haller, *William O'Brien and the Irish Land War* (Dublin, 1990), pp 124–8, for a discussion of O'Brien's novel *When We Were Boys* (London, 1890) which touched on these themes. His position was marginally more ambiguous than the Y.I.S. oration implied: 'A rising is (I may not quite say, used to be)', wrote O'Brien, 'a sort of Silver Jubilee in every generous Irish life. Young men look forward to their own rising, and old men look back upon theirs.' See also William O'Brien, 'Was Fenianism Ever Formidable?', *Contemporary Review*, lxxi (1897), pp 680–93, for a less sanguine view.
[78] *W.F.*, 19 Jan. 1884.

class, some R. C. clergymen and a few ladies'.[79] These M.P.s hoped to moderate the character of the organisation in the eyes of those who were targeted by these membership drives. It was a delicate balancing act: in attending and speaking at such meetings the constitutionalists were involved in the continuous game of placating advanced opinion, while at the same time conferring respectability on men associated with militarism. One anonymous polemicist warning against 'incipient Irish revolution' in 1889 was alert to these ambiguities. The author argued of the members of the Y.I.S. that they were 'not compelled to join the I.R.B. Circle, but association and force of opinion almost invariably' drove 'the whole of one into the other'.[80]

IV

Once the initial excitement and press attention had subsided the return from exile of John O'Leary was something of an anti-climax. Considerable hope had been vested in his return. In 1885 he was 55, in good health, and familiar to advanced nationalists owing to his regular correspondence with *The Irishman*.[81] He was readily elected by a large majority to the presidency of the Y.I.S. and was called upon to address the inaugural meeting of the 1885 session of the society at the Rotunda.[82] The society had been well primed for his return. A letter to Fred Allan of November 1883 enclosed a contribution to the nascent National Monuments Committee, as well as expressing resolute advanced views:

> Recreant rebels have taken to preaching to you a different sort of creed of late but I have too much confidence in the rising manhood of Ireland to believe that the new moral force delusion can be any more lasting than the old pestilent heresy of O'Connell's time.[83]

O'Leary's letter of acceptance of the honorary presidency of the Glasgow Y.I.S. of June 1884 suggested a similar intransigence, although signs of tempering were emerging. 'You are right in thinking my political opinions have undergone little, if any, change since '48. . . . I have little faith in Parliamentary action, which does not, however, involve want of faith in all public action, and still less in Parliamentary men.'[84] The Invincibles and the use of dynamite

---

[79] N.A. C.S.O.R.P. 22535/84.
[80] *Incipient Irish Revolution: An Exposé of Fenianism of To-day* (London, 1889), p. 4.
[81] *Irishman*, 24 Jan. 1880, 31 Jan. 1880, 8 May 1880, 29 May 1880, 5 Feb. 1881, 26 Feb. 1881, 19 Mar. 1881, 12 Nov. 1881.
[82] *Irishman*, 10 Jan. 1885. O'Leary's future rival for influence Charles McCarthy Teeling was in the chair.
[83] Papers found among the D.M.P. papers of 1889.
[84] *W.F.*, 14 June 1884, front page.

were condemned as 'the Irish form of that general Nihilistic movement which, in some shape or other, seems spreading everywhere at present'. O'Leary, more monarchist than republican, had been deeply shaken by the assassination of Tsar Alexander II in March 1881. The letter concludes without belligerence; education ought to be their only aim: 'we none of us, can be so certain of our wisdom as to be entitled to condemn a man simply because he differs from us.' Gavan Duffy dryly expressed a similar view in a letter to O'Leary from Monaco: 'I have come long ago to understand that uniformity of opinion is impracticable among men who think for themselves. It is not so much right views I seek in a friend as upright views – right views being of course those of which I have the monopoly.'[85] With age, it would seem, had come pluralism, eroding a position that gained much of its force from tunnel vision.

Both the *Weekly Freeman* and the *Nation* thoroughly reported the O'Leary speech and gave considered editorial comment. To a densely crowded Rotunda, O'Leary delivered his lecture 'Young Ireland – the Old and the New'. To the attentive listener this was no bland rehearsal of tired rhetoric. Having reiterated the need to educate, O'Leary launched a blistering attack on the current nationalist generation, urging them to live up to their past namesakes. It was not their timidity he castigated but their intolerance; this was a speech laced with classic free-thinking secularist ideas picked up in France.

> In no way are we more different from the Young Irelanders than in this; and by the 'we' here I mean to include all creeds, classes, and conditions of Irishmen in the present time. The Young Irelanders not only proclaimed the 'right to differ', but, having availed themselves pretty largely of the right themselves, were certainly as willing as any body of men I have ever heard of to concede it full to others. In the Ireland of today, on the contrary, there is no right so steadily denied, and assertion of which is so severely punished. . . . If we have good reason for believing that a man means well for Ireland we should take him to our heart of hearts, no matter what his way of thinking may be . . . there is no need that a man should be right, but only that he should be upright (cheers).[86]

Gavan Duffy must have smiled on reading this. What was more, although remaining unchanged in 'principles and aspirations', O'Leary's view had altered 'in many matters of practice and detail'.[87] As a returned exile, O'Leary acknowledged he had to resist the tendency to regard opinion as unchanged, and had to adapt to the tenor of the times.

Not even the most imaginative Fenian could claim O'Leary hoped to build an insurrectionary body out of the scattered branches of the Y.I.S. He advocated a 'central advising, guiding, and directing council', but repudiated Stephensite centralism, urging that the 'amplest latitude of choice should in

[85] N.L.I., MS 5927, 26 Nov. 1884.
[86] W.F., 24 Jan. 1885.
[87] Nation, 24 Jan. 1885.

all these matters be left to the separate branches, and that the last thing that should be thought of for societies, as for individuals, is that they should be forced into any Procrustian bed of uniformity'. O'Leary's peroration attempted a rebel cry:

> I believe firmly still what I first learned to believe some forty years ago, when I first read the poems of Thomas Davis, that it is the bounden duty of every born Irishman to live, and if needs die, that Ireland may be free (loud and prolonged cheers).[88]

William O'Brien, as ever on hand to clear up any ambiguity, stood to a 'tremendous ovation' and provided implicit praise of constitutionalism while echoing O'Leary's sentiment: 'Something has been done to reduce their [Irish nationalists'] principles and aspirations to practice (cheers). Something has been done to loosen the grip of England on Ireland (cheers).' John Redmond spoke after O'Brien.[89]

O'Leary's speech had been almost uniformly moderate: he had shown a hesitancy regarding his rightful role in 1880s Ireland as well as implying that his age put him beyond any desire to claim an overall leadership – O'Leary had a tendency to exaggerate his decrepitude. He curtailed his role to that of the literary guru, happily providing reading lists and guidance. Privately, O'Leary was even more pragmatic. Shortly after Gladstone's opening speech on the first home rule bill, O'Leary wrote an approving letter to the Liberal politician James Bryce:

> [A]s well as I can form an opinion as yet the scheme is, barring a few details, satisfactory – as much as most reasonable Irishmen could expect, and, I fear, more than most Englishmen, who are mostly most unreasonable in regard to Ireland, will be willing to concede. God grant, however, that it may be otherwise, and God bless Mr Gladstone anyhow.[90]

O'Leary's recognition of the nationalist legitimacy of reasonable expectations pointed to an ideological flexibility not normally associated with Fenianism. Although a clear vindication of Parnell's progress since Kilmainham – there was even a veiled reference to the effectiveness of agrarian agitation ('"the price of peace is Ireland" as Sir Chas. Duffy phrased it') – O'Leary suspected home rule was 'probably more than England is willing to give' and was 'certainly the least that Ireland will be permanently satisfied with'.[91]

---

[88] W.F. and *Irishman*, 24 Jan. 1885.

[89] Ibid.

[90] O'Leary to Bryce, 9 Apr. 1886, Bryce Papers, Folio 95–101 (Bodleian MSS 213). My thanks to Dr Ian Sheehy for this reference.

[91] Cf. O'Leary in *Irishman*, 8 May 1880: 'Mr Parnell promises vastly more than Mr Butt, and is as much more energetic as he is less intelligent, but as his pace is so much rapider, so, in all human probability, will he more quickly reach that inevitable goal of all agitators – failure.'

Nevertheless, the Rotunda speech was pitched correctly if O'Leary was looking for warm editorial comment. 'John O'Leary on a platform in the Rotunda', cooed the *Weekly Freeman*, 'is like a vision from the days of twenty golden years ago. But his reception shows that decades may roll by and the spirit of his country remains unchanged.' Echoing O'Brien, both the *Freeman* and the *Nation* praised O'Leary's moderation. *The Irishman*, limping through its final months of publication, grabbed the opportunity lent by O'Leary's speech to editorialise orthodox Fenianism once more. The paper is worth quoting at length as an example of the type of screed O'Leary counselled against:

> Liberty won by heroism in battle, by the highest sacrifice that man can make for justice and natural right is cheaply purchased, more dearly prized, and possibly more lasting. As human nature is constituted, man is invigorated by supreme efforts, and the memory of a victory over the enemies of freedom inspires the pride and dignity which preserve nations from decrepitude and decay. Had we a choice, none of us would hesitate to take the shortest and manliest road to Liberty, cutting our way with the sword through the solid ranks of our adversary.[92]

Although it is not possible to identify two clearly defined factions operating within the Y.I.S., the impact of O'Leary and the rising generation of Irish nationalists came into focus through O'Leary's clash with Charles McCarthy Teeling in February 1886. The row had been brewing for some time. In August 1885 the society organised a memorial service at Mullinahone to mark the third anniversary of the death of Kickham, then president of the Supreme Council. O'Leary gave another moderate speech, praising Kickham's determination but acknowledging Parnell's current national leadership and the need for tolerance. Teeling spoke too, declaring himself 'no humanitarian or philanthropist', caring not how much of his own or his country's blood should be shed in the fight for freedom. O'Leary admonished him sharply, retorting, 'What nonsense. You should care.'[93]

As tensions escalated it is possible to trace the gradual rejection of Teeling by the society. In the session of January 1885 to June 1885, Teeling was elected vice-president, a position he retained for the remainder of the year. From January to June 1886 he held no committee post, having lost the joint vice-presidency to T. W. Rolleston and C. H. Oldham. The trend culminated in February 1886: Teeling belligerently insisted upon proposing a resolution before that week's paper was read and therefore before the general public. O'Leary ruled from the chair that this violated procedure and on Teeling's insistence on reading his resolution, O'Leary felt compelled to adjourn the meeting. In 1914 W. B. Yeats claimed that the controversy arose when Teeling attempted

[92] *Irishman*, 24 Jan. 1885. A characteristic product of its notorious editor Richard Pigott.
[93] W.F., 29 Aug. 1885.

to move a vote of censure against O'Leary for his condemnation of the Dynamitards,[94] while a police observer stated that the breach was triggered by Teeling's objection to the admittance of a socialist to the society.[95] The matter was settled at a well-attended special general meeting of 19 February. Despite the attempts made to heal the divisions, Teeling proved unrepentant and was expelled from the society by a convincing majority.

Teeling was later described by Yeats as 'an excitable man who had fought for the Pope against the Italian patriots and who always rode a white horse in our nationalist processions'.[96] Teeling was O'Leary's first blood, proof that an adherence to tolerance did not mean an uncritical acceptance of any revolutionary methods. However, whether provoked by a particular controversy concerning socialism or by dynamite, the long-term significance of the clash was largely symbolic. Teeling's electoral defeat at the hands of Rolleston and Oldham represented an expansion of the legitimate social constituency of grass-roots separatism. Rolleston, Trinity don and journalist, and Oldham, at 25 a Trinity star, were a long way from the D.M.P.'s list of 'dangerous Fenians'. Together they had founded the *Dublin University Review* in 1885 in emulation of Isaac Butt's *Dublin University Magazine*, and Oldham the Contemporary Club, both venues for primarily moderate discussion of contemporary issues.[97] Moderate perhaps, though it was around this time Oldham claimed to have lost his rooms at Trinity for having 'taken too prominent a part in politics to please the powers that be'.[98] Having controlled the Dublin branch of the Y.I.S., the I.R.B. had been upstaged by respectable cultural nationalists who now treated it as their own. Allan's orthodox attempts to keep the Fenian propensities of the society concealed had been subverted by O'Leary. Not only had an eirenic O'Leary openly discussed the relative merits of constitutionalism and separatism given the current political context, he had effectively advocated coexistence. The insult for Teeling and his ilk can only have been compounded by a lecture delivered by Oldham in April 1886 criticising the past work of the society and advocating the formation of a student circle as a corrective.[99]

'The Young Ireland Society, which a short time ago was an influential medium for disseminating Fenianism in Dublin and the provinces', the D.M.P. reported in June 1887, 'has lately ever since John O'Leary took it up, withdrawn

---

[94] Ó Broin, *Revolutionary Underground*, p. 40 and Marcus Bourke, *John O'Leary: A Study in Irish Separatism* (Tralee, 1967), pp 180–1 both follow W. B. Yeats, *Autobiographies* (London and Basingstoke, 1955), pp 99–100.

[95] C.O. 904 18/988.

[96] Yeats, *Autobiographies*.

[97] John Kelly and Eric Domville (ed.), *The Collected Letters of W. B. Yeats, Volume 1 1865–1895* (Oxford, 1986), pp 481–2, 508.

[98] Oldham to F. J. Bigger, 25 Feb. 1888 (Bigger Collection, Belfast Central Library, OL3).

[99] N.L.I., MS 19158.

from active service and is now out of favour with the Extreme Party.'[100] The implications of this estrangement would become apparent only in retrospect. O'Leary had provided an environment for the nourishment of a sophisticated cultural separatism under the leadership of an emergent intelligentsia. It was in the York Street rooms of the Y.I.S. that the precedent was set for the prominence of individuals in the mould of W. B. Yeats, Maud Gonne, and Douglas Hyde. Similarly, in the Teeling episode a precedent might be sought for the turn of the century debate between the Irish-Ireland movement and the Anglo-Irish literati over who constituted the legitimate leaders of Irish nationalism. An emergent generation of Anglo-Irish cultural separatists perceived itself nearing the end of its apprenticeship and was primed to assume the mantle of leadership.

Despite contemplating in October 1888 publishing a map of Glasnevin cemetery showing the position of graves of 'notable patriotic leaders',[101] the Y.I.S. was by this point beginning to lose its distinctive identity. Oldham once again lectured in the York Street rooms in March 1888,[102] but was introduced by Davitt as the honorary secretary of the Protestant Home Rule Association. His lecture on Emmet was well received, but as Davitt's introductory speech and the M.P. T. D. Sullivan's closing remarks indicated, the distinction between constitutionalist and separatist had increasingly weakened in the public mind. Their aim, Davitt proclaimed to cheers, was to 'capture the Castle'. They

> might not be able to do it by similar methods to those Emmet used, but by methods that prove themselves more efficacious. . . . they found his name [Emmet's] a memory as deeply reverenced by moderate as by advanced nationalists, who, of course, claim him as their typical leader. . . . as long as they cherished a reverential love of Robert Emmet so long would they not be wanting in recruits for their movement or admirers for their cause (cheers).

Both were able to embrace Emmet's legacy but the militancy of M.P.s like O'Brien attracted a great deal more support than the eupeptic platitudes of the Fenian ideologues. Superintendent Reddy had observed as far back as October 1885: 'Practically there is no real difference now between a nationalist and a Fenian. They both have the same object in view; and would both resort to extreme [recte non-] parliamentary measures, if they thought it would be to their advantage to do so.'[103]

This was an exaggeration that was to become increasingly true. The estrangement of the Y.I.S. under John O'Leary from the more orthodox Fenians probably contributed to the society's growing financial difficulties in 1886.

---

[100] D.M.P. 1887 'Fenian doings in Dublin City 16th May to 7th June 1887'.
[101] W.F., 20 Oct. 1888.
[102] D.M.P. 1888/990 & 992.
[103] D.M.P. 19 Sep. 1885

Notably, plans to open a reading room in emulation of the Young Irelanders of the 1840s had to be scrapped.

V

The inevitable question this account raises is in what sense was the Y.I.S. under O'Leary Fenian? R. V. Comerford's influential argument is helpful here, that it is most profitable to regard the Fenians from a functional rather than an ideological perspective.[104] If defined primarily as a social phenomenon and painted as rather inept military organisers little committed to the battlefield, the Fenians in the 1860s and '70s fit into a materialist paradigm of an insecure rising petit-bourgeoisie seeking purpose against a background of rural and provincial tedium. Similarly, Fenianism in the 1880s was not an efficient military organisation pursuing definitive revolutionary goals, but was a subversive subculture, with ill-defined separatist propensities. Fenianism provided an alternative political environment, independent of Westminster, Dublin Castle, and the offices of petit-bourgeois employment. It is in this primarily tonal sense, that Yeats and other members of the emergent cultural avant garde identified with Fenianism. In the 1880s, it is not entirely spurious to see Fenianism reconceived as bohemianism.

Contrary to usual assumptions, the political successes of Parnell did not render the ideals of the Fenians redundant, but heightened the urgency to assert a separatist identity distinct from the constitutionalism of the home rule party and Westminster. The more sophisticated Fenians understood that the means by which Ireland achieved self-government, in whatever form, would to a great extent dictate the character of that emergent Irish state and nation. Ideologically Ireland was up for grabs, and the apparently imminent success of constitutional nationalism had thrown the Fenians into something of an existential dilemma. Could they afford to reject outright the political successes of Parnellism? Both O'Leary and William O'Brien, from different sides of the political divide, faced the problem of reconciling their separatist inheritance with the success of the home rule campaign. To a greater or lesser extent, this conflict was felt by many of their generation of Irish nationalists. Consequently, the timing of O'Leary's return to Ireland was crucial. He provided a focus for the accelerated development of Irish cultural nationalism, ensuring that Fenianism ideologically and organisationally remained a critical force. Implicit in O'Leary's approach was the belief that although Parnellism had compounded the emasculation of revolutionary Fenianism, the organisation could be used to fortify a separatist mentality that would not be satisfied by home rule. Despite his social conservatism ('The constant talk about the abolition of landlordism

---

[104] V. E. Vaughan (ed.), *A New History of Ireland: Ireland Under the Union, 1870–1921* (Oxford, 1996), p. 6.

is semi-socialism and whole nonsense'),[105] O'Leary emerges as a bizarrely progressive figure, providing for a younger generation a model of Fenianism less bound by a dichotomous conception of Irish nationalism as divided between constitutionalism and separatism, which was more constructive at a time of constitutional ascendancy. On the other hand, the Y.I.S. embodied the social tensions that existed within the advanced nationalist milieu, which brings to mind the rather disdainful tone with which O'Leary writes about the non-literary Fenians of the 1860s in On Fenians and Fenianism. More generally, the history of the Y.I.S. highlights the ambiguous relationship between Fenianism and constitutionalism, suggesting a greater incidence of interaction than is often supposed.

Yet this was not simply the New Departure operating in the more subdued mode appropriate to the post-Kilmainham dispensation. Y.I.S. activity was predominantly an urban phenomenon and through cultural nationalism urban separatists found the radical impulse denied them by the land agitation of 1879–82. After 1879 urban and rural advanced nationalists were increasingly set upon divergent trajectories; this would prove starkly the case during the split. Agrarian agitation periodically absorbed the energies of rural radicals; various forms of separatist nationalism functioned similarly in urban areas. Both tendencies had a troubled relationship with the home rule party, but it was evident the party could more readily absorb agrarian agitation. Consequently, it can be seen that the pattern of support for Parnellites and anti-Parnellites during the Irish parliamentary party split of the 1890s ran deep. There was a striking congruence between the Kilmainham treaty, Parnell's discountenancing of the Plan of Campaign, and his separatist support during the split.

In Yeats's identification of this milieu as presaging 'the Irish culture of the future' lies a final irony. Yeats's primary political opponent of the early 1900s too cut his nationalist teeth in the Y.I.S. Aged 14, Arthur Griffith was the secretary of the Junior Young Ireland Society in Dublin and gave a paper on John Mitchel in February 1885.[106] Their paths must surely have crossed.

[105] Irishman, 29 May 1880.
[106] Nation, 7 & 14 Feb. 1885.

2

Parnell and the Fenians

Structuring the split

I

Accustomed as many historians are to diminishing the impact of the individual on the broader process of historical change, the course of the Parnell split appears to defy expectations. The actions of a single individual of tremendous prestige and influence shattered a political consensus carefully established over a decade of intense political organisation and party discipline. The home rule party was centrally controlled and disciplined to an extent unique to late nineteenth-century British politics. Parnell was the undisputed leader of the party and, for many, the primary cause of its political success: he appeared to be indispensable. For F. S. L. Lyons, Parnell's most important modern biographer, the split was the final act of a tragic life. With 'the Chief' exposed as an adulterer and rejected by Gladstone because he was afraid ballasting Parnell would alienate his party's core nonconformist constituency, the majority of Parnell's parliamentary colleagues eschewed him in favour of the Liberal alliance.[1] Parnell's personal animus overrode the strategic necessity of preserving the 'union of hearts', an action Conor Cruise O'Brien finds 'indefensible'.[2] A later generation of historians have viewed the split as a catalyst, facilitating the establishment of a fresh Parnellite dynamic along non-sectarian lines, as intimated in the late 1880s. Frank Callanan is aggressively Parnell's advocate, intent upon discerning a political strategy that would restore independence to the home rule party and free Irish nationalism of its endemic Catholic 'supremacism'.[3] This argument is congruent with the more cautiously expressed hypotheses of Paul Bew and Philip Bull. Bew suggests Parnell's later speeches were an attempt to re-conceive home rule in a non-sectarian mode that would appeal to Irish unionists.[4] Bull perceives Parnell's recognition of the diminishing returns of the Liberal alliance and the need to position himself

---

[1] F. S. L. Lyons, *Charles Stewart Parnell* (London, 1977), pp 546–8.
[2] Conor Cruise O'Brien, *Parnell and his Party 1880–90* (Oxford, 1957), p. 348.
[3] Frank Callanan, *The Parnell Split 1890–1* (Cork, 1992), pp 260–7.
[4] Paul Bew, *C. S. Parnell* (Dublin, 1980), pp 127–32.

to assume the leadership of an independent home rule party that might resort to a tactical withdrawal from Westminster.[5] In essence, Lyons detects an aberration, Callanan (and to a lesser extent Bull and Bew) seek to recover Parnell's reputation, lending shape to a career previously considered foreshortened by irrationalism.

Both Lyons and Callanan focus primarily on Parnell: Lyons's elegant narrative, tinged with distress, and Callanan's dense analysis of Parnell's rhetoric, place the fallen leader emphatically at the centre of the story.[6] Katharine Tynan, an ardent Parnellite, 'burnt out, exhausted', and reduced to ennui by the campaign, gave romantic expression to the intensity of Parnell's actions that year:

> I see now, after twenty-one years, that Parnell lives and shines by that one year. To the Muse of History it matters very little whether movements fall or succeed, whether men live or die untimely. She is concerned only with men. And here is a man to whom longer living would have added nothing of lustre, of splendour. To the Muse of History it matters little that Parnell died when he did. He had reached his full height. His place is secure.[7]

It would be grossly simplistic to attribute this fixation simply to the appeal of a dramatic tale, and as has been suggested, the history of the period was 'inescapably linked with the personality of one man'.[8] Nonetheless, Parnell's centrality to analyses of the split has risked inhibiting a wider historical understanding of what these events revealed about Irish political culture in general. The split was the result of identifiable historical pressures, of colliding social, cultural, and sociological forces, which are obscured if the history of Ireland during these ten months is reduced to the dénouement and death of a personality.

By attempting to decentre Parnell and establish the dynamic driving his campaign, it should be possible to begin to delineate the structures and motivations within Irish nationalism from which he drew support. Fundamentally, the split exposed the fragility of the Parnellite hegemony; it released pent-up energies that had been restrained by the belief that the home rule party offered the best chance of extending Ireland's self-government. Parnell's overthrow and his struggle to retain the leadership put these uneasy compromises under severe strain and his support base necessarily had to shift. Rejected by

---

[5] Philip Bull, 'The Fall of Parnell: The Political Context of his Intransigence' in D. George Boyce and Alan O'Day (ed.), *Parnell in Perspective* (London, 1991), pp 129–47.

[6] For Callanan's extraordinary, and extraordinarily sustained, analysis of Healy's rhetoric during the split see his *T. M. Healy* (Cork, 1996), pp 257–404.

[7] Katharine Tynan, *Twenty-five Years: Reminiscences* (London, 1913), p. 333. Tynan appears to owe something to Standish O'Grady's description of Parnell's fall in *The Story of Ireland*: quoted in Malcolm Brown, *The Politics of Irish Literature* (Chatham, 1972), p. 374.

[8] R. F. Foster, *Modern Ireland, 1600–1972* (London, 1988), p. 400.

Gladstone and the catholic hierarchy,[9] he made his 'appeal to the hillside men'. This notorious phrase was popularised by Healy following O'Shea's use of it before the Special Commission. It infuriated the separatists, sensitised by a culture wittily replete with urban contempt for the rural: the police observed during the Kilkenny by-election that 'the I.R.B. are swearing vengeance against T. M. Healy M.P. for calling them hillside men.'[10]

Subject to much debate, the 'appeal' has been largely interpreted in terms of what it revealed about Parnell's political beliefs. Although historians are near unanimous in agreeing that Parnell did not deviate from his constitutional ethic,[11] there is some disagreement regarding the wider implications of Parnell's actions. Callanan argues that Parnell induced 'Fenian sympathies to impute to him a deeper affinity with their views than he actually possessed'.[12] Parnell's rhetoric was a cunning subterfuge: 'With masterly elusiveness Parnell cheated Fenian ideologues of any substantive concessions.'[13] Parnell certainly defended constitutional methods – sometimes obliquely, sometimes not – but it is hard to accept that his words did not legitimise a renewed questioning of orthodox home rule's strict constitutionalism, raising Fenian expectations.[14] During an address made in Meath in March 1891 he declaimed 'Men of Royal Meath, perhaps some day or other in the long, waiting future, some one may arise who may have the privilege of addressing you as men of Republican Meath (loud cheers).'[15] This evoked his early nationalist rhetoric, departing from the language of finality associated with the 1886 Parnellite case for home rule. That Parnell had appealed to the Fenians along similar lines during the Land War led the anti-Parnellite *Nation* to observe scathingly:

> Mr Parnell now largely indulges in reminiscences, and in quotations from speeches made before 1883. He can find nothing apposite to the present since the Kilmainham Treaty, not to speak of the home rule bill and Hawarden conference.[16]

The progress of the split is a reminder that Parnellism was first and foremost a political dynamic and not a set of clearly delineated political principles flawlessly melded to a consistent political strategy.

---

[9] See Emmet Larkin, *The Fall of Parnell and the Roman Catholic Church in Ireland* (Liverpool, 1979).

[10] N.A., misc. police reports 1882–1921, box 3 [hereafter M.P.R.3], 20 Dec. 1890.

[11] An exception is Margaret O'Callaghan. In a brief consideration of the split, she refers to 'Parnell's fall into the hands of the hillside men in 1891' and 'his final rejection of constitutionalism', in *British High Politics and a Nationalist Ireland* (Cork, 1994), pp 120–1.

[12] Callanan, *Parnell Split*, p. 243.

[13] Ibid., p. 239.

[14] Cf. Lyons, *Parnell*, p. 540.

[15] *The Times*, 2 Mar. 1891, quoted in James H. Murphy, *Abject Loyalty: Nationalism and Monarchy in Ireland During the Reign of Queen Victoria* (Cork, 2001), p. 199.

[16] *Nation*, 24 Jan. 1891.

The I.R.B. renewed its purpose in response to – in Robert Kee's vigilantly understated phrase – the 'unconstitutional nuances' of Parnell's rhetoric.[17] A detectable reshuffling was evident within Fenianism itself. The split rejuvenated the leaders of more traditional advanced nationalism, particularly those now drawing on G.A.A. support, who had been undermined by the literary Fenians of the 1880s. Fenianism was rendered visible, vocal, and newly legitimated by the split – and to some extent cleansed of the Phoenix Park murders. This stemmed from Parnell's rhetoric and the crucial role the I.R.B. played in structuring Parnell's support base and running his electoral machine. Force of association with the Fenians conditioned the reception of Parnell's speeches, ensuring they were recognised as suggestively radical. The challenge, therefore, is less to exonerate Parnell from accusations of Fenianism than to examine how the context of the split shaped the meaning of his campaign.

Paradoxically, the most significant 'hillside men' were urban working-class nationalists. In a letter infused with class hostility, Archbishop Croke described the bedrock of Parnell's support as follows:

> The lower stratum of society in Ireland is almost entirely for him. Cornerboys, blackguards of every hue, discontented labourers, lazy and drunken artisans, aspiring politicians, Fenians, and in a word, all irreligious and anticlerical scoundrels in the country are at his back. But on the other hand, every thoughtful, intelligent, industrious and Christian man, is strenuously opposed to him.[18]

The 1892 general election affirmed the urban basis of Parnell's support. With large majorities Parnellites won the Dublin seats of College Green, Dublin Harbour,[19] and St Patrick's; they suffered a narrow defeat to a Liberal unionist in St Stephen's Green (unionists won the two Dublin University seats). Parnellites won comfortably in Dublin County North and came ahead of the anti-Parnellite in Dublin County South, but were defeated by the unionist Horace Plunkett. In Meath, the adjacent county to the north, they were strong losers. Despite consistently failing to take either of the Cork City seats, they nonetheless polled approximately two-thirds of the anti-Parnellite total. From the beginning clerical opinion saw the conflict in stark terms: 'In Cork there is much division – the mob is for Parnell, and the priests were insulted and hooted lately in the streets.'[20] John Redmond won in Waterford City; Parnellites lost both Waterford county seats. In the small electorate of Galway City the Parnellite Arthur Lynch was defeated by fifty-one votes; in Kilkenny

---

[17] Robert Kee, *The Laurel and the Ivy* (London, 1993), p. 589.
[18] Croke to Kirby, 29 Jan. 1891, reproduced in M. Tierney, 'Dr Croke, the Irish Bishops and the Parnell Crisis, 18 Nov. 1890–21 April 1891' in *Collectanea Hibernica*, 11 (1968), p. 139.
[19] This was Timothy Harrington's seat. When he died in 1910 he was succeeded by the Parnellite William Abraham, who was prominent in Dublin politics in the 1890s.
[20] Bishop T. A. O'Callaghan to Kirby, 27 Dec. 1890 (Tierney, 'Croke', p. 127).

City and Limerick City there were strong Parnellite showings but anti-Parnellite victories. By contrast, Parnellites were badly beaten in Limerick County and fielded no candidates in Kilkenny County, although Colonel John Nolan took Galway County North. Parnellites were strong in the anomalous Roscommon and Clare. Matthias Bodkin's narrow defeat of the old Fenian J. J. O'Kelly in the Clare County North seat had an emblematic quality. Luke Hayden, Parnellite, defeated Andrew Commins in Clare County South. In Clare East and West the Parnellites William Redmond and James Rochfort Maguire were victorious, but not overwhelmingly so. Redmond and Nolan's success has been attributed to the solid Parnellism of the towns of Ennis and Tuam.[21] Parnellites lost in Mayo, Connemara, Kerry, Tipperary, Westmeath, and Wicklow.

However, the narrow basis of the franchise means that an analysis of election results runs the danger of distorting analyses of the distribution of political support. Since O'Connell's Monster Meetings, Irish nationalism was predicated on mass popular movements of the largely unenfranchised. Irish political activists did not necessarily have the vote, and it is striking that (according to police figures from September 1891) the National League's membership was only a little less than half that of the new anti-Parnellite organisation, the Irish National Federation (I.N.F.), (29,486 to 68,491).[22] Moreover, the main Parnellite organisation, the Irish National League (I.N.L.), was larger than the I.N.F. in Dublin City and in Counties Roscommon, Limerick, Mayo, Galway, Londonderry, Wicklow, Meath, and Dublin. There were relatively strong I.N.L. branches in Tipperary, Louth, Sligo, Kildare, Cork, and Kilkenny. Unfortunately, with the exception of Dublin, the figures do not distinguish between urban and rural branches. Police and clerical observers predicted Parnellite victories during the by-elections of 1890–1 but, as Michael Davitt recognised, there were good reasons for mistakenly exaggerating Parnellite chances. Although 'Mr Parnell's former clerical and episcopal supporters went with the majority. The minority in the country however, included a majority of the most active of the local leaders.'[23]

Reflective of these changed circumstances was the second Parnellite takeover of the United Ireland office on the night of 10 December 1890.[24] A Parnellite crowd, torch-lit and angry ('John Clancy's new crowbar brigade'),[25] marched to the Dublin office and ejected the anti-Parnellites. Parnell appeared transformed, his aloof self-control given way to an impassioned physicality.[26]

---

[21] Richard Barrett, 'The Politics and Political Character of the Parnellite Party 1891–99' (M.A. thesis, University College, Dublin, 1983), p. 9.

[22] C.B.S. Box 3, 4208, 30 Sept. 1891.

[23] Michael Davitt, The Fall of Feudalism in Ireland (London, 1904), p. 643.

[24] The first saw the memorable exchange between John Clancy and the editor Matthias Bodkin: '"Will you walk out, Matty?" he asked, "or will you be thrown out?" Matty walked out.' Tynan, Twenty-five Years, p. 325.

[25] Nation, 24 June 1891.

[26] For a description see F. S. L. Lyons, The Fall of Parnell (London, 1960), p. 160.

This was the dominant characteristic of the two most powerful images of the split, both dating from these first few weeks: Parnell, pounding at the door of the *United Ireland* office with a crowbar, his Gothic shadow thrown against the wall, and Parnell, speech-making in the pouring rain, fist aloft and face shrouded in bandages after quicklime was thrown on him during a Kilkenny hustings.[27] At the Irishtown meeting of April 1891 to commemorate the launch of the Land League twelve years earlier, the Parnellite alliance of 1879 was symbolically reaffirmed. Thomas S. Ryan presented Parnell with the blackthorn stick he had confiscated from Bodkin on the night of 10 December. Ryan was a commercial traveller from County Mayo, a well-known I.R.B. organiser in Roscommon, Galway, and Mayo, and his sister was married to P. W. Nally.[28] Formerly a member of the Supreme Council and close to James Boland, Nally was much championed by Fred Allan following his imprisonment for conspiring to murder eight officials in Mayo at the height of the Land War – the so-called Crossmolina conspiracy. He died in Mountjoy jail in November 1891 and the resultant Nally G.A.A. Club was closely associated with Allan, Boland, and working-class Dublin Fenianism in the 1890s.

The symbolic significance of the blackthorn incident can be easily overplayed, but that stick seems a strangely appropriate Parnellite symbol. It was recognised as such by the *Nation* in a sarcastic description of the Parnellite army addressed by Pierce Mahony M.P. and Father O'Kelly during the North Sligo by-election of April. 'Some carried the regulation blackthorn, others ashplants, and pokers, railings, hurdle posts, and even a couple of broken boat oars, made up the mixed medley of their armament.'[29] In its semiotic awkwardness, caught somewhere between the Fenian pike, the Gael's càman, and the common weapon of the agrarian agitator, the blackthorn bespeaks the impossibility of fixing the meaning of the split. Anti-Parnellites, however, exploited such images in order to traduce Parnellite and Fenian politics as little more than 'Rowdyism'. 'We know that wherever the Redmondites are in force', William O'Brien told an Irish National Federation convention held in Galway during December 1891, 'there is no argument except the *bludgeon* and the *paving stone*'.[30] Although Callanan has argued that the ardour of Fenian support for Parnell as the split progressed did not suggest that revolutionary calculations were uppermost in their minds,[31] the split did generate a situation in which the range of political possibilities, albeit ambiguously articulated, appeared expanded. With Parnell's rejection by the majority of his parliamentary

---

[27] See cartoon reproduced in Kee, *Laurel and the Ivy*.

[28] Ryan attempted to establish a branch of the Y.I.S. as an I.R.B. front organisation and was to remain an active organiser until his death on 2 October 1897. C.O. 904/18, Register of Suspects, no. 923; *F.J.*, 20 Apr. 1891.

[29] *Nation*, 4 Apr. 1891.

[30] C.O. 903/2, misc. notes – series xiv, p.34, quoting *National Press*, 18 Dec. 1891. O'Brien's sensitivity to political 'rowdyism' was something of a leitmotif. Cf. his later abhorrence for the A.O.H., see p. 229 above.

[31] Callanan, *Parnell Split*, p. 254.

colleagues, and Irish nationalist politics descending into a confused scrap, the political settlement of the 1880s, with its endemic ideological uncertainties, appeared open to reconfiguration.

II

As the tangled history of the Y.I.S. suggested, advanced nationalism comprised a broad spectrum of separatist nationalists that included dynamiters, Phoenix Park murderers, American agitators, city gang members, agrarian agitators, and littérateurs. The gulf between the Invincibles and Katharine Tynan or W. B. Yeats was indeed a large one, and although a shared romantic nationalist outlook suggests a superficial resemblance, such sentiment was clearly not the exclusive preserve of advanced nationalism. Indeed, the lines of demarcation within Irish separatism could be sharper than those between separatists and home rulers. As a result the reasons for separatists supporting Parnell were equally complex and varied. At the most basic level, the 'appeal to the hillside men' was a request for the support of the Fenians against church and Gladstonian dictation in politics, manipulating sympathies that were already present. There 'might have been talk of Parnell welcoming "the hillside men", but the process was also the reverse: the hillside men were welcoming him.'[32]

Parnell was not guaranteed the support of the I.R.B. from the outset. There were strong indications of a growing hostility to Parnell from advanced elements, particularly following his repudiation of the Fenians during the Special Commission hearings. Under close questioning Parnell had described the 'New Departure' as 'a combination of the political with the agrarian movement', claiming that 'the physical force organisation has been consistently hostile to us since 1880'.[33] At an amnesty demonstration in Cork just before Parnell's condemnation of Gladstone and the Liberal alliance,[34] Tim Healy attempted to propose a resolution in favour of Parnell, but 'were told that if they did, they & the platform should be knocked into the river, & they then withdrew with some boos'. Colonel A. E. Turner continued in this letter to Chief Secretary Arthur Balfour: 'So far the feeling of the [Irish National L]eague is in favour of Parnell, but I imagine they are ready to throw him up, for they do not really like him, & all the extremists are dead against him – they have never forgiven him for many things.'[35] Shortly before the split, Fenian

---

[32] Kee, *Laurel and the Ivy*, p. 600.

[33] Quoted in Frank Callanan, '"In the name of God and of the dead generations": Nationalism and Republicanism in Ireland' in Richard English and Joseph Morrison Skelly (ed.), *Ideas Matter: Essays in Honour of Conor Cruise O'Brien* (Dublin, 1998), pp 113–14.

[34] The campaign for the amnesty of Irish political prisoners is analysed in the following chapter.

[35] Colonel A. E. Turner to A. J. Balfour, 27 Nov. 1890, in Robin Harcourt Williams (ed.), *Salisbury–Balfour Correspondence* (Cambridge, 1988), pp 334–5.

activists in the Cork Y.I.S. organised a boycott of a meeting addressed by Justin McCarthy M.P. on the grounds that his views were not advanced enough, and after Parnell's death, Parnellite M.P.s heaped abuse on McCarthy for political feebleness.[36] Advanced nationalist feeling in Cork changed quickly. As Bishop O'Callaghan noted, Parnell's 'crowd . . . is the Fenian Society, which hitherto was opposed to him, but is now his main support, and this is perhaps the greatest point of danger'.[37] Although these examples detail only minor incidences of overt separatist ambivalence for Parnell in the early stages of the controversy, they demonstrate that I.R.B. support for Parnell was not a foregone conclusion.

Further police reports suggest that some I.R.B. organisers took a strongly cynical line on the opportunity afforded by the split. In the west the police supposed the I.R.B. supported Parnell in the hope he would therefore take a bolder stand against the opposition. By supporting the weaker party, the I.R.B. reasoned, the split would be prolonged, making an amicable settlement less likely. In Cork they hoped to keep the party factions at it, 'until – like the Kilkenny cats – "they eat each other to the tails"'.[38] With the consequent weakening of the home rule party, it was supposed disillusioned members of the Irish National League would switch allegiance to the I.R.B. 'and give a new vitality to their now effete organisation'.[39] Such strategic hopes were paralleled in Conservative party hopes that a Parnellite victory would weaken the Liberals.[40]

In Belfast the I.R.B.'s frustration with the progress of constitutional politics was evident in the months immediately prior to the split. At one meeting it was hoped a Conservative would be returned for West Belfast at the next general election. This would highlight the inadequacy of the Irish National League, again persuading I.N.L. members to return to the I.R.B. Intriguingly, the police noted the I.R.B. now regretted passing money to the I.N.L.[41] On 22 January Edward Madden, a leading member of the organisation in County Monaghan, reputedly persuaded a secret meeting of the I.R.B. in Belfast to support Parnell for the same reasons.[42] Several days later an I.R.B. gang disrupted an anti-Parnellite meeting in support of Thomas Sexton M.P. at St Mary's Hall, Belfast. Other responses included the Belfast Young Ireland Society's criticism of member J. B. Killen for announcing he was Parnellite in contravention of the society's professed neutrality.[43] During an I.R.B. meeting in Belfast at the Forresters' Hall on 7 December 1891, Thomas Kelly advised

---

[36] C.O. 903/2, misc. notes – series xiv.
[37] O'Callaghan to Kirby, 27 Dec. 1890 (Tierney, 'Croke', p. 127).
[38] C.B.S. Box 3, Crime Special Precis, Dec. 1890.
[39] P.R.O. 30/60/4, Balfour Papers, Intelligence Notes, 16–31 Dec. 1890.
[40] O'Callaghan, British High Politics, p. 120.
[41] P.R.O. 30/60/3, 16 Oct.–1 Nov. 1890; P.R.O. 30/60/1, 15–30 Nov. 1889.
[42] P.R.O. 30/60/4, 15 Feb. 1891.
[43] M.P.R.3, 23 Jan. 1891; Nation, 14 Feb. 1891.

the adoption of a neutral stance: 'they had no cause to love Parnell, and if any chance offers they must try and make good use of it . . . the constitutional sham must come to an end . . . force was the only remedy.'[44] In general, however, Parnellism had less impact on the northern counties.[45] 'The North, priests and people, is solid against Parnell', wrote Archbishop Logue to Monsignor Kirby, 'A small clique in Belfast and Newry are trying to make a noise, but nobody heeds them.'[46] At the 1892 general election the Parnellite Fenian Robert Johnston contested the Newry parliamentary seat and won fifty-four votes. He was soundly beaten by the victorious anti-Parnellite. The unionist candidate came second.

P. N. Fitzgerald and P. J. Hoctor, long-time I.R.B. colleagues and G.A.A. organisers, fell out over the legitimacy of these cynical calculations.[47] Fitzgerald privately justified his support for Parnell on the grounds that the I.R.B. was receiving money from the Parnellites in order to assist in the campaign.[48] Hoctor considered this irrelevant because Parnell elicited Fenian support not out of 'respect' for the organisation, 'but for his own purposes'. At an Amnesty Association meeting Hoctor interrupted Parnell, claiming that he had 'stood on amnesty platforms before Mr Parnell had the pleasure of doing so (loud interruptions)'.[49] He continued in a mode that repudiated the separatist modus operandi of the 1880s and prefigured the separatist debates of the 1900s. 'I am not a Healyite nor a Parnellite either (groans and interruptions)', Hoctor declared, 'I come here as an Irish nationalist, having nothing to do with current politics at all (interruptions).'[50] He maintained this position throughout the 1890s. At a meeting in April, Fred Allan reportedly endorsed Hoctor's views,[51] despite remaining a stalwart member of the Parnell Leadership Committee in Dublin. During the Boulogne negotiations unreconstructed Fenians like the

---

[44] C.B.S. Box 3, Crime Special Precis, Dec. 1890.

[45] Membership in Ulster: I.N.L. 4,812, I.N.F 12,383. Poor Law guardians elections 1891 (1892) for Ulster: Parnellite 100 (63), anti-Parnellite 306 (331), Conservative 395 (400), Liberal Unionist 228 (222), Neutral 13 (14). No Conservatives or Liberal Unionists elected in Louth. C.B.S. Box 4, 5002, Mar. 1892 [There was a slight error in the official totals producing twelve more guardians in 1891 than 1892.]

[46] Logue to Kirby, 5 Feb. 1891 (Tierney, 'Croke', pp 139–40).

[47] Fitzgerald's Fenianism was unambiguous: in November he had delivered a 'very strong Fenian speech' to the Manchester Martyrs commemoration at Glasnevin cemetery. There were 7–8,000 onlookers. P.R.O. 30/60/2, 16–30 Nov. 1890.

[48] It was a frequent complaint of the bishops that Parnellite money was used to encourage rowdiness and hostility to the clergy (Tierney, 'Croke', pp 123, 127). There was a certain irony in Fitzgerald's concern for the financial fortunes of the I.R.B. In 1890 he had been suspected of misappropriating £1,000 – a fantastic sum – of I.R.B. funds. John O'Leary, president of the Supreme Council, took a direct role in the investigation. It appears no conclusion was reached. T.N.A (P.R.O.) 30/60/2, 1–15 Jan. 1890, 15–28 Feb. 1890.

[49] The amnesty issue is considered at length in Chapter 3.

[50] W.F., 11 Apr. 1891.

[51] P.R.O. 30/60/4, 1–15 Apr. 1891.

ex-Invincible James Boland denounced Parnell as a 'traitor and a coward'.[52] John Redmond steadied nerves at a meeting of the Arran Quay branch of the National League in early March by refuting rumours that Parnell planned to retire.[53]

John O'Leary's open support for Parnell from December 1890 was broadly consistent with his earlier sympathy for Parnell as expressed at the public meetings of the Y.I.S. in Ireland and England. Then he had been impressed by Parnell's character and resolve; now, couching his adherence in terms critical of Parnell's earlier activity, he reasserted his radical credentials by implying the novelty of his sympathy.

> It was for the Grand Young Man to get out of his scrape as well as he could. I was not going to trouble my head about him. But when the Grand Old Man interfered, that gave a new aspect to the affair. It then became a question of submitting to the dictation of an Englishman, and for the first time I resolved to support Parnell.[54]

With Parnell assailed by the catholic church and advocating independent political action, an ideal opportunity emerged for O'Leary to depart from his temperate rhetoric into a newly radicalised political arena.[55]

In the opening stages of the split the Fenian veteran Denis Mulcahy stated in a letter to O'Leary, 'While I am with him in this fight I have very little reliance on his revolutionary hints or threats.'[56] Mulcahy further considered Parnell's strategy and appeal, indicating that the ambiguous character of Parnell's rhetoric was not lost on those witnessing events through the Irish-American press.

> From what the telegrams tell us ye are having a lovely time just right now in England and Ireland. Parnell is beginning to assert himself. His speech in Dublin very ably [sic] and very vague – means anything or nothing. The Fenians whom he saw fit to ignore for a decade of years, he now warns the home rulers that those same Fenians may by & by voice the opinion of a majority of the Irish people and then he would find himself a Fenian.

More valuable than simply a comment on Parnell's position in December 1890, Mulcahy encapsulated the problems faced in defining Parnellism. This was Parnell as ideologically indistinct, a cipher for the structural imperatives of Irish nationalism – an agrarian agitator when the Irish people were agrarian

---

[52] D.M.P. 1891/2003, 7 Feb. 1891 and /2025, 14 Feb. 1891.
[53] F.J., 13 Mar. 1891.
[54] R. Barry O'Brien, *The Life of Charles Stewart Parnell* (London, 1898, 1910), p. 477.
[55] Cf. Callanan, *Parnell Split*, p. 250.
[56] Denis Mulcahy to John O'Leary, 12 Dec. 1890 (N.L.I., MS 5926). Mulcahy was a leading Fenian of the 1860s and remained close to Thomas Clarke Luby. O'Leary regularly corresponded with Luby while writing his *Recollections of Fenians and Fenianism* (1896).

agitators, a constitutionalist when the Irish people were constitutionalist, a Fenian when the Irish people were Fenian. Not so much an empty vessel but the arch-pragmatist who comprehended the nature of the forces, English and Irish, at his disposal. In mildly admonishing terms Parnell himself articulated this analysis from the balcony of the National Club on 3 August 1891:

> I want to justify my own faith in constitutional action, which I proclaimed to you many years ago (hear, hear). I trust that it will be justified. In the face of every difficulty I believe in it still (applause). But there is an end of all things, and if the Irish constituencies show that they know not the use of this powerful and keen weapon and that they do not understand how to employ the gigantic forces which are at their disposal, than all true Irishmen will have to reconsider their position upon this subject (hear, hear).[57]

These abstractions did not concern Mulcahy. He supported Parnell not for 'his defiance . . . of the despicable Davitts or the howling Healys', but, for 'his open defiance of the bishops who until the grand old man spoke had nothing to say about the O'Shea verdict'.

Davitt's anti-Parnellism is of particular interest. Redmondite and advanced nationalist suspicion dogged his later career. Timothy Harrington considered Davitt's anti-Parnellism to be motivated by personal grievance,[58] while the contrast between Mulcahy's 'despicable' and 'howling' reflected the intensity of this emergent bitterness. In general, Davitt's purpose after 1882 is under-explored,[59] but there seems to be a consistency between his anti-Parnellism during the split and his socialist politics. Parnell's distancing from the Plan of Campaign undermined his popular appeal in Ireland and his efforts to avoid a resurgence of agitation over the winter of 1889–90 by securing relief underlined his desire to neutralise the agrarian issue.[60] In contrast, Davitt continued to look to the nationalisation of Irish land and the creation of an Irish trade union movement. To Davitt's chagrin, Parnell made his opposition to the Irish Democratic Labour Federation clear in early 1890.[61] Davitt,

---

[57] D.M.P. 1891/ 2147; *F.J.*, 3 Aug. 1891.

[58] Harrington to Father Hogan, 5 Jan. 1891 (Tierney, 'Croke', pp 130–1): 'Davitt is a horribly jealous and vindictive man who has never forgiven Parnell for depriving him (Davitt) of the Irish leadership.'

[59] For a survey highlighting Davitt's role in the wider British labour movement, see T. W. Moody, 'Michael Davitt and the British Labour Movement 1882–1906' in *T.R.H.S*, 5th ser., 3 (1953), pp 53–76; closing chapter of Moody, *Davitt*; also, Carla King, 'Michael Davitt, Irish Nationalism and the British Empire in the Late Nineteenth Century' in Peter Gray (ed.), *Victoria's Ireland? Irishness and Britishness, 1837–1901* (Dublin, 2004), pp 116–30.

[60] At the Irishtown meeting Parnell rejected claims that support for home rule stemmed principally from economic grievances, Lyons, *Fall*, p. 256.

[61] For Davitt's commitment to land nationalisation see his *Fall of Feudalism*; Parnell's hostility to Irish trade unions is at pp 636–7.

O'Brien, and Dillon's shared commitment to an agrarian strategy was an important dimension of their tetchy co-operation after 1890. Consequently, Davitt's push for Parnell's retirement before Gladstone's fait accompli,[62] and the slight evidence of him encouraging opposition to Parnell in 1890,[63] suggests that the split might have served political purposes similar to those underlining the creation of the United Irish League in 1898.[64] Parnell's semi-detachment and the waning dynamism of the parliamentary party invited the rejuvenation of the home rule movement through radical grass-roots politics. Consequently, although it was likely that Davitt's sense of personal betrayal following assurances from Parnell that the O'Shea divorce would not prove damaging can only have compounded memories of the Kilmainham Treaty,[65] it seems unlikely that this wholly explains Davitt's anti-Parnellism.

However, as Maura Cronin has shown of Cork, class solidarity was undermined by the stratifications that existed within the working classes and the overwhelming political dominance of the national issue.[66] This left Davitt and others unable to build an effective labour politics as an adjunct to the home rule movement. Parnell's attitude to agrarianism enhanced the affinity for him felt by urban nationalists, and separatists in particular. Despite his labour sympathies, Davitt found the working men hostile to him when he stood against John Redmond during the November 1891 Waterford City by-election.[67] This was not so much based on hostility to agrarianism, as on the extent to which home rule, by deriving its principal energies from agrarianism, had marginalised the urban political voice. Parnell conceded at Ballina in April 1891 that the party had done 'absolutely nothing' for the labouring class.[68] The agricultural crisis of the late 1870s had generated high unemployment in Dublin and other urban centres, but Anti-Rack Rent Associations and the House League had little success in linking up with the Land League. After the Kilmainham treaty, short-lived Dublin-based organisations like the Irish Labour League and the National Labour League failed to generate a stable working-class politics. This provoked widespread working-class resentment of philanthropic, Land League, and National League efforts to relieve the rural destitute.[69] On the other hand, the Land War had rejuvenated rural and

---

[62] Lyons, *Parnell*, p. 482.

[63] Colonel Turner attributed the hostility shown to Parnell at the amnesty meeting to Davitt's manoeuvrings, see n. 35 above.

[64] See Chapter 5 of this book.

[65] Davitt, *Fall*, p. 637.

[66] Maura Cronin, *Country, Class or Craft? The Politicisation of the Skilled Artisan in Nineteenth-Century Cork* (Cork, 1994), pp 184, 189, 196.

[67] C.O. 903/2, misc. notes – series xiv, p.18.

[68] *U.I.*, 25 Apr. 1891.

[69] Gerard Moran, 'The Land War, Urban Destitution and Town Tenant Protest, 1879–1882' in *Saothar*, 20 (1995), pp 17–30; Fintan Lane, *The Origins of Modern Irish Socialism 1881–1896* (Cork, 1997), pp 147–52, 174–6.

small town Fenianism, providing radical activists with a political purpose.[70] By contrast, activists in the cities had to satisfy their nationalism and socio-economic discontent by attending meetings in support of home rule and separatists increasingly complained that they were reduced to passing resolutions. One response was the radicalisation of the G.A.A. in the late 1880s and this dynamic helps to explain its consequent support for Parnell during the split. The Fenian ascendancy established at the Thurles annual national convention of January 1889 was understood by Dublin Castle to have been achieved by young Irish men frustrated with the home rule party, raising the prospect of them 'adopting once more the lines of the Fenian party'.[71]

If the Invincibles were an earlier separatist response to these urban frustrations, a more controlled response was the I.R.B.'s penetration of Dublin trades and friendly societies such as the Gasworkers' Union, the Mechanics Institute, the Railway Workmen's Club in Inchicore, various Dublin temperance societies,[72] and, as has been indicated with respect to the Young Ireland Society, Dublin's largest Workingmen's Club at York Street. During 1891 the trend continued. In particular, the I.R.B. extended its operations through the Labour Leagues and Workingmen's Clubs of Kilkenny, Galway, and Enniscorthy.[73] Parnellite overtures to the urban working man were seized upon by activists such as Fred Allan, Adolphus Shields, Myles Kavanagh, and James Poole. Allan, Shields, and Kavanagh were members of the Gasworkers' Union and the Parnell Leadership Committee in Dublin; Poole associated with literary Fenian groups throughout the period. The Gasworkers were the leading organisers of the Dublin labour conference of 14 March addressed by Parnell, who provided an ambiguous endorsement of its radical programme. Despite this, the newly established Irish Labour League dissolved over the following months.

In the absence of a dynamic urban movement for social reform, urban nationalist legitimacy relied heavily on the celebration of the separatist traditions of '98, '48, and '67. Consequently, although not explicitly aligning himself with these aspirations, Parnell's re-centring of the rhetoric of nation in effect re-centred urban nationalist politics. In Inchicore Parnell asserted that his opponents fought against 'the elite of the intelligence of the working class, artisans, traders, merchants of Ireland and of Dublin. They are contending

---

[70] The complexities can be followed in part two of Donald Jordan, *Land and Popular Politics in Ireland: County Mayo from the Plantation to the Land War* (Cambridge, 1994); also, Sam Clark, 'The Social Composition of the Land League' in *I.H.S.*, xvii, no. 68 (Sept. 1971), pp 447–69.

[71] C.O. 903/2, series 8, pp 7–8, 'Memo. on G.A.A.'; W. F. Mandle, *The Gaelic Association and Irish Nationalist Politics 1884–1924* (Dublin, 1987), pp 72–3, 80–6.

[72] Eoin McGee, '"God save Ireland": Manchester Martyr Demonstrations in Dublin 1867–1916' in *Eire–Ireland*, Fall–Winter 2001, p. 12; Lane, *Irish Socialism*, p. 173.

[73] M.P.R.3, Kilkenny, 30 Dec. 1890, 18 & 28 Jan. 1891, Galway, 14 Jan. 1891, Enniscorthy, 16 Feb. 1891.

against the voices of the great cities like Cork, Limerick, Waterford, Tralee, and [the] Nationalists of Belfast.'[74]

Parnell's association with Fenianism became increasingly formal.[75] Leadership committees, set up throughout Ireland, welcomed prominent members of the I.R.B. onto their committees, while the National Club in Rutland Square, Dublin, 'the effective headquarters of Dublin Parnellism',[76] was of a distinctly Fenian origin. In March 1886 the Y.I.S. charged Fred Allan, Foley, and J. J. O'Brien with setting up the 'National Club of the Young Ireland Society'.[77] Financial problems saw the opening delayed until November 1887, under the control of John Clancy, M. J. Seery, and J. K. Shannon.[78] The D.M.P. described it as having 'obtained very large support from the better classes of the physical force party,' and existing in opposition to the Catholic Club, Sackville St. 'The clerical party have not supported it', which strongly suggested a membership unsympathetic to constitutionalism. A sceptical Superintendent Reddy received reports of a number of I.R.B. meetings, including those of the Supreme Council, taking place in the club in 1888–9.[79] On 23 December 1890 the leading I.R.B. men of the city and the county, including John Clancy, met in the club. They held an excitable meeting. The impression the meeting had, according to the police, was that 'Parnell is trying for support of the I.R.B.'. If 'constitutional means do not succeed he will favour physical force' and on this basis 'all agreed to support Parnell.' P. N. Fitzgerald claimed Parnell admitted he 'favours physical force, & is willing to take the oath'.[80] Fitzgerald was more diplomatic at a Cork Leadership Committee meeting of January 1891. Sharing a platform with John O'Connor M.P., he explained his support for Parnell:

---

[74] Quoted in Callanan, *Parnell Split*, p. 278.

[75] The police reports suggest occasional incidences of money being passed directly to the I.R.B., particularly from the I.N.L. I.N.L. money was given to the Belfast election gang, in April Parnellite money was being distributed amongst the I.R.B. in County Mayo (I.R.B. man Edward Cavan of Kiltemagh received £20 expenses), and in July in Counties Kildare and Leitrim. P.R.O. 30/60/4, 1–15 Apr. 1891, 16–31 July 1891.

[76] Lyons, *Parnell*, p. 530.

[77] N.L.I., MS 19518.

[78] D.M.P. 1887/793.

[79] D.M.P. 1888 and 1889.

[80] C.B.S. Box 3, Crime Special Precis, Dec. 1890. Callanan notes that Parnell regularly spoke to Fitzgerald throughout his career, *Parnell Split*, p. 249. Fitzgerald's claim that Parnell might be willing to take the oath is curious in the light of Patrick Maume's consideration of the possibility that Parnell took the oath on 2 or 3 May 1882, between his release from Kilmainham and the Phoenix Park murders. The Invincible Patrick Joseph Sheridan, an associate of Fitzgerald's, allegedly administered the oath to Parnell in Trinity College library. Maume posits no more than the circumstantial possibility that Parnell took the oath. However, had Parnell taken the oath it seems likely that Fitzgerald and other leading Fenians would have known and consequently it is surprising that the police did not hear of its mention at I.R.B. meetings during the split. Patrick Maume, 'Parnell and the I.R.B. oath' in *I.H.S.*, xxix, no. 115 (May 1995), pp 363–70.

He had never adopted Mr Parnell's programme although he supported him now. But when he saw a man struggling against adversity, and kicked at the bidding of an English faction by those people who ought to help him, he thought that it was his duty, putting all political creeds aside, to stand by the man against the faction (cheers). He begged them to remember that he did not surrender one jot of his principles. They were the same now as when he stood in the dock at Green Street (cheers).[81]

Parnell and Timothy Harrington were proposed to membership of the National Club by John Clancy and John O'Connor at the beginning of 1891. Michael Davitt's membership was allowed to lapse at the same time.[82] In March, Clancy was elected to the Parnell branch of the National League in the presence of John Redmond, Timothy Harrington, and Edmund Leamy.[83] On 24 August 1890 the I.R.B. met, including representatives of England and Scotland. Clancy, Fitzgerald, and Seery were among those present.[84] A few days later Patrick O'Brien M.P., a steady Parnellite who acted as a conduit between Fenianism and the party in the 1890s,[85] stayed at the club and was visited by the leading I.R.B. men of the city. It is conceivable a report of the I.R.B. meeting was made to O'Brien. Of meetings held in the National Club during the split Superintendent John Mallon – the D.M.P.'s leading authority on Fenianism – commented, 'It is somewhat remarkable that the Fenian or I.R.B. element is prominent at all the Parnellite meetings.'[86]

Circumstances were similar in Belfast, although the scale was smaller. Robert Johnston chaired the Parnell Leadership Committee in Belfast. He was exposed at the Special Commission as representative for Ulster on the Supreme Council and was the father of Anna Johnston (later manager of the separatist monthly *Shan Van Vocht*, edited by fellow Ulster separatist Alice Milligan). Katharine Tynan remembered Johnston as 'an old hillside man'.[87] James Johnston, Robert's solicitor son, worked with other Belfast Fenians for the Parnellites at the Sligo by-election. One of the party, Hugh Ferris, was thought to have brought revolvers with him.[88] A similar contingent, this time including Robert Johnston, came down from Belfast for the Carlow by-election.[89]

A little noted exchange recounted in R. Barry O'Brien's 1898 biography of Parnell further clarifies the character of Fenian co-operation with Parnell. At

---

[81] *W.F.*, 3 Jan. 1891.
[82] *U.I.*, 10 Jan. 1891.
[83] *F.J.*, 13 Mar. 1891; D.M.P. 1891/2025.
[84] P.R.O. 30/60/4, 1–16 Aug. 1890.
[85] For example, O'Brien attended the Dublin Manchester Martyrs commemoration in 1889 organised by James Boland, D.M.P. 1889/1609, 25 Nov. 1889.
[86] D.M.P. 1891/2018, 4 Mar. 1891.
[87] Tynan, *Twenty-five Years*, p. 345.
[88] P.R.O. 30/60/4, 1–15 Apr. 1891.
[89] P.R.O. 30/60/4, 1–15 July 1891.

the time of the Kilkenny by-election Parnell failed to attend a pre-arranged meeting with an unnamed Fenian drafted in to provide organisational ballast. The Fenian, clearly annoyed, warns a 'parliamentarian': 'We are here to help Mr Parnell; we are not paid by him. We are not his people. He must keep his appointments.'[90] That O'Brien does not name the Fenian or the parliamentarian indicated the continued sensitivity of these connections.[91] As with the New Departure, and in line with the 1873 I.R.B. constitution, Fenian support was provisional. The Fenian was almost certainly P. N. Fitzgerald, for in an important letter on the early stages of the split, O'Brien told John O'Leary of the Kilkenny campaign:

> The disorganisation was terrible, and without P. N. Fitzgerald and his men we could have not carried on the war at all though P[arnell] fought like a lion at every turn. I like P. N. Fitzgerald. He said that he would hang me when he got the chance, and I agreed to deal equally liberally with him when I became Chief Secretary. On this basis we worked smoothly together.[92]

Michael Conway M.P. showed less scruple when he complimented Fitzgerald for his services during the Kilkenny and Sligo campaigns at a Parnellite meeting at Broadford, County Clare.[93]

Police reports on the Kilkenny campaign further testify to the Fenian presence. The sub-sheriff, John Fanning, was thought to risk I.R.B. reprisals owing to his support for the anti-Parnellite candidate Sir J. P. Hennessy. If Parnell is defeated, speculated one officer, 'the I.R.B. boys will make it hot for him [Fanning] for they are very determined about it and they say there is nothing else [apart from the I.R.B.] to beat him [Hennessy].'[94] Fifty I.R.B. men assembled on the railway platform to 'vigorously' groan Hennessy and cheer Parnellite M.P. Pierce Mahony on 11 December; nine days later a Parnellite majority of 500 was predicted, before it became clear that the clergy would ensure an anti-Parnellite victory.[95] As Dr Brownrigg, bishop of Ossory, acknowledged, the result might have been different if it had been an election for the Kilkenny City constituency. 'The whole city of Kilkenny, corporation and all, have *gone* solid for Parnell. Fortunately they have no votes, or the day was lost.'[96]

Parnell's appeal to the advanced nationalists took on a more concrete form when leading Parnellites became involved in the burgeoning amnesty move-

---

[90] Barry O'Brien, *Parnell*, pp 514–15.
[91] O'Brien was similarly discreet regarding the 'old Fenian leader' converted to Parnellism by Gladstone's letter. This was probably O'Leary.
[92] R. Barry O'Brien to John O'Leary, 15 Mar. 1891 (N.L.I., MS 5927).
[93] P.R.O. 30/60/4, 16–30 Apr. 1891.
[94] D.M.P. 1891/ 2225.
[95] C.B.S. S Files, Box 2, 2267, 11, 20 & 21 Dec. 1890.
[96] Brownrigg to Croke, 12 Dec. 1890 (Tierney, 'Croke', p. 123).

ment. At the end of March Dublin Castle was informed that in Limerick the 'I.R.B. Society are anxiously waiting the statement that Mr Parnell will make on the subject of John Daly & others. If satisfactory he will have in them strong support in Limerick City.'[97] At a meeting in Phoenix Park in April 1891 attended by 12–13,000 supporters, Parnell shared the platform with the M.P.s Joseph Kenny and Colonel John Nolan, both stalwart Parnellites. P. N. Fitzgerald and city councillor M. Hutchinson presided and the principal focus was on the treason-felon John Daly.[98] Dr Kenny's speech strongly appealed to Fenian sensibilities and the rhetorical confession of ignorance regarding the constitutionalism of their activities would become a standard refrain at amnesty meetings in the 1890s:

> My friend Mr Moran when he spoke to you said that we were proceeding constitutionally here today, well I do not know whether we are or not, and what is more I do not care a damn, we never got anything except by breaking the constitution, all we know of the constitution – this boasted constitution – is persecution and imprisonment, and the more we break of it the better.

Although the *Freeman's* coverage of the meeting had a Fenian ambience – 'Old comrades, who in the times of danger risked so much, came together again, not alone from Dublin, but from all parts of Ireland, and there was an air of reality and purpose about the proceedings which impressed all who were present' – the newspaper did not record Kenny's outburst.[99]

Parnell's speech, however, concerned the basis of his political leadership. He contrasted the 'strength' he took from the Irish people's 'spirit of patriotism and nationality' with the anti-Parnellite 'handing over the future of Ireland to the Liberal party'. Looking to the sovereignty of the Irish people, Parnell combined defiance with a confession of vulnerability that positioned him not above the electoral fray in the guise of a pre-ordained leader, but as the representative of an increasingly enfranchised electorate.[100] A similar perspective informed the very moderate speech Parnell made in Wicklow in June. With its focus on the practical benefits to be gained from home rule, as well as its nonchalant dismissal of separatism, it showed him to be the model constitutionalist nationalist.

> I have always been convinced that with the extension of the suffrage which we obtained in 1885, and by the cordial acceptance by the people of that suffrage as a means for enabling them to wield the constitutional weapon with effect, that all things would come in time to Ireland (hear, hear) – that she would regain her legitimate freedom. I don't mean separation from England or anything of that kind,

[97] M.P.R.3, Limerick, 30 Mar. 1891.
[98] P.R.O. 30/60/4, 1–15 Apr. 1891. W.F., 11 Apr. 1891.
[99] W.F., 11 Apr. 1891.
[100] Ibid.

but power to attend to her own affairs (hear, hear), to look after the industries of her country, to protect the tenant-farmer (hear, hear), to keep our population at home (hear, hear), to supply employment for our labourers (hear, hear), to supply new fields and avenues for the enterprise of our citizens (hear, hear), in fact to do all these things for ourselves which in these days of progress and improvement go to make a nation (cheers). I have been convinced that all these things are possible for Ireland.[101]

Here, the 'imperishable force' that gave Parnell his 'vitality and power' was not the 'spirit of the nation' but his authority as an elected representative in a modern democracy. These phrases were used by Parnell in the Rotunda immediately after his defeat in Committee Room 15 during what is considered the archetypal 'appeal to the hillside speech'.[102]

The most important Parnellite event of the summer of 1891 was the Dublin convention held in July. The purpose of the convention was to consolidate the movement in preparation for future elections. It was a fairly impressive occasion, attracting 24 M.P.s, 1,648 official delegates, and a further 5,000 supporters. It was evident that certain areas of the country were over-represented. Dublin, Meath, Kildare, and Wicklow accounted for 50 per cent of the delegates, Dublin City and County for a third, while Ulster had only fifty-two delegates.[103] Given that Meath and Wicklow were only two of the nine counties where the Irish National League was a larger organisation than the Irish National Federation, the July convention did not accurately reflect Parnellite strength.

The convention proceedings were divided between a formal meeting at Leinster Hall for the revision of the I.N.L. constitution and a public meeting in the evening. Over the course of the day Parnell made several addresses, along with Pierce Mahony, William Redmond, Edmund Leamy, Edward Harrington, Patrick O'Brien, and Dr Kenny. Among the Dublin organisations represented were the Leinster Literary Society,[104] the Amnesty Association,[105] the National Club, the Gaelic Athletic Association, the Protestant Home Rule Association,[106] and the Parnell Leadership Committee, under whose banner Fred Allan attended. Representatives of several hundred I.N.L. branches far outnumbered these sectional interests.

The available records suggest that a systematic analysis of the I.R.B. presence was not made, but reports submitted by the western division of the

[101] W.F., 6 June 1891.
[102] Callanan, Parnell Split, pp 238–9.
[103] P.R.O. 30/60/4, 16–31 July 1891; F.J., 24 July 1891, reported 2,500 delegates; Lyons, Fall, p. 278.
[104] Represented by J. G. Fitzgerald, J. Clegg, E. R. Whelan, J. R. Whelan, C. R. Doyle.
[105] Represented by Henry Dixon, T. Lambert, J. P. Moran, J. Hopper, W. J. Hickey, F. McGonigal, W. J. Leahy.
[106] Represented by C. H. Oldham.

Royal Irish Constabulary (R.I.C.) are suggestive. During the convention officers of the division identified fourteen delegates as I.R.B. suspects including P. J. Kelly, president of the G.A.A. and an I.R.B. county centre;[107] of the eighteen Mayo delegates twelve were of the I.R.B., and two were described as 'old Fenians'. They variously represented the G.A.A., the Parnell Leadership Committees, and the Irish National League; among them were several town commissioners.[108] In general, the I.R.B. was 'very strongly represented'; Robert Johnston and P. N. Fitzgerald were present and suspects John McCarthy and P. J. Kelly were seen lobbying delegates.[109] I.R.B. significance again depended on their effectiveness as organisers: their presence at the preceding county conventions seems to have been equally decisive.[110]

The importance of the I.R.B. presence was reinforced by the debate concerning the make-up of the executive committee and the vexed question of which organisations had a right to claim direct representation on this body. In April Mallon had commented 'that the more respectable of Mr Parnell's supporters are trying to avoid being committed to the policy of the I.R.B.'[111] Timothy Harrington forcefully argued the case for restricting representation as far as possible to the Irish National League. William Redmond put the case for including a greater variety of sectional interests on the council. Harrington and William Redmond's respective positions commenced a tension that would run through Redmondite politics in the 1890s. Henry Dixon, leading member of the Young Ireland Society and prominent Dublin Parnellite in 1891, made an important intervention. He argued that the constituency of Parnellism had broadened since the split: 'The fact could not be denied that after the proceedings in Committee Room 15 Dublin proved absolutely solid in support of Mr Parnell's leadership, and still the men who formed the national movement were men who had never been members of the National League (hear, hear).' An irritated Edward Harrington, speaking as a regional representative, said the organisation was not to be governed by Dublin and activists whose only qualification was membership of the Amnesty Association. An unnamed delegate retorted with the familiar refrain, 'The Amnesty Association was in existence before the National League (cries of "Order").' William Redmond, his populist instincts intact, favoured recognition of the Amnesty Association: 'one of the best things I know about Mr Parnell is that twenty years ago he was the treasurer of the Amnesty Association (cheers).'

The meeting closed by resolving that as soon as the chairmen of the county councils were elected the Parnellite movement would reconvene in Dublin with its MPs to elect twenty further members to complete the central

---

[107] D.M.P. 1891/2120.
[108] D.M.P. 1891/2128.
[109] P.R.O. 30/60/4, 16–31 July 1891.
[110] M.P.R.3, Thurles, 3 July 1891.
[111] D.M.P. 1891/2044, 5 Apr. 1891.

executive. The associations who could send representatives to consult with the convention were as follows: the Parnell Leadership Committees, the City and County Dublin branches of the Irish National League, the National Registration Associations in the cities and counties, the Amnesty Associations, the Protestant Home Rule Association, the Trades and Labour Organisations, and the Gaelic Athletic Association. Besides affirming the weakness of the Parnellites outside of Dublin, the list formally recognised organisations with a distinct separatist identity that had become important to the Parnellite cause. This was a wary Parnellite attempt to formalise an alternative coalition representative of a wide range of marginal political interests and it is important to note that the constituent parts were to retain their separate identities rather than be wholly subsumed by the league. On the whole, however, advanced nationalism sat more easily with the informal connexions permitted by the Parnell Leadership Committees.

IV

In its centrifugal sundering the split was Parnellism's epiphany, revealing the violently contradictory forces that had structured home rule's support base. With rural Ireland tending to support anti-Parnellism, the elements within the Parnellite coalition were re-ordered, extending greater priority to the sensibilities of urban nationalism, recognising in particular its stronger affinity with advanced nationalism. That said, a local study of Westmeath serves as a necessary corrective to any explanation of Parnell's urban support that is based exclusively on an analysis of advanced nationalism and labour. In Westmeath alignments during the split have been characterised in terms of tensions in the 1880s between young, educated townsmen and the farmers, shopkeepers, and clergymen faithful to Dr Thomas Nulty, catholic bishop of Meath.[112] As suggested, one approach to explaining the Parnellite tilt towards advanced nationalism is to see it as the urban equivalent of agrarian radicalism. Boycotting and hostility to (protestant) landlordism gave expression to rural ambivalence, if not outright opposition, to English government in Ireland. In urban Ireland similar sentiments found expression in advanced nationalism, and the prominence given to the working man in Parnell's rhetoric reflected their resurgent importance. Fred Allan, in combining Fenianism with Dublin labour politics and links to English radicalism, personified this aspect of Parnell's support base. Nonetheless, as the Mulcahy letter suggested, advanced nationalists found in Parnell not the answer to their political aspirations but a reflection of their attitude towards the British political system. They did not impute to Parnell orthodox Fenianism, but recognised in him the rebel

---

[112] A. C. Murray, 'Nationality and Local Politics in Late Nineteenth Century Ireland: The Case of County Westmeath' in *I.H.S.*, xxv, no. 98 (Nov. 1986), pp 144–58.

archetype they found most charismatic in Irish nationalist history. Parnell's glorious failure renewed a tradition that prized principle over pragmatism. *United Ireland*, rejecting anti-Parnellite calls for unity in the aftermath of Parnell's funeral, not least from the *Freeman's Journal*, expressed the Parnellite paradigm in the most basic terms:

> We are a predestined nation. More than once in our brave island story we faltered; more than once the Teuton tripped us up; more than once, alas! our enemies prevailed not alone over our swords, but what was a million times worse, over our judgement, our sense, and our pure love for the honour and glory of our motherland. But GOD guarded Erin. When SARSFIELD failed He raised a force of men who manned the regiments of the Volunteers; when TONE failed He gave us DAVIS and MITCHEL; when they failed He gave us STEPHENS and his Fenian boys; and, last kind gift from Heaven, when STEPHENS failed, He gave us our glorious PARNELL, noblest, bravest, kindliest Roman of them all.[113]

This was the apostolic succession of Irish failure, clearly privileging the romantic tradition over the successes of the mass catholic politics of Daniel O'Connell.

If technically Parnell did not compromise his constitutional ethic, his rhetoric bolstered the legitimacy of advanced nationalist sensibilities and Parnellite politicians did little to dilute this effect. For example, a few days after Parnell's funeral, James Stephens came to pay his respects at the graveside. Accompanied by Patrick O'Brien, John Clancy, William Bardon, and James Boland, the visit took on the air of an official visit. *United Ireland* put a cartoon of Stephens laying his wreath on its front cover and reported his words as: 'I place this with all reverence on the grave of the noblest Irishman of our time.' As he bent to lay his tribute he was reported, like Joyce's Mr Casey, to have 'sobbed aloud'.[114] The meaning of Parnell's discourse during the split and his historical legacy were determined by political theatre of this sort, which was partly or entirely outside his control. Nevertheless, his speeches did strongly evoke the historical tradition delineated in the *United Ireland* editorial and his attitude and defiance resonated with popular notions of the authentic Irish patriot.

Moreover, the meaning of Parnell's speeches was shaped by the complexion of his audience, and in particular the widespread recognition that he appealed to nationalists who identified with the advanced tradition. This effect was heightened by anti-Parnellite characterisations of Parnell as beholden to the Fenians. In their mockery of the apparent foolishness of the 'hillside men' they sought to denigrate the Parnellite–Fenian combination as a serious alternative

---

[113] *U.I.*, 12 Oct. 1891.
[114] *U.I.*, 31 Oct. 1891.

to the 'union of hearts':[115] it was not advisable for the anti-Parnellites to suggest that there might be some future for the rather nebulous idea of the Fenian home ruler. Rather, they worked to render redundant the conceit that Parnell was essential to the maintenance of the advanced nationalist commitment to home rule. Parnellites attempted to escape this trap by conceiving more clearly the principles on which the Parnellite campaign rested and by imagining the basis of a Parnellite politics without Parnell. In July 1891 at a Parnellite convention in Ennis, County Clare, Mahony argued:

> This was no longer a personal matter. If Mr Parnell were removed, they would still carry on the fight (cheers), for a year, for ten years, for the whole of their lives, on it should go, because the independence of their country and their people, was at stake (cheers). . . . It was very easy to say 'Ireland a nation', and to toast Ireland a nation, but that they were now on their trial to show that they meant what they said, when they said 'Ireland a nation'. No act of parliament could make them free and independent. Independence must come from the fact that the Irish earth had produced men with independent spirits and free minds. If they were men they should make Ireland free; if they were not men they would remain slaves as they deserved to be (cheers).[116]

Increasingly, Parnellites outlined a political platform that regarded the legitimacy of any Irish nationalist politics as dependent on the extent to which it was rooted in Irish cultural identity. They could not be defeated by the priests, Mahony continued, because 'they had the undying force of Irish nationality on their side, and that force would yet enable them to plant the banner of their country over the field of final victory (loud applause).' The idea that authentic Irishness was predicated on a masculine independence of spirit and thought was an important legacy of the split. It was central to advanced nationalism's mockery of Justin McCarthy's anti-Parnellite leadership in the early 1890s and later Redmondite constitutionalism. Failure within this masculine paradigm enhanced Irish dignity; failure outside it enhanced Irish ignominy.

Parnell's funeral provided a powerful evocation of what Parnellism meant during the split and to a great extent how it would be remembered in the nationalist imaginary. More than an expression of grief, it was the most formidable political spectacular of late nineteenth-century Ireland and was structured to give expression to the political complexion of Parnellism as constructed by the split. In proving impenetrable to anti-Parnellite overtures

---

[115] For example, in the *Nation*, 7 Feb. 1891, 'a hillside man' considered 'The Humours of Parnellism': 'I remind my readers that Jeremiah Francis D. T. Flabbergaster has been a sterling nationalist during the long, dangerous years since 1887, and that Hugh Roe O'Dempsey O'Dooly has been in the midst of the fight for freedom, since the early days of distant '89.'

[116] *Clare Saturday Record*, 18 July 1891. Edward Harrington and Leamy were also present.

the funeral symbolised continued Parnellite opposition to reunion. And in the accompanying host of aggressively political statements, from the hysterical assertion that Parnell's death amounted to a murder to the Parnell Leadership Committee's rejection of any possibility of reunion, it embodied further defiance.[117] Newspaper reports emphasised the solemnity and good behaviour of the crowd, and although there seems little basis on which to doubt this, Yeats wrote to his sister Lily:

> The Funeral is just over. The people are breathing fire & slaughter. The wreathes have such inscriptions as 'Murdered by the Priests' & a number of Wexford men were heard by a man I know promising to remove a bishop & seven priests before next Sunday. Tomorrow will bring them cooler heads I doubt not.[118]

Parnell's funeral was Fenian in tone and separatist in implication.[119] The escort of Gaels – 'And they are there, John Clancy and his "boys" guarding the Chief's body. Guarding it in death as they supported it in life' – was redolent of a state funeral, an expression of the honours due 'the uncrowned King of Ireland'. Given the politics of the 1889 G.A.A. convention, the escort was also unambiguously separatist and secular, compounding the impression created by the absence of an official catholic presence. In the rigorously organised processional order, the leadership executive led, headed by John Clancy, R. McCoy (a city councillor), John Wyse Power, Fred Allan, and regional representatives. The hearse followed draped in the Avondale Volunteer flags; Parnell's favourite horse, the 25-year-old Home Rule, walked behind. The remaining Parnellite M.P.s and the G.A.A. escort accompanied the bier. Then followed the carriages carrying the chief mourners. The first two carried Parnell's family, the third the protestant clergymen who were to conduct the burial, and the fourth John O'Leary, James Stephens, and P. N. Fitzgerald. This gave remarkable prominence to Fenianism, and, through the inclusion of Fitzgerald, to the present generation of separatists that had been so central to the campaign. As with the high profile of the G.A.A., in part this prominence reflected the strength of the advanced nationalists on the National Club Parnell Leadership Committee. It also was a nod to Parnell's celebrated visit to James Stephens on 29 September, one of his last public acts.[120]

In ascribing meaning to Parnellism care must be taken in emphasising the breaks over the continuities. Rather than a seismic shift in the character of

---

[117] In Dame Street a number of handbills were distributed with a deep mourning border headed with 'Murderer!' in large letters.

[118] W. B. Yeats to Susan Mary Yeats, 11 Oct. 1891 (*Yeats C.L.1*, p. 265). The I.N.L. was particularly weak in Wexford and these violent instincts, however short-lived, might have been a product of a sense of helplessness: the Invincibles once again.

[119] Detail taken from *F.J.* 10 Oct. 1891 and *F.J. & U.I.*, 12 Oct. 1891; for description based on these reports see Kee, *Laurel and Ivy*, pp 3–12.

[120] D.M.P. 1891/ 2198.

Parnellite political doctrine, the split represented a re-ordering of its priorities. Parnellism was a coalition between radical agrarians, constitutional nationalists, and Fenians. Each of these elements had been part of the mix between 1879 and 1891. Full clerical approval of the home rule campaign only followed Parnell's distancing from the Fenians and radical agrarians, but as the involvement of home rule M.P.s in the Young Ireland Societies shows, separatist sentiment continued to be carefully placated. Although rather overstated, the R.I.C. captured something of this relationship in its 1889 description of the Young Ireland Societies as 'educators or feeders to the great organisation of the [Irish National] League'.[121] The split saw Parnellism revive its capacity for recognising the cultural capital of the separatists.

Moreover, the affinity between Parnellism and advanced nationalism, as highlighted by the Parnellites during the split, was in continuity with the historical paradigm adumbrated by William O'Brien in his speeches to the Y.I.S. Pierce Mahony M.P. reframed this evolution from Fenianism to Parnellism in a speech at Tralee in 1891. Central to his historical analysis was the effect on nationalist morale in Ireland of the acceptance, with clerical approval, of positions in the Aberdeen government in 1852 by the independent Irish M.P.s John Sadlier and William Keogh. Long established among Irish nationalists as the archetypal modern traitors to the national cause, Mahony argued that Sadlier and Keogh's decision 'threw the organisation back into the melting pot, and that produced a state of deadness and dullness in Ireland from which the actions of the men of '67 alone roused the nation (applause)'. Tralee had a marked Fenian presence and Mahony played to this in his denigration of the men of Carlow, who, at the July by-election, elected an anti-Parnellite.

> He might mention that at a large meeting in the town of Carlow he made some reference to the men of '67, and there was only one man in the crowd who took any notice of his remarks. He thought that was a very significant incident, which almost foretold the result of the [by-]election.[122]

This was of a piece with Parnell's repeated celebration of the men of Dublin. Mahony praised the Fenians and elicited the inevitable applause, while arguing that Fenianism arose from Sadlier and Keogh's reliance on the clergy. In other words, the resurgence of the physical force tradition was the result of an avoidable political misjudgement. This placed his concluding remarks into an ambiguous context. By not responding to his notice of the Fenians the Carlow audience appeared to accept the legitimacy of the decision of Keogh and Sadlier to come under direct clerical influence. The contemporary meaning of this speech becomes clear: a failure to acknowledge the necessity of the Fenians in the 1860s implied an acceptance of the anti-Parnellite position.

---

[121] C.O. 903/2, misc. notes – series x, Nov. 1889, p. 82.
[122] D.M.P. 1891/2116.

This assigned the same structural role to the I.R.B. in the 1860s and the Parnellites in the 1890s. Parnellite resistance to clerical and Gladstonian dictation in politics was formulated as Fenianism by other means. The Parnellite present legitimised the Fenian past and acknowledged its possible future. This provided a more sophisticated version of O'Leary's dictum that a successful nationalist leader needed either the support of the Fenians or the priests.

Mahony made a similar appeal at the Parnellite conference of 24 July. Speaking at the evening meeting when the conclusions of the convention were presented to the general public, Mahony conflated the separatist militarist tradition with the independence stance.

> Those memories of our history that we cherish most tenderly, most dearly, are those of men who have failed as some count failure, but when they died upon the battlefield or upon the scaffold or in the chilly shade of exile from their native land, they died as victors in the fight (cheers). And why? Because they did that which was nearest to their heart, they kept aloft the banner of Irish independence, and they handed it on to the care of others who followed after (cheers). It is ours now to bear it aloft and keep it high; to keep it unsullied and unstained (cheers); and we can feel that we have done our duty in this matter (renewed cheering).[123]

When Parnell was in Wicklow in June, Mahony's sentiment took a literal turn. The two 'sadly tattered and faded' ensigns first carried by the Wicklow Volunteers of 1782 under the leadership of Colonel Sir John Parnell were displayed.[124]

R. Barry O'Brien posited a similar argument in his letter to O'Leary:

> The business, the villainy, the [indecipherable], are all to be found among the Irish men who acted like craven cowards by deserting their leader because an Englishman said 'I won't work with him'. Oh! the infamy of the thing. What will be said of us in a hundred years hence unless we wipe out these seceders, reconstruct our army, and advance once more in solid phalanx. When I was a boy public opinion in Ireland was contemptible. The country was dead. The Fenians breathed the breath of life into it. Fenianism was crushed and the country went to the d[evil] again. And Fenianism though morally changed saved the country again. The country is going to the d[evil] now. Can Fenianism save it again? That is the question that we have to face. We are again going the round of the old circle.[125]

The key moment in this passage is O'Brien's characterisation of Parnellism as a 'morally changed' Fenianism. In less oblique terms, O'Brien restated this position for public consumption in the Parnell biography. 'From the moment he [Parnell] thought seriously about politics he saw, as if by instinct, that

---

[123] F.J., 24 July 1891.
[124] W.F., 6 June 1891.
[125] R. Barry O'Brien to John O'Leary, 31 Mar. 1891 (N.L.I., MS 5927).

Fenianism was the key to Irish nationality . . . he ultimately rode to power on their shoulders. . . . Fenians are the real nationalist force in Ireland.'[126] Although it is likely O'Brien was alert to the popular appeal of this mode of rhetoric in 1898, the centenary year of the United Irishmen rising, it is clear he idealised Fenianism as Irish nationalism in its purest and most authentic form, perhaps a nationalism 'racy of the soil'.[127] Douglas Hyde expressed similar sentiments to O'Leary shortly after Parnell's death. In a strongly anti-clerical vein, Hyde admitted to only belatedly recognising Parnell's 'transcendent vigour': 'Fool that I was I thought that the party had made him more than he the party.'[128]

The common characteristics identified by the Parnellites as shared between themselves and the separatists of the United Irishmen, Young Ireland, and the I.R.B., were independence of thought and attitude. Opposition to clerical dictation in politics was further underpinned by a loose adherence to the enlightened values of republicanism and the associational culture of urban life, the Fenian ideal. On the night of 3 August 1891, Parnell spoke from the balcony of the National Club: 'Dublin says with the instinct and knowledge which come from experience, culture and reading, if this man is a traitor, why is he supported by the best of Irishmen?'[129] Similarly, William Redmond celebrated the split as ensuring 'that the grain had been sifted from the chaff'; Pierce Mahony compared it to the fire of London when the city was 'purified by fire'; and twenty years later Katharine Tynan stated, 'I still believe it was a sifting, and that the best took the side of Mr Parnell.'[130]

V

Parnellite articulations of 'independent opposition' exercised the imaginations of a small group of serious young men who met in Dublin to discuss literary, political, and social issues. Whereas the Young Ireland Society had readily given way to its offspring the National Club, the Leinster Debating Society gained an overt political identity from its decision to support Parnell. Established in October 1888, its most striking rule was that 'all questions relating

---

[126] Barry O'Brien, *Parnell*, pp 73, 81–2, 540.

[127] O'Brien's latent Fenianism was further suggested in the O'Leary letter where he intoned: 'During the fight in Committee Room 15 I met Parnell. I said "when your star was in the ascendant I did not come to join your forces. Things are now changed and I do come. I shall stick to you in the fight to the end of the battle." He looked as if he didn't care a ___ whether I did join his forces or not, or whether anybody else formed his forces. Cool, self-reliant, independent, defiant: He said "Thank you very much. I won't forget that." and [sic] then we parted.'

[128] Hyde to O'Leary, 10 Oct. 1891 (N.L.I., MS 5927).

[129] Callanan, *Parnell Split*, p. 144.

[130] *W.F.*, 25 July 1891; *F.J.*, 24 July 1891; Tynan, *Twenty-five Years*, p. 330.

to the religious creed of the members shall be strictly excluded from discussion.'[131] Probably inspired by the Contemporary Club and the Young Ireland Society, these young men approached serious matters with a wry and knowing irony (they did, however, reject an offer to amalgamate with the Jovial Littérateurs). In the minute book there is a strong sense of young adults playing with adulthood, self-consciously parodying the platitudinous pretensions of their elders. For example, having dealt with the meeting's business on 14 February 1890,

> the meeting resolved itself into a bohemian choral association, and selections from ancient and modern composers, having been rendered à la Wilhelm Ludwig, to the satisfaction of all, and to the complete annihilation of another, but less gifted musical association which meets below, the meeting adjourned, elated with success and resolved to meet again on Friday February 21st, 1890.

In October 1890 the secretary ironically lamented the decision to change the meeting day from the Friday, 'which was always the night in the good old days now fast-fading into the shadows of a half forgotten but ever living past'. Unlike the Y.I.S., the Young Ireland League, the National Literary Society, or the Irish Literary Society, London,[132] the Leinster Debating Society did not attract prestigious speakers or benefit from the patronage of home rule politicians. It could not rely on the pre-existing network of I.R.B. organisers or the I.N.L. to establish branches elsewhere. It was essentially a private club of very young insignificant people. Although deciding to advertise their meetings in the *Freeman's Journal* in December 1889, in November 1890 they decided to restrict its membership to a maximum of twenty. In June 1891 they were invited to co-operate with the National Club Literary Society. It appears this invitation was a precursor of the Young Ireland League initiative of September – similar feelers were put out to regional Y.I.S. branches.[133] The Leinster put off a decision, the Y.I.L. failed, and the Leinster was relaunched as the Celtic Literary Society in February 1893.

An early member was Arthur Griffith, present from December 1888 and occasionally chairing from February 1889; he was variously a committee member, vice-president, and, during 1891, president. Party to the society's playfully ironic mode, the Leinster was a key stage in Griffith's development of the brisk, muscular, and fresh polemical style of his maturity. Other members

---

[131] Unless otherwise stated, information in this section is gleaned from the Minute Book of the Leinster Debating Society [from January 1891 the Leinster Literary Society] (N.L.I., MS 19935).
[132] The National Literary Society was established in Dublin in 1892 following a letter writing campaign in *United Ireland*; the Irish Literary Society, London grew out of the Southwark Literary Society, founded in 1883. See *Yeats C.L.1*, pp 495–6, 499–500.
[133] *D.E.T.*, 30 May, 8, 12, & 19 June 1891.

included William Rooney, vice-president from December 1891, president from August 1892; the brothers John and Edward Whelan, who both held various positions; and Peter White, who was president from December 1891. Little is know of the latter three, but each played roles in the various political organisations with which Griffith associated before 1914.

The political atmosphere of the society was suggested by one speaker's 'unsparing' treatment of 'those who had differed with his estimate of the political career of John Mitchel'; by Griffith's condemnation in February 1889 of the imprisonment of William O'Brien at Clonmel; by the majority of five in favour of capital punishment; by the anti-clerical leanings suggested by the majority of only one vote against Griffith's proposal that the church was 'opposed to civilisation'; and J. R. Whelan's advocacy of 'state socialism' as a means to avoid strikes and the uncertainties of industrial arbitration. The mounting political crisis saw the society assert its distance from contemporary politics by defining its objectives on 14 November 1890 as the study of Dublin literature and characters and the establishment of a Dublin parliament.

On 28 November Griffith, identifying as 'a non-Parnellite and an independent nationalist', proposed a motion in support of Parnell. He did not explicitly support Parnell's politics but denied 'the right of any but the Irish people to depose him from the leadership'. Moreover, they pledged 'to use every honourable means' in their power 'to prevent the return to parliament of any Irish members who shall at this momentous crisis in our history betray their country by voting against Parnell'. The Leinster telegraphed Parnell and it is difficult not to see this as evidence of Griffith's developing sense of the importance of grandiose public gestures: 'Dublin supports you. We are confident you will vanquish your enemies, and win the day.' Like Yeats, Griffith had a powerful sense of the need to nurture the agenda and atmosphere within which his work, opinions, and self could develop. The telegram was followed by an address to the 'Men of North Kilkenny' during the Kilkenny by-election of December 1890: 'It is for you to decide whether you will be represented in the British house of commons by the follower of an English statesman, or by the supporter of Ireland's leader and Ireland's cause.'

Leinster debates and lectures in 1891 were dominated by the exposition of historical examples intended to prove the political efficacy of independent opposition. Christopher Doyle argued that it was the 'hillside men' and the 'records of their deeds' that had 'preserved intact the spirit of nationality in the Irish race'. Griffith established his lifelong adherence to Henry Flood as a model of patriotic 'self-reliance', typically contrasted with Henry Grattan's political naivety. Although Griffith would develop a more sophisticated mode of historical explanation, his continued readiness to illuminate Irish nationalist quandaries by identifying great moments of decision with the position of individuals gave his work a forceful simplicity. Most importantly, Grattan and Flood were later joined by Deak and Kossuth of the Hungarian parallel. Interestingly, Griffith rarely manipulated the O'Connell/Mitchel dichotomy. For though identifying with the latter, he recognised the complexities of the dynamic between moral and physical force nationalism and cannot have failed to appreciate the importance of O'Connell's method and achievement.

Edward Whelan continued the theme in his comparison of 1641 with 1891, 'a parallel'. He thought the 1641 rebellion had failed because the lack of unity among the Irish chieftains stemmed from their too great confidence in 'English promises'. The anti-Parnellites were likened to Ormond and his supporters, and Whelan urged that they did not give up their support for Parnell 'who was guiding them by the correct road to national independence'. John Gaynor questioned the parallel, making the classic purist observation that the *'revolutionary* movement of 1641' could not be paralleled with 'the present *political* crisis'.[134] At something of a tangent, Griffith 'showed by numerous historical allusions how fatal had been the influence of priests in politics'. James Doyle spoke on how the 'hopes of an over-confident people were shattered by the treachery of Sadlier and his associates'. The secretary reported: 'The majority of the speakers were of opinion that when priests interfered in politics, they should not use the spiritual weapons of the Church to terrify their flocks to follow the political party they support.' William Rooney tacked the required formula onto his treatment of Art McMurrough O'Kavanagh:

> Art successfully battled every attempt of Richard II to conquer him, by self-reliance, and by disdaining to place trust in the promises of an English monarch whose sole desire was the destruction of one of the greatest warriors and statesmen of the Middle Ages.

Following explorations of the respective value of English and Irish literatures, the French Revolution, and the parliaments of the ancient Irish – they were proof of Irish suitability for self-government – the society reached the summer of 1891. As Parnell travelled back to Dublin from Thurles the society prepared an address to present to the leader on his arrival:

> To us it matters not whether most or any of those representatives desert that policy and seek fusion with any English party. To us, it matters not whether ecclesiastical domination on the one side, or Dublin Castle influence on the other prevail, our duty is imperative – the path of independence is before us. Independent of English politicians, and without Irish traitors and cowards, we will seek for freedom; or failing to obtain it, we will, like the Carthaginians of old retire behind the embattlements of our nights, and refuse to obey the dictates of any leader of an alien people. And we hereby emphasise that resolve by declaring in the words of John Mitchel: 'all whig professions about conciliatory and impartial government in Ireland were as false as the father of whiggery himself.'

This address was remarkably revealing about the half-formed ideas of Griffith, Rooney, the Whelans, and White. Allusion and metaphor disguised a half-formed trajectory for the furtherance of home rule. The basic ideas of Sinn

---

[134] My italics.

Féin can be read back into this passage. Rather than advocating insurrection in the event of the demonstrable failure of home rule, it suggested a withdrawal from Westminster and resistance to British rule in Ireland. In a sense, rather than the bones of Sinn Féin, here was the flesh, the vision of an alternative political strategy. Griffith is often identified as a Parnellite, but as this passage suggests, his Parnellism stemmed from his identification of Parnell as Mitchel's successor. Mitchel was the Leinster's principal spiritual guide, reflecting both their separatist inclinations and their partial detachment from the verities of the Fenian tradition. Clearly the Leinster debates shaped by the Parnell split were predicated on the Mitchelite mistrust of British (more often, English) actions, which in their self-interest were underlaid with a profound urge to destroy Irish nationality. As Griffith's articulation of these beliefs grew more sophisticated, he tended to emphasise the self-interested aspect of the Mitchelite case. If Parnell's aim in the split was to reconfigure constitutionalism in order to make it work more effectively, Griffith pictured for Parnellism a much more radical agenda. Whereas Philip Bull's suggestion that Parnell considered the possibility of a tactical withdrawal from Westminster implied the possibility of a return under more favourable conditions, Griffith looked to something more permanent. Griffith's position was more of a piece with the conventional, uncritical reading of the 'appeal to hillside men' than the constitutionalist subtleties of recent historiography. Giving constitutionalism one more chance in this case did not reserve the possibility of a return to Westminster. Griffith's Carthaginians, and later Sinn Féin, offered the same non-negotiable position. The enlistment of Griffith in Parnell's Parnellism risks denuding Griffith of his radicalism and creating an alternative and fallacious apostolic succession of Irish nationalist leaders. As recent historio-graphical trends suggest, it is apposite to ask just how Parnellite was Parnell. As Redmond would discover in the 1890s, Parnell had left a highly problematic legacy.

3

'Parnell's Old Brigade'

The Redmondite–Fenian nexus in the 1890s

I

On 13 October 1896 P. J. O'Keeffe, member of the Kilkenny corporation, held a meeting at which 300 people gathered with lighted torches and two bands. Having denounced and burnt an effigy of the mayor, Major O'Leary, the gathering processed to the town hall. Asserting his right to enter as a member of the corporation, O'Keeffe with his crowd forced an entry to the town hall and ensured a resolution was passed condemning the mayor. With this done the crowd dispersed. Two days later an ordinary meeting of the corporation broke up in confusion when O'Keeffe refused to give up the borough treasurer's chair at the request of O'Leary. Following a coarse exchange, in which O'Leary insulted O'Keeffe's father and O'Keeffe twisted O'Leary's nose in recompense, the mayor left the chamber. On his return he found an empty porter barrel in his chair. The cause of these extraordinary scenes was the mayor's attempt to comply with a request of the Navy League that the Union Jack be hoisted on the anniversary of the battle of Trafalgar. The local police were deeply embarrassed by the attention these scenes attracted throughout Ireland and the United Kingdom.[1]

Although hardly a threat to the fabric of the state, P. J. O'Keeffe's particular brand of political ruffianism was very familiar to the police of the south eastern division of the R.I.C.[2] He had joined the I.R.B. when he was 15 years old and had taken a prominent role in corporation politics for some years. In 1888 he had been similarly upset by the corporation and had again raised a crowd that on this occasion was responsible for smashing nearly all the public lamps in the centre of the town. Hauled up before the magistrates, O'Keeffe was freed when all witnesses to the destruction denied they had seen him vandalise any public property. He was similarly freed when brought before the magistrates for threatening to shoot a sergeant leading a patrol in December 1890.[3]

---

[1] C.O. 904/57, south eastern division, Oct. 1896; *Kilkenny People*, 17 Oct. 1896.
[2] The account of the affair in the *Kilkenny People*, 17 Oct. 1896, conveys the style of O'Keeffe's politics very effectively.
[3] C.B.S. Box 4, 5405 S, 29 June 1892. O'Keeffe was fined £1 in August 1891 for leading

According to police commentary O'Keeffe had caused an affray on a number of other occasions. He was elected to the town council in December 1894 and was the I.R.B. centre for the county and city of Kilkenny.[4] O'Keeffe combined his Fenianism with staunch Parnellism. He worked with the Cork Parnell Leadership Committee in 1891[5] and identified as a Parnellite member of the Limerick corporation. He established a Parnellite newspaper, the *Kilkenny People*, with his close Fenian friend Edward J. Kane. O'Keeffe worked as the paper's manager, Kane as its editor, with both attending I.R.B. meetings at the Workingmen's Club in Kilkenny.[6] At a Parnellite meeting in Kilkenny of 250 people in December 1898 addressed by John Redmond on 'Irish Popular Leaders from Swift to Parnell' O'Keeffe once again showed his readiness to pitch in for the cause. He was fined £10 at the Kilkenny quarter sessions on 12 January 1899 for assaulting W. M. Kenealy, a reporter with the anti-Parnellite *Kilkenny Journal*, when he became involved in having him ejected from the meeting.[7]

Although P. J. O'Keeffe might have appeared an irrelevance to the national scene in the 1890s, with attention drawn to him only when he was able to engineer the type of publicity stunt described here, at a local level he was a figure of significant influence. He headed the poll when three vacant seats were filled in the municipal elections of December 1895, beating three anti-Parnellites with a combination of Parnellite and I.R.B. votes.[8] In many respects O'Keefe was an unusually prominent example of a typical figure – in his unashamed marrying of Fenianism and Redmondism, his involvement in organisations such as the Amnesty Association and his prominence at the annual Manchester Martyrs commemorations, he was representative of that awkward coalition of forces that Redmond came to rely on as organisational ballast in the 1890s. Patrick O'Brien M.P. was among those who wrote letters in support of O'Keeffe during the Major O'Leary controversy. In the loyalty he showed towards Redmond and his involvement in electoral politics, O'Keeffe clearly did not strictly adhere to the shibboleths of Fenian orthodoxy. Like many Fenians he distinguished what he could achieve in the short term without compromising his separatist ambitions.

---

an assault on an anti-Parnellite excursion party and damaging their musical instruments. For a few months in 1892 he moved to Dublin to work for the *Daily Independent*, but returned to Kilkenny in June. O'Keeffe and his three siblings were brought up and educated by the clergy of St Patrick's when his father died leaving them destitute. The children came under the influence of the Halligan family, many of whom were '67 veterans. Halligan senior's grave was the assembly point in Kilkenny for the annual Manchester Martyrs commemorations.

4 C.O. 904/18, Register of Suspects (Home), vol. 2, 821.
5 M.P.R.3, Kilkenny, 11 Mar. 1891.
6 C.O. 904/18, 653.
7 C.O. 903/6, intelligence notes, B series, xxxv, Nov. & Dec. 1898.
8 C.O. 903/5, B series, no. v, Nov. & Dec. 1895.

O'Keeffe is emblematic of many of the chief concerns of this chapter. The energies of advanced nationalists such as O'Keeffe could not be confined to the traditional activities of Fenianism. Although the I.R.B. continued to function and attract a significant membership, no attempt was made in the 1890s to organise a military campaign – there is almost no evidence of drilling. Instead this chapter will posit a characterisation of the I.R.B. as the home of particular brand of inveterate political activism, with the separatists finding themselves useful to the myriad of, often unsuccessful, Redmondite initiatives. Rather than merely a hangover from the split, it is argued that the close interaction between Fenianism and the structures of Redmondism contributed towards the survival of John Redmond as a viable politician. Just as with Parnell's lieutenants in the 1880s, Redmondites in the 1890s worked to retain Fenian sympathy (while the chief kept a suitable distance). The speeches of William Redmond in particular contained extremist nuances calculated to appeal to the Fenians. This appeal provoked dissension among the Redmondite ranks, notably from Timothy Harrington M.P., who saw the Redmondite–Fenian nexus as inhibiting the likelihood of the party reunifying.

Naturally the relationship between advanced nationalists and the Redmondites was symbiotic. Throughout the 1890s separatists battled to overcome their organisational fragmentation and to maintain a sense of momentum. As well as satisfying a need for political involvement among locally influential Fenians, the Redmondite cause, with its provision of clearly defined opponents, provided the I.R.B. with the sense of direction required in order to avoid the crippling stagnation and paralysis that inaction would inevitably precipitate. It is for this reason that the 1798 centenary celebrations came to acquire such importance. But a lack of ideological ambition and coherence coupled with inadequate organisational rigour ensured that this great chronological rallying point, remorselessly advancing and then rapidly receding, became the great lost moment of late nineteenth-century separatism.

Parnell's death provoked an outpouring of grief and recrimination, and it was clear that the rift would not be immediately closed. The Parnell Leadership Committee reconstituted itself as the Parnell Independent Union and the remaining Parnellite M.P.s issued a manifesto declaring, 'with the men immediately responsible for the disruption of the National Party, who, in obedience to foreign dictation, have loaded with calumny and hounded to death the foremost man of our race we can have no fellowship, and in their guidance Ireland can have no safety.' Henry Dixon junior, in the 1880s a member of the Young Ireland Society, and a prominent member of the Parnell Leadership Committee in 1891, gave voice to the bitterness and resentment that convulsed the movement: 'Crocodile tears had been shed, and they had had sympathy from men who were, in his opinion, responsible for the murder of Mr Parnell (cheers).'[9]

---

[9] *Weekly Freeman*, 17 Oct. 1891.

During 1891 John Redmond had emerged as the clear successor to Parnell. Known for his classical oratory, but clearly lacking the charisma, political instinct, and daring of his predecessor, Redmond has not been generously treated by historians. Despite leading the home rule party from its reunification in 1900 until his death in March 1918 there is neither a modern full-length scholarly biography of Redmond nor a sustained analysis of the movement he led.[10] The best recent single study of Redmondism is Paul Bew's *Conflict and Conciliation 1890–1910: Parnellites and Radical Agrarians*. The bulk of Bew's path-breaking work is concerned with the re-emergence of radical agrarian politics from 1898 under the inspiration of the newly constituted United Irish League. This is contextualised through a characterisation of Redmond's strategy in the 1890s. Bew contends that Redmond, unable to see the return to power of the Liberal party for a number of years, sought to build an alternative coalition of interests that could be used to appeal to the Conservative government.[11] The most visible aspect of this strategy was Redmond's cultivation of the Tory and unionist M.P. for South Dublin Sir Horace Plunkett.[12]

Bew's aim is to explore the 'grass-roots' and the '"popular" politics' of the period,[13] but his account runs the danger of sanitising the Redmondism of the 1890s. The focus on Redmond's conciliatory tactics at this stage in the development of the party obscures the ambiguity of his support base in Ireland, effectively sidestepping the grass-roots. The Redmondites appealed to the I.R.B. in a direct continuation of Parnell's strategy in 1891. They campaigned for the release of I.R.B. prisoners convicted in the early 1880s of terrorist activity, they jockeyed for position in the organisation of the centenary celebrations of the 1798 risings, they allowed the offices of the *Independent* newspaper group to become the Dublin I.R.B. headquarters, and, on occasion, their rhetoric took on a strongly anti-imperialist and separatist tone. As an embittered William O'Brien put it in an account that held Redmond principally responsible for the continuation of the split:

> He [Redmond] who was constitutionally an Irish nationalist of the most moderate type threw out hints and vague demands which alarmed a good many honest but uninformed Britons, and gave the Whiggish section of the Liberal party a plausible pretext for separating themselves from what they nicknamed 'Fenian home rule'.[14]

---

[10] For biographical detail see Denis Gwyn, *The Life of John Redmond* (London, 1932) and Stephen Gwynn, *John Redmond's Last Years* (London, 1919). More recent accounts include Paul Bew's brief study *John Redmond* (Dundalk, 1996) and Michael Laffan's essay 'John Redmond (1856–1918) and Home Rule' in Ciaran Brady (ed.), *Worsted in the Game: Losers in Irish History* (Dublin, 1989).

[11] Paul Bew, *Conflict and Conciliation in Ireland 1890–1910: Parnellites and Radical Agrarians* (Oxford, 1987), pp 23–4.

[12] Ibid., pp 26–7.

[13] Ibid., p. 13.

[14] William O'Brien, *An Olive Branch in Ireland and its History* (London, 1910), p. 69.

In their turn, Fenian activists contested local elections in the Redmondite interest, helping to ensure that Redmondites retained a voice as poor law guardians, coroners, and town councillors. In doing so, local Fenians worked to enhance their own reputations and positions within the locale, pursuing the faction fights and local rivalries so characteristic of the milieu. It is this symbiotic relationship that is the subject of this chapter. The tendency of the police to demean the social status of the I.R.B. also needs to be questioned. Far from consisting merely of young men and 'corner boys', it was not uncommon for prosperous businessmen and professionals, in particular medical doctors – who could use the I.R.B. to strengthen their local influence – to maintain close links with the organisation.[15] Despite, if not because of, its lack of readiness to take to arms against the British, the I.R.B. functioned as an integral part of the social and political fabric of the 1890s.

II

Assessing the numerical strength of the I.R.B. is notoriously difficult. As the organisation was secret and oath-bound, any assessment of its strength depends upon the use of police estimates. Two factors militate against confident assertion. The first was the tendency of the police to minimise the importance of the I.R.B. – their immediate concern was the extent to which the I.R.B. represented a threat to the peace. Second, much police information was gathered with the assistance of paid informers, who often exaggerated the significance of their information, thereby inflating its value. Much police correspondence was taken up with the assessment of this information.[16] A further conditioning factor is the weight of historical opinion, which holds that Fenianism was largely moribund, with a decrepit and fragmented organisation.[17] It is therefore surprising to note that the police estimates point

[15] Michael Laffan challenges the same police assumptions regarding Sinn Féin in *The Resurrection of Ireland* (Cambridge, 1999), pp 190–3; Peter Hart demonstrates how the Volunteers defined themselves against these very groups, *The IRA and Its Enemies: Violence and Community in County Cork 1916–1923* (Oxford, 1998), p. 148. Examples of medics manipulating their I.R.B. links to further their positions in the locale include Dr Mathew Grey of Drumlish, County Longford, at one point the local I.R.B. treasurer, and Dr M. M. Sheehy of Kilmallock, County Limerick, Land Leaguer, Parnellite and Amnesty Association campaigner. C.B.S. Box 7, 7453; C.B.S. Box 11, 12844, 29 Dec. 1896; C.B.S. Box 12, 14851.
[16] Senior police officers often provided moderating commentary on the bold claims of their juniors. For example, compare the monthly report of October 1892 submitted by the County Kildare inspector with that of his divisional commissioner. C.O. 904/60, Midland Division Monthly Report [M.D.M.R.], Oct. 1892.
[17] Leon Ó Broin, *Revolutionary Underground: The Story of the Irish Republican Brotherhood 1858–1924*, p. 49; R. F. Foster, 'Thinking from Hand to Mouth: Anglo-Irish Literature, Gaelic Nationalism and Irish Politics in the 1890s' in *Paddy and Mr Punch: Connections in Irish and English History* (London, 1993), pp 262–80; cf. W. F. Mandle, *The Gaelic Athletic*

towards two general conclusions. The first was that the I.R.B. had a larger active membership than the Irish National League, the main Parnellite organisation – in 1892 these figures were 11,051 and 8,076 respectively.[18] The second was that I.R.B. membership held up in the years 1896–8 when the membership of the I.N.L. and the Irish National Federation collapsed – I.N.F. membership fell from 56,000 members to 9,000, the I.N.L. from 3,338 to 160, while I.R.B. totals held up with 8,500. This goes some way towards justifying the I.R.B. mythology of a hard-core of activists immune to the ebb and flow of popular politics. The divisional inspector of the western division of the R.I.C. gave some indication of the extent of I.R.B. sentiment in his claim that the most powerful Parnellite organisation in his division was the I.R.B., with a possible 10,000 supporters; despite clerical condemnation, young men 'seem as keen to join the I.R.B. as ever'.[19]

Direct co-operation between the Redmondites and the Fenians occurred at the offices of the *Independent* newspapers. Set up during the split and owned by Redmond and Timothy Harrington, the papers were the chief disseminators of Redmondite propaganda throughout the 1890s. Between 1895 and 1898 the average circulation of the *Independent* newspapers was approximately half that of the leading Federationist journals, the *Freeman's Journal* and the *Weekly Freeman*.[20] Redmond appeared to have made no effort to prevent Fred Allan, business manager of the group, from holding I.R.B. meetings on the *Independent* premises; one informer claimed it was a condition of Allan's employment that he could do so.[21] Moreover, the *Independent* employed many I.R.B. suspects at all levels in the organisation. In March 1896 the police named sixteen suspects working for the organisation: in addition to Fred Allan and John O'Mahony, the sub-editor of the *Weekly Independent*, there were two canvassers, three working in the commercial branch, two compositors, two printers, a vanman, an engine cleaner, a fitter, a night watchman, and a stationary engine driver.[22] The employment of John Merna and John Nolan (they probably murdered the suspected I.R.B. informer Patrick Reid) respectively as an engine cleaner and as a fitter strongly suggests that Allan used his position to provide employment

---

Association and Irish Nationalist Politics (Dublin, 1987), pp 80–124 for the high level of factious I.R.B. activity in the G.A.A.

[18] C.O. 903/6, misc. notes, B series, no. xxxvii, Jan. & Feb. 1899. These police estimates are taken seriously by Tom Garvin, *The Evolution of Irish Nationalist Politics* (Dublin, 1981), p. 91, and David Fitzpatrick, *The Two Irelands 1912–1939* (Oxford, 1998), p. 15, n. 6.

[19] C.B.S. Box 6, 6186, Annual Report of the Crime Special Report for 1892, western division.

[20] C.B.S. Box 13, 16247; T.N.A. (P.R.O.) C.O. 903/5, misc. notes, B series, no. vii, Jan. 1896. Prior to the split the *Freeman's Journal* sold 50,000 copies daily.

[21] C.B.S. Box 10, 10712, 25 Oct. 1895. Allan was paid £4 a week, a low wage for the job; John Wyse Power took on his role as I.R.B. co-ordinator when Allan was away.

[22] C.B.S. Box 11, 11411. Mallon remarked, 'Of course there are a lot of others who are regarded as of no consequence, but who follow Allan on public occasions.'

for men whose reputations for extremism and violence might otherwise leave them unemployed.[23] In April 1894 Assistant Police Commissioner John Mallon highlighted the importance of the *Independent* newspapers with their close I.R.B. links to the Redmondite strategy:

> The Parnellite M.P.s [are] feeling their position gradually weakening, Dublin is their stronghold[,] the existence of the 'Daily Independent' is of the first importance, and hence they are practically in the hands of Wyse Power, Fred Allan, and a few others who have the confidence of the I.R.B.[24]

The most important visible link between the Redmondites and the I.R.B. was the involvement of the constitutionalists in the amnesty movement. Demands for the amnesty of Irish political prisoners periodically emerged as an important focus for Irish nationalists, regardless of their specific position on the Irish nationalist spectrum. Amnesty had a universal patriotic appeal, uniting constitutionalists and physical force nationalists and providing a cover for their more fundamental ideological divisions. For Isaac Butt, president of both the Amnesty Association from 1869 and the early home rule movement, amnesty was a central component of a political strategy that sought to reconcile the Irish to the union and empire through the grant of a measure of devolved government. By adopting the amnesty cause, Butt and the liberal home rulers were seen to be sympathetic to the popular passions roused by Fenianism, while maintaining their distance from the aims of Fenianism.[25] For Redmond the role of amnesty was equally ambiguous. Besides John Redmond, the Parnellite M.P.s William Redmond, William Field, Timothy Harrington, Patrick O'Brien, Pierce Mahony, and Dr St Lawrence ffrench-Mullen all made regular appearances on amnesty platforms alongside well-known members of the I.R.B. The Redmondites annually tabled amendments to the Queen's Speech requesting an investigation into the case for amnesty of Irish political prisoners and the issue was given substantial coverage in the *Independent* newspapers. In contrast to Isaac Butt, John Redmond had little need to placate British liberalism.

The second wave of amnesty campaigners had their origins in the convictions for treason-felony secured by the state against the dynamiters of the early 1880s.[26] The movement's spiritual home in the 1890s was Limerick, the home of the most prominent of the prisoners, John Daly. Daly attracted a combination of opprobrium and hero worship – the police, in particular,

---

[23] For details of the murder see Ó Broin, *Revolutionary Underground*, pp 50–5.
[24] C.B.S. Box 8, 8454.
[25] R. V. Comerford, *The Fenians in Context: Irish Politics and Society 1848–1882* (Dublin, 1985, 1998), pp 169–79; David Thornley, *Isaac Butt and Home Rule* (London, 1964), pp 53–6, 65–82.
[26] For a differently focused account of the politics of dynamite, see Seán McConville, *Irish Political Prisoners, 1848–1922: Theatres of War* (London, 2003), pp 326–404.

despised him. He was among those Fenians who had actively supported Butt's home rule movement, but withdrew in 1876, apparently in line with the I.R.B.'s undertaking to do so should the campaign have appeared to be a failure.[27] Along with a handful of other Fenians he was convicted of treason-felony in 1884 for planning to drop bombs into the chamber of the house of commons and sentenced to penal servitude for life.[28] He had been arrested at Birkenhead station in possession of three brass-cased bombs. When released in the summer of 1896 he did not deny the charges.

The Limerick Amnesty Association was formed in November 1889 – there were simultaneous meetings in Cork – and after publishing a pamphlet or two branches were established in Waterford, Tipperary, Kilkenny, and Tralee, often through the Irish National League.[29] Initially, the movement attracted little attention, although the authorities were concerned that Daly's supporters accorded him the status of a political prisoner and emphasised his apparent ill-treatment in prison.[30] The prominent Limerick Fenian P. J. Hoctor, an early champion of the campaign, complained of the lack of press coverage of an amnesty demonstration in June 1890, when 750 people processed to the O'Connell monument in Enniscorthy to hear him speak.[31] Hoctor's repeated attacks on the 'union of hearts' cannot have helped his media profile.[32] During the split, amnesty meetings became increasingly inhospitable for the anti-Parnellites – Parnellite resolutions passed at meetings made a mockery of anti-Parnellite speakers.[33] According to the police, Parnell's stance on amnesty reinforced I.R.B. support in Limerick and it seems likely that this was the case elsewhere.[34] Allan later posited the patent logic of the link between Irish nationalism and the amnesty campaign, arguing that Gladstone's rejection of Parnell 'took away the last shred of excuse from any man of independent spirit in Ireland against supporting the movement for amnesty'.[35]

Lacking a sound organisational basis, the movement was reorganised in August 1892 following a large demonstration in Phoenix Park and a conference. The officers of the Irish National Amnesty Association represented the range of political interests subsumed under Redmondism.[36] Pierce Mahony

[27] Thornley, *Isaac Butt*, pp 87–90, 135–7, 188–9, 290.
[28] T.N.A. (P.R.O.) CAB. 37/14/5 Case of John Daly 1885, report by E. G. Jenkinson (from August 1882 he was the head of special branch at Dublin Castle).
[29] C.O. 904/16, Register of Home Associations 1890–3, p. 413/1–4.
[30] C.O. 903/1, misc. notes – series ix, p. 80.
[31] C.B.S. Box 1, 838, 824, 876.
[32] C.O. 903/2, misc. notes, no. xii; *Munster Express*, 25 Oct. 1890.
[33] C.B.S. Box 9, 9156.
[34] M.P.R.3, Limerick, 30 Mar. 1891.
[35] *W.I.*, 28 Apr. 1894. Allan claimed, 'Even Mr Parnell himself (as I learned from his own lips) had up to then been carried away with the idea that the quickest way to get the men out was to get Home Rule.'
[36] In November 1896 the *Independent* decided to publish the appeal of the John Daly

M.P. was elected president of the association; Allan, William Redmond, and Henry Harrison, a moderate Parnellite, were made vice-presidents; Dr Mark Ryan, P. N. Fitzgerald, and Thomas O'Gorman, a Limerick activist, were made honorary vice-presidents; and William Field and Dr ffrench-Mullen were appointed treasurers.[37] It is noteworthy that I.R.B. members were not put in control of the organisation's finances, particularly the impecunious Fitzgerald.

There was a certain inevitability in the failure of these diverse individuals to work together peacefully for long. The first break came when Allan, pursuing a classic radical strategy that would allow Fenian activists a disproportionate influence, temporarily withdrew with eight others when ffrench-Mullen and Mahony refused to adopt a resolution that placed the policy of the association solely in the charge of the committee.[38] Allan argued:

> very many of them who had never followed parliamentary lines in their political action, and who never would, while always glad to work in harmony with independent parliamentary action, could not fall in with an association which was worked strictly according to the lines laid down by the parliamentary party.

This division between the extremists and moderates resurfaced in a different form two months later when Redmondites Lambert and Patrick O'Brien led the opposition to a proposal to make the release of the Invincibles the association's priority. Evidently, the Invincibles remained untouchable and O'Brien attempted to deflect criticism from the Redmondites by focusing on the Federationists 'who by their inactivity, had helped to keep the prison doors closed'. M. A. Manning, the editor of the *Weekly Independent*, had a simple explanation for the refusal of the authorities to release the prisoners:

> The English people had an opportunity to release prisoners on the occasion of the Royal Marriage, but they missed it. Even the autocrat of all the Russians would feel his heart soften on such an occasion, and some men and women would be freed from Siberia. But the English people are less tender.[39]

In directing his fire at the Federationists and the Liberals Manning adhered to the strategy that allowed the co-operation between the advanced and constitutionalist Parnellites. The belief that chief secretary Morley had reneged on assurances given prior to his appointment became the cornerstone of the amnesty movement's rhetorical strategy in the early 1890s. John Redmond highlighted the issue in a speech at Newcastle, England, in November 1893.[40]

Testimonial Committee in the news columns free of charge. Minutes editorial committee Irish Independent 1896–7 (N.L.I., MS 14915).
[37] C.B.S. Box 9, 9156.
[38] Ibid. & *W.I.*, 2 Sept. 1893.
[39] *D.I.*, 4 Oct. 1893.
[40] J. E. Redmond, *Historical and Political Addresses* (Dublin, 1898), p. 364.

Each group could then play the role allotted to it by the Parnellite theatre of the split. The Liberal party remained the vaudevillian traitor to the nationalist cause and the Federationists the ineffectual stooges. This facilitated the perpetual reaffirmation of the illicit liaison between the Parnellites and the I.R.B. To Mallon's consternation, in November 1894, Morley and Gladstone's unfriendly reception of a Dublin corporation amnesty resolution[41] saw the *Daily Independent* launch a vitriolic attack on the chief secretary,[42] which concluded:

> He is a plagiarist of Balfour, without Balfour's strength and worth. . . . John Morley is revealed to the Irish public as a person of lath and plaster, a stucco litterateur, a shoddy statesman, an inchoate and empirical infidel coquetting with croziers, and cozening Christianity.[43]

Contempt for writers and journalists often featured in Irish nationalist abuse; Justin McCarthy, historian as well as anti-Parnellite leader, faced similar onslaughts. Irrespective of this, the chief secretary always featured prominently in nationalist rhetoric, especially between 1887 and 1891 when Arthur Balfour occupied Dublin Castle. Then a unified and powerful home rule movement in its repeated and alliterative calls for 'boos for Balfour' and the soubriquet 'bloody Balfour' exhibited a certain respect for an awe-inspiring enemy; Balfour personified a resolute anti-Irish imperial Toryism. Conversely, Morley was portrayed as vacillating, hypocritical, and weak; a typically well-meaning but misguided liberal, very much a suitable ally for Dillon, Healy, and O'Brien.

Although the campaign for amnesty could maintain a certain momentum by highlighting the inequity of the Federationist alliance with the Liberals, to be sustained it needed firmer, more positive foundations. Allan responded by delineating the amnesty case in a series of articles under the heading 'Behind Prison Bars' in the *Weekly Independent*. In promulgating these arguments Allan was representative of those attempting to build bridges between the I.R.B. and mainstream Irish nationalism. Like so many appalled by the actions of the Dynamitards, Allan suggested, with 'the most moderate of parliamentarians', that he did not approve of the actions, but argued,

---

[41] *F.J.*, 13 Nov. 1894.

[42] C.B.S. Box 9, 9238.

[43] *D.I.*, 13 Nov. 1894. Morley was similarly condemned following the execution of John Twiss, hanged at Cork jail, 9 February 1895. Twiss was convicted of the murder of the Earl of Cork's bailiff James Donovan on the morning of 21 April 1894. Donovan was the caretaker of a farm in the townland of Glenlara, near Newmarket, County Kerry. Nationalist opinion considered Twiss innocent, targeted for his history of moonlighting. Meetings calling for his reprieve exemplified the Redmondite–Fenian nexus. C.B.S. Box 10, 9545; *D.I.*, 4 Feb. 1895; *Evening Herald*, 9 Feb. 1895. See also Pat Lynch, *They Hanged John Twiss* (Tralee, 1982, 1983) for a picturesque account of the murder, trial, and apparent miscarriage of justice.

that these men and others have just as much right to think that the time has come for the use of these methods as others of us have to consider that the time has not yet arrived for this; or as the most modern constitutionalist has to believe that such methods should not be used at all. It is merely a matter of opinion, not a question of degree of patriotism. The men now in jail for Ireland were above and before all things honourable, high minded and self-sacrificing patriots. They believed that the adoption of a certain course would benefit Ireland, and they entered upon it nobly, fully cogniscent of the risk, but taking that unhesitatingly.[44]

This was Allan at his most conciliatory, suggesting that the issue that divided Irishmen was primarily one of tactics rather than ideology or morality. William Redmond at an Irish National League meeting in May 1892 made his appeal on behalf of the prisoners on very similar grounds. This was a remarkably seditious speech by a sitting member of the house of commons:

> He (Mr Redmond) did not care whether these men were twenty times dynamiters. If they did use it, and he refused to believe it in the case of Daly and Egan and other men, they were driven into the use of it because of the intolerable tyranny put upon this country by successive British governments. . . . Whether these men used dynamite or whether they did not, they acted for the best motives, and from the desire to liberate Ireland and benefit the Irish people.[45]

At Newcastle, John Redmond, urging that the prisoners be granted political status, was equally provocative: 'It is believed in Ireland, and by many of our best friends in England, that these acts were committed, not from any selfish, sordid, or degraded motive, but committed to advance the cause of popular freedom or of national right.'[46] The Redmonds and Allan legitimised activities they considered inappropriate by praising their patriotic motivations; they distinguished between ends and means, attempting to generate support on the basis of abstract ideals. The relativist logic of this argument may not be convincing, but the appeal was made to a romantic nationalist sensibility that prized bravery and self-sacrifice more highly than efficacy. Reinforcing this was the general uncertainty regarding the very legitimacy of the British legal system in Ireland.[47] Fundamentally, the Amnesty Association was built on the assumption that, among Parnellites at least, nationalist solidarity was a more powerful emotion than an abhorrence of terrorism.

Central to the maintenance of this emotional appeal were accounts of the ill-treatment of Irish political prisoners in British jails. Conditions were harsh,

---

[44] W.I., 28 Apr. 1894

[45] C.B.S. Box 4, 5052; D.I., 13 May 1892.

[46] Redmond, *Historical and Political Addresses*, p. 360.

[47] On this subject see the fascinating article by Donald Jordan, 'The Irish National League and the "Unwritten Law": Rural Protest and Nation-Building in Ireland 1882–1890' in *Past and Present*, no. 158 (1998), pp 146–71.

abusive, and primitive but the Dynamitards do not seem to have been singled out for exceptional treatment.[48] Mallon reported of the alarm in I.R.B. circles when William Manahan returned from visiting Daly in May 1896 and reported to the association in Limerick that Daly was 'stout and strong . . . [of] robust frame . . . [with] a glow of health about his countenance'.[49] That this description was published in the *Limerick Leader*, a paper with marked Fenian tendencies, suggests an unusual lapse in news management. John Redmond was reported to have made the same slip in April at an amnesty convention in Dublin where he described Daly 'as sound in mind and body as any man he was addressing'.[50] Redmond was rather more on-message following his visit to Daly in July, with the *Daily Independent* reporting his alarm when confronted with Daly's deteriorating health.

In parliament the Redmonds, Harrington, Mahony, and Clancy made powerful arguments for amnesty based on four major strands: the dynamite prisoners were political prisoners; the convictions were legally dubious; those that were sound had served sufficiently long sentences; and the prisoners had been subjected to particularly harsh conditions. Harrington pointed up the irony that although the Explosive Substances Act in 1883 was forced through parliament with extraordinary speed – it passed three readings in a night – the Irish prisoners were tried under the treason-felony statutes of 1848, which carried much heavier sentences, on account of their supposed connections to the I.R.B. John Redmond compared the treatment of the so-called Dynamitards with that of the Walsall Anarchists, who were tried under the Explosive Substances Act in 1892 and received ten years' penal servitude.[51] Asquith's response was blunt. Yes, Egan's release after eight-and-a-half years' imprisonment had been announced because it was clear there was no evidence linking him to dynamite, but his punishment to date was entirely just given his link to the I.R.B. and history of treasonable activity. Little, Asquith continued, could be compared to the heinousness of dynamite crimes and the convicts could expect thorough punishment.[52] Predictably, William Redmond upped the ante. He

had the greatest admiration for the motives which induced the action of John Daly, and his fellow prisoners. ['Hear, hear!'] He might be told that they committed the most horrible crime, but crime begot crime; and he said that these men, horrible as their methods of action might be, were the outcome of the system of government in Ireland. The whole meaning of the home rule movement was that the past

---

[48] McConville, *Irish Political Prisoners*, pp 365–73.
[49] C.B.S. Box 11, 12211; *Limerick Leader*, 8 May 1896.
[50] C.B.S. Box 11, 11642.
[51] See also Redmond, *Historical and Political Addresses*, pp 371–2 and Redmond, 'A Plea for Amnesty' in *Fortnightly Review*, 52, no. 212 (1 Dec. 1892), pp 722–93.
[52] McConville, *Irish Political Prisoners*, p. 387.

government of Ireland had been based upon injustice and upon despotism, which they were going to remove.[53]

The debate on the Queen's Speech of February 1892 elicited a remarkable exchange in which the Redmondites defended the revolutionary heritage of Fenianism against the charge made by Home Secretary Sir William Harcourt that the I.R.B. was 'a secret association which professes to accomplish revolutionary objects by violence and outrage (cries of 'No, no' from the Irish benches)'. The Irish representatives accepted Harcourt's adapted definition: 'Fenianism is a secret association which professes to bring about revolutionary objects by force.' In response to Harcourt's 'sneer' at the mention of Fenianism, William Redmond pointed out the necessity of placating the 'considerable section' of the Irish population who retained sympathy for the efforts of the I.R.B. 'years ago':

> if we are going to have a genuine treaty of real and lasting peace between England and Ireland, let it be with the whole of Ireland – not excluding a considerable section of the Irish people from that treaty with a sneer at them because they belonged to the movement years ago, which now, apparently, is strongly condemned on both sides.[54]

Redmond's ambiguous 'apparently' suggested some uncertainty concerning Fenianism's contemporary status. Moreover, what was more striking was Redmond's open acknowledgement of the necessity of any political settlement being satisfactory to Fenianism and his demand that the organisation be treated respectfully in the house of commons. In an unusually moderate speech proposing an amnesty amendment to the Queen's Speech of February 1898, William Redmond again underscored the sympathy the remaining prisoners evoked in Ireland: 'It is a strange reflection that these men are honoured in Ireland; representative men are glad to call them friends, and they are looked up to as men who are suffering in the interests of the people at large.' Parnellite M.P. William Abraham, speaking after Redmond, aligned himself forcefully with the '98 centenary movement, admitted the moral legitimacy of orthodox Fenianism, and asserted the continuity between Fenianism and constitutionalism:

> I admit that we have adopted revolutionary methods in the past. I do not know whether in the future revolutionary methods may be adopted in Ireland, but you

---

[53] Hansard, *Parliamentary Debates*, 4th series, vol. III, 992, 9 Feb. 1893.

[54] Hansard, *Parliamentary Debates*, 4th series, vol. 1, 292–3, 334–5, 341, 12 Feb. 1892. Justin McCarthy's defence of Fenianism was more ambivalent, resisting the alignment of the Federationists with Fenian sentiment: 'Fenianism and dynamite have absolutely nothing to do with each other. The Fenians were a revolutionary party, but they never had anything to do with outrage or dynamite or any other crime of that kind.'

will never find us using dynamite. We shall meet you openly on the field, as our forefathers did in 1798, and for that you cannot condemn us.[55]

An officer of the south western division of the R.I.C. referred in January 1894 to 'the "Parnellites" and members of the Amnesty Association which is almost one and the same body'.[56] However, the police were not consistent in their taxonomy of the Limerick branch and it is clear they found it difficult to understand the exact nature of the relationship between the I.R.B. and the Redmondites. In February 1893 they referred to the extreme section of the 'Amnesty Party' as being unwilling to accept any form of home rule unless Daly was released as well,[57] while the following month the members of the Limerick Amnesty Association were described as permanent members of the I.R.B.[58] This inconsistency reflected the uncertainty that the I.R.B. exhibited throughout this period. Unable fully to reject the achievements of the home rule party, and in some cases being among the most fervent home rule activists,[59] the demand for Daly's release provided an emasculated Fenianism with a radical project. However, their position was perpetually compromised, since it was arguable that once an I.R.B. cause had been adopted by the constitutionalists it lost its radical edge. Conversely, if amnesty was not adopted the chance of its generating any recognition diminished. Consequently, minor successes, like the passage of an amnesty resolution by Limerick corporation in April 1894, had ambiguous resonances.[60] The irony at the heart of much I.R.B. activity during the 1890s was that relative success risked further ideological marginalisation. Any I.R.B. campaign, short of armed uprising, could be rendered impotent from a separatist perspective when adopted by the Redmondites. That the I.R.B. were alert to this dilemma was demonstrated in September 1894 when Mark Ryan, on a visit to Limerick to discuss the strength of the I.R.B. and the progress of the amnesty campaign, criticised them for working 'too constitutionally'.[61] P. J. Hoctor made the same complaint in September 1895, arguing that through the Amnesty Association

---

[55] Hansard, *Parliamentary Debates*, 4th series, vol. LIII, 438, 441, 11 Feb. 1898.

[56] C.O. 903/63, south west division [S.W.D.] M.R., Jan. 1894.

[57] A common demand: a resolution put to the Workingmen's Club in Dublin said a home rule bill had to include the release of Irish political prisoners if it were to be satisfactory. *W.I.*, 2 Sept. 1893.

[58] S.W.D. M.R., Feb. & Mar. 1893.

[59] As William Redmond pointed out during the 1892 Queen's Speech debate: 'I tell him that some of these men who have been most active, have done most to promote the cause of good will between the two countries upon the lines laid down by the Right Hon. Gentleman the Member for Midlothian.' Hansard, 4th series, vol. i, 292–3, 11 Feb. 1892.

[60] C.O. 904/63, S.W.D. M.R., Apr. 1894.

[61] C.O. 904/64, S.W.D. M.R., Sept. 1894. Ryan was perhaps purging himself of impure influences. In August 1894 he had been present in his capacity as president of the Amnesty Association of Great Britain at an amnesty convention in Liverpool where it was agreed that all parliamentary candidates should be called upon to take an amnesty pledge. It read,

working with the Redmondites the old cause was being compromised.[62] However, work within the constitutional framework brought dividends in July 1895 when John Daly was elected M.P. for Limerick with no opposition. This was a classic gesture of defiance – while in prison Jeremiah O'Donovan Rossa was returned unopposed in the Tipperary by-election of 1870; John Mitchel, separatist polemicist, Young Irelander of the 1840s, and convicted felon, won in Tipperary in 1875 – in each case done in full knowledge that the election would be annulled. However, the broader context of the 1895 general election was the continued failure of the Redmondites to dislodge the Federationist stranglehold on the electorate. In Cork, despite slightly stronger showings than in 1892, the Parnellite candidates, J. C. Blake, a solicitor, and the popular ex-mayor Alderman Michael Roche, failed to dislodge the sitting anti-Parnellite M.P.s J. F. X. O'Brien and Maurice Healy. In East Clare William Redmond's majority was reduced to fifty-seven, with the police surprised he retained the seat at all.[63]

As is evident, the rhetoric of William Redmond played an important role in bridging the gap between the aspirations of the I.R.B. and the Redmondites. He had long been placed in the more radical section of the parliamentary party. In May 1885, for example, he described Irish loyalty to the Queen as merely that which 'the strict letter of the law enforces'.[64] An 1887 police report re-circulated in 1894 characterised him as 'a very advanced nationalist and a fiery speaker. He is strongly believed to be connected with Fenianism; has associated with well-known Fenians about the country.'[65] William Redmond was particularly active towards the end of 1895. In Dublin in November he achieved that peculiar blend of extremism and paralysis so characteristic of those who straddled the separatist–constitutionalist divide and, as such, is worth quoting at length:

No nation was conquered which kept green the memory of the men who died for its freedom. . . . In spirit Ireland has never bent to the yoke of England, and has never consented to her rule. . . . Their hearts during the struggle in England's parliament never turned away from the men whose memory they were met that

---

'I hereby declare that should I be elected to parliament, I will on all occasions that arise in the house of commons, vote for the immediate and unconditional release of all prisoners incarcerated in prisons for offences rising out of the political struggle in Ireland, and I will further take every opportunity in parliament and in all public discussion of advocating the cause of amnesty with regard to these prisoners.' C.O. 903/5, misc. notes, B series 1895–97, Aug. 1894.

[62] C.B.S. Box 10, 10819.

[63] C.O. 903/5, July 1895.

[64] Quoted in James H. Murphy, *Abject Loyalty: Nationalism and Monarchy in Ireland During the Reign of Queen Victoria* (Cork, 2001), p. 242.

[65] C.B.S. Box 8 also identified the sometime Parnellite M.P. Dr Kenny as a Fenian of high standing.

night to honour. They always loved and ever would love those men who were hunted by England, and whose crime was love of Ireland. He (Mr Redmond) was proud and happy as an Irish representative to stand there that night and to publicly declare his respect for the dead rebels of Ireland and his sympathy with their struggles.[66]

Although the speech contained the odd enigmatic hint of possible action along I.R.B. lines – 'Freedom might come sooner than they expected' – it was primarily concerned with the necessity of remembrance as a means to keeping a more exalted spirit of national identity alive. This mode of rhetoric was the expression of marginalism and it confirmed the I.R.B. as still caught in the backwash of the 1860s and unable to formulate a strategy for renewed action. There is no need to doubt that William Redmond could combine separatist aspirations with a constitutionalist strategy, just as it would be fanciful to suppose that his apparent radicalism was an assigned role cast to keep the I.R.B. in line; nonetheless this speech confirmed Redmond's limited intentions. Remembering had become an alternative to action.

William Redmond struck an increasingly hard-line note at a series of Parnellite conventions aimed at bolstering the Irish National League and raising cash for the Independent Home Rule Fund. A thousand Corkonians were treated to the following:

He knew that in many parts . . . the young men were getting a bit tired of parliamentary inaction, and he knew it was small blame for them. Since Parnell's death five years ago, parliamentary action had brought little to Ireland but shame and disgrace, and he would say to these young men whose hearts beat as his own, that before they gave up all hope from the British parliament, let them make one more rally around the few Parnellites of Parnell's Old Brigade (cheers), and then, if they would not bring back from Parliament something in the way of legislative reform, he would join heart and hand with those who said the time had come for Irishmen to decide themselves instead of signing ballot papers (cheers).[67]

[66] C.B.S. Box 10, 10825; *D.I.*, 14 Nov. 1895, also *D.I.*, 25 Nov. 1895; cf. William Redmond addressing his East Clare constituents on the second home rule bill: 'Sooner than stand up and allow his lips to frame the words that the bill was the final settlement of Ireland's national demand he would not only give up being their representative and leave public life, but if any man said that he should either say that this was the settlement of Ireland's claims or lose his life, he believed, if God gave him strength, he would lose his life before he would accept that bill as a final settlement of the demand for which their forefathers had fought and died. That was the difference between the McCarthyite members and the Parnellites. With that bill or without they would go on until the epitaph of Robert Emmet could be written (cheers).' *W.I.*, 23 Sept. 1893.

[67] Patrick O'Brien addressed a Waterford meeting in January 1895 in similar terms: 'Constitutional agitation was now on its trial, and if it succeeded at all it could only succeed on the lines laid down by Parnell, on the lines of John Redmond, and if did not succeed the opportunity would come for the good and true men to adopt other means (loud cheers),

Police observers confirmed that although the *Daily Independent* reported the phrase in the closing sentence of this speech as 'decide themselves', William Redmond said 'drill themselves', as reported in the *Cork Examiner* and the *Cork Herald*.[68]

III

The tensions thrown up by the contradictions inherent to the Fenian–Redmondite nexus spilled over into a series of public disputes from late 1895. Timothy Harrington, after John Redmond the most prominent Parnellite, used his newspaper *United Ireland* to articulate his opposition to the co-operation between the two political traditions. Harrington favoured unity among constitutional nationalists and his actions clearly demonstrated that not only did he believe that the Federationists and the Parnellites had politically more in common than the Parnellites and the Fenians, but that the political prestige of the remaining Parnellites was sufficient to achieve a measure of unity without relying on the I.R.B. He corresponded with Michael Davitt throughout the 1890s and was treated warmly in William O'Brien's embittered account of the period: it was Harrington's 'fondness rather than his political judgement which led him to side with Parnell'.[69] Harrington's attempts to rise above the factional fray, to position himself in the grey area where Redmondism and Federationism blended, saw him risk alienating Parnellite support in key areas. For example, in March 1895 Harrington and John Redmond gave St Patrick's Day speeches in Limerick and Cork respectively. Both cities retained a strong Parnellite faction, within which an I.R.B. element was prominent and in both cases the speakers were criticised by 'advanced Parnellites' for being too moderate.[70] Harrington's reputation as a conciliator was reflected in his meagre audience of fifty; Redmond's audience of 2,600 was proportionally much larger. In Limerick politics was fiercely divided, not only between Parnellites and Federationists, but, owing to the prominence of the amnesty campaign, the tension between Fenianism and Redmondism was more acute than elsewhere.[71]

---

to realise the dreams of Emmet and Fitzgerald. When that day came he knew at least one man who would not funk the fight then any more than he was not funking the fight now (cheers).' *D.I.*, 23 Jan. 1895.

[68] C.O. 903/5 intelligence notes, B series, no. v, Nov. & Dec. 1895, pp 11–12; *D.I.*, *Cork Herald*, *Cork Examiner*, 9 Dec. 1895. Secret society men were prominent at similar December meetings in Tuam and Newry, but were not noted at Sligo, Enniscorthy, Wicklow, Aughamore, and Kilkenny.

[69] O'Brien, *An Olive Branch in Ireland and its History*, p. 6.

[70] C.O. 904/64, S.W.D. M.R., Mar. 1895; T.N.A. (P.R.O.) H.O. 184/65 intelligence notes, misc. – M series, xxxvi, Mar. 1895, p. 97.

[71] The political division was confirmed at the municipal elections for Limerick of December 1895. The Parnellites gained one seat with twenty-two, the Federationists got fourteen

With the lines of demarcation sharply drawn, expectation demanded that speeches fortify the resolve of local activists and supporters in their defiance of the majority of the nationalist population and the catholic clergy. In a city like Limerick Harrington's reputation for conciliation had little appeal. Nonetheless, Harrington remained capable of making the expedient gesture. Shortly before the Limerick speech, Harrington joined the funeral procession of James Boland, a Dublin Fenian, who had died on 11 March 1895.[72] Harrington's presence on foot in a procession of little more than 300 people, at which Allan's Nally Club represented the 'cream of the extremists', was clearly a calculated gesture from the Dublin Harbour M.P. to his constituents.[73] Field, Clancy, and Mahony's decision to drive to the cemetery rather than join the procession was resented.[74]

Harrington chose to take the Fenians on in both his and their Dublin territory, first in the National Club and then in the municipal elections of December. With the club facing bankruptcy in 1895, Redmond and Harrington stepped in to save it, believing it essential to preserve it as a place where protestant and catholic nationalists could meet.[75] Harrington's first action was to bar as guests a handful of Fenians, including Nolan and Merna, arguing that he did not want to alienate young commercial men, presumably protestants, from the movement. The influential Fenian Patrick Gregan led the opposition, but Harrington proved impervious to their appeal by petition.

Harrington's next move was to run Thomas O'Hanlon in opposition to Patrick Gregan in the municipal elections of December 1895. Gregan won the central Dublin Rotunda Ward seat and Harrington responded by printing an article in *United Ireland* characterising Fenians as those who 'spent half their time drinking with detectives, and the other half cursing the government'.[76] Gregan and Allan were furious and a National Club meeting was secretly moved from eight o'clock in the evening to two o'clock in the afternoon to avoid disruption from Gregan's supporters. Despite this, 200 protesters attended the meeting. Following a tip-off, swift action by the police prevented a serious disturbance and halted a determined effort to set fire to the *United Ireland* and *Independent* offices.[77]

Although Harrington prevailed with regard to the National Club, he and Redmond remained unable to restrain 'the troublesome fellows'. The Greganites continued to press for recognition of their political legitimacy, with Allan

---

seats, the Unionists one seat, and three candidates were elected as neutrals. C.O. 903/5, misc. notes, B series, no. v, pp 57–8.

[72] *D.I.*, 12 Mar. 1895.

[73] C.B.S. Box 10, 9702. The *D.I.*, 15 Mar. 1895, reported that the procession swelled to around 1,500 people en route to the cemetery.

[74] C.B.S. Box 10, 9707.

[75] C.B.S. Box 10, 9532; *D.I.*, 30 Jan. 1895.

[76] C.O. 903/5, misc. notes, B series, no. viii, p. 11.

[77] C.B.S. Box 11, 11316. Mallon reports that Redmond and Harrington resolved to have Allan removed from his job; if so, this was not acted upon.

having the audacity to hold a meeting of two hundred sympathisers at the *Independent* office in March.[78] Eventually a reconciliatory interview was arranged between Allan, Gregan, and Harrington, which saw Harrington deny that the *United Ireland* article referred to the Nally Club. In the brief article reporting the meeting Allan made a statement that, for all its imprecision, summarised the peculiar political texture of Parnellism in the 1890s. 'The policy of Mr Parnell after the split embraced more than his policy previous to it, just as the movement after the split embraced many sections of the people who could not consistently belong to it before that period.'[79] In July 1896, a Dublin informant claimed:

> That Mr Timothy Harrington has nothing to do with the 'Independent' at present, and that he and Mr J. E. Redmond do not agree on vital points of policy. Mr Harrington is in favour of constitutional agitation under the policy of Parnellism, and does not regard Fenianism in any form as necessary to promote that policy. Mr Redmond considers it more necessary now than ever to keep close to the Fenians, and in order to keep some of them, who are well known to him, from starving he actually has money paid to them.[80]

The Harrington controversy refocused a year later when the Redmondites attempted to revivify their organisation by replacing the Irish National League with the newly inaugurated Irish Independent League. This was not a success for a number of reasons. It brought into contention the supposed divergence of interests between Redmond's rural and urban supporters, it exposed the controversy regarding the role of the I.R.B. in Redmondite politics, and it served to highlight the crippling disillusionment that was afflicting all forms of political organisation wedded to the models of the 1880s. The police were especially scathing in their accounts of the new organisation's inauguration. The Dublin convention of 20 April 'was really a gathering of Mr Redmond's personal friends' and the I.R.B. had 'practically convened the meeting'.[81]

---

[78] C.B.S. Box 11, 11477.

[79] *D.I.*, 12 Mar. 1896.

[80] C.B.S. 12013, July 1896. The informant goes on to claim that Redmond's party was being kept afloat thanks to the financial generosity of Cecil Rhodes. Patrick Maume also points out this connection with reference to the 'sinister Rhodes associate' J. Rochfort Maguire, M.P. for West Clare 1892–5, *The Long Gestation* (Dublin, 1999), p.16.

[81] C.B.S. Box 12, 13478. Mallon goes on: 'Most people are laughing at the whole thing as a good joke. Some say that Secret Society money is spent so freely on both sides of the Atlantic that it is impossible for any honest [i.e. constitutionalist] nationalist to join any organisation pretending to be Irish nationalist, and that nothing serious will arise out of them. Others say that between Harringtonites, Healyites, Dillonites, I.R.B. and I.N.A. it is easy to keep the country quiet, especially as no one seems disposed to trust either party with large sums of money.' *The Spectator* was equally snide: 'When in doubt call a conference and found a new association. That appears to be the rule on which the Irish patriot now acts.' Reprinted in the *Weekly Nation*, 1 May 1897.

Fifty-two separatists were among the 107 members elected to the League's provisional executive.[82] An enthusiastic report in the *Daily Independent* listed the Irish Independent League's objectives as national self-government, full civil and religious liberty, independence of all British political parties, manhood suffrage, immediate redress of Ireland's financial grievances, amnesty for all political prisoners, land law reform, and the encouragement of the labour and industrial resources of Ireland.[83] 'We want a parliament with full powers to manage Irish affairs without entrenching on imperial prerogatives,' the provisional executive demanded, 'but a parliament we must have that will be supreme with regard to Irish questions. We will have no English veto.'[84] Despite its vagueness, or even because of it, this was a classic definition of home rule.

A letter from Michael Davitt suggested that at this time Harrington seriously considered resigning his seat. Davitt urged him not to, arguing that he could not hope to regain it if opposed by the Redmondite press. He could do more good working within the movement than in taking Redmond on from without.[85] The rows that were to follow were prefigured in the defeat at the convention of Harrington's proposition that the Irish National League be consulted before the existing organisation was altered. John Redmond argued that the I.N.L. was in the 'main an agrarian organisation (hear, hear)', and that the Irish Independent League was an attempt to redress this imbalance and to attract the support lost during the split.[86] However, Harrington raised the stakes in an overt criticism of the connections Redmond appeared to be nurturing with the I.R.B. He 'knew the forces which were sought to be placated, and he for one at least would never lend himself to an effort to fight Ireland's cause other than by rational means. He appealed to the meeting to support him in his effort to keep the flag flying which Parnell gave into the care of those who followed the true principles of national effort.'[87] This incursion was indicative of the continued controversy surrounding the ownership of Parnell's inheritance and implied that the separatists were an exclusively urban element. This interpretation was reinforced by a sober report from the south western division of the R.I.C. that suggested Redmond's core support in the region came from the shopkeeper, artisanal, and labouring classes of the towns, particularly in Cork and Limerick. In a rather oblique assertion, the report stated that the presence of leading secret society men at the

---

[82] C.B.S. Box 12, 13748.

[83] *D.I.*, 21 Apr. 1897.

[84] *D.I.*, 5 May 1897.

[85] Michael Davitt to Timothy Harrington, 20 Mar. 1897 (Harrington Papers, N.L.I., MS 8576/11).

[86] At a National Club meeting in January 1895 Redmond addressed the crowd outside: Dublin 'had always been the centre of the national spirit of Ireland'. The *D.I.* claimed 2,000 were present; the D.M.P. said not more than 500 at any one time. *D.I.*, 21 Jan. 1895; C.B.S. Box 10, 9502.

[87] *F.J.*, 21 Apr. 1897.

Independent League's inaugural convention accurately reflected Redmond's support base.[88] John O'Leary joined the controversy with a letter to the press displaying his characteristic disregard for the conventions of constitutional and advanced nationalism:

> Mr Harrington, at the conference, seemed to fear that the new movement was a bid for Fenian support; but if so, why not? Mr Harrington seems to forget, or at least to ignore, the fact that the Land League, in its inception and during the greater part of its course, was a purely opportunistic Fenian movement. . . . I am thoroughly with the new movement, or, at least, with the ideas that underlie it – a full measure of self-government, and an appeal from the less national to the more national sections of the community.[89]

It might seem odd that the *Daily Independent* would print this letter, it apparently being in the Redmondite interest to keep its connections with Fenianism obscured. However, O'Leary occupied a peculiar position within the nationalist debate in the 1890s. Having spoken of Fenianism openly since his return to Ireland in 1885, he had fashioned a rhetorical mode that purported to see no danger in uttering the apparent truths that others feared to acknowledge. The advantage of this from Redmond's point of view was that a Fenianism openly discussed was a Fenianism demystified and consequently rather less dangerous.

Attempts to set up branches throughout the country were far from successful. Harrington's oppositionism increased the hostility met by Field when he attempted to establish an Usher's Quay branch in Dublin city. Field was driven to argue that he was not attempting to coerce the I.N.L. into becoming the Irish Independent League, but that it was the case that the I.N.L. had 'practically ceased to exist'. According to the Federationist *Freeman's Journal*, Field 'dwelt especially on the item of the programme in reference to the right of people to carry arms, and said that what the country wanted was men, money, and arms'.[90] Mallon pointed up the awkwardness of Field's position: he 'has a reputation of a man of peace and is really so, and his allusion to arms etc. provoked a good deal of chafing.'[91] However, Field's use of martial rhetoric was more metaphoric than literal. When a branch was established in Wicklow in late April, Field extolled, they

> were struggling for national self-government, for an independent parliament (cheers). . . . If their opponents thought they were going to lay down their arms they were very much mistaken, as the old fight would be carried on until the crown

---

[88] C.O. 904/65, S.W.D. M.R., Apr. 1897.
[89] *D.I.*, 30 Apr. 1897; C.B.S. Box 12, 13531.
[90] *F.J.*, 20 May 1897.
[91] C.B.S. Box 12, 13652.

of freedom was placed on the brow of the nation (loud cheers) . . . Ireland for the Irish.[92]

Insofar as this speech contained undeniable Fenian resonances, it also tapped into a discourse that sought to equate Parnellism with the 'old fight', implying a continuity between Fenianism, Parnellism, and the Irish Independent League.[93] The emphasis on an 'independent parliament' suggested that the Redmondite conception of home rule went further than that of the collaborationist Federationists. In underlining the affinity of the Redmondites for the advanced nationalists Field reaffirmed the affinity of the Redmondites for the Fenians.

At one dismal meeting at Cork in June Patrick O'Brien, despite hiring two bands, could only attract a crowd of 600. Police hyperbole proclaimed it 'the most insignificant public meeting ever held in Cork', while one moderate Parnellite was reputed to admit that more people would collect on a Sunday 'to witness the arrest of a drunken man'.[94] By the end of the year it was evident that the Irish Independent League would not provide the basis of a resurgent Parnellite politics. There were branches only in Counties Armagh (1), Meath (3), Galway (2), Mayo (3), Roscommon (3), Clare (3), Limerick (1), Carlow (1), Kildare (1), and Wicklow (8). This did not represent an expansion of Parnellite operations. Of these twenty-six branches with a combined membership of only 1,758, eighteen featured physical force nationalists among the executive officers of president, treasurer, or secretary.[95] Indeed, the south western division of the R.I.C. made the extraordinary claim that three-quarters of the circulars issued by the central Dublin branch of the Irish Independent League were addressed to I.R.B. suspects.[96]

Rather than attributing the failure of the Irish Independent League to the preponderance of the I.R.B. among its organisers, the real explanation lies in the widespread disengagement among the nationalist population from the structures of constitutionalism. Although the general population was not moving towards physical force separatism, there was undoubtedly a burst of separatist enthusiasm linked to the 1798 commemorations, but the primary trend was the accelerating disillusionment with the potential of organised

---

[92] D.I., 29 Apr. 1897.

[93] During the 1892 Queen's Speech debates William Redmond argued that the Fenians 'paved the way for the movement of Mr Parnell', while both Redmond and Harrington agreed that Parnell had been responsible for ensuring the Fenians supported home rule. Hansard, *Parliamentary Debates*, 4th series, vol. 1, 292, 336–7, 11 Feb. 1892.

[94] C.O. 904/66, S.W.D. M.R., June 1897. William Redmond communicated with leading supporters in County Clare about the possibility of his setting up a branch of the Irish Independent League, but there was no interest and the suggestion was dropped. C.O. 903/6, misc. notes, B series, no. xxiv, July 1897, p. 15.

[95] C.B.S. Box 12, 14826 S.

[96] C.O. 904/65, S.W.D. M.R., May 1897.

politics.[97] The failure of the second home rule bill, the disengagement of the Liberal party from Irish nationalist politics, and the demoralising impact of a strong Conservative government pursuing 'constructive unionism', rendered Redmondism and Federationism politically bankrupt.[98] It seems evident that had Harrington succeeded in distancing the Redmondites from the I.R.B. and achieved political unity it would have made little difference to the medium-term fortunes of the home rule party. The resurgence in I.R.B. sentiment, if not long-term commitment, generated by the 1798 centenary saw the various I.R.B.-controlled '98 Centenary Associations achieve a membership of over 10,000 by December 1897,[99] and over 30,000 by the close of 1898. At the same time, William O'Brien's United Irish League, with which Harrington cagily associated, boasted a nominal membership of 10,844 and an active membership of 3,200 and 121 branches.[100] This was soon to undergo a dramatic increase. 'There is grave uneasiness', commented one police report in November 1897, 'among moderate nationalists who cannot afford to cut adrift the knot of extremists who are working under the cover of the '98 movement in Dublin.'[101]

IV

The split had exposed the illusion of the Parnellite hegemony; in the forces unleashed were revealed the myriad of political opinions and aspirations that Parnellism embraced, if not disguised. In 1891 the dazzling artifice stood exposed and the silent dissident voices ungagged. Parnell's overt courting of the I.R.B., whatever its ambiguous complexities, extended towards separatism the political legitimacy it had lacked in the decade since the Land War. Fenianism once more took its place in the nationalist discourse, once more provoking the passion and division it had engendered in the 1860s and 1870s.

By inheriting the Parnellite leadership, Redmond inherited the same coalition of contradictory elements that Parnell had assembled in 1891. The

---

[97] In May 1897 the editors of the *Weekly Independent* decided they could arrest the decline in circulation of the paper by reducing the number of political reports it carried. Minutes editorial committee Irish Independent 1896–7, 13 May 1897 (N.L.I., MS 14915).

[98] Cf. 'In the mid-1890s Parnellism was firmly placed in a ghetto within Irish politics.' Bew, *Conflict and Conciliation*, p. 26.

[99] Calculation based on the figures in C.O. 903/6, misc. notes, B series, no. xxviii, 'The '98 Centenary Movement'.

[100] C.O. 903/6, misc. notes, B series, no. xxxvii, Jan. & Feb. 1899. At the height of the I.I.L. controversy Harrington shared a platform with William O'Brien, ex-M.P., and Abraham M.P. at an agrarian meeting held at Glanworth, Mitchelstown, Cork East Riding. The district inspector reported that the overt object of the meeting was to aid the Evicted Tenants Fund, but the real object was 'unity'. O'Brien's speech was a eulogy of Harrington; the usual resolutions calling for aid for evicted tenants, the denunciation of land grabbing, and the release of political prisoners were passed. C.O. 904/65, S.W.D. M.R., May 1897.

[101] C.B.S. Box 12, 14781.

opinion of the police observers and the sheer time and energy devoted to advanced nationalist causes by the Redmondites strongly suggests that without them Redmond's political survival was far from assured. Davitt lectured Harrington in January 1896,

> the spirit which underlines your own and Redmond's pronouncements shows clearly that neither of you have the courage of your moral convictions – to despise the Fred Allans and ignore their truculent [?illegible] 'sympathy'. Believe me my friend you will have more than enough of your old-time 'troublesome lads' before you have done with them.[102]

Redmond was caught in an impossible dilemma. Without the Fenians, the Redmondites would have found it more difficult, if not impossible, to maintain a functioning organisation; with them, they could not hope to attract a majority of Irish nationalist support. Vitally, Redmond could never have shaken off the stigma of the adulterer and won the trust of the catholic hierarchy.

To sustain the Parnellite position Redmond conducted a series of rhetorical sleights of hand worthy of his predecessor. On St Patrick's Day in 1892 he addressed a crowded Rotunda on the national demand: 'Aye, and I assert without fear of contradiction, that the insurrectionary movement of 1848, and the insurrectionary movement of 1867, were both of them the direct result of the refusal to grant the national demand for the repeal of the union.'[103] Redmond argued that the home rule demand went beyond mere repeal, implying that the origins of the home rule cry were more radical than that of Young Ireland or Fenianism. In Redmond's formulation Poynings's Law had rendered the independence of Grattan's parliament illusory. Conversely, the 'federal parliament which Isaac Butt proposed was a parliament which, in name, was dependent, but in reality was independent. . . . it would have had absolutely supreme power, from any interference or control of the English parliament, over exclusively Irish matters.' This line of argument broke the essential congruence of separatism with insurrection that was identified by the I.R.B. as their exclusive ideological inheritance. By interpreting 1848 and 1867 in this way, Redmond suggested that advanced nationalists could support the home rule movement without betraying their political heritage. In essence, his interpretation radicalised the home rule cry and depoliticised the earlier impulses to insurrection. Involuntary shivers aside, the terrorists of the early 1880s could be integrated into the Redmondite system; the I.R.B. could be drawn in and made safe.

Indeed, Redmond's reaching out towards sympathetic conservatives, as described by Paul Bew, might be additionally understood as an attempt to free

---

[102] Michael Davitt to Timothy Harrington, 15 Jan. 1896 (Harrington Papers, N.L.I., MS 8576/11).
[103] Redmond, *Historical and Political Addresses*, pp 324–6.

Parnellism of the Fenians as part of his construction of a coalition of interests that would free home rule of dependence on the Liberal party. Ultimately, the reunification of the home rule party in 1900–1 was built upon the re-emergence of agrarianism and the struggle against the graziers instigated by the United Ireland League.[104] Central to this process was the severing of Redmond's links with the I.R.B. – the *Independent* newspapers were sold to the conservative home ruler William Martin Murphy; Fred Allan and others were sacked. By 1900 the amnesty cry was rendered obsolete by the gradual release on licence of all the political prisoners.[105]

On a general note the earnestness attributed by historians to professions of separatism needs to be seen in the context of the overwhelming military superiority inherent in British rule. Owing to their relative weakness there is the temptation to treat the separatists as faintly ridiculous, particularly in their attachment to an untenable military ideal. To do so would be to ignore a current in Irish nationalism as variegated and tenacious as the constitutional tradition. As one astute county inspector commented in January 1900 with respect to the widespread sympathy for the Boers:

> The sentiment of disloyalty is undoubtedly strong and widespread, but all efforts to give effect to it by seducing the young men of the country into a great secret organisation, have up to the present been failures. This illustrates the fact that the young Irish enthusiast of today is a different man to the young fellow of 1866. He may be as disloyal at heart as his prototype, but the present day Fenian is too well educated to risk the consequences of open rebellion. He will talk freely but go no further.[106]

A sense of the futility of an armed uprising and a commitment to separatism were not incompatible: indeed, Sinn Féin's emergence was a bid to solve this very conundrum.

[104] This process is considered at length in Chapter 5 of this book.
[105] C.B.S. Box 15, 20299, 31 Aug. 1899.
[106] C.O. 904/69, Jan. 1900.

4

Literary Fenianism and Fenian faction

'In the past of a nation lives the protection of its future and the advancement of its present'[1]

I

It has become a truism in Irish history that the death of Parnell marked a watershed. Yeats gave the most famous and most frequently quoted expression to this insight in his 1923 Nobel lecture:

> The modern literature of Ireland, and indeed all that stir of thought that prepared for the Anglo-Irish war, began when Parnell fell from power in 1891. A disillusioned and embittered Ireland turned from parliamentary politics; an event was conceived; and the race began, as I think, to be troubled by that event's long gestation.[2]

Yeats shared this historicising mindset with many of his contemporaries and it is interesting to find that the specific shape Yeats later imposed on the development of Irish nationalism after 1891 was anticipated by William Rooney in the 1890s. Proto-Sinn Féiner and Irish language enthusiast, Rooney addressed the Celtic Literary Society on 20 January 1899 using the metaphor that Yeats would make his own:[3]

> Some little semblance of interest in the tongue of the Gael marked every generation before ours; but we, with our backs turned to everything native, our eyes perpetually on the parliament of the foreigner, dazed by joyous anticipation of a 'Union of Hearts', forgot everything but the shibboleth of the hour, and were gradually degenerating into mere automata, until a crash came, and in the rending of the veil we saw for the first time what was before us and paused.[4]

It was the conceit of separatists like Rooney that the parliamentary nationalists had failed to learn the lesson taught by the fall of Parnell: this being, the danger

[1] John R. Whelan of the Celtic Literary Society, *Shan Van Vocht*, 5 Feb. 1897.
[2] W. B. Yeats, 'The Irish Dramatic Movement' in *Autobiographies* (London, 1961), p. 559.
[3] Yeats's 1914 autobiographical treatment of his youth was entitled *The Trembling of the Veil*; the metaphor of the veil was adopted from Mallarmé.
[4] William Rooney, 'A Recent Irish Literature' in *Prose Writings* (Dublin, 1909?), p. 14.

of dependency on English political benevolence and co-operation. The key phrase here is 'forgot everything'. The 'union of hearts' had done more than entrap Irish nationalism in an unproductive strategy, it had begun to diminish the distrust Ireland should have for perfidious Albion. Identifying moments of sudden and great illumination was characteristic of separatist thinking, and, as suggested, the Parnell split awakened the young men of Rooney's circle to what they thought to be the pernicious realities of British politics. Separatists interpreted the Ulster Crisis of 1912–14 in the same way,[5] while the 1916 rising was in part an attempt to create such a moment. Consequently, by caricaturing the constitutionalists as slow learners, the separatist position in the 1890s could increasingly cohere around the amalgam of continued allegiance to physical force – as the ultimate and inevitable solution to the Irish national question – and the cultural nationalism of the revival. Broadly speaking, separatists claimed possession of the revival, challenging claims that cultural nationalism was not teleologically fastened to a separatist trajectory, and that the revivalist idea of Irish life did not necessarily seek reification in a separate nation-state. In reality the revival was malleable: it attracted committed artists (both talented and untalented) and their inevitable coterie of fellow travellers; it could be moulded to both unionist and nationalist agendas; it could be insular and exclusivist, laying its emphasis on the cultural uniqueness of the Gael – often with racial or ethnic connotations – or fashionably international, embracing the world community of the Celt. To a varying extent, poetry, theatre, antiquarianism, and language scholarship suffused a self-help co-operative ethos:[6] revivalism was a matter of 'Creameries and Dreameries'.[7] Regardless of the specific political agenda at work, the revival in all its forms increased the consciousness of the different racial or ethnic characteristics of the Gael or Celt and the English. The Gael's qualities of spirituality, anti-materialism, egalitarianism, and heroism could be grasped only through contrast with the supposedly opposite qualities of the English. Joep Leerssen has discussed this in terms of the Irish tendency to auto-exoticism.[8] It should be noted that these inclusivist notions of Irishness were, paradoxically, at odds with unionist identity. Moreover, constitutionalists could accommodate this agenda without it radicalising their overall strategy, allowing nationalist audiences to absorb revivalism uncritically as a heightened version of long familiar political forms. Indeed, the dogged pursuit of the rhetoric of independence by the Redmondites as part of a devolutionist stratagem, and their

---

[5] See Chapter 6.

[6] For a (wicked) deconstruction of the currents at work see R. F. Foster, 'Thinking from Hand to Mouth: Anglo-Irish Literature, Gaelic Nationalism and Irish Politics in the 1890s' in *Paddy and Mr Punch* (London, 1993), pp 262–80. See also P. J. Mathews, *Revival: The Abbey Theatre, Sinn Féin, the Gaelic League and the Co-operative Movement* (Cork, 2003).

[7] Filton Young, *Ireland at the Cross Roads* (London, 1903), p. 98.

[8] Joep Leerssen, *Remembrance and Imagination* (Cork, 1996), pp 66–7.

continual alignment with the heroes of the separatist pantheon, chimed with a popular idea of the revival.

With this in mind, Yeats's sentences might just bear the burden of another close reading. Implicit to the poet's reproductive simile was a quintessentially Irish nationalist imagination in which events – risings, rebellions, betrayals, defeats – are re-enacted by successive generations wedded to the same cause. Yeats appears to fit into an Irish historical mentality that conceived of events within a cyclical rather than a linear temporal mindset.[9] The poet, however, also made a specific case for the cause of the 1916 rising, in which poets and littérateurs are granted extraordinary historical agency. For just as 'conceived' implies the careful formulation of ideas and understanding, so too does it suggest the unpredictable outcome of a pregnancy. For, the pregnancy was troubling, and as with any birth, the progeny was unexpected and autonomous. Something apart from the parents was present in the child, and the teleology apparently embedded in the Yeatsian paradigm is subtly undermined in this mixing of determinism with the unexpected course of events.

That the Yeatsian view of Irish history contains manifold falsehoods is obvious: as the history of the Y.I.S. suggests, the Irish literary revival of the late nineteenth century – itself one of several nineteenth-century Irish literary revivals[10] – had its origins in the 1880s and was initially defined in relation to Parnellism. The foundation of the Young Ireland League preceded Parnell's death by several weeks and reflected the complexities of Parnell's coalition of 1891.[11] Nonetheless, despite this scepticism for the schematic mythologising of the poet, it is difficult not to see a great deal of elemental truth in Yeats's grand and ambiguous claims.[12] One way in which they can be refined is to suggest that November 1890 marked a greater break than October 1891. As Rooney argued, it was the exposure of the reality of the 'union of hearts' that transformed his politics and, as shown, the progress of the Leinster Literary Society confirmed this. According to Rooney, the significance of the crisis in Committee Room 15 was that it precipitated a cultural awakening by demonstrating how 'perilously near' the Irish had come to West Britonism.[13]

The purpose of this chapter is to explore the organisational manifestations of the literary revival and the cultural nationalism of the 1890s from the separatist perspective. Some during this period might have looked forward to

[9] Oliver MacDonagh, *States of Mind: Two Centuries of Anglo-Irish Conflict 1780–1980* (London, 1983, 1992), pp 1–14.

[10] F. S. L. Lyons, *Culture and Anarchy in Ireland 1890–1939* (Oxford, 1982), pp 27–8; Leerssen, *Remembrance and Imagination*.

[11] R. F. Foster, *W. B. Yeats: A Life. I: The Apprentice Mage* (Oxford, 1997), p. 115; *F.J.*, 18 Sept. 1891; C.O. 904/16, Register of Home Associations 1890–93.

[12] Roy Foster addresses the flaws in Yeats's schema, but ultimately structures his treatment along similar lines, *Modern Ireland, 1600–1972* (London, 1988), pp 431–3.

[13] Rooney, writing as Shel-Martin, member of the Celtic Literary Society, *Irish Patriot*, vol. 1, no. xii, 9 Oct. 1896.

an event similar to the rebellions of 1798 or 1867, but there is no evidence of any concerted effort to prepare for that day.[14] If, as Roy Foster has argued, the approach of the year 1900 bred millenarian expectations among the theosophists (providers of the 'ghost discourse of the revival'),[15] this did not manifest itself as military preparation or planning. But this was emphatically not a period of stasis in separatist politics, despite the predominance of the Redmondite–Fenian nexus. Although the progress of Irish separatism between the outset of the Parnell split and the emergence of Sinn Féin in the early 1900s remains obscure, historians have long recognised the significance of the '98 centenary, the organised opposition to the Boer War, and the hostility to the royal visits of 1900 and 1903 as crucial to the emergence of Sinn Féin in the early 1900s. But the medium-term organisational and intellectual origins of these developments have been only partially traced.

Here it is argued that the creation of the Irish National Brotherhood in the 1890s was partly an attempt to conceive of a Fenianism more in line with the developments in literary Fenian thinking. Marking a repudiation of Fred Allan's Fenianism, and by extension the Redmondite–Fenian nexus, the I.N.B. also reflected unease with Dublin Fenianism's links to labour politics. This was in line with the socially conservative and petit-bourgeois character of early Sinn Féin.

II

Division and factionalism were endemic to Fenianism and in this the general character of grass-roots Fenianism had changed little since the early 1880s. While differences remained concerning the legitimacy of the Invincibles and the Dynamitards, the Amnesty Association successfully made the case for co-operation. As Fenian support for Parnell had shown, intelligent and effective associates of the Invincibles like James Boland were readily accepted back into the fold. At the same time, the progress of the split itself and the Patrick Gregan controversy indicated the essential foothold Fenianism retained in the tough working-class politics of urban Ireland. Here advanced nationalism underpinned Fred Allan's gang of activists – the Nally Club – as it did the Old Guard Benevolent Union, a social club for an older Fenian generation somewhat alienated from the formal structures of the I.R.B. The 'cream of the extremists were in Allan's following', Mallon noted of the Manchester Martyrs parade of

---

[14] Dublin Castle found no evidence to substantiate the rumour that arms were being imported for 1898. C.B.S. Box 12, 14651, 19 Nov. 1897.
[15] Foster, *The Story of Ireland* (Oxford, 1995), pp 25–6. It is Selina Guinness's phrase: 'Ireland through the Stereoscope: Reading the Cultural Politics of Theosophy in the Irish Literary Revival' in Betsey Taylor Fitzsimon and James H. Murphy, *The Irish Revival Reappraised* (Dublin, 2004), p. 32.

November 1895, while the 'Old Guard following are many of them fossils & dreamers'.[16] Given the absence of an efficacious revolutionary strategy, the Supreme Council could happily tolerate these various affiliations without feeling its authority challenged. The connection to the Clan na Gael remained intact and the intersection between the amnesty campaign and the opportunity afforded by the split provided Fenianism, as a mass organisation, with the focus it had lacked in the 1880s.

This situation was significantly altered by the I.R.B. split, which produced a rival organisation that actively competed with the I.R.B., claiming the older organisation's role and membership. Leon Ó Broin first drew sustained attention to the secession of the Irish National Brotherhood, or Association, and structured his treatment of the I.R.B. in the 1890s around what he regarded as a classic power struggle within advanced nationalism that originated in divisions in U.S. Fenianism.[17] The I.R.B./I.N.A. rivalry has since been further highlighted in the growing number of studies of the 1798 centenary cele-brations.[18] The origins of the split lay in the parlous state of Irish-American politics in the 1880s. The Chicago political power broker Alexander Sullivan became the head of Clan na Gael and aligned with the Republican party. The party reciprocated by providing Clan members with jobs at various levels in the administration. In 1884 the organisation severed its links with the I.R.B. owing to the Supreme Council's opposition to the Clan's dynamite campaign.[19] John Devoy opposed this move, regarding the I.R.B. Supreme Council as the provisional government of Ireland and consequently the rightful determinant of actions against the British. In early 1887, Devoy and his New York followers formally seceded from the Clan and were immediately recognised by the I.R.B. Fearing the charges Devoy had prepared against him, Sullivan resigned as head of the Clan shortly before its convention of June 1888. Devoy argued that Sullivan had neglected the families of men killed or imprisoned as a result of the dynamite campaign, had embezzled $110,000, and had acted incorrectly

---

[16] C.B.S. Box 10, 10885, 25 Nov. 1895.

[17] Leon Ó Broin, *Revolutionary Underground: The Story of the Irish Republican Brotherhood 1858–1924* (Dublin, 1976), pp 60–83.

[18] In general see: T. J. O'Keefe, 'The 1898 Efforts to Celebrate the United Irishmen: The '98 Centennial' in *Eire–Ireland*, 23 (1988), pp 51–73, and '"Who Fears to Speak of '98?": The Rhetoric and Rituals of the United Irishmen Centennial, 1898' ion ibid., 28 (1992), pp 67–91; Senia Pašeta, '1798 in 1898: The Politics of Commemoration' in *Irish Review*, 22 (Summer 1998), pp 46–53; Warwick Gould, John Kelly, and Deidre Toomey (ed.), *The Collected Letters of W. B. Yeats: Vol. II 1896–1900 [C.L. II]* (Oxford, 1997), pp 695–707; Deirdre Toomey, 'Who Dares to Speak of Ninety-Eight?' in Warwick Gould (ed.), *Yeats and the Nineties: Yeats Annual*, 14 (London, 2001), pp 216–17; and R. F. Foster, *Apprentice Mage* and 'Remembering 1798' in *The Irish Story: Telling Tales and Making It Up in Ireland* (London, 2001), pp 211–34.

[19] This narrative account is based upon that given in Terry Golway, *Irish Rebel: John Devoy and America's Fight for Ireland's Freedom* (New York, 1998), pp 155–68, 178–80.

in breaking the link with the I.R.B. The nine-member executive committee that replaced Sullivan contained four of Devoy's allies including Dr Philip Cronin. They investigated Sullivan's actions over the summer of 1888, despite the potential damage the exposure of Clan dealings might do Parnellism at the time of the Special Commission.[20] Cronin publicly dissented from the tribunal's decision to clear Sullivan of the serious charges and, contrary to a prior agreement, refused to give up the evidence he possessed against Sullivan, regurgitating the original accusations in a pamphlet. In May 1889, Cronin was murdered.

A month later, Sullivan and three others were found responsible, arrested, and released with the charges dropped. Politically isolated, Devoy moved to Chicago, intent on continuing to pursue Sullivan. By the early 1890s, the leadership of the Sullivanites had effectively passed to William Lyman, a Bostonian building contractor and owner of the newspaper the *Irish Republic*.[21] It was during Lyman's period of ascendancy that the split impacted on the internecine rivalries of the I.R.B.

Ó Broin's account of the controversy was written from Devoy's perspective, with Sullivan and Lyman represented as a crude plutocratic disruption of the established balance of power in Irish-American politics. Sullivan's failure to discountenance the use of dynamite debased his Fenianism, distinguishing him ideologically from the noble transatlantic duet sustained by Allan and Devoy in the long period of I.R.B. decline in the 1880s and 1890s. Yet, as Golway has commented, Devoy's pursuit of Sullivan was not wholly in line with the long-term interests of Irish-American politics,[22] nor, it should be added, was the Clan's record of opposition to dynamite pristine. Devoy's actions undermined the unity of Irish-American separatism and his pursuit of Sullivan does seem to have been inspired by a personal vendetta. However, Sullivan *had* undermined Devoy's Fenian ideals. As has been shown, the prisoners championed by the Amnesty Association might attract plaudits from separatist platforms in Ireland and at times in the house of commons, but the strategy they represented received unambiguous approval only from the fringes of Irish separatism. Underlying the squabble for political influence that the

---

[20] Golway makes the extraordinary claim that J. J. O'Kelly was despatched to the U.S. by Parnell to prevent the revelation that Egan had handed over $100,000 of Land League money to the Clan that was used for the dynamite campaign. This was exactly the revelation the Special Commission was looking for. Golway's evidence is a report in the *Gaelic American*, 7 Feb. 1925. See *Irish Rebel*, pp 163–4.

[21] Ó Broin, *Revolutionary Underground*, p. 62. Lyman was from Ballyfarnon, near Boyle and had been a member of the Ballyfarnon I.R.B. He emigrated to the U.S. in the early 1870s where he made his fortune and was said to be worth $500,000 by June 1892. In October 1891 he was elected treasurer of the Irish National League at its Chicago Convention while head of the executive of the Sullivan wing of the Clan na Gael. C.O. 904/19, 252.

[22] Golway, *Irish Rebel*, pp 162–4.

I.R.B./I.N.A. split undoubtedly represented, Devoy detected a challenge to the ideological precepts of the I.R.B. The oddity of the secession in Ireland was that the division was not predicated on these terms. By maintaining a steady attack on its enemies in Ireland the *Irish Republic* served a useful purpose, but its apparent countenance of the Dynamitards caused grave concern among Lyman's nominal supporters in Ireland. Ultimately, the U.S. crisis provided a convenient framework for a division based on a very different indigenous agenda. U.S. divisions were not required to focus the multiple ideological and strategic complexities advanced nationalism had grappled with since the rise of Parnell.

It was the quality of the seceders and the supposed riches available from the United States that ensured the secession posed a grave threat to the I.R.B. and the authority of the Supreme Council. Whereas the Old Guard Benevolent Union primarily comprised men past their peak and did not appeal to the young, the I.N.A. attracted many of the leading separatists of the day. Chief among them was Mark Ryan, the long-established focus of separatist activity in London. His circle included Yeats, John MacBride (the future husband of Maud Gonne and signatory of the 1916 proclamation), and Arthur Lynch. Lynch frequently contributed to the *Independent* newspapers and was the unsuccessful Parnellite candidate for Galway in the 1892 general election. Major Gosselin thought Lynch was bankrolled by Lyman and an important revolutionary. In April 1894 Lynch resigned as president of the Amnesty Association in Great Britain following his election as president of the Irish National League of Great Britain. This suggests a continuity with the earlier I.R.B. influence within the Home Rule Association of Great Britain. In August 1896 Lynch was appointed Paris correspondent of the *Daily Mail*, which surely provided him ample opportunity to work with Gonne and on her newspaper *L'Irlande Libre*.[23] He led one of the two Irish brigades in the Boer War; MacBride shared the leadership of the other with the Irish-American Colonel John Blake.

Belfast, Limerick, and London proved important centres of a secession that was in part an assertion of autonomy from the Supreme Council and Allan. Resentment of Allan's leadership was part of a broader provincial frustration with the strategy of the Dublin leadership. It is difficult to pin this down in precise terms, although it is a theme which runs through the history of advanced nationalism and was to become a particularly acute problem in the late 1900s. It is evident that the Redmondite–Fenian nexus relied heavily on the insular advanced nationalist politics of Dublin, enhancing Allan's influence over the I.R.B.'s agenda in general. Hoctor's secession, for instance, was directly attributed to his resentment of Allan's ascendancy, especially during the preparation of the '98 celebrations.[24] Other influences were also at work. In the north of Ireland, where Redmondism was weak, co-operation with constitutionalism paid Fenianism few dividends, while back in Limerick John

---

[23] C.O. 904/18, 681. Lynch's politics are discussed in Chapter 5.
[24] C.B.S. Box 14, 17762, 16 Nov. 1898. Mallon disputed Hoctor's membership of the

Daly was something of a law unto himself, a tendency legitimised by his prison experience.

The secession of Dr Mark Ryan and the London separatists has long been noted, but as striking was the secession of the Belfast cultural separatists focused on the periodical, *Shan Van Vocht*, edited and managed by Alice Milligan and Anna Johnston. Another key seceder was Yeats, who through his presidency of the London '98 organisation advertised his seniority within the new organisation. At the higher echelons, the I.N.A. represented an attempt to break free of the narrow, antiquated Fenianism of Allan, with its tedious and disreputable feuds and factions. Crucially, despite O'Leary's continued loyalty to the Supreme Council, there was some continuity of mood between the Young Ireland Society under his tutelage and the I.N.A. Mallon, in particular, associated the I.N.A. with the organisations of the literary revival and among the Dublin leadership was John Whelan of the Celtic Literary Society. Recruits were also drawn from the National Monuments Committee (an offshoot of the Young Ireland Society of the 1880s), the Young Ireland League, the Sheridan Literary Club, the Dublin Literary Society (sometimes addressed by James Connolly),[25] and the G.A.A., as well as the Old Guard Benevolent Union and the Amnesty Association.[26] The police noted that O'Leary Curtis, secretary of the National Literary Society, presided at an I.N.A. meeting in Dublin on 11 October 1896. Overall, Mallon considered them 'rather a respectable class', 'practically literary fanatics' that 'dream away about new Republics and so on'. Although he noted that on the fringes there was 'a low bad lot connected with them' who were 'in sympathy with dynamiters', it is clear the I.N.A. drew on a higher social class than the men typically associated with Dublin Fenianism.[27] To some extent the new organisation replicated more successfully the Young Ireland League's intended purpose as an umbrella organisation for literary Fenianism. Indeed, in October 1893 the Celtic Literary Society noted M. Walsh's argument in favour of amalgamating the many Dublin nationalist societies in order to improve their effectiveness:

> Now the first point that must strike the general reader is that all these societies are within a stone's throw of each other. Three in Marlboro' Street (two in the same house, 87), one in Talbot Street, one on Ormond-quay, one in Great-Britain Street, one in Upper Abbey-Street, and one in Capel Street.[28]

I.N.A., suggesting that his criticism of Allan's leadership was personal. C.B.S. Box 14, 17910, 2 Dec. 1898.

[25] *D.E.T.*, 11 Nov. 1896.

[26] C.B.S. Box 11, 12674, 28 Oct. 1896.

[27] C.B.S. Box 11, 12656, 5 Nov. 1896 & 12730, 13 Nov. 1896. Cf. Edward Martyn's scathing reference to the 'considerable bevy of female and male mediocrities interested in intellectual things' that surrounded Yeats. *Yeats C.L. II*, p. 695.

[28] News clipping from *United Ireland* (23 Oct. 1893) preserved in Celtic Literary Society Minute Book (N.L.I., MS 200).

In March 1897, the *Irish Republic* made a similar case, declaring the 'mission of the Alliance is and will be the linking together of all existing organisations and societies'.[29] Although by the time of the '98 centenary it was evident the I.N.A. would fail to sustain a long-term challenge to the I.R.B., the effectiveness of the I.N.A. publicists, notably Yeats and Milligan, ensured that the seceders had a disproportionate influence.

The American split itself generated considerable confusion in the Fenian ranks in Ireland. In the summer of 1894 Major Gosselin was more than usually baffled by the divisions in the nationalist parties, both constitutional and separatist, though he was confident that Mark Ryan had spent six weeks in Ireland organising on behalf of the I.N.A.[30] Closer to the ground, Mallon could be more confident, observing in October, 'I am perfectly satisfied that there are at least four factions of them [secret society men] in Dublin, and while there is mutual reciprocity of design, there is a corresponding mutual distrust.'[31] Further records suggest that the Supreme Council naturally enough aligned itself initially with Lyman. When the Supreme Council was reorganised in July, Allan was made chair,[32] presiding over a committee comprised of James Boland, Denis P. Seery,[33] Patrick Tobin,[34] P. J. Hoctor, James Connor,[35] P. N. Fitzgerald, James A. Egan,[36] one of the Nallys of Balla, and James

---

[29] *I.R.*, 31 Mar. 1897.

[30] C.B.S. Box 8, 9117, 15 Oct. 1894, report for the under secretary.

[31] C.B.S. Box 9, 9246, 30 Oct. 1894.

[32] C.B.S. Box 8, 8806, based on a D.M.P. report, 30 July 1894.

[33] Denis P. Seery became an active Fenian following his involvement in the G.A.A. and was connected to the minor explosions in December 1893 at Tyrone Place and Aldboro' Barracks; he was consequently sacked as a clerk at Darcy's Brewery. He was also an active Parnellite. He assisted C. J. O'Farrell with the reorganisation of the I.R.B. in Enniscorthy in January 1896 and remained loyal to the I.R.B. throughout the secession. The police variously described him as a 'mischievous little coward' and a 'mean wicked little fellow of the John Nolan type'. He appears to have sometimes gone under the name of Denis Sheehan. C.O. 904/18, 963, 965.

[34] Patrick Tobin was born in 1858 and worked as a clerk in the Irish Railway Clearing House in Kildare Street, Dublin. He was active in the G.A.A. and as a Parnellite during the split, particularly at the Carlow by-election. Nolan and Merna were at his house prior to the Reid murder. In Mallon's words a 'most important fellow'. He supported the I.N.A. and Mark Ryan from the outset of the secession and was a member of the I.N.A. executive for Leinster. C.O. 904/18, 991.

[35] James Connor was born in 1854 and was a purveyor's assistant in Dublin. He was close to Allan, had Invincible connections, was a member of the Nally Club, and was suspected of involvement in the murder of John Kenny in Seville Place in 1882. In 1896 he was the treasurer of the Dublin Directory of the I.R.B. C.O. 904/17, 123.

[36] James A. Egan was born in c. 1860 and was convicted with John Daly; on his release he worked for the Amnesty Association. He stood for election to the rate collectorship of Limerick with the support of the National Club. It was alleged that the mayor of Limerick had promised Egan a paid job on his release, but failed to produce. His most important role was as a fundraiser in the United States in 1895–6; before his departure in November 1895,

Moore.[37] A month later O'Keeffe of Kilkenny, C. J. O'Farrell of Enniscorthy,[38] and Robert Johnston and Henry Dobbyn of Belfast,[39] were co-opted onto the council.[40] Johnston, Dobbyn, Tobin, and Hoctor would be later associated with the I.N.A. – Dobbyn and John MacBride attended the I.N.A. inaugural convention in Chicago in September 1895.[41] At the National Club meeting the possibility of a change in name was debated, with Irish National Brotherhood eventually favoured. Intriguingly, the informant claimed that a good many preferred the decidedly Redmondesque Irish Independent Brotherhood. This contrasted with a later report claiming the I.R.B. had decided to work independently of Parnellism on the recommendation of P. N. Fitzgerald, which seemed to chime with the lower Fenian presence noted at the Parnell anniversary that year.[42]

In 1894 Fitzgerald travelled to the U.S.A. hoping to reconcile the two Irish-American factions; he failed and returned from Philadelphia in October, his loyalty to Devoy rekindled. On 8 October he faced a hostile meeting at the National Club owing to his criticism of Allan while in the U.S.A. and he failed to convince members of the necessity of returning to the old nomenclature and alignment with Devoy. Fitzgerald stormed off

he fell out with Allan. Around this time, he seceded to the I.N.A. and worked in the U.S. on behalf of Henry Dobbyn, Mark Ryan, Robert Johnston, and John MacBride. The *Irish Republic* (10 October 1895), in one of its periodic attacks on Allan, described Egan as 'one of the glorious "Felons of our land"'; the police thought him 'an ill-tempered little man'. C.O. 904/17, 200; C.B.S. Box 10, 9583, 10712, 25 Oct. 1895, 10835, 19 Nov. 1895, 10878; D.I., 11 Feb. 1895.

[37] James Moore was a publican of Park Street, Dundalk and an I.R.B. centre. He had paid for delegates to attend the 1889 Thurles G.A.A. convention in support of P. N. Fitzgerald and the I.R.B. takeover of the organisation. He was the secretary of the Irish National Forresters in Dundalk and was close to Allan. C.O. 904/18, 712.

[38] Charles J. O'Farrell was born in c. 1845 in Enniscorthy, Co. Wexford and was a clerk in a distillery; he was unmarried, lived with his mother and sister, and could speak French fluently. He had a fine Fenian lineage having been suspected of importing arms in 1867 and he served a six-month prison sentence in 1868 for illegal possession of firearms. He had opposed the Land League and National League because they diverted attention and funds from the I.R.B. He was the secretary of the Ennis I.R.B., which was thought to have 600 members, and was the principal organiser of the Amnesty Association in the town. His prestige was evidenced at the Nally funeral when O'Farrell shared a carriage with James Stephens; he opposed the I.N.A. during the secession. C.O. 904/18, 815.

[39] Dobbyn was a builder and contractor, and came to Belfast from Bellaghy, Co. Derry in September 1892; he was on good terms with Johnston and was president of the Independent (Parnell) Branch Y.I.S., Belfast. Since Johnston went to the U.S.A. in 1893 Dobbyn was the dominant force in Belfast Fenianism, but his domineering attitude made him unpopular, especially since attending the I.N.A. Chicago Convention of September 1895 without informing his colleagues and allegedly returning with plenty of I.N.A. money. C.O. 904/17, 155.

[40] C.B.S. Box 8, 8882, Aug. 1894.

[41] C.O. 903/5, misc. notes, B series, no. xiii, June 1896, pp 28–9.

[42] C.B.S. Box 9, 9317, 10 Oct. 1894.

in so excited a state that he came out of the Club & down Rutland Square with his hat in his hand and was followed by Pat Gregan who wanted him back, but Fitzgerald declined the invitation and both proceeded to the Crown Hotel where they were subsequently joined by John Mallon.[43]

What should be made of this last comment is unclear. Perhaps Fitzgerald's dubious reputation was built on correct suspicions that he associated with the Dublin detectives. Can the same be said of Gregan? Fitzgerald and Allan reportedly resolved their differences in the emotional maelstrom of the Nally anniversary at the end of November, and Allan's uncertainty regarding the I.N.A. soon resolved itself into overt hostility.[44]

Although the evidence is slight, it is clear that Allan was not steadfast in his allegiance to Devoy and the I.R.B. traditions the Clan leader represented. It is not clear, however, that the controversy was recognised in Ireland as one regarding the precepts of the I.R.B. First, the Irish-American Dynamitards had become inactive and in any case maintained weak links with the Irish organisation. Second, a series of very minor Dublin explosions in 1892 were of little consequence and appear to have been generally tolerated by the I.R.B. as acts of defiance. It was over a decade since the Invincibles murders and the decline of Fenian aggression had blurred the distinction regarding what could be legitimately done in the name of the I.R.B. Nonetheless, the unease provoked by the *Irish Republic's* apparent advocacy of dynamite was revealed in a letter intercepted by the police from Anthony MacBride[45] and the London I.N.A. leadership addressed to the I.N.A. leaders Thomas Walsh of Kinsale, Joseph MacBride of Westport,[46] Patrick Tobin, and Henry Dobbyn. MacBride asserted that Lyman 'does not countenance dynamite, and neither does his paper', and that the signed letters and articles in the paper that did so did not reflect the views of the editor.[47] Although Mallon investigated the distribution of the *Irish Republic* in response to concerns regarding dynamite raised by Gosselin,[48] he took Anthony MacBride's letter at face value. Allan's initial seduction by Lyman represented less of a betrayal of Devoy's principles than a

---

[43] Ibid.

[44] C.B.S. Box 10, 10574.

[45] Anthony MacBride, the brother of John and Joseph, was a medical doctor and worked in the Chancery Lane practice headed by Dr Mark Ryan. He took a prominent role in many London-based nationalist initiatives, including holding the position of treasurer of the Amnesty Association and the I.N.A. Although the police thought him 'v. timid and nervous', his periodic trips to Mayo were as an I.R.B. organiser. C.O. 904/18, 761.

[46] Joseph MacBride was born in 1860 in Westport and from 1890 worked as secretary to the Westport harbour commissioners. Unlike his brothers, Dublin Castle believed that before joining the I.N.A. he had not been involved in secret society work. C.O. 904/18, 762.

[47] C.B.S. Box 11, 12599, letter dated 16 Oct. 1896.

[48] The distribution of the *Irish Republic* was very low. In October 1896 250 copies were distributed in Dublin, with the rest of Ireland receiving about 170 (this figure was about 90

pragmatic alignment with the most powerful element in advanced Irish-American nationalism.

The I.N.A. was formally launched in Ireland on 6 May 1895 at a meeting in Blessington Street, Dublin. Shortly afterwards, John O'Mahony[49] and J. A. O'Sullivan[50] drew up a constitution and rules which broadly emulated those of the I.R.B. The I.N.A.'s object was the achievement of the independence of Ireland and the fostering of 'national feeling among all classes of Irishmen'. Mallon's characterisation of the I.N.A. was confirmed by the integration of the precepts of the literary revival into the I.N.A.'s core values. The third clause of the constitution stated: 'The officers and members shall encourage as much as possible the study of Irish history, of the Irish language and of all subjects likely to promote the national spirit.' The constitution also aspired to provide a blueprint for the values of an independent Ireland and affirmed enlightenment and liberal secular ideals. All 'Irishmen' were to be equal in the sight of the law, there would be no established religion, and a system of free education would be available to all. The remainder of the thirty-eight points dealt primarily with the structure and governance of the organisation. This placed full responsibility of leadership onto an eleven-member Directory similar to the I.R.B. Supreme Council. Each of the four provinces of Ireland elected a member, a further member was elected each by the south and the north of England, and a seventh by Scotland. These seven members co-opted a further four members. They held office for three years and from among their number elected a president, treasurer, and secretary to hold office for the same length of time. The Directory had full control over the organisation's finances, but the organisation was intended to function along democratic lines through a system of elected delegates. As with the I.R.B., a pyramidal structure was intended to protect the I.N.A. from informers by limiting the access of members to information concerning the overall functioning and membership of the organisation. Despite this, the constitution had a strong bureaucratic thrust, demanding quarterly reports from individual sections, and the election of secretaries and treasurers at all levels. The constitution gave no indication as to what would happen to this sensitive information, which if ever supplied appears not to have survived.

---

in October 1895). Only eight counties received ten or more copies each week and they were Longford (20), Roscommon (50), Tipperary (20), Kilkenny (12), Mayo (10), Tyrone (10), Waterford (12), and Galway (11). It is probable that these papers were read aloud at meetings. C.B.S. Box 11, 12631, 8 Oct. 1896.

[49] John O'Mahony was born in 1857 and lived in Mary's Lane, Dublin. He was a labourer and second hand clothes dealer. Not to be confused with J. O'Mahony, native of Cork, who worked in Dublin as the sub-editor of the *Independent* and spent his spare time at the National Club. C.O. 904/18, 846 & 844.

[50] J. A. O'Sullivan was from London and associated with the London Y.I.L. He came to Clonmel in November 1895 and worked as an Amnesty Association and I.N.A. organiser thereafter. C.O. 904/18, 843.

A year later it was evident that the I.N.A. was failing. Part of the explanation for this lies in how deeply embedded communal I.R.B. loyalties were. The organisation could be in a state of near-dormancy, but if a reason for rekindling advanced nationalist activity emerged there was automatic recourse to the I.R.B. This was strongly evident in the organisation of the '98 centenary. Obviously this owed much to the organisation's historical legacy and the authority accrued by individuals believed to have been 'out' in '67. The *Irish Republic* recognised this problem, challenging the I.R.B.'s self-identification as the exclusive guardian of Irish separatism and the virtual government of Ireland. In a striking formulation, it asserted the I.N.A.'s claim to Fenianism: "'Fenian' is a sort of generic term which embraces all species of Irish revolutionists, and incidently it may be remembered that it is a term synonymous with terror of the paralysis producing sort so far as the English mind is concerned.'[51]

In March 1897, Mallon thought that the I.N.A. was disintegrating, particularly in Cork and Limerick.[52] The new mood of advanced nationalist conciliation now evident in *Irish Republic* editorials did not generate a consistent attitude to the split in Ireland. I.N.A. recruits ceased to maintain a connexion with the I.R.B. in Queen's County, and Counties Tipperary, Waterford, and Wexford. In Gorey the factions were friendly but operated as distinct organisations and made separate collections. In Longford the county inspector reported that the I.N.A. and the I.R.B. were on good terms and 'freely discuss revolutionary matters', with the I.N.A. adopting the newly conciliatory tone of the *Irish Republic*. The I.R.B. in Longford contended, probably rightly, that an organisation that recruited from the whole spectrum of nationalist organisations could not hope to be run on a secret basis. In the west there were cases of I.R.B. members retaining their membership after joining the I.N.A., but the new organisation was generally understood to be an attempt to replace the I.R.B. In the south west the I.R.B. and the I.N.A. worked together most effectively through the Amnesty Association: John Daly supported 'unity amongst the brethren, but with a more open and forward programme than he knew existed amongst the I.R.B.'[53]. In early 1898 tensions between the I.N.A. and the I.R.B. were high. P. J. White of Clara, King's County, and O'Keeffe of Kilkenny threatened the seceders with arms.[54]

III

There is mild disagreement as to who or which group initiated the organisation of the '98 centenary. Whether the idea originated with the Celtic Literary

[51] *Irish Republic*, 31 May 1896.
[52] C.B.S. Box 12, 13244, 9 Mar. 1897.
[53] These reports are collected in C.B.S. Box 12, 13699, Apr.–May 1897.
[54] C.B.S. Box 13, 15231.

Society, the Young Ireland League, or the letter from Patrick Gregan to the *Daily Independent* of 31 December 1896 is unimportant. Given the necrophilia of the 1890s, particularly among separatists and revivalists, sustained efforts to celebrate the centenary of 1798 were likely.[55] In an anticipation of the debates that would surround the origins of the Irish Volunteers in 1913, Federationist efforts to establish a '98 organisation to rival that dominated by the I.R.B. emphasised the spontaneous or non-aligned origins of the movement.[56] It was equally predictable that the I.R.B., the I.N.A., and the myriad social and literary associations would be heavily involved, and that the constitutional politicians would attempt to direct the movement towards their own ends. The deeds of the United Irishmen had been in the air since the death of Parnell.

Nonetheless, the size of the movement produced and the overwhelming influence of advanced nationalists, in particular the I.R.B., at all levels in the organisation were remarkable. Despite the '98 Centenary Committee executive council pontificating that it was not a party platform,[57] it had a clear separatist complexion and its declared aims reflected a well-established literary Fenian agenda. The initial circular issued in February 1897 by the provisional committee stated their intention to lay a foundation stone for a lasting memorial to Tone and the United Irishmen and to publish the unpublished records of '98 at affordable prices.[58] It was signed by John O'Leary, M. J. Quinn, P. Lavelle, P. F. O'Loughlin, and Patrick Tobin. A central purpose was to encourage a 'monster excursion' of Irish delegates from the U.S., Australia, and South Africa, and the prominence given to this aspect of the movement in its propaganda points to the considerable feeling in Ireland that only with the participation of the diaspora could full advantage be taken of the centenary's promise. Large numbers of overseas delegates would ensure world opinion recognised the significance of the occasion. The influx of overseas celebrants would confer legitimacy, status, and a higher profile on the separatist organisers. Dublin Castle regarded the arrival of the Irish-Americans as key to any possible political significance that might evolve from the celebration, fearing the visitors might consolidate the revival of the I.R.B. that the celebrations intimated.[59] Without the visitors there was the strong chance that the centenary would expose the separatists' political marginality. Consequently, the outbreak of war between Spain and the U.S.A. had a severe effect on the progress of the centenary. Dublin Castle thought the 'longer-tongued' nationalists, the extremists, supported the U.S.A., while the *Freeman's Journal*

---

[55] This section draws particularly on C.O. 903/6, misc. notes, B series, no. xxviii, 'The '98 Centenary Movement' [hereafter: '98 C.M.], pp 1–56.

[56] *F.J.*, 15 Jan. 1898; '98 C.M., p. 16; see p. 205ff of this book.

[57] *D.I.*, 13 Sept. 1897.

[58] '98 C.M., pp 5–6.

[59] C.O. 904/68, Feb. 1898.

sympathised with Spain as a fellow catholic nation: it objected to the transfer of the West and East Indian possessions from a catholic to a protestant country. The Celtic Literary Society overwhelmingly supported Spain for cultural and historic rather than religious reasons. P. Lavelle thought 'Cuba was, by right of discovery, colonisation, language, and blood, Spanish, and had received from Spain rights still denied to Ireland, and that the rebellion of the blacks was maintained for ulterior objects by the gold bugs of New York.' Moreover, Spain's historic sympathy for the Irish national cause, particularly during the home rule crisis of 1886, suggested where Irish sympathies should lie. Rooney concurred, arguing against the occupation of Cuba by the U.S.A. because this would lead to Anglicisation.[60] Despite these differing interpretations of the significance of the war, Steve Ickringill has argued that nationalist and unionist opinion in Ulster was more generally supportive of the U.S.A. than these examples might suggest: unionists heralded the triumph of Anglo-Saxon virtue; nationalists celebrated an American intervention on behalf of an oppressed people.[61] According to one source, an M.P. who spoke to Gosselin, the Spanish–American war 'has completely strangled the '98 movement as far as America is concerned, and, of course, the influx from there would have been the soul of the anniversary celebrations'.[62]

Over the course of 1897 the I.R.B. and the I.N.A., from their respective strongholds in Dublin and London, struggled to control the '98 organisation. Later on, the effort to protect the movement from home rule contamination drew them closer together. I.N.A. members J. K. Bracken of Templemore, P. J. Hoctor, Alice Milligan, and F. H. O'Donnell objected to the preponderance of Dublin men on the initial general committee, a problem addressed with the election of the executive committee following the national convention of 22 June.[63] Dublin and the four provinces of Ireland were represented chiefly by members of the I.R.B. or the I.N.A., and most prominent separatists, including Maud Gonne, Alice Milligan, and Anna Johnston, were included. Later efforts to combat accusations that the committee was unrepresentative encouraged affiliation and consequently representation from the Amnesty Association, the Trades Councils, the National Forresters, the G.A.A., and the innumerable '98 committees. This constellation was strongly reminiscent of Parnell's last coalition.

The I.R.B. initially worked to prohibit the M.P.s from taking places on the organising committee, highlighting the incongruency of constitutionalist

---

[60] *D.E.T.*, 17 May 1898; N.L.I., MS 19934 (i), Minute Book of the Celtic Literary Society, 1896–1901.
[61] C.O. 904/68, Apr. 1898. See Steve J. S. Ickringill, 'Silence and Celebration in Ulster: William McKinlay and the Spanish–American War' in Sylvia L. Hilton and Steve J. S. Ickringill (ed.), *European Perceptions of the Spanish–American War of 1898* (Bern, 1999), pp 95–110.
[62] C.B.S. Box 13, 16285, 20 May 1898.
[63] '98 C.M., pp 8–10.

nationalists organising the celebration of the most successful physical force nationalists of Irish history. At the City Hall convention of 22 June 1897 a strongly separatist tone was set in the speeches following the conclusion of business. Maud Gonne identified the celebrations as an appropriate riposte to the Queen's jubilee of that year; P. N. Fitzgerald urged his listeners to 'emulate the men of '98, and carry on the national movement until they achieved the independence of their country'; C. G. Doran urged Irish nationalists to take the opportunity to break free of constitutionalism:

> Now, if they were to unite under this '98 centenary celebration, it must not be a union of words; it must be a union of action. It must not be a union of putting one foot on Vinegar Hill and the other in Westminster; it must be a union of Irishmen for the independence of Ireland.[64]

The national secretary of the I.N.A. in the U.S.A. expressed the separatist position in similarly blunt terms:

> To give 'parliamentarianism', or constitutionalism as properly understood, a showing in the connection with the '98 movement, would be to place the Irish people in a false position before the nations. It would be an outrage on the sacred memory of Ireland's glorious dead. It would be casting to the winds a grand opportunity for revivifying and glorifying the spirit of Irish nationality.[65]

However, the perceptive author of the extensive Dublin Castle report on the organisation noted that the relative detachment of the Redmondite M.P.s from the early stages of the organisation should be set against the fact that 'the I.R.B. and other secret societies are principally manned by sympathisers with the Parnellites.'[66] In contrast, the Federationists established a rival organisation in November 1897 and attracted support from some disgruntled I.N.A. members, including Tobin and the newly apostate Gregan.[67] The Federationist position benefited from a generalised hostility to I.R.B. domination of the '98 association and the inclusivism of the emergent United Irishmen's Centennial Association generated some unlikely couplings, not least in Patrick Gregan and Timothy Harrington sharing committee duties respectively among the honorary treasurers and secretaries.[68]

Detailed records tabulating the political affiliation, number of members, and planned activities of the 160 branches of the centenary movement were prepared for the government in February 1898, and presumed to be accurate to 31 December 1897. With the major divisions unresolved, the government

---

[64] *D.I.*, 23 June 1897, quoted ibid., p. 9.
[65] *D.I.*, 29 Nov. 1897.
[66] '98 C.M., p. 15.
[67] Ibid., p. 13.
[68] Ibid., p. 17.

statistics indicate the balance of power within the movement. '98 clubs were reported in all counties except Westmeath, Down, Leitrim, and Roscommon. Of the 482 officers elected to the leadership of the clubs, 258 and 26 were identified by name as members of the I.R.B. and the I.N.A. respectively; the remainder included Redmondites, Federationists, and members of the Irish National Forresters and the Ancient Order of Hibernians. The I.N.A. controlled seven branches, sharing this control with the I.R.B. in three County Wexford branches and with the Irish National Federation in a County Galway branch.

The dominance of the City Hall executive in Dublin was indicated by the 96 clubs that acted under its direction – only 24 did not, of which some were controlled by the Federationists and some the I.R.B. The 26 committees and 960 members in County Wexford (including the 260 members of the Wexford town branch) were directed by the Wexford county committee and its three I.R.B. executive members, the president M. Brown, the secretary Edward O'Cullen, and the assistant secretary M. J. Furlong.[69] A similar situation pertained in Limerick city where the Limerick Committee No. 1 directed seven branches with a total membership of 330. John Daly led this branch with his I.R.B. colleagues (and fellow veterans of the Amnesty Association) William Whelan, Michael Prenderghast, Henry Mathews, and James H. Moran.[70] In Belfast, the more complex range of nationalist affiliations was reflected in a large number of competing branches.[71] The I.R.B. controlled eight branches with a total membership of 1,210. This compared favourably with the I.N.A., who controlled two branches with 450 members. The larger of the latter two was based at the National Club under the direction of Henry Dobbyn, and, despite its leanings towards the I.N.A., was affiliated to the central executive in Dublin. The I.N.A. co-operated with the I.R.B. where it was clear the constitutionalists would dominate the celebrations.[72]

The Federationists were most successful in Belfast: they controlled the James Hope branch (with 245 members); a further five branches, with a combined membership of 840, were controlled by the Irish National Forresters. Interestingly, the James Hope branch was led by two members of the I.R.B. – Matthew Mullen and E. McGuinness – a reminder that an affinity between the Fenians and the Redmondites was not de rigueur. The largest of the Forrester branches (450 members) was led by the emergent anti-Parnellite Belfast power-broker Joseph Devlin, who put the Federationist '98 clubs to work in the 1897 municipal elections.[73] The creation of the Federationist

[69] Ibid., pp 49–50.
[70] Ibid., p. 55.
[71] Ibid., pp 44–5.
[72] Ibid., p. 19.
[73] Ibid., pp 19–21. Dillon, Harrington and O'Brien shared a platform with the clerical candidates in a celebration of William Orr. O'Brien gave a very effective speech that was

Ulster Council of '98 clubs on 31 October 1897 provoked the I.R.B. into similar action and, accordingly, on 9 November a Belfast convention chaired by Henry Dixon produced the Ulster Provincial Council with James Stephens as president.[74] These developments are a reminder of the tendency of nationalism in Ulster to develop independent identities. And, although the I.R.B. dominated, the inclusion of members of the I.N.A. and, indeed, Dixon's presence, demonstrated the superficiality of the I.R.B./I.N.A. split in the face of the Federationist challenge. Overall, Belfast contained the largest concentration of '98 clubs in Ireland, with a total membership in January 1898 of 3,005 compared to Dublin's 1,200. One Belfast club, for women only, had 300 members.[75] In an undated report written in the late spring of 1898, these figures had increased to a total membership of 5,000 for Belfast and 1,400 for Dublin.[76]

The numerical weakness of the I.N.A. and their tendency to submit to the direction of the City Hall executive demonstrated their relative weakness. In May 1898 Dublin Castle received a copy of a return from Mark Ryan to Lyman declaring that the I.N.A. had 10,000 members. Ryan's figures make impressive reading, claiming a membership for Dublin city and county of 6,000. Mallon rejected these figures unreservedly. There were not more than 500 members in Dublin, he said, and rumour had it that Ryan was considering withdrawing from the splinter group anyway.[77] The official figures prepared by Dublin Castle for I.N.A. membership suggest very different orders of magnitude. In 1896 membership was thought to be at 1,533 (728 in good standing); the figure for 1898 was 1,270 (479 in good standing).[78] The two '98 branches dominated by the I.N.A. in Dublin boasted twenty members between them in January 1898.[79] As in Belfast, this weakness was indicated by the co-operation between the two organisations in the City Hall executive.[80] At the important '98 meeting in Phoenix Park on 13 March 1898 M. Maginn (I.R.B.) and Henry Dobbyn (I.N.A.) shared the Ulster platform, and Anthony Mackay (I.N.A.),[81] Yeats (I.N.A.), and Rooney spoke from the Connaught platform. Unimpressed by

---

reminiscent of those he gave in the 1880s to the Y.I.S. with its intoxicating mixture celebrating heroic deeds and affirming constitutionalism. See *F.J.*, 15 Oct. 1897. Cf. Patrick Maume, *The Long Gestation* (Dublin, 1999), p. 38.

[74] '98 C.M., pp 22–3; *D.I.*, 10 Nov. 1897.

[75] C.B.S. Box 13, 15984, Apr. 1898.

[76] C.B.S. Box 13, 16235.

[77] C.B.S. Box 13, 16160, 6 May 1898.

[78] C.O. 903/6, B series, no. xxxvii, Jan. & Feb. 1899.

[79] '98 C.M., p. 45.

[80] Ibid.

[81] Anthony Mackey was a prosperous hotelier and the tenant of numerous eel weirs held from the Board of Works at £2,000 a year at Athlone, Killaloe, and Castleconnell. He used his position on the Fisheries Conservation Board to further his interests and was said to have caused the bankruptcy of Thomas O'Gorman, president of the Amnesty Association, who died shortly afterwards. Although a friend of Mark Ryan, he was not considered a danger to the peace and was removed from the B list of suspects in May 1904. C.O. 904/18, 713.

the affair, the police described it as 'simply a wholesale turnout of Dublin middle-class shopkeepers and their assistants, clerks, artisans and labourers who had not had the opportunity of demonstrating recently'.[82]

In Cork tensions between inclusivist and purist members of the I.R.B. saw Fitzgerald and P. H. Meade, wealthy pawnbroker and sometime Lord Mayor, manoeuvre behind the backs of their separatist colleagues. Both attended the Dublin meeting of 4 March 1897 and later secretly co-ordinated the formation of a Cork committee. This was an exclusively Fenian affair run by John O'Keeffe, a rarely noticed I.R.B. organiser who acted in close cahoots with Fitzgerald.[83] The desire to keep off the committee elected public figures who had taken the oath of allegiance to the Queen was undermined by the need to tap their cash, and Fitzgerald and Meade both advocated the inclusion of local public figures associated with either constitutionalist politics and/or public office. The activists of the secret committee refused. At the public launch of the movement on 14 May, and before an audience of 300, Michael Power led the committee against attempts by Fitzgerald and Meade to place it on a more inclusive footing. Chiefly they objected to the nomination of Alderman Eugene Crean (one of the city's M.P.s), Alderman Madden, and Alderman Roche as vice-presidents. Power won the day, and the police sources suggest that the financial complacency of the 'irreconcilables' stemmed from their belief in the largesse of Irish-America.[84] Over the summer of 1897 repeated attempts by Meade and Fitzgerald failed to generate a compromise and on 26 September they set up a secret committee of Parnellites and Federationists and invited sympathetic constitutionalists to a meeting in November.[85] The executive committee elected at this meeting not only mixed constitutionalist and separatist, but also Parnellite and Federationist. Meade took the presidency; the M.P.s J. F. X. O'Brien and T. M. Healy shared the vice-presidency with the I.R.B.–Parnellite J. Slattery. Two Federationist town councillors were elected treasurers, a further Federationist joined John O'Keeffe as elected secretaries.

---

[82] C.B.S. Box 13, 15647; *D.I.* 14 Mar. 1898. 'The speeches were short; not violent and advised unity. None of the speakers, except Mr Yeates [*sic*] of London and Anthony Mackey of Castleconnell seemed capable of making a speech. The old speakers indulged in commonplace claptrap and sentimental balderdash and provoked no enthusiasm whatsoever.' O'Leary appeared bored by the whole '98 exercise already. The *Daily Independent* quoted the old Fenian: 'He had no power and no inclination to roll out sonorous phrases, generally signifying next to nothing at all. Besides he did not wish to strain his voice.'

[83] The initial committee comprised the familiar I.R.B. social strata: John O'Keeffe (engineer), William O'Shea (publican), John Sullivan (clerk), Daniel O'Leary (porter), Michael Power (pig-buyer), John Buckley (publican), Gerald Fitzgerald (clerk), John Connell (carpenter), Patrick Broderick (fitter), and Simon Potter (tallyman). '98 C.M., p. 25.

[84] Ibid., pp 26–7.

[85] This committee comprised Meade, John Slattery, T.C., Alderman Crowley, Thomas Goggin, Michael O'Brien, John O'Keeffe, and Thomas Dooley. Ibid., p. 27.

The I.R.B., objecting to the proceedings throughout, were appeased with the inclusion of twenty-five members of the Bryan Dillon Club (of which Meade, Fitzgerald, and O'Keeffe were members) on the various organising committees.

Meade's conciliatory tactics gave off deeply ambiguous signals. In November he presided at the Cork Manchester Martyrs commemoration organised by the Bryan Dillon Club – 5,500 marchers heard C. G. Doran's oration.[86] Whereas the Manchester Martyrs commemorations had generally been politically ecumenical in the past, the absence of the Trades Associations in 1897 confirmed that the '98 controversy over representation had intensified the distinctions between the constitutionalist and the separatist. Meade faced the consequences in January when he was threatened with expulsion from the Bryan Dillon Club if he did not resign from the Redmondite Independent Club (of which he was a founding member). Meade, now Lord Mayor, capitulated and realigned with the extremists, thereby confirming the basis of his political support: his refusal would have brought months of abuse and harassment at the many public meetings and events planned for 1898.[87] Despite the exclusion of the Redmondites, the torch-lit procession organised by the Bryan Dillon Club for 31 December attracted 6,000 marchers and many sympathetic onlookers. Meade can only have been impressed by the popular passions the centenary had generated and the political dividends to be reaped by close alignment.

John Daly's determination to dominate the movement in Limerick ensured that the political balancing act attempted by the separatist leaders in Cork was not replicated.[88] Daly's chronic self-aggrandisement exacerbated his unpopularity with Limerick's constitutional political class. If it were the case that the most popular separatist genus was the dead Fenian, then the progress of Daly's career demonstrated that the nearest rival of the dead was the imprisoned. Daly was fêted as a hero in the mould of Ireland's historic nationalist martyrs. Unfortunately he took this at face value, and emerged from prison expecting to fill Tone's shoes. 'He appears to be a man of over-weening vanity,' wrote Dublin Castle, 'regarding himself as a born leader of men, and as destined to bring about the unity of the Irish race in its struggle for freedom.' Daly's personal ambition might be contrasted with the preparedness of Dobbyn and Fitzgerald – both acknowledged leaders, but personally unpopular figures – to accept the leadership of others. The less blatant posturing by advanced men in Cork ensured a workable united front was more viable. Squabbles between the I.N.A. and the I.R.B. saw the occasional unco-operative period, but on the whole Limerick divided between constitutionalists and advanced nationalists, with the catholic clergy increasingly mobilising against Daly.

Momentum, the Holy Grail for separatism in the 1890s, was hard to maintain. By May 1898 Henry Dixon and twenty others had stopped attending

---

[86] C.B.S. Box 10, 14851.
[87] '98 C.M., p. 28.
[88] Ibid., pp 29–32.

'98 committee meetings in Dublin. They were troubled by the influx of constitutional politicians following the amalgamation of the principal '98 organisations in April.[89] By June the movement was in a 'dull and disorganised state' owing to want of funds, although it has been suggested that evidence of the commercial opportunities afforded by the celebrations had generated some popular enthusiasm.[90] This was clearly demonstrated on the day of the laying of the foundation stone of the Wolfe Tone memorial. Undoubtedly a triumph of I.R.B. organisation, it was Dublin's largest procession since O'Connell's funeral. Some 27,000 people arrived by train, including 7,000 from Belfast and 2–3,000 from Cork. The procession took one hour and forty-five minutes to pass a given spot, and was said to number 12,000, with a further 20,000 spectators – as usual, advantage was taken of the reduced ticket prices for a day out in Dublin. Allan, as chief marshal, was the leading organiser, and despite the more co-operative attitudes of recent months, worked to exclude the I.N.A. Mallon described it as a 'monster I.R.B. turn-out' and likely to precipitate 'an absorption of all revolutionary associations by the I.R.B. and then an attempt to shape the course of the constitutionalists'.[91] Moreover, during the summer the mood of the centenary provoked insurrectionary threats from unlikely quarters. In June at the Rotunda, William Field said the centenary taught 'that the people of Ireland were determined if they got the chance to revert to the old methods of the men of '98, and that their hearts were as ready for the fray as in '98 (applause)'.[92] Following the laying of the foundation stone, the *Daily Independent* editorial reflected this mood. It observed that American visitors must have been convinced that if Ireland's opportunity arose, the 'entire nation would be ready to rise up in insurrection'.[93] Despite this, Dillon and Redmond dominated the speech-making and the insurrectionary talk of the preceding months was largely absent from the official proceedings.[94]

The euphoria soon passed. The bust of Wolfe Tone displayed at the top of Grafton Street was pushed off its pedestal and the head stolen. A resentful I.N.A. were blamed.[95] In County Mayo activists were relieved when the French delegates invited by Maud Gonne departed: they 'left a very bad impression'.[96]

---

[89] O'Leary chaired the meeting in the council chamber, City Hall, at which the amalgamated organisation was launched. P. N. Fitzgerald was unimpressed and P. J. Hoctor withdrew from '98 activity. *F.J.*, 7 Apr. 1898, *D.I.*, 25 Apr. 1898, C.B.S. Box 13, 16074, 16133, 16515, 27 May 1898.
[90] C.B.S. Box 13, 16515, 13 June 1898; cf. Toomey, 'Who Dares', p. 245.
[91] C.B.S. Box 14, 17025, 17 Aug. 1898.
[92] *D.I.*, 21 June 1898.
[93] *D.I.*, 16 Aug. 1898.
[94] Toomey, 'Who Dares', p. 249.
[95] C.B.S. Box 14, 17087, 19 Aug. 1898.
[96] C.B.S. Box 14, 17115, 30 Aug. 1898.

IV

Since John Mitchel's complaint that England had the 'ear of the world' and could determine the outside impression of the Irish situation, separatists were aware of the importance of appealing directly to foreign governments and opinion. Maud Gonne argued that the purpose of *L'Irlande Libre*, her Paris-based separatist newspaper, was to counteract the effect of 'English' accounts of Irish satisfaction with the 'British' government. 'I attach great importance to these ['98] celebrations', she wrote, they were 'a means of proving to the world that Ireland is separated from England in feeling, in sentiment, in ideals, in policy, and is only waiting for an occasion to become separate in fact'.[97] William Rooney went further than this, believing that the debate was stifled within Ireland itself, and that the purpose of commemoration was to demonstrate that a 'considerable section of our people are [not] content to become mere citizens of the British Empire'. Refuting Redmond's infamous claim before the Cambridge Union that separation was neither desired or desirable, Rooney asserted, with a Parnellian ring, 'that no man, or section of men, has a right to set a limit to the demands expressed or otherwise of our people.'[98] For the separatists the '98 centenary had two audiences, namely British imperialists and Irish constitutionalists.

Literary Fenianism is a useful generic term to describe the range of writings, produced in particular during the 1890s, that attempted to counter Mitchel's diagnosis and inculcate a separatist mentality. This propaganda included poetry, ballads, journalism, history, and public lectures. Its principal aims were to generate strong nationalist sentiment and to provide the intellectual justification for a culturally based Irish separatism. As with the work of the Young Ireland Societies it sought to justify and exalt the history of Irish separatism, in particular the United Irishmen rebellion of 1798 and the I.R.B. rising of 1867. By glorifying self-sacrifice, the now familiar claim that failure in the cause of Irish separatism represented a moral victory was repeatedly reiterated. To recognise this was to reject the materialist discourse of empire, which rewarded might and strove for cultural homogeneity, in favour of the family of nations, each of which embodied and celebrated differences of race, language, and custom. William Rooney,[99] one of the most effective and productive literary Fenians, summarised their thinking as follows:

---

[97] *W.I.*, 3 Apr. 1897.

[98] *The Parnellite*, 25 May 1895.

[99] William Rooney was born on 20 October 1873 and was educated by the Christian Brothers. He was a member of Rose Kavanagh's Irish Fireside Club before joining the Leinster Literary Society, which was relaunched as the Celtic Literary Society in 1893 with Rooney as president. He co-authored a series of articles on 'Notable Irish Graves in and around Dublin' for the *Dublin Evening Herald*, edited the Celtic's monthly manuscript journal *Seanachuidhe*, and had poems published in *United Ireland* and *Shamrock*. He was also a member of the Young Ireland League, wrote and edited a series of '98 pamphlets, and

Nationality, to my mind, is that all-embracing quality which holds everything characteristic of the country as sacred, which concerns itself with the minutest fragments that typify and define a distinct civilisation, which zealously guards and fosters everything that keeps the land and the people in it *one* amongst the peoples of the world, and to that end educates every inhabitant to the errors of the past, the needs of the present, and the possibilities of the future.[100]

Rooney's literary Fenianism corresponded with some of the essentialist nationalist ideas of J. G. Herder that shaped ideals of nation in late eighteenth- and nineteenth-century Europe.[101] Rooney even suggested that Wolfe Tone was implicitly an Irish language enthusiast.[102] By defining nationality in cultural rather than racial or religious terms Rooney's Irishness was ostensibly inclusive; it could only be authentically accessed through the Irish language which anyone could learn. However, Rooney's Gaelicism was an ideology of restoration and recovery, meaning that an individual could not achieve authentic Irishness unless they had a Gaelic lineage. D. P. Moran infamously claimed that 'the Gael must be the element that absorbs' and, though more temperate in his formulations, Rooney's Gaelicism strongly implied a view of Irish ethnicity that was similarly hierarchical. He shared these ideas with Douglas Hyde who, in a highly coloured passage arguing that the Irish should study Irish literature rather than the classics of Greece and Rome, encapsulated the theoretical basis of the language movement as follows:

> It was because every fibre in their being would pulsate and thrill to something or other in that language. Every chord, obeying some certain but mysterious law of racial necessity, will give forth with ease and freedom its fullest note only when struck by the bow of its ancestral lyre, while it required a minute, tedious, classical training to make Celt or Teuton appreciate Greek or Roman literature, which, in many cases, they failed to do, while in most they did so very imperfectly. The fact was that a man could not very readily feel what none of his ancestors ever felt before him, while he was much more likely to be touched with what they had for countless generations been touched with.[103]

was an enthusiastic Gaelic Leaguer, despite opposing its apolitical identity. He died in May 1901 and attracted extravagant praise from Arthur Griffith: 'the greatest Irishman I have known or can ever expect to know.' See Patrick Bradley, 'William Rooney: A Sketch of His Career' in William Rooney, *Poems and Ballads* (Dublin, 1902), pp xiii–xlv; Brian Maye, Arthur *Griffith* (Dublin, 1997), p. 16. Rooney's ideas are summarised but the anti-imperial dimension analysed here neglected in Shane O'Neill, 'The Politics of Culture in Ireland, 1899–1910' (unpublished D.Phil. thesis, Oxford 1982), pp 140–8.

[100] Rooney, *Poems and Ballads*, pp xxviii–xxix.
[101] A good place to start an exploration of Herder's ideas is Isaiah Berlin, *Vico and Herder* (London, 1976), pp 143–216.
[102] At the Celtic Literary Society, Dublin, 5 Jan. 1900: Rooney, 'The Development of the National Ideal' in *Prose Writings*, p. 98.
[103] 'The Irish Language and Literature: Its Characteristics and Value', reproduced in the

Rooney shared much of Hyde's analysis but consistently denied the efficacy of his apolitical conception of the language movement.[104] Only through separation from England could Ireland hope to be de-Anglicised. Rooney advocated a politicised Gaelic League that would make common cause with nationalist political movements and this could only succeed by making 'a fearless appeal to the people on the broad grounds of Ireland versus England'.[105] This fearlessness demanded a frank appraisal of Ireland's political history and its bearing on the present. Rejecting the nationalist orthodoxy that Grattan's parliament marked a high point in Irish history, Rooney regarded such celebrations as a typically tendentious polemical strategy by constitutional nationalists. Again, his argument was framed to emphasise the overriding importance of language revivalism, demonstrating that an Irish life conducted in Gaelic could function autonomously of the British government, generating de facto independence:

> As long as Gaelic remained among our people they were practically free – they had their own customs and their own laws. Did the bills passed in College Green affect the people outside a half-dozen English-speaking towns? Certainly not. . . . It should be understood by all, as it can become evident to any one who seeks the truth, the universal use of Irish in Ireland means the government of Ireland by Irishmen . . . the government by Gaelic-speaking Irishmen means something more than home rule.[106]

Consequently, 'by refusing to take part in the commemoration of the anniversary of '98, [the Gaelic League] took up a position occupied by every anti-Irish and West-British individual in the country.'[107]

Clearly, for Fenians of Rooney's stamp, to prioritise the achievement of separation over the needs of the language movement was to create a false dichotomy. Cultural nationalism was not an appealing adjunct to less culturally sensitive forms of political separatism, it embodied the very essence of their

---

W.I., 20 Jan. 1894. This National Literary Society meeting attracted a prestigious audience: John Redmond, John O'Leary, Edmund Leamy, Dr George Coffey, Miss [Mary?] Rooney, John McBride, J. F. Taylor, Michael Cusack, P. J. McCann, P. Lavelle, George Coffey, and Jennie Wyse Power. Cf. William Rooney: 'How much easier would it be to teach those Irish speakers of English good Gaelic than to persist in a hopeless crusade to graft on them a tongue antagonistic, even in its most elementary parts, to the idiom and accent of the people.' *W.I.*, 29 Aug. 1896. Cf. James Joyce, *A Portrait of the Artist as a Young Man* (Oxford, 2000), p. 159. The Celtic Literary Society expressed their condolences to the Rooney brothers on the death of their sister Mary in November 1895. See Minute Book (N.L.I., MS 200).

[104] For a discussion of Hyde's ideas see Oliver MacDonagh, *States of Mind* (London, 1983), pp 109–13.

[105] Rooney, *Prose Writings*, p. 253.

[106] *W.I.*, 29 August 1896.

[107] Rooney, *Prose Writings*, p. 244.

commitment. Their separatism was inconceivable outside of this revivalist agenda. Consequently, Rooney's demand for a politicised Gaelic League was accompanied by a scornful rejection of the pieties of the Gaelicists. Condemning the 'hyper-Gaelic element' for their 'vendetta' against the English language Young Ireland tradition,[108] Rooney incredulously wondered what Irish nationalists were to read until they had achieved fluency in the Irish language. '[U]ntil we are independent', he argued, 'we shall have to use English in our daily life.'[109] Although readily accepting that the Young Ireland tradition was not a 'distinctly national literature' because it was not written in Irish, Rooney grasped its utilitarian value as propaganda. As a 'nationalist' literature (note the distinction) it had effectively preserved 'a political ideal for the people': 'the separate and individual entity of the Irish nation'.[110]

Sometimes Rooney framed the argument in more polemical terms. His stark evaluation of the Young Ireland oeuvre as their 'most national' writing because it was their 'most anti-English' writing reflected a further aspect of revivalist thinking.[111] This was a crude articulation of the belief that Irishness could be identified in part as a series of values diametrically opposed to those associated with Englishness. More characteristically, literary Fenians described their Irishness in absolutist terms that were historically predetermined. John Whelan suggested that 'no man can be false to his country who is true to its history, and only with a knowledge of it can that truth come.'[112] Whereas abstract political thought provided the basis for revolutionising a nation into a fundamentally different entity, by being beholden to history, the possibility of reinventing the nation was denied: 'In the past of a nation lives the protection of its future and the advancement of its present.'[113] By this formulation, the past circumscribed the legitimate future of the nation, for to transcend the past was to corrupt, if not destroy, the very essence of that historic nation. As Whelan argued at a Young Ireland League demonstration memorialising Owen Roe O'Neill, 'The nation ignorant of the history of its ancestors and willing to remain in ignorance was no nation (hear, hear).'[114] Such argument strengthened the literary Fenian challenge to the legitimacy of home rule as a means to achieve Irish nationhood. Again, as Rooney postulates, prior to the union the so-called 'native parliament' had operated entirely in the interests of the anti-Irish. Eliding the 1782 constitutional arrangements with home rule, allowed home rule to be labelled 'wholly foreign, utterly un-Irish', and any attempt to marshal an historical justification for it was fallacious. History taught

---

[108] Ibid., p. 229.
[109] Ibid., p. 68.
[110] Ibid., pp 67, 225.
[111] Rooney, 'Is there an Anglo-Irish Literature?' in *Prose Writings*, p. 227.
[112] S.V.V., 8 Jan. 1897.
[113] Ibid.
[114] W.I., 9 Sept. 1893.

that home rule was a means to transform the Irish 'from restless and opportunist irreconcilables to plodding, placid citizens of the empire';[115] its aim was pacification rather than the fulfilment of nationhood.

With separation as the prerequisite for the restoration of Irishness, literary Fenians implicitly depicted the union as a fiction. Ireland was not England's equal, but its colonial subject and increasingly separatists identified the British imperial dynamic as more than simply economic or social exploitation. Its power rested on far more insidious and effective processes dependent not merely on the exercise of crude political power but predicated on cultural penetration. That home rule might be satisfactory to Irish nationalists was symptomatic of this process and, like Douglas Hyde, Rooney fastened onto the culturally numbing 'penny dreadfuls' and 'shilling shockers'[116] as symbolic of this market-driven mode of imperial subjugation. Only by nurturing a Gaelic culture could a 'barrier' be erected against the 'insipid and colourless' cultural life generated by the English in Ireland:

> By the adoption of Gaelic we shall gradually wean ourselves away from fashions and habits that have grown on us unknowingly, we shall become what we claim to be, and strengthen to an almost incalculable extent our claim to individual nationhood.[117]

Arthur Griffith framed this argument much more forcefully in a lecture on the 'English Invasion' given to the Young Ireland League in November 1893. In this analysis Irish–British relations were understood as a series of intersecting struggles between nation, empire, and race.

> This seven-centuried war was one of Ireland against England, nationality against empire, Celt against Saxon. . . . The struggle of nationality against empire is the struggle known for all time to the world. The result of empire is to crush out nationality, and destroy or impede expansion of individual national life. . . . The ideal state of progress would be the destruction of empire, and the consequent expansion of national life.[118]

Griffith's cultural nationalist critique of empire also rejected contemporary efforts to conceive of the empire in federal terms. Notably promoted by Joseph Chamberlain as an alternative to Gladstonian home rule, 'home rule all round' attracted some attention in Irish political circles thanks in part to the links

---

[115] Rooney, 'Our Native Parliament' in *Prose Writings*, pp 156–66.
[116] Hyde's phrase, see Douglas Hyde, 'Necessity for De-Anglicising Ireland' in Charles Gavan Duffy, George Sigerson, and Douglas Hyde (ed.), *The Revival of Irish Literature* (London, 1894), p. 159.
[117] Rooney, *Prose Writings*, pp 65–6.
[118] *W.I.*, 25 Nov. 1893.

between Cecil Rhodes and the Redmondites.[119] Rather than a positive reconstruction of the empire to the benefit of each of its constituent parts, Griffith recognised in this idea another manifestation of British imperial self-interest. Again, race and culture provided the bedrock of Griffith's rejection:

> Latterly the methods of the Teuton were cosmopolitanism – the parliament of men in the federation of the world. And it was curious that most of the promoters of the cosmopolitanism came from the same branch of the Teuton race. The worst thing that the peoples of the world may fear is the cosmopolitanism that would lead to the subjection of the Celt by the Teuton, particularly the Saxon branch of the race. It may be that the fight between the Celt and the Saxon would in the near future assume great dimensions; in that day it would be found that the Irish, who for seven hundred years have resisted its domination, would lead the van.[120]

This preoccupation with the debilitating and culturally eroding influence of cosmopolitanism and the increasing linkage of these ideas to anti-imperialism was a more general feature of the revival. Yeats had joked (with all seriousness) at the inaugural meeting of the Y.I.L.: 'One man only they would not welcome – they would have nothing to do with the cosmopolitan. The cosmopolitan was no concern of theirs, nor the concern of any nation. He was a very extravagant and eccentric being (laughter).'[121] George Coffey, archaeologist, antiquarian, friend of the Yeats family and moderate nationalist,[122] pursued this line when he lectured on Thomas Davis in 1895 at the Antient Concert Rooms. Davis, Coffey argued, 'sought to sting them into some sense of their provincialism; to make them feel that as Irishmen they would be respected, as imitators of English thought and ways they must be despised (hear).' As a good Yeatsian, but also, as has been shown, in line with Rooney's thought, Coffey praised the didactic effectiveness of Davis rather than the quality of his poetry. By acknowledging the radical implications of his argument and concluding that 'Empire means averages, not excellence',[123] Coffey demonstrated that British imperialism ensured the impossibility of sustaining Douglas Hyde's apolitical agenda.

Griffith's belief that Ireland's peculiar relationship with the British empire presented it with certain international obligations was developed by Alice

---

[119] In March 1895 a 'home rule all round' motion was put in the house of commons. It attracted Balfour's scorn and perfunctory debate. John Redmond argued that Irish, Welsh, and Scottish claims were not equivalent. Ireland demanded the restitution of rights taken by force and therefore home rule should precede federation, not least because the Irish were not prepared to await the required change in Scottish and Welsh public opinion. See John Kendle, *Ireland and the Federal Solution: The Debates over the United Kingdom Constitution, 1870–1921* (Kingston and Montreal, 1989), pp 81–2.

[120] *W.I.*, 25 Nov. 1893.

[121] *F.J.*, 18 Sept. 1891.

[122] Foster, *Apprentice Mage*, p. 97.

[123] *W.I.*, 9 Nov. 1895.

Milligan in strikingly messianic (and Mazzinian) terms. Not merely witness to the clash of civilisations, Milligan perceived a titanic struggle between the material forces of modernisation and the spiritual bedrock of national cultures. Protecting Irish specificity was to make the country the agent of a more generalised quality, or spirit, of national individualism that transcended Ireland's individual national cultural interests. Milligan, contra Hyde,[124] firmly repudiated unionist revivalists who celebrated 'the link with the mightiest empire in the world' and believed Ireland could 'develop her genius in the domain of literature and music, as Scotland had done'.[125] Rather:

> We live in an era which in spite of its advance along the line of material civilisation, is retrograding towards utilitarian philosophy and mere paganism, an age which has lost or is losing faith in immortality and things divine, and which is necessarily becoming debased. A redeemer is called for among nations, and where should we look for an awakening impulse towards higher, nobler, and more christian [sic] views of human life and rule but in our own Ireland. . . . we believe that our nation has a high and noble destiny to fulfil, a part to play in the advancement of the human race along the upward path of progress.[126]

Here Milligan asserted the classic link made by romantic nationalists between the nation-state and the progress of civilisation. Empire, if not necessarily destructive of prosperity, destroyed the moral foundations of civilisation. Although not explicitly stated, the anti-imperial critique of the literary Fenians implied that the destruction of empire would also serve to regenerate English culture. It was not clear, however, whether England's imperial penetration of Ireland and elsewhere brought the penetration of English culture or a peculiarly imperial culture that was as equally at odds with Englishness as it was Irishness.

In this separatist polemic the actions of historic individuals continued to be emphasised as models for emulation. 'History has never been made by the millions', argued Rooney, 'the few who sacrificed did all that the world is proud of. The single seed eventually fills the corn field; the silent, earnest thinker moves the masses.'[127] There was not, however, a very developed sense that the actions of a small group of dedicated revolutionaries could awaken the masses to the structural realities of their material conditions. Nor did the discourse of the cultural separatists suggest that they had much faith in the Irish nationalist masses being moved to act on the basis of abstract political

---

[124] Hyde, 'Necessity', pp 117–18.

[125] S.V.V., 7 Aug. 1896.

[126] Mazzini believed the people of the Italian peninsula 'were destined to achieve great things for the welfare of humanity' and to do so 'must one day or another be constituted a nation'. Quoted in Anthony D. Smith, *Nationalism in the Twentieth Century* (Oxford, 1979), p. 121.

[127] 'The Importance of Being in Earnest' in Rooney, *Prose Writings*, pp 237–8, an essay on the necessity of organisation and tenacity in the nationalist project.

principles. Consequently, in the post-Parnellite context of the 1890s, *Shan Van Vocht* explained the significance of the '98 celebrations in very straightforward terms: 'With no pre-eminent figure among living Irishmen to command their adherence and inspire their confidence, they had looked back into the past and taken for their hero one of the greatest of our race.'[128]

Wolfe Tone's legacy, however, was a matter of dispute and the struggle to control the '98 centenary married factional rivalry to the political need to determine the meaning of the 1798 rising. There were three basic models in circulation in 1898. The dominant model was that propagated by Father Patrick Kavanagh from platforms throughout the country and in his *The Wexford Rebellion*.[129] Kavanagh regarded the rising as unplanned and provoked by the oppressive activities of the Orange Society. He promoted the ideal of the heroic priest as separatist leader and rejected the efficacy of oath-bound underground organisations. Given the papacy's prohibition of secret societies an uprising of this sort in a catholic country was bound to fail. Although admiring the heroism of the priests during the rising, the separatists resented Kavanagh's subtext that the clergy were the natural political leaders of the Irish people.

More intolerable still was the common argument that the rebellion was an unorganised response to English provocation, itself part of a wider governmental strategy intended to necessitate the Act of Union. In the *New Century Review* J. A. O'Sullivan of the London Young Ireland League objected to W. T. Stead's description of the rebellion as 'the mere maddened welter of a peasantry deliberately driven frantic by the wholesale violation of their wives and daughters'.[130] John Redmond had shared Stead's interpretation of '98 since at least 1886.[131] *Shan Van Vocht* criticised Stead for 'suppressing all mention of revolutionary leaders and organisation, and showing that the whole thing was designed by Pitt and Castlereagh'.[132] To attribute the rebellion to pre-political instinct rather than the revolutionary agency of the United Irishmen was to render memorial of Tone and the United Irishmen redundant. O'Sullivan argued that Tone was a separatist from the founding of the first United Irishmen club in 1791 and that it was circumstances that destroyed the chances of an Irish revolution inspired by the French example. Preparations were particularly

---

[128] *S.V.V.*, 5 Sept. 1898.

[129] See Anna Kinsella, 'The Nineteenth Century Interpretation of 1798', M.Litt, Trinity College, Dublin, 1992, pp 15–35.

[130] J. A. O'Sullivan, 'The True Character of "Ninety-Eight"' in *New Century Review*, vol. iv (24 Dec. 1898), p. 480; see W. T. Stead, 'The Topic of the Month: The Centenary of 1798', *Review of Reviews*, vol. xviii (July 1898), pp 66–76, repr. with second essay as W. T. Stead, *The Centenary of 1798 and its Bearing on the Practical Politics of To-day* (London, 1898), p. 47.

[131] J. E. Redmond, 'The Truth About '98' in *The Irish Question*, no. 6 (London, 1886), pp 1–36.

[132] *S.V.V.*, 1 Aug. 1898.

advanced in the north of Ireland where Cromwellian rule by the Orangemen had ensured the Defenders and United Irishmen were 'arm in arm' preparing for 'a bloody war'.[133] It was the failure of the French landing at Bantry Bay, the arrest of the leadership, and the declaration of martial law, which caused the rising to fail. Just as separatists argued that the Fenians of the 1860s might have succeeded if they had risen in 1865 when the movement was believed to be at its greatest strength, the delineation of specific explanations of the failure of the 1798 rising was equally driven by the conviction that insurrection remained a viable strategy. As history taught Rooney:

> The question of Irish freedom must eventually be settled by the same means that gave independence to America, Greece, Belgium and Italy; but it would be folly to invite a pitched battle yet. Our forces need to be concentrated and organised; they need discipline and education. These in our hands, the hour will come, and coming, shall find us prepared to grasp the opportunity.[134]

Constitutional politicians derived very different lessons from the rebellion. Both John Redmond and William O'Brien interpreted 1798 within the familiar Whiggish historical paradigm of insurrectionism preparing the way for the effective constitutionalism of Parnellism.[135] O'Brien's line was entirely consistent with his Young Ireland Society addresses. O'Sullivan was scathingly critical of O'Brien's 'exasperating incoherence', but above all he was incensed by O'Brien's suggestion that rebellion could have been avoided in 1798 if the English had provided for the 'amicable adjustment of matters'. In the same way, O'Brien argued that any sense of 'an incipient revolutionary feeling' in contemporary Ireland had yet to fundamentally undermine 'the belief in a peaceful arrangement'.[136]

O'Sullivan mocked O'Brien's polemical suggestion that Davitt be sent to Washington to 'play Wolfe Tone' and suggested that the Irish would prefer to rely upon 'themselves alone' – an early use of the most common translation into English of Sinn Féin. In the meantime advanced nationalist support for Redmond was a temporary exigency aimed at obtaining 'sure measures of temporary relief'.[137] This was an interesting admission. By criticising O'Brien and positing the contingent nature of separatist support for Redmond,

---

133 O'Sullivan, 'True Character', p. 480.
134 Rooney, *Poems and Ballads*, p. xlv.
135 Redmond's '98 speeches are considered in Kinsella, 'Nineteenth Century Interpretations of 1798', pp 37–52 and Paseta, '1798 in 1898', p. 49. Redmond wrote a series of long articles on 1798 for the press, e.g. *Limerick Leader*, 10, 14, 17, 21, 24, 26, & 28 Jan. 1898, 'The Centenary of '98', *Nineteenth Century*, xliii (1898), pp 612–24, and 'Ireland since '98', *North American Review*, clxvi (1898), pp 385–97; William O'Brien, '"Who Fears to Speak of Ninety-Eight"', *Contemporary Review*, lxxiii (Jan. 1898), pp 14–34.
136 O'Sullivan, 'True Character', p. 482.
137 Ibid.

O'Sullivan acknowledged the Redmondite–Fenian nexus as the temporary repository of authentic nationalist sentiment. Orthodox Fenians and independent oppositionists with their apparently opportunistic constitutionalism could both legitimately claim the United Irishmen legacy, but the nationalist credentials of all those who stood outside of this combination were highly dubious.

V

Although the link between the 1916 rising and the 1798 centenary seems extremely tenuous, behind the scenes of the preparations for the centenary was a mounting frustration with the established leadership and, to some extent, the established dictums of the Irish Republican Brotherhood. The coincidence of members of the I.N.A. and the more energetic promoters of a politicised literary revival cannot be ignored. Despite the I.N.A. failing to replace the I.R.B. as the separatist organisation of choice – the *Irish Republic* ceased publication in June 1898[138] – it nonetheless sounded a warning to Allan, Fitzgerald, and the motley crew of the Nally Club. The Redmondite–Fenian nexus might have proved an effective means to pursue a separatist agenda through the Amnesty Association and the pseudo-separatism of the rhetoric of independence, but it was clear that it did not offer a long-term solution to the strategic dilemmas of Fenianism. 'I am a Parnellite on the two broad questions of clerical and English dictation', wrote Allan to the *Irish Republic*, 'but I need scarcely say that I nor those who think like me ever take the remotest interest in the parliamentary work of the party, for we regard it as so much waste of time.'[139]

Lyman's challenge to the Supreme Council was backed with cash and it was to this combination that Mark Ryan, Dobbyn, Milligan, and Yeats responded. Ideologically, the I.N.A. offered a more sophisticated Irish separatism than that associated with the I.R.B., but its cultural nationalism ultimately failed to make a strategic breakthrough comparable to Arthur Griffith and Bulmer Hobson's later doctrines of passive resistance. Its aspiration to form a nationalist umbrella group that would become the pre-eminent political organisation in Ireland placed the I.N.A. in competition with the major constitutional organisations and, as such, was unrealistic. Moreover, despite the irreconcilable tone of the *Independent*, with Timothy Harrington building informal links with the Federationists – which were reinforced by the Federationist and Parnellite M.P.s on the joint executive committee running the amalgamated '98 movement – and William O'Brien's launch of the United Irish League, it was clear that the reunion of the Irish parliamentary party was imminent. Redmond's

---

[138] C.B.S. Box 13, 16462, May 1898: Lyman 'is tired putting up money for it'.
[139] Republished in *W.I.*, 22 Sept. 1894.

attempt through the Irish Independent League to secure an urban following that could challenge the political authority of the Irish National Federation had signally failed and from its inception the United Irish League, identified as the inheritor of the Land League, promised the rejuvenation of agrarian constitutionalism. Advanced nationalism needed a new home and a new identity.

At the opening of the centenary year and some years before the foundation of Sinn Féin, the *Shan Van Vocht* urged, 'so let our strength come from ourselves alone.'[140] A month later the journal reproduced the following fiery extract from John Mitchel's *Jail Journal* as a reminder of its ultimate objectives and reasoning:

> Hungary is henceforth and forever a great nation – how much greater now than before her bloody agony! How much grander her history! How much richer her treasury of heroic memories! How much surer and higher her destiny! It is through this bloody travail and by virtue of this baptism of fire, and only so, that the nations ever spring forth, great, generous, and free. If Ireland in '82, instead of winning her independence from the coward foe by the mere flash of unbloodied swords, had like America waded through carnage to her freedom, like America she had been free this day. A disastrous war ever had been better than a triumphant parade.[141]

Though the Mitchelite mode would remain central to the separatist rhetorical battery, this was also the age of the financial relations committee, of radical discussion of the economics of empire, of the *Manchester Guardian* and its emergent 'New Liberalism'. Although there is no evidence that Griffith had read the works of J. A. Hobson – the influence on his thought of the protectionist economist Friedrich List is, however, well documented – this atmosphere of economic radicalism had begun to condition advanced nationalist thinking. It would be another six years before Griffith wrote his seminal articles on 'The Resurrection of Hungary', but the tropes and economic ideas characteristic of Sinn Féin were emerging. In terms of the 'new nationalism', the lecture David Fagan gave to the Young Ireland Society in 1893 on 'The Industrial Resources of Ireland' was indicative of a strain of thought Griffith would develop.[142] Fagan advocated increasing the acreage of flax grown in Ireland in order to end the import of cloth. He also focused on the benefits of increasing the capacity of Ireland's quarries and on the need to educate the Irish in the commercial opportunities represented by Ireland's untapped natural resources. Two years later, the Celtic Literary Society debated whether Ireland should have an industrial or an agricultural future. Joseph T. Doyle suggested that Ireland was rapidly becoming a pastoral country and that

---

[140] S.V.V., 3 Jan. 1898.
[141] Quoted in S.V.V., 1 Feb. 1898.
[142] W.I., 23 Dec. 1893.

no nation could exist without the development of its other resources. Probably drawing on the German example, he argued that 'the hand of parental government was the first essential towards prosperity.' And although Patrick Gregan poured cold water on this by suggesting the industrial future envisaged for Ireland was impossible owing to its coal shortage, these discussions nonetheless indicated the emergence of a more far-sighted separatist style of debate.[143] William Rooney's essays were one outcome of these developments but to see his pluralist anti-imperialism, his blending of the rhetoric of self-reliance and Gaelicism with Fenian conviction, as a civic republicanism is somewhat problematic.[144] Undoubtedly non-sectarian, Rooney's arguments nonetheless strengthened an essentialist nationalist tradition that determined membership of the nation in terms of ethnic origin rather than the active citizen bound and protected by the rights and obligations enshrined in a constitution.

If revolution impoverishes language, so too must interminably anticipated revolution. Yeats may have struggled to create a high literature against a stultifying popular taste, but he too was capable of banal aspiration. 'Next year they would celebrate the glories of defeated causes, causes which rose afresh on their great pilgrimage, knowing that their final triumph was inevitable.'[145] Again, the Fenian ideal. Assistant Commissioner Mallon, however, indicated just how huge was the task the separatists faced:

> It is marvellous how apathetic the people are, about Dublin at all events, about this '98 movement. I suppose the Spanish–american [sic] war had an effect on it; but the Local Government Bill was undoubtedly the great factor in drawing public attention from the '98 movement.
>
> The dozen or two Dublin miscreants who are ready for anything are really very tame, no party will own them at present, and whatever money they have they are receiving from America.[146]

In a less considered but inadvertently more revealing vein, the policeman noted that the '98 centenary did not reach the 'pitch of enthusiasm' he associated with the Land League, sniping: 'In Dublin, at all events, the most ardent allusions to physical force are criticised as "clap-trap" and impracticable, mere sentiment seems to predominate.'[147] Mallon may have been scornful of this 'mere sentiment' but his observation that Fenianism was rejected because 'impracticable' is a reminder of the complexities of Irish nationalist allegiance in this period. It is difficult to read these words without thinking of the seismic

---

[143] *The Parnellite*, 19 Jan. 1895.
[144] Cf. Mathews, *Revival*, pp 94–103.
[145] From a speech to a '98 convention held in Manchester chaired by Yeats, *W.I.*, 9 Oct. 1897.
[146] C.B.S. Box 14, 16660, 1 July 1898.
[147] C.B.S. Box 13, 15438, 21 Feb. 1898.

upheavals of the 1912–1923 period and reflecting on the seminal influence the '98 centenary had on a generation of Irish nationalists. Despite the I.R.B.'s failure to solve the problem of strategy it had successfully sustained the Fenian ideal, not least through its tenacious adherence to the ideal of an armed uprising. The apparent predilection of the Irish nationalist population for the ideals of '98 and the determination of the politicians to align themselves with a sanitised separatism was indicative of their success. On balance, however, once the political holiday of 1898 was over, most were happy, stimulated but under-challenged, to return to their constitutionalist homes.

5

The end of Parnellism and the ideological dilemmas of Sinn Féin

I

Apocalyptic bloodlusts in expectation of the redrawing of the political map of Europe were two-a-penny at the turn of the twentieth century. As British politicians debated the best way to manage the empire – simultaneously near the peak of its territorial expansion and under pressure from ambitious European powers – the New Imperialists conceived of these rivalries as a pseudo-Darwinian struggle for the survival.[1] Spurred on by the Boer War, Irish political debate was infected with this discourse, the moth-balled adage 'England's difficulty, Ireland's opportunity' emerging freshly laundered for the new century. 'Clovis', writing in the *United Irishman*, prophesied a struggle of magnificent proportions:

> Her [Ireland's] people uneasy, dissatisfied, apathetic, despairing, agitated by conflicting counsels and impulses, face the coming century without a leader whom they can trust or a plan which they can confidently follow. . . . we await the coming of the chosen one . . . She [Ireland] bids us look to the East, beyond her once invincible but now failing enemy, to where the nations of Europe are girding their loins for the greatest struggle the human race has ever engaged in.[2]

The Christological metaphors that became so characteristic of Pearse's later oratory are evident here, implicitly transfiguring Parnell, an earlier chosen one, into a sacrificed Christ. Packed with presentiment, this passage was also a call for clarity amid the confusion of turn of the century Irish politics. The Irish parliamentary party, although still divided, remained the dominant political force in Ireland. However, expectations were fuelled by the 1898 centenary and advanced nationalists hoped that the energies the celebrations marshalled

---

[1] E. H. H. Green, 'The Political Economy of Empire, 1880–1914' in Andrew Porter (ed.), *Oxford History of the British Empire. Volume III: The Nineteenth Century* (Oxford, 1999), pp 346–68.
[2] *United Irishman*, 6 Jan. 1900.

could be channelled into a resurgent activism and organisation. In its second number the *United Irishman* urged that the '98 clubs be maintained as the 'rallying centre of nationalism',[3] but 'Celt' was soon decrying committees that resolved too much and did too little. He parodied the innumerable resolutions chalked up:

> That we the members of 'This and That' hereby commend (or condemn) the action of 'Somewhere else' &c., prefaced by long platitudes and followed by lugubrious ratiocination is not a task productive of enthusiasm or of the exercise of any qualities of mind or body.

This sarcasm became astute commentary, identifying the problem often faced by frustrated ideological ambition:

> an over-zeal in the practice and exposition of principles repels by its very monotony and turgid reiteration. . . . anyone that has experience of political, even patriotic and literary, societies in Ireland, can bear testimony to the negative pleasure given by their variation of the old theme.[4]

Over the next decade the '98 organisation gradually disintegrated, dominated by internal disputes over expenditure and undermined by a plethora of embarrassingly unfinished building projects.[5]

Overall, however, Irish politics was entering a period of realignment and retrenchment. It was evident that separatists would cease to channel their energies through the Redmondite–Fenian nexus and with the reunification of the party Redmond became a particular target for abuse, vitriol, and obsessive scrutiny. On his election to the chair of the party, the *United Irishman* revived memories of his notorious Cambridge speech of 1895, inaccurately claiming that this marked Redmond's break with the advanced nationalists:

> But his imperialistic sentiment was strong enough to allow him to part company without a pang with the men who had fought beside him for five years under the delusion that he, too, was an Irish nationalist.[6]

Mockingly referred to as an 'ex-Hillsider',[7] Redmond's apparently friendly response to the royal visit of 1900 exposed his fickleness and hypocrisy: he was dubbed 'John Genuflection Redmond, Hillsider, Foundation-Stoner, and

---

[3] *U.I.*, 11 Mar. 1899.
[4] *U.I.*, 26 May 1900.
[5] For example, a dispute over an alleged embezzlement caused a split in the Cork Y.I.S. C.B.S. Precis, Box 3, 22 Nov. 1901, 9 Oct. 1902, 17 Oct. 1902, 5 Nov. 1902.
[6] *U.I.*, 10 Feb. 1900.
[7] *U.I.*, 24 Feb. 1900.

British Army Panegyrist'.[8] The reference to Hillsider carried a particular satirical resonance, repudiating constitutionalist underestimation of the separatists as unreflective pike-carriers. Indeed, central to this separatist assertion of political independence was a determination to define themselves on their own terms. If in the 1890s the I.R.B. primarily functioned as a mildly alarming adjunct to Parnellism, in the 1900s separatism determined upon self-definition. Rejecting the Parnellite conceit that constitutional nationalism was Fenianism by other means, separatists increasingly distinguished themselves in terms of first principles. P. J. Hoctor, deploring Lord Mayor Pile's welcome to Queen Victoria, asserted,

> The fact of his lordship being connected with the 98 Centenary Committee and having posed as a believer in Wolfe Tone's principles may lead him to suppose that he may have what would be known as a strong national support behind him to justify his present conduct. I wish to remind him that he or any other man will not be permitted to degrade the principles for which Wolfe Tone died, and which the majority of our country-men believe in.[9]

William Rooney argued along similar lines. Objecting to the use of 'advanced' to describe his nationalism, he admonished that there was 'no earthly reason why the adjective should be applied' because only the separatist demand could be considered an expression of nationalism.

> The movement of '48 and Fenianism were decidedly nationalist movements, but not one whit more 'advanced' than any legitimate national movement has ever been. It is a mistake to call the nationalism of any period a policy; it is a tradition, a belief, an ideal, an end, but in no sense the means which a policy is most certainly. . . . its means are merely determined by the circumstances of each generation.[10]

This insistence on the ideological purity of nationalism was reiterated in the *United Irishman*'s puff for the Cumann na nGaedhael convention of November 1900. Keen to underline that the organisation did not represent a departure in separatist politics – it was 'merely a combination of a series of existing national bodies' – it repudiated constitutionalism, insisting 'on the difference between the ideals of '98, '48, and '67 and those which, in our time, are sought to be identified with them'.[11]

On an adjacent tack, Joseph Ryan accounted for the pervasive confusion of the contemporary political scene by fastening on the resurgence of agrarian politics and the pernicious influence of the United Irish League. Ryan explored

---

[8] *U.I.*, 17 Mar. 1900. In the 1903 municipal elections the *U.I.*, 3 Jan. 1903, advocated the Labour candidate Dowd over the U.I.L. candidate Harrington.
[9] *U.I.*, 17 Mar. 1900.
[10] *U.I.*, 7 Apr. 1900. Also, *U.I.*, 29 June 1901, 20 June 1903.
[11] *U.I.*, 17 Nov. 1900.

a familiar theme, arguing that support for home rule stemmed from agrarian self-interest. Constitutional nationalism was a beneficiary by default:

> if the League had never been started the political atmosphere would be clearer today, for the end of the last parliament would have ended the power for mischief of most of our national party. They would simply not have had the funds to go forward for election.[12]

If self-interest were removed from the political equation, the separatists would see the mass of the population gathered around them and their beliefs. Agrarianism, Ryan supposed, distorted the authentic political aspirations of the Irish population.

Such ideological assertiveness was reflected in Terence MacSwiney's confidence, as recorded in his diary in November 1902, that the authority of the Irish party had diminished. The young demanded something 'more consistent, more vigorous and more national in the true sense of the word'.[13] Nevertheless, the separatists clearly had much to fear from the reunified party. Owing to the exigencies of I.P.P. politics the Parnell anniversary took on an increasingly minor note in the nationalist calendar. Now known as Decoration Day – it saw the decoration of the graves of past nationalist leaders and exemplars – during the 1890s it had symbolically linked Parnell with separatist martyrs. In October 1900 only a thousand people formed the Dublin procession, although among the dutiful were Redmond, Field, Patrick O'Brien, John P. Hayden, and the recently elected M.P. for College Green, P. J. Nannetti.[14] Standing at the grave of Paddy Dignam in June 1904, hat in hand, Joyce's Leopold Bloom accounted for the decline of the Parnell anniversary in a meditation on mortality and the quality of Ned Lambert's tweed. 'Bam! expires. Gone at last. People talk about you a bit: forget you. Don't forget to pray for him. Remember him in your prayers. Even Parnell. Ivy day dying out.'[15] But deceased nationalist leaders are not so easily forgotten and the political explanation of a Cork special branch officer offers a more satisfactory explanation: 'Many of its former supporters believe that holding the usual funeral here would tend to raise ill-feeling, a matter which they are anxious to avoid.'[16] Shortly afterwards, following resolutions passed at a national convention in the Rotunda, Redmond was reconfirmed as chair of the unified party.[17]

---

[12] Joseph Ryan, 'Provincialism in Politics' in *U.I.*, 15 Dec. 1900.
[13] MacSwiney Diary, 26 Nov. 1902, MacSwiney Papers (U.C.D. P48c/99).
[14] C.B.S. Box 18, 22986, 9 Oct. 1900. Nannetti was selected for College Green in place of the Redmondite J. L. Carew. An active trade unionist with strong separatist contacts, he took a leading role in the testimonial raised in 1899 for the Invincible Joseph Mullet. C.B.S. Box 16, 19779, 18 Aug. 1899.
[15] James Joyce, *Ulysses* (Paris, 1922, London 1992), p. 146.
[16] C.B.S. Box 18, 23002. Two hundred Corkonians took the train to Dublin.
[17] *F.J.*, 14 Dec. 1900.

Building on its west Mayo base, the new constitutionalist organisation the United Irish League (U.I.L.) returned agrarian politics to the centre of Irish political life, eclipsing the '98 clubs and becoming Ireland's most popular mass political organisation.[18] In response the I.R.B. resorted to a characteristically ill co-ordinated complex of infiltration, subversion, resistance, and association. James Daly of Castlebar, the leading Land League veteran, immediately recognised the importance of the new organisation and as president of the Redmondite–Fenian Connaught '98 Council sought accommodation with O'Brien. Talks quickly broke down over political differences; at the same time the catholic bishops gave guarded approval to the organisation as an agent of social justice.[19] The U.I.L.'s failure to accommodate advanced nationalism and its success in attracting the support of the catholic hierarchy gave notice of how Irish politics would function after the reunification of the parliamentary party. Elsewhere – and away from the U.I.L. activist epicentre – advanced nationalist responses were more confused. In Templederry, County Tipperary, the local president of the '98 Centenary Club, I.R.B. suspect Thomas O'Donohoe, worked with J. K. Bracken to establish a branch of the U.I.L. It was thought they hoped it would function as a separatist recruiting centre, possibly in the interest of the remnants of the I.N.A.[20] In Galway, Peter J. Kelly, reputedly the acting representative for Connaught on the Supreme Council, led overt I.R.B. opposition to the U.I.L. and the leadership of John Roche. Kelly denounced the organisation as inimical to Parnellism, providing further instance of the construction of Parnellism as Fenianism by other means.[21] In Longford, Patrick E. Fitzgerald led the charge against the League. He was particularly aggrieved by William O'Brien's opposition to John MacBride's South Mayo candidature in 1900 and Thomas Fenlon's expulsion from the League for failing to vote for its chosen candidate for the chair of Longford county council. This combination triggered talk of I.R.B. members who had joined the League being forced to resign their U.I.L. membership.[22] A curious report by the Mayo county inspector claimed that Joseph MacBride planned to infiltrate each local branch with twelve reliable men who, although working in line with League precepts, would seek to bypass the leadership of William O'Brien. Almost certainly working under instruction from London, MacBride had enlisted the help of John McHale, president of the West Mayo U.I.L. executive and Manus Malloy of Westport, both I.R.B. suspects.[23]

Fenian polemic and this scattered and anecdotal evidence does little to challenge the view that advanced nationalism was a marginal force in 1900.

---

[18] Philip Bull, 'The Formation of the United Irish League, 1898–1900: The Dynamic of the Irish Agrarian Agitation' in *I.H.S*, xxxiii, no. 132 (Nov. 2003), pp 404–23.
[19] Ibid., pp 411–15.
[20] C.B.S. Precis, Box 2, 3 Feb. 1899.
[21] Ibid., 22 Feb. 1899.
[22] Ibid., 21 Aug. 1900, Box 3, 2 Nov. 1900.
[23] Ibid., 3 Nov. 1899.

William O'Brien had been right to argue in 1885 that the Irish population had been convinced of the efficacy of parliamentarianism, but this only provides part of the explanation. Ireland in the 1890s was a profoundly different place from the Ireland of the 1790s, the previous period of most fervent republican activity. Despite the political uncertainty caused by the split and the existence of a Conservative government closely identified with unionism, the relative stability and prosperity of Irish society diminished the likelihood of a resurgence of physical force nationalism. Violence had increasingly polluted the domestic and international politics of the 1790s, fuelling the militarisation of the United Irishmen. In the 1890s this conditioning atmosphere was largely absent, producing a population less psychologically and physically acclimatised to political violence and defiance. The occasional outbreak of collective violence aggravated by agrarian unrest belonged to a specific historical and political context. Over twenty years of intermittent agrarian unrest had seen the construction of a series of legitimate enemies, primarily the landlord, the land grabber, and, in the later phase, the grazier. Coeval with this were a series of communally sanctioned and codified militant strategies that provided moral justification and direction for collective action. Outside the agrarian context a framework for collective resistance to the forces of the crown did not exist. The abstract demand for a republic, however 'virtually' established, and the exaltation of separatist martyrs were not an effective substitute. Fenianism demanded a leap of faith: to fight for one abstract, the Irish republic, against another, the British empire. One *United Irishman* contributor, almost certainly Bulmer Hobson, grasped this difficulty. In a fascinating piece on 'Defensive Warfare', Hobson rehearsed ideas that would later form the basis of his iconic 1909 pamphlet of the same name. He adumbrated a system of resistance that would distinguish the enemy, rendering the nebulous manifest:

> The underlying principle of it is that whereas the traditional method, the attack, proceeded upon the basis of the enemy being in possession of the country, and aimed at retaking it from its hands, the aggressive defence proceeds upon the basis of the people being in possession of the country, treats the enemy as an invading force, throws upon him the necessity of crushing out the popular centres of resistance[,] the necessity, practically, of reconquering the whole country.[24]

'Defensive Warfare' would expose the reality of the ostensibly liberal, relatively democratic, and increasingly 'green' (or nationalist-friendly) regime of Dublin Castle,[25] revealing the apparatus of a military occupation.

---

[24] *U.I.*, 17 Feb. 1900.
[25] For an analysis of the development of an Irish administration increasingly friendly to home rule, see Lawrence MacBride, *The Greening of Dublin Castle: The Transformation of Bureaucratic and Judicial Personnel in Dublin Castle in Ireland, 1892–1922* (Washington, 1991).

Hobson's ideas were the military equivalent of Rooney's Gaelicism and Griffith's emergent Hungarian policy. In each case implementation would place the onus of reaction on the British, requiring that they regain the authority the Irish had chosen to assume. Bypassing the British, these strategies subverted the rules of engagement, forcing the initiative onto the British. Oliver MacDonagh has argued that the classic pattern of organised Irish nationalism was to create instability and wait for the British government to propose a solution to the grievance to which the instability gave expression.[26] By this measure, Defensive Warfare, separatist Gaelicism, and the Hungarian policy fit into the same mode as radical constitutionalism, but the distinctive aims of each should not be blurred.

Hobson's innovative approach to the problem of creating an activist dynamic can be contrasted with Alice Milligan's more orthodox optimism. Milligan wrote an article on the 'The Republican Ideal', where she described the I.R.B. in the 1860s as 'pre-eminently the uprising of the people of Ireland, the insurgence of the masses, organising themselves in secrecy in vast numbers, inspired with a great hope that a call would come to them'. Unfortunately, despite his genius for conspiracy and organisation, James Stephens was not a military strategist.[27] Milligan's faith in physical force separatism led her to conclude that Fenianism's failure in the 1860s was one of leadership rather than of the popular will. Like many others, her political convictions were rooted in the belief that in the right circumstances Ireland could inflict a defeat on England. Like many others, her heart fed on fantasy, Milligan harboured fantastic expectations of the readiness of ordinary people to take to arms. Even James Joyce was susceptible to the romance of '67 in terms akin to Milligan's. In his 1907 *pièce d'occasion* 'The Last Fenian', written on the death of John O'Leary, Joyce attributed the failure to establish a republic not to the numerical weakness of the Fenian movement but to the network of spies and informers.[28] In his account there was no sense that Fenianism was anything less than a national movement that could have led the population of Ireland (inflated to 'over eight million') to inflict a military defeat on the British. This passage should be considered alongside the 'Cyclops' episode of *Ulysses* where the chauvinism of a vulgar Fenianism was savagely exposed.[29]

The appeal of the constellation of ideas that became subsumed under the Sinn Féin name was twofold. To those frustrated by the apparent failure of the Irish parliamentary party the policy raised the prospect of a viable non-violent and non-clandestine alternative. To more orthodox separatists Sinn Féin offered a pragmatic escape from the strategic dilemmas Fenianism had faced

[26] Oliver MacDonagh, *States of Mind: A Study of Anglo-Irish Conflict, 1780–1980* (London, 1983).

[27] *U.I.*, 7 Dec. 1901.

[28] James Joyce, 'Fenianism: The Last Fenian' in *Occasional, Critical, and Political Writing* (Oxford, 2000), pp 138–41.

[29] Joyce, *Ulysses*, pp 376–449.

for thirty years. Satisfying the demand for new ideas generated by the literary revival, the '98 centenary, the Boer War, and the opposition to the royal visits, the policy was adopted by the network of separatist organisations, providing a framework for sustained separatist debate, speculation, and meditation. As a foundational text Arthur Griffith's *The Resurrection of Hungary* remains undeniably seminal. However, the defections to Sinn Féin of the home rule M.P.s John Sweetman, Thomas Esmonde, James O'Mara,[30] and C. J. Dolan, though providing high profile support and fuelling the Sinn Féin publicity machine, arguably pushed the movement towards a premature engagement with conventional political activity. Sinn Féin made much of Dolan's votes, heralding a new 'political era' and dating 'Ireland's resurrection from the day when 1,200 Irishmen in the poorest and most remote county in Ireland, voted for Sinn Féin'.[31] But the weakness of the movement against the parliamentary party machine and the re-adoption by the Liberal party of home rule cut short any triumphalism.

There is a well-established narrative of the consolidation of the Sinn Féin movement into a political organisation.[32] Its main constituents were the National Council, which grew out of pro-Boer agitation and was established to organise opposition to the royal visit of 1900 – it was not a membership organisation but a co-ordinating committee on which Griffith was the leading light; Cumann na nGaedhael, a cultural nationalist organisation strongly influenced by the *United Irishman*; Inginidhe na hÉireann, established along similar lines but for women only as the title suggests ('Daughters of Erin'); and the Dungannon Clubs, northern republican groups under the direction of Bulmer Hobson. Each had its own character and core constituency and these differences complicated the amalgamation and arguably undermined the emergent organisation. Furthermore, Griffith's pamphlet appeared to confer onto a fairly narrow Dublin clique possession of the revival and the authority to pronounce on its projects. The National Council, and later Sinn Féin, became the dominant force in separatist politics, but its apparent authority masked a submerged narrative of ideological dissent and resistance to the Griffithite centralising tendency. Indeed, Griffith and the National Council can be compared to Isaac Butt and the Home Government Association of the early 1860s. Just as Butt resisted the formation of a popular political organisation, the National Council tended to pose as an autonomous leadership clique, alienating the Fenian membership of the Cumann and the Inginidhe. Moreover, as Sinn Féin became more organisationally consolidated, the compromises this coalition required of radicalised home rulers and Fenians

---

[30] See Patricia Lavelle, *James O'Mara: A Staunch Sinn-Féiner 1873–1948* (Dublin, 1961).
[31] *Sinn Féin*, 29 Feb. 1908.
[32] Richard Davis, *Arthur Griffith and Non-violent Sinn Féin* (Dublin, 1974); Michael Laffan, *The Resurrection of Ireland* (Cambridge, 1999). Senia Pašeta, 'Nationalist Responses to Two Royal Visits to Ireland, 1900 and 1903' in *I.H.S.*, xxxi, no. 124 (Nov. 1999), pp 488–504.

became ever more problematic. As Tom Kettle put it, the policy faced the 'inertia of tradition'.[33]

Although the '98 centenary and the publication of the *United Irishman* increased the currency of advanced nationalist sentiment, the obverse of this was a defensiveness caused by constitutionalist absorption of some of their radical ideas. Just as the adoption by the Redmondites of the amnesty cry had removed some of its radical ambience, so too could the Irish Ireland agenda be made safe. Although ultimately regarding Griffith's Hungarian policy, which demanded Irish M.P.s withdraw from Westminster and establish an Irish government in emulation of the Hungarian nationalists of 1867, as unworkable, by emphasising the 'wise tolerance' of the Hungarian nationalist Kossuth, Tom Kettle configured the Hungarian policy as a possible means for constitutionalists and separatists to work together, thus fulfilling what he regarded as the conciliatory promise of the earliest issues of *United Irishman*.[34] Both the greatest strength and greatest weakness of the policy lay in this ideological flexibility. By the same token, a new generation of constitutional nationalist newspapers such as *Derry People and Donegal News*, first published on 20 September 1902, could effortlessly fuse constitutionalism with the cultural nationalist agenda. With a circulation of 5,500, chiefly in the city of Derry, the paper was judged by the police to be more radical than the *Derry Journal*, itself a supporter of the U.I.L., the Gaelic League, and the anti-recruiting campaign.[35] A remarkable early editorial historicised the reception of Irish Ireland ideas, indicating the narrowness of the ground conceded to the separatists.

> Irish nationality in its political aspect received a whole-hearted support while in its spiritual and material side it was treated with neglect. Irishmen worked hard and worked well for the restoration of their native parliament, but in their ardour and enthusiasm for that, they well nigh forgot the necessity that also existed for the development of their native industries, and the preservation of their language, and the distinctive traits and characteristics of their race and nation.
>
> A few years ago this was recognised – just in time to save our Celtic distinctiveness – and a new movement was inaugurated to do for the language, customs, and industries of Ireland what the Irish parliamentary party were doing for national self-government. At first it was looked on by many with suspicion and distrust. Irishmen, honest at heart, imagined that it was an attempt to interfere with the policy of the Irish party, and, where they did not stand entirely aloof, they approached it with hesitation and caution. At length, however, its true character, as a great national movement, came to be known, the spirit that it created got abroad in the land, and

---

[33] Tom Kettle, 'Would the Hungarian Policy Work' in *New Ireland Review*, xxii, no. 6 (Feb. 1905), p. 328.

[34] Ibid., pp 321–2.

[35] C.B.S. Box 22, 28166, 2 Feb. 1903; *Derry People and Donegal News*, 24 Jan. 1903.

today it is incontestably admitted that no man can rightly call himself a real home ruler who is not also a real Irish Irelander.[36]

This assimilation of supposedly radical ideas to the constitutionalist paradigm and the claim that they were essential to respectable nationalist politics provided both an opportunity and a challenge to the separatists. As Rooney grasped, they had to seek to expand the separatist constituency through the medium of Irish Ireland by arguing that this agenda could only be fulfilled through complete separation. The corollary of this was the need to maintain a posture of hyper vigilance, ever ready to expose the shortcomings of the constitutionalists and any conciliatory drift on the part of advanced nationalists. For example, the *United Irishman* was quick to condemn a Redmond speech for stating that the basis of an alliance between the Irish parliamentary party and the Liberals would have to rest on the following demands: the remedy of the defects of the Land Act and the Labourer's Act, legislation that would finally settle the Irish university question, and finally home rule. Home rule, it would seem, had become the party's fourth priority because it was clear the Liberals would not commit to it.[37] These tensions were thrown into sharp relief by the Hungarian policy, generating a disturbing debate concerning separatist strategy and ideals.

II

The new-found prominence of separatism at the turn of the century owed most to the leadership cadre associated with the *United Irishman*, the first national separatist newspaper since *The Irishman* ceased publication in 1885.[38] The *United Irishman* liberated separatist activity from the small-print columns adjacent to the agricultural news, unambiguously promoting the separatist case. In May 1902 John MacBride wrote that the newspaper 'at present supplies the place of organisers in Ireland, and is at least equal to a dozen'.[39] Moreover it provided advanced nationalism with a continual spectacle, allowing

---

[36] *Derry People and Donegal News*, 20 Sept. 1902.

[37] *U.I.*, 23 Sept. 1905.

[38] The directors variously were Griffith, O'Leary, Gonne, Thomas Kelly, Seumas MacManus, Henry Dixon, Walter Cole, and John O'Mahony. For Dublin Castle's assessment of the seditious content of *United Irishman* and its reluctance to seize issues, see appropriate file in C.O. 904/159; also, Victoria Glandon, *Arthur Griffith and the Advanced-Nationalist Press, 1900–1922* (New York, 1985), pp 17–19. Abuse of Queen Victoria attracted particular attention, prompting the seizure of 14 April and 1 September 1900 issues, though without 'forcible entry'. Of the latter, 200 copies were seized from Easons in Dublin, 214 from Griffith; elsewhere copies were seized in Belfast (150), Derry City (57), Limerick (52), and Ennis (25).

[39] MacBride to Devoy, 29 May 1902, *D.P.B. II*, pp 349–50.

those outside the Fenian networks it reinforced to passively engage with the machinations of the separatists. Griffith's journalism invited response, generating a series of symbiotically antagonistic relationships with other recently established nationalist periodicals: in particular, the Jesuit *New Ireland Review* and D. P. Moran's *Leader*, the former aspiring to reasoned commentary, the latter to caustic debunking.[40] Consequently, much of the interest of turn of the century separatism is to be found in the teratological study of these debates and the separatist elite. Nonetheless, all was not spectacle, and Fenianism continued to function beneath this journalistic carapace, in particular developing its relationship with the nascent labour movement through co-operation in local government. Below the Griffithite Dublin milieu and the Dublin–London–Paris adventuring of Yeats, Gonne, and MacBride, can be constructed a submerged narrative of locally orientated, grass-roots separatism.

In 1902 the police took great care to compile an accurate head count of the membership of Irish political organisations.[41] Although problematic, the figures are interesting for what they suggest about the geographical spread of Fenianism. Again there was the now familiar classification of nominal and active membership: the total was 20,317, the number in 'good standing' was 8,690. This was an increase of 1,000 members in 'good standing' since 1899, but an overall decrease of 5,000. It is tempting to see this as evidence that with the disintegration of the '98 movement the I.R.B. had tightened up its structure, removing some of the dead wood. Equally, it appears to be the case that the police took greater care in producing a more accurate count. The weakness of the formal structures of the I.R.B. in Dublin is striking; the active membership was put at 56 out of 114, with only nine circles. This vindicated Assistant Commissioner Mallon's earlier claim that he could put his hands on the entire Dublin membership.[42] Some time in early 1903 the police observed that the only secret society activity of any significance in Dublin was the Fenian section of the Cumann na nGaedhael; this included most of the members of the Wolfe Tone Committee, the Oliver Bond '98 Club, and the mysterious Red Hand Clubs, probably a remnant of the '98 organisations, possibly with a Belfast connexion.[43] The Cumann's membership was greater than that of any separatist organisation of recent years. But with no exact membership figures, it is hard to accept that the Cumann outnumbered the membership of the Fenian-influenced branches of the Dublin '98 organisation; this police claim might be interpreted as attesting to the earnestness and organisational effectiveness of the new organisation. The list of the Cumann's most prominent

[40] For Moran see Patrick Maume, *The Long Gestation* (Dublin, 1999), pp 59–63, and *idem*, *D. P. Moran* (Dundalk, 1995).
[41] C.B.S. Box 20, 26268.
[42] Cited in R. F. Foster, 'Thinking from Hand to Mouth: Anglo-Irish Literature, Gaelic Nationalism and Irish Politics in the 1890s' in *Paddy and Mr Punch* (London, 1993), p. 271.
[43] C.B.S. Box 22, 29274, n/d.

Fenian members is striking for its unfamiliarity. P. T. Daly, increasingly the most dominant Fenian in Dublin, figured, but the remaining names are unknown both to the Allan milieu and the propagandists surrounding Griffith.[44] Nonetheless, the Cumann had made its presence felt with its opposition to the U.I.L. and unionist candidates in local elections, notably when P. T. Daly was the successful National Council candidate for the Rotunda Ward in Dublin in September 1903.[45] In 1904, the year Sinn Féin first appeared as an organised Dublin corporation group, the Cumann successfully secured the election of Walter L. Cole, also on the National Council, against the U.I.L. candidate for the vacant aldermanship in Inns Quay Ward.

P. T. Daly, elected to the presidency of the Sinn Féin League, personified all that was most dynamic at an organisational level at this time. He was the official organiser of the Cumann, received a salary for his trouble, and was to establish a branch wherever twelve men would join.[46] He was equally involved in the Dublin labour movement – within which Daly's I.R.B. involvement was generally unknown, according to the reminiscences of the Dublin labour activist William O'Brien.[47] His name was a constant feature of the police reports of the period. He cropped up in Cork in October 1902 attempting to reconcile the divided city branch of the Y.I.S.; he was in close touch with a multi-aliased Clan na Gael emissary in January 1903; he was in Cavan in February meeting with Terence Fitzpatrick and five other I.R.B. members; in Armagh and Tyrone in March (where an informer claimed he promoted membership of the I.R.B. as a good way of getting work); and in April he met eleven prominent suspects in Glasgow. In Dungannon I.R.B. members formed the Emmet Centenary Club shortly after Daly had visited; it soon had eighty members. In June he attended the Irish Trades Congress at Newry as representative of the Typographical Provident Society; he was elected a member of the standing order committee and made delegate to the Scottish Congress to be held in October. He was heavily involved in the entertainment of John T. Keating of Chicago, Clan emissary. This included attending the Wolfe Tone anniversary at Bodenstown, which attracted a crowd of 4,000, and speaking at the Glasnevin Emmet centenary commemoration (a small affair).[48] In August

---

[44] They were J. Hanlon, J. Connor, P. J. Devlin, P. Ryan, J. W. Kenny, J. Berkley, L. Reddy, M. Quinn, O. Ryan, J. J. O'Brien, J. Snitch, J. Short, and M. Cusack jnr, presumably the son of the G.A.A. founder.

[45] C.B.S. Precis, Box 3, 3 Oct. 1903. Daly worked with the Labour and Trades Council interests.

[46] C.B.S. Precis, Box 3, 26 Nov. 1902.

[47] Edward MacLysaght (ed.), *Forth the Banners Go: Reminiscences of William O'Brien* (Dublin, 1969), pp 64–5.

[48] C.B.S. Precis, Box 3, 9 Oct. 1902, 16 Jan. 1903, 17 Apr. 1903, 1 May 1903, 13 June 1903, 7 July 1903, 31 July 1903. Dublin Castle wrote, 'the Irish Republican Brotherhood has been greatly strengthened and reorganised about Belfast and the adjoining counties by the exertions of P. T. Daly, who stated lately that "the I.R.B. was now stronger than in the days of James Stephens".'

1904 an informer reported that Daly, with Mark Ryan and P. N. Fitzgerald, was working in the interest of the Hungarian policy.[49] Until this point, Daly's work had been seen by the police as being in the interest of the I.R.B., and to a great extent it was. Cumann na nGaedhael was an I.R.B. front organisation and in 1907 Daly was reputedly elected to the presidency of the Supreme Council.[50]

Outside of Dublin the I.R.B. had pockets of isolated strength, suggesting strong regional tendencies. A glance at the U.I.L. figures for early 1903 (1,150 branches, nominal membership 121,443, active membership 84,335) puts the following discussion into context. In Cavan the ongoing squabble with the Ancient Order of Hibernians[51] maintained the Fenian dynamic, the police figures indicating that Cavan remained Fenianism's most active county. Of 1,630 members, 1,120 were active. The A.O.H. boasted respective figures of 520 and 440. In Clare, the location of William Redmond's constituency, there was an active cohort of 894 out of 1,100. In Longford, a county identified as particularly active in the 1890s, 450 of 650 members were active. Conversely, in a number of counties notorious for their Fenianism, the raw figures suggest unexpected conclusions. Limerick boasted a nominal membership of 2,852, the highest of any county, but an active membership of only 277. This put it on a par with Londonderry, 250 (300), and Meath 200 (605), and strongly suggests that the influence of John Daly and his gang made I.R.B. membership a social imperative. Similarly, in Roscommon, notable for its Parnellite pockets in the 1890s,[52] the nominal membership was an impressive 1,241, but the activists totalled a meagre 190. On the whole, the Fenians were concentrated in particular regions. The eastern counties of Queen's (later Laois), Kilkenny, Wexford, and Wicklow boasted 2,000 active members, squeezing Carlow and Kildare with their total of 60. Relatively high levels of membership were evident in the north east, with a total activist cohort of 2,650 in Counties Longford, Cavan, Monaghan, Armagh, Meath, and Louth. It is striking that the small but relatively densely populated and impoverished County Louth (it included the towns of Dundalk and Drogheda), had 580 active Fenians. Louth was highly urbanised and the branch of the Y.I.S. with 320 active members suggested a lively urban associational culture. The large western counties of Galway and Clare had 1,294 activists, but it is unclear whether they were concentrated in particular areas. Given the MacBride presence in Westport and its history of agrarian activism, it is surprising that the activist count in Mayo was only 40. Possibly the poverty of the county discouraged membership

---

[49] Ibid., 15 Oct. 1904.
[50] Davis, *Non-violent Sinn Féin*, pp 32–3.
[51] See following chapter for discussion.
[52] Paul Bew, *Conflict and Conciliation in Ireland 1890–1910: Parnellites and Radical Agrarians* (Oxford, 1987), p. 34, mentions the involvement of Parnellites in the De Freyne estate agitation of 1895. My thanks to David Anderson for alerting me to Roscommon Parnellism.

of the I.R.B., while it is likely that the MacBride connexion enforced a more rigorous assessment of who should be designated an I.R.B. member. With MacBride in close connexion with the national leadership, those who did come under his immediate influence must have appeared irrelevant; the presence of a national figure throwing into sharp relief the marginalism of the local membership.

Sligo was equally curious. Michael Farry has suggested that the virulent anti-Treatyism of the Sligo I.R.A. during the civil war can be best understood by close attention to short-term causes: most particularly, the readiness of the I.R.A. to fill the power vacuum created by the withdrawal of the British and the desire to atone for its inactivity during the Anglo-Irish war.[53] That Sligo was not habitually a centre of republican radicalism is borne out by these figures: Sligo, with Kerry, Waterford, and the Tipperary south riding appeared to boast no I.R.B. activists, although Kerry and the Tipperary south riding both had branches of the Y.I.S. with a respective active membership of 97 and 60. Later reports characterised the ageing membership of the Young Ireland Societies of Castleisland, Listowel, and Tralee as the last redoubt of the Kerry I.R.B.,[54] despite Maurice Moynihan's high profile as a speech maker.

The situation looked little brighter in the first quarter of 1903.[55] The regional variation was still evident. In Wicklow separatist organisation remained effective. The Father Murphy '98 committee looked forward to spending £450 on a statue in time for an unveiling on or around 9 June, the anniversary of the 'battle' of Arklow. Political discussion was dominated by chief secretary George Wyndham's expected land bill to extend the provision for tenant purchase; the I.R.B. remained the dominant force in the very active local G.A.A.; and ten Gaelic League classes were regularly held throughout the county – an impressive 130 people attended one class in Bray. In the north riding of Tipperary the I.R.B. remained relevant through its support for the U.I.L.'s campaign against the eleven months grazing system, and in Thurles it controlled a number of very active branches of the Gaelic League. Things looked a little more positive in Cork, where Gonne and MacBride subsidised a branch of the Inghinidhe na hÉireann and the Cork Literary Society, a breakaway section of the Cork Y.I.S. Spiritual guidance in Cork was provided by the austere and unpredictable Terence MacSwiney. Later a reluctant chair, he was prone to withdraw from organisations that failed to adhere to the high standards he set. More extreme than the Y.I.S., the Cork Literary Society had proved impregnable to informers. The Y.I.S. itself was largely inactive, but looking to spend £1,000 through the National Monuments Fund – it needed more money and hoped to unveil a '98 monument in time for the king's

---

[53] Michael Farry, *The Aftermath of Revolution: Sligo 1921–23* (Dublin, 2000), pp 14–16, 50–74.

[54] C.B.S. Box 11, 28288, 1 Mar. 1903.

[55] Ibid.

expected visit. In February 1903 Dublin Castle summarised these patterns of political sentiment in a manner that perhaps relied more on cliché than judgement:

> Politics in the north largely resolve into pounds, shillings and pence, and it is chiefly in the west that the sentimental idea takes any hold; and although there are a good many I.R.B. men in the north, chiefly in Co. Armagh, Monaghan and Louth, it is in Connaught and the midland counties adjoining it that the I.R.B. organisers meet with most success.[56]

Advanced nationalists had, however, become more visible following the passage of the 1898 Local Government Act. It was immediately grasped as a development of great significance by the I.R.B., who put up numerous candidates for the first election held under its terms. The bulk of these candidates identified with the labour interest, although it is likely that their separatist proclivities were known – the Dublin Trades Council had established a Labour Electoral Association in response to the act.[57] Overall the act resolved the paradox at the heart of Irish political representation: unionists would no longer dominate local government in constituencies with a nationalist M.P. Andrew Gailey has shown how the passage of the act was motivated less by a desire to placate nationalist Ireland than by a need to rationalise certain financial mechanisms and a unionist obligation to achieve constitutional consistency throughout the United Kingdom.[58] The first election held under its terms was shaped by the relative weakness of the Irish parliamentary party. With the Irish National League and the Irish National Federation in a state of virtual collapse and the United Irish League not yet fully integrated into mainstream constitutional politics, the field was laid open to an unexpectedly wide range of political influences. Given the local nature of the contests the presence of known separatists would be expected; the disarray of the I.P.P. allowed their profusion in 1899.

Electoral results immediately registered the impact of the act. Before the passage of the act, unionists filled 704 grand jury places, while only 47 were occupied by nationalists. From March 1899 nationalists held 774 county council seats which accounted for 75 per cent of the total and compared to the unionist tally of 265, most of which were in Ulster.[59] Yet these figures hardly do justice to the dramatic increase in local autonomy that the act represented. The main effect of the act was to sweep away the fiscal powers of the grand juries, transferring their authority to newly constituted county councils, rural district councils, urban district councils, and boards of guardians. These were

[56] C.B.S. Precis, Box 3, 3 Feb. 1903.
[57] MacLysaght, *Forth the Banners Go*, p. 30.
[58] Andrew Gailey, *Ireland and the Death of Kindness: The Experience of Constructive Unionism 1890–1905* (Cork, 1987), pp 40–50.
[59] Virginia Crossman, *Local Government in Nineteenth-century Ireland* (Belfast, 1994), p. 96.

under the supervision of the local government board. The elections took place on the basis of the parliamentary franchise, with the addition of women and peers. Furthermore, women were eligible to stand for election in all but the county councils,[60] which were the sole rating authority and were responsible for approving expenditure by the rural district councils. With the abolition of separate elections of poor law guardians, rural district councils became responsible for the administration of the poor law.[61] Among the tasks the new councils inherited from the grand juries was the construction and repair of county institutions such as the court house, prison, and infirmary as well as the main roads and important bridges.

Virginia Crossman suggests that the police reports of these first elections 'left little doubt that the elections would in most cases be a simple contest between nationalists/tenants and unionists/landlords'.[62] Although broadly the case, these elections had hidden complexities, that allowed for the representation of a wide range of Irish nationalist interests and gave an enormous boost to labour interests. One police summary of the results identified the successful candidates as nationalist or labour.[63] The nationalists were sub-divided into unionists, Dillonites, Redmondites, Healyites, neutrals, and undefined. 'Labour' was sub-divided into candidates representing constitutional and separatist nationalists, unionists, and the, rather Delphic, non-nationalists. A comparison between the figures for 1898 and 1899 reveals the full extent of the expansion in representation facilitated by the new act. In 1898 only Ulster had any labour unionist representation, comprising eight councillors; Ulster also boasted the only labour councillor aligned with neither the nationalists nor the unionists. There were three labour nationalists in Munster and three in Dublin. In 1899 the overall labour representation had increased to 303 and was a feature of the new local politics in each of the provinces and Dublin. Of these representatives, 218 were 'nationalist', that is, were affiliated to one of the factions of the I.P.P., and fifty-six were 'extremist', in other words had an association with the I.R.B.[64] The unionist labour representation was also increased, with small showings in each of the provinces (Ulster 14, Munster 4, Leinster 2, Connaught 1), but none in Dublin.

---

[60] R. Barry O'Brien, *Dublin Castle and the Irish People* (2nd ed., London, 1912), pp 183–4.
[61] Crossman, *Local Government*, p. 93.
[62] Ibid., p. 95.
[63] C.B.S. 1899, Box 15, *Summary of County, Borough and Urban District Council elections January 1899 contrasted with number of previous bodies.*
[64] These figures represent a conservative description of the election outcome. A Dublin Castle attempt of January 1899 compiled from that month's reports stated that in Cavan, Louth, Monaghan, and Sligo the I.R.B. comprised 66 of the 168 district councillors; in the remainder of the northern counties they held fourteen seats. In the midland and western counties they garnered 133 of 520 seats, while in the south they were judged similarly successful but no figures were given. Again their success was attributed to the labour vote. C.B.S. Precis, Box 2, 22 Feb. 1899.

The enfranchisement of the labour vote reduced the comparative representation of each of the conventional nationalist parties, except in Ulster where there was a small increase owing to the loss of 53 unionist seats.[65] Notably, the Dillonites lost 80 seats in Munster, to the benefit of the 'Extremists', who gained 36 seats and the labour nationalists 114. In Dublin, the twenty seats lost by the unionists were shared predominantly between the labour nationalists, who gained nine, and the Redmondites, who gained eight.

The police division of the nationalist vote into labour and nationalist was significant and stemmed from two basic insights. First, labour was regarded as operating independently, or semi-independently, of the I.P.P., and second, labour politicians often worked in tandem with the I.R.B. Labour politics were based on the labour and trades organisations established in many towns. Although these organisations did not necessarily form an opposition to the Irish Independent League, I.N.F., and U.I.L., they nonetheless had an independent existence not reliant on the patronage and prestige of the local nationalist M.P. Labour in this context referred to working-class candidates who articulated their political interests as opposed to those of the wealthier members of the community who traditionally directed local affairs. In Cork after 1899 there were incidences of the property-owning classes, unionist or nationalist, co-operating against the labour interest.[66] On balance, labour candidates represented the little man against the big, rather than socialism against capitalism. Their reformist agenda reflected trade union demands across the United Kingdom: fair conditions and wages, with only, preferably local, trade union members employed on public contracts.[67] The I.R.B. was quick to capitalise on the emergence of labour as a separate electoral identity. Reports suggested that 15 per cent of members elected to the Longford, Ballymahon, and Granard district council belonged to the I.R.B.[68] For the Granard district council, County Longford, sixteen of the twenty-three nominees were identified as I.R.B. suspects. They worked with the labour interest in a coalition against the 'monied class' in the county.[69] Their most prominent opponent was the catholic bishop Dr Hoare.[70] I.R.B. county centre Thomas Fenlon was

---

[65] The unionist tally overall was not disastrous. In Ulster they were reduced from 400 to 347, in Munster from 70 to 30, in Leinster from 76 to 59, in Connaught from 23 to 18, and in Dublin from 89 to 69.

[66] Ian d'Alton, 'Southern Irish Unionism: A Study of Cork City and County Unionists, 1885–1914' (M.A. thesis, University College Cork, 1972), pp 181–2.

[67] Joseph V. O'Brien, *'Dear Dirty Dublin': A City in Distress, 1899–1916* (Los Angeles, 1982), p. 78.

[68] Return of Local Government Elections 1899 (C.O. 904/184/1), p. 27.

[69] C.B.S. Precis, Box 2, 20 Jan. 1899, 3 Feb. 1899.

[70] C.B.S. 1899, Box 15, 18168. Numerous condemnations of secret societies by R.C. priests are collected in C.B.S. 1899, Box 16, 20400, 7 Nov. 1899. The majority were from the northern counties.

elected for Edgeworthstown on the labour ticket.[71] He joined a further four I.R.B. suspects on the county council, alongside five Redmondites, two Dillonites, and four unaligned councillors. Tellingly, the I.R.B. councillors are sub-divided as two Redmondites and three Dillonites. The under-secretary was right to comment that the various electoral addresses were 'quite innocuous'.[72] In County Meath the I.R.B. put forward fifteen candidates for the Navan urban district council. Their reported strategy was to advocate labour views as a means to counteract the clergy's likely opposition to their campaign.[73] In the local government context, the I.R.B. designation appeared to have been broadly synonymous with parochial anti-establishment sentiment.

In grouping the various I.P.P. factions under one heading the police recognised the increasing co-operation between Parnellites and anti-Parnellites. In Armagh Parnellites refused to attend meetings presided over by the catholic clergy but promised to support nationalist candidates against the unionist opposition. In County Monaghan there was more overt co-operation, including with the I.R.B., which nominated six candidates to represent it on Clones town council and nine in Monaghan itself.[74]

A further measure of the influence of advanced nationalists in this election lay in the number subsequently elected to chair their urban district councils. This was the case in Clonakilty, Skibbereen, and Bantry in County Cork; Thurles, Templemore, Tipperary, and Nenagh in County Tipperary; Listowel in County Kerry; Ennis and Kilrush in County Clare; Naas and Athy in County Kildare; Clones and Monaghan in County Monaghan; Loughrea in County Galway; Castlebar in County Mayo; Tullamore in King's County; Dundalk in County Louth; Cootehill in County Cavan; and Waterford, Kilkenny, and Wexford.[75] Of these twenty-two, twelve were sworn in as magistrates, in direct contravention of the law. The chairs L. C. Strange, P. J. O'Keeffe, and John Daly were also respectively mayors of Waterford, Kilkenny, and Limerick.[76] In Dublin labour candidates led the poll in three wards, depriving Harrington, Nannetti, and the late lord mayor, Daniel Tallon of aldermanic honours. Labour failed to extend its representation with the enlargement of the council in 1901, but the successful passage of resolutions by the Dublin Trades Council indicated co-operation between mainstream nationalists and the labour interest. Given previous controversies, it is not surprising that labour councillors distrusted Harrington.[77]

---

[71] Ibid., Box 15, 19079, 18257.

[72] Ibid., 19073.

[73] C.B.S. Precis, Box 2, 20 Jan. 1899, 3 Feb. 1899.

[74] C.B.S. 1899, Box 15, 18168.

[75] Gosselin was surprised that only one I.R.B. candidate was identified among the nominees in the four rural electoral divisions of County Wexford. C.B.S. Precis, Box 2, 22 Mar. 1899.

[76] C.B.S. 1899, Box 16, 19203.

[77] O'Brien, 'Dear Dirty Dublin', pp 78–84.

With the advent of nationalist majorities, the various council bodies provided a new venue for the expression of nationalist sentiment, often of a fairly advanced hue. This was particularly the case during the Boer War, when the Irish Transvaal Committee lobbied council members and provided draft resolutions. Mildly subversive gestures included Cork county council deciding in November 1899 to fly a green flag from the court house when the council was in session. According to one speaker, 'A glimpse of the old green flag would do more to stir the people than all the speeches and resolutions of the last 100 years.'[78] Pro-Boer resolutions were passed by county councils in King's County, Counties Limerick, Kilkenny, Cork, Mayo, and Sligo and by approximately thirty other official bodies.[79] When John Clancy proposed a pro-Boer resolution to Dublin city council, the lord mayor responded, 'the present war in South Africa is a war of wanton and unprovoked aggression (cheers from the gallery).'[80] To Mayo county council P. O'Donnell proposed a motion trusting 'that as Babylon fell and as Rome fell, so also must fall the race and nation whose creed is the creed of greed, and whose God is the god of Mammon.' Similar motions were put to Mullingar rural district council[81] and Castlebar urban council, the latter proposed by James Daly, J.P.[82] Castlerea district council declared itself a catholic and nationalist body that disapproved of any attempts by the people of Ireland to celebrate the succession of Edward VII, especially given the blasphemy of the coronation oath.[83] Waterford county council voted to hoist a black flag over its offices in coronation week, 'as a protest against the continued misgovernment of our country'.[84]

Rebellious posturing, however, could not disguise the limited leverage the I.R.B. had over the patronage in the power of the councils. This was amply demonstrated by its failure to acquire a position for the recently released Dynamitard and future 1916 signatory Tom Clarke. From March 1899 Clarke, in the care of his future father-in-law John Daly, sought election to a salaried public position. According to the police, Daly was impressed by Clarke's straightforward attitude towards the dynamite conspiracy – he had not attempted to deny his culpability in court – and hoped to use Clarke to ingratiate himself with Dublin Fenianism.[85] Initial approaches were made to Mackay regarding a job in London, but when this failed Clarke focused on the vacant clerkship to the Rathdown union. He worked to promote himself, lecturing in Dublin on his prison experiences while the I.R.B. held meetings in support

---

[78] C.B.S. Box 15, 20561; *Cork Examiner*, 24 Nov. 1899.
[79] Inspector-general's report on 'Effect of the War Excitement and Pro Boer Agitation on Irish Nationalist Organisation', 6 Jan. 1900, in Balfour Papers, T.N.A. (P.R.O.), 30/60/28.
[80] C.B.S. Box 15, 20684; *Nation*, 12 Dec. 1899. The meeting was inquorate.
[81] C.B.S. Box 15, 20754; *Westmeath Guardian*, 15 Dec. 1899.
[82] C.B.S. Box 17, 23235; *F.J.*, 7 Nov. 1900.
[83] C.B.S. Box 21, 27502; *Roscommon Herald*, 16 Aug. 1902.
[84] C.B.S. Box 21, 27241; *Waterford News*, 27 June 1902. 11 J.P.s assented.
[85] C.B.S. Precis, Box 2, 13 Apr. 1899.

of his candidature, including one in Bray on 18 May.[86] Unelected, Clarke returned to Limerick where Daly attempted to shoehorn him into a local position; he was opposed by the labour interest on the council who objected to having a stranger foisted upon them.[87] This despite both Daly's support of the candidature of thirty-four labour representatives in the elections – twenty-four were elected – and the council's conferral of the freedom of the city on Clarke in January.[88] On 27 September 1899 Clarke left for America.[89] The following year he was tempted back to Ireland with the promise of his likely election by Dublin city council to the position of superintendent of the abattoir. He left New York on 15 September 1900, arrived in Limerick on 6 October and discovered he has not been elected, despite Gonne's efforts to secure him the position. Enraged, Clarke allegedly pledged to stop the flow of cash to Ireland for political purposes, and sailed for Boston on 10 October.[90]

Sinn Féin had great hopes for local government. Griffith argued that owing to its political and budgetary autonomy Irish local government provided a legitimate means through which to pursue their programme. By purchasing Irish products, local government could be used to nurture Irish industries. To this end, the National Council was constitutionally bound to nationalise the local representatives of the country.[91] John Sweetman argued in 1907:

> as Mr Gladstone's Land Act of 1871 first gave hope to the farmers, and enabled them to combine, so the local councils have given hope to us Irishmen, and shown that it is possible to work ourselves for the creation of a prosperous nation; one way being by our local councils buying only Irish manufactured goods.[92]

A modicum of success was evident by 1904 when a Sinn Féin grouping was formed in the Dublin corporation. Working with labour councillors, Sinn Féin had consolidated by 1906 into the main opposition force under the leadership of the fruit merchant Walter Cole. The labour–advanced nationalist coalition was co-ordinated by Alderman Thomas Kelly, the Sinn Féiner and secretary of the Workmen's Hall, York Street.[93]

---

[86] Ibid., 8 June 1899.
[87] Ibid., 24 Aug. 1899.
[88] C.B.S. 1899, Box 15, 18261; C.B.S. Precis, Box 2, 22 Feb. 1899.
[89] C.B.S. Precis, Box 2, 6 Oct. 1899.
[90] C.B.S. Precis, Box 3, 3 Oct. 1900, 16 Oct. 1900.
[91] U.I., 8 Aug. 1903
[92] John Sweetman, 'The New Spirit' in *New Ireland Review*, vol. xxvii, no. 4 (June 1907), pp 224–5. The annual report of the Local Government Board for 1902 reported that, 'Attention has been directed to certain political differences which have been introduced by some of the smaller bodies into their ordinary business transactions with reference to the appointment of officers and the giving of contracts; but it is only fair to state that these cases have been quite the exception, and not the rule.' Quoted in R. Barry O'Brien, *Dublin Castle and the Irish People*, p. 187.
[93] O'Brien, '*Dear, Dirty Dublin*', pp 89–90; Maume, *Long Gestation*, pp 58, 224.

Ultimately, local government did not provide the means to disturb the U.I.L. and home rule party dominance. The vacuum briefly opened up by the discombobulation of the I.P.P. allowed members of the I.R.B. to be elected to positions reflecting their local influence. And in the un-programmatic localism of the 1899 Irish local government elections there was something engagingly democratic and pre-political. After 1899 the U.I.L. dominated local elections.[94] Nonetheless, although these elections demonstrated the existence of a section of the electorate aligned with labour and/or the I.R.B., they do not provide conclusive evidence of a democratic dividend awaiting the separatists. Moreover, Ian d'Alton has found that over the longer term the labour representatives in Cork tended to align with the U.I.L.,[95] disturbing any easy assumption of cohabitation between labour, Parnellism, and the I.R.B.

In Dublin, labour representation was reduced from eight councillors in 1899 to two by January 1912. Under the direction of John T. Kelly (Sean T. O Ceallaigh, future president of the Irish republic) Sinn Féin peaked with twelve members in 1910, but was reduced to four by 1913.[96] During the mayoralty of Nannetti, and at the height of Sinn Féin's influence, Dublin corporation decided in September 1907 against adopting Sinn Féin principles by 31 to 14. Those 1899 councils were the Indian summer of a particularly ineffective form of Fenianism, '67's last hurrah.

III

The involvement of separatists in local government elections was not alone in being characterised by the absence of a centralised campaign – to a great extent this was the case too with the constitutionalist groupings. The separatists also lacked a single national voice, whether newspaper or leader, to give expression to a general advanced nationalist platform. Despite the developments in separatist thinking, despite the extensive '98 organisation, Irish separatist organisation remained fragmentary and scattered. Arthur Griffith was not the only observer to recognise this problem, and although possessed of determination and journalistic ability of a high order, he did not return from South Africa in late 1898 with a clear blueprint for action.[97] Nonetheless, the publication of the *United Irishman* was immediately recognised by the I.R.B. as an important development and Griffith's circular promoting the newspaper initially relied for its distribution on well-established Fenian networks. This was evident at the 1899 pilgrimage to Tone's grave

---

[94] Detailed local work would need to be done to determine how far the U.I.L. absorbed or replaced dissident elements.
[95] d'Alton, 'Southern Irish Unionism', pp 186, 189.
[96] O'Brien, *'Dear, Dirty Dublin'*, pp 89–91. Kelly lost four bids for the mayoralty.
[97] Griffith was in South Africa from early 1897.

at Bodenstown. At the height of the centenary celebrations in 1898, it had attracted an exceptional 10,000 pilgrims. In 1899 the momentum was main-tained, with 8,000 making the journey, including 4,000 from Dublin and fourteen bands.[98] The event had all the trappings of a conventional Fenian muster. P. N. Fitzgerald introduced Maurice Moynihan of Tralee as orator and the communicants took away small pieces of ivy from the wall over Tone's grave. Among the crowd was Dublin suspect Michael J. Quinn and 'a young man named Griffin [sic] who has recently returned from South Africa'. They were distributing copies of the United Irishman, named by Moynihan as the only paper every Irishman should read. He also advised they set up associations that would bide their time until an opportunity arose.[99] Moynihan's ambiguous words were suggestive of non-clandestine separatist organisations such as the Y.I.S. and the '98 associations. Also circulating were James Connolly and Daniel O'Brien of the Irish Socialist Republican League. Moynihan's embrace of the United Irishman did not generate goodwill on all fronts. Allan's crowd ensured that O'Brien went home with a black eye in recompense for the Worker's Republic criticism of Allan's alleged toast to the Queen. Allan denied making the toast.[100] In London, the United Irishman was adopted by the Irish National Club at a meeting presided over by Mark Ryan.[101] The club, 'the foster-parent of . . . Cumann na nGaedheal and Sinn Féin', was the latest in a long line of advanced nationalist groups based at Ryan's Chancery Lane medical practice.[102] Meanwhile, in September 1899 P. J. Hoctor was actively promoting the United Irishman in Limerick, Thurles, Nenagh, Templemore, and Roscrea, only to find his business rival James Butler in hot pursuit brandishing copies of the Irish People.[103]

In November 1900 John Daly, lecturing on the I.R.B. to the Y.I.S. in Limerick, echoed Moynihan's Bodenstown oration. Although maintaining that the I.R.B. must remain in readiness should an opportune insurrectionary moment arise, Daly recognised the centrality of the Irish Ireland dynamic to the current phase of Irish separatism:

> When [I] stepped into the ranks in 1863, it was not then a movement to educate the people as their movement was now, but it was an effort to close up the ranks and be prepared to await the opportunity which was then believed to be near at hand. The idea was to suffer in an effort to free Ireland, and not to make capital out of the failings of a nation as the parliamentarians were doing at the present day.[104]

[98] C.B.S. Box 16, 19572, 10 July 1899.
[99] Ibid. For the unambiguous separatism of early U.I., see Glandon, Arthur Griffith, pp 14–16.
[100] Workers Republic, 1 July 1899.
[101] C.B.S. Box 16, 19492, 26 June 1899. The police noted in July 1900 that the U.I. could be bought at Eason's, Dublin's leading newsagent. C.B.S. Box 17, 22234, 16 July 1900.
[102] Mark Ryan, Fenian Memories (Dublin, 1945), pp 190–194.
[103] C.B.S. Precis, Box 2, 6 Oct. 1899.
[104] C.B.S. Box 18, 23337; Limerick Echo, 17 Nov. 1900.

Notwithstanding this apparent openness to new ideas, older Fenians found it difficult to stay abreast of developments; and however genuine their openness to the Irish Ireland agenda, their gradual marginalisation was inevitable. Inspector Waters commented on this tendency in Cork: 'The old Fenians . . . distrust the younger sections; and the latter affect to despise the older men as effete and past their work.'[105] Shortly afterwards an attempt to extend the operations of the Cork Y.I.S. westwards failed because 'the old Fenians there fight shy of the theories of the younger enthusiasts and openly declare that the present is not the time for conceiving plans for a physical force movement.'[106]

Despite these caveats, it was the evolution of a more flexible separatist mentality that allowed the Irish Transvaal Committee to flourish. In October 1899 the committee first assembled in the rooms of the Celtic Literary Society at 32 Lower Abbey Street.[107] It was the progeny of the C.L.S. and the I.N.A. Maud Gonne took the chair, and among those present were Griffith, Rooney, G. A. Lyons, Frank Dorr, and Alice Milligan. According to a brusque D.M.P. assessment the committee was comprised of 'Fenians of the worst type'.[108] These 'Fenians' had recently organised the successful pro-Boer public demonstration at Beresford Place at which, according to the *Daily Nation*, 20,000 people attended.[109] In addition to Gonne, John O'Leary, T. D. Sullivan M.P., Michael Davitt M.P., Patrick O'Brien M.P., W. B. Yeats, John Plunkett, town councillor for Bray, and Lambert, members of the Old Guard Benevolent Union and fifty Gaels attended. The meeting was informed that MacBride had raised one hundred Irishmen, including sixty from Dublin, to fight for Kruger. C. G. Doran, a good metaphor always to hand, proclaimed, 'England was like an octopus. Kruger was going to lop off one of its arms, and they all fervently hoped that Ireland would knock another off before long.' At another October demonstration pictures of Kruger and General Joubert were displayed by limelight at the *Independent* offices and M. A. Manning gave a speech.[110] Although a few stones were thrown, the police prevented clashes between the crowd and around fifty Trinity College students.[111]

---

[105] C.B.S. Precis, Box 3, 21 Feb. 1901.

[106] C.B.S. Precis, Box 3, 17 May 1901. A branch of the Y.I.S. was formed in Skibbereen in August.

[107] *Daily Nation*, 11 Oct. 1899.

[108] C.B.S. Box 16, 20142, 16 Oct. 1899. Gonne's wealth was important to the movement. Prior to the Bereford Place meeting she financed the printing of 2,000 leaflets and a number anti-recruiting posters (apparently 1,500). They were printed by Bernand Doyle, printer of the *United Irishman* and editor and printer of *Irish Worker*.

[109] *Daily Nation*, 2 Oct. 1899.

[110] C.B.S. Box 16, 20299; *D.I.*, 20 Oct. 1899.

[111] The *Daily Nation*, 20 Oct. 1899, claimed a crowd of 10,000 with a complement of 200 police.

Manipulation of the press played as significant a role in the anti-recruiting campaign as it had in earlier separatist causes. The *Freeman's Journal* in October 1900 recorded an important Irish Transvaal Committee meeting at which it was resolved to present President Kruger with an address on his arrival in Europe and to ask the Dublin corporation to confer the freedom of the city on the President. The address was to be printed in Irish, Dutch, French, and English. Present at the meeting were O'Leary, Egan, Hoctor, O'Leary Curtis, O'Beirne, Quinn, White, Rooney, Griffith, Gonne, Johnston, and Yeats. The Cork Y.I.S. was also a signatory.[112] Sergeant Robert Montgomery reported that the meeting was concocted by Gonne, Johnston, and Yeats, who were all staying at J. W. O'Beirne's Derrydawn Hotel, Lower Mount Street, Dublin.[113] Clearly, it was acceptable for the names of the campaign leadership to be so used. This incident underlines the importance the separatists attached to creating an impression of great activity. The presentation of addresses, the passing of resolutions by councils, and the reporting of meetings all contributed towards the impression of fevered, committed activity. This was the *raison d'être* of the emergent leadership. As an exhausted Griffith told John O'Leary, 'Though I loathe and hate writing, I kept firing away because I believe it is only by dogged insistence on obvious truths we can get the hypnotised Irish sometime or other to realise them and make an effort to prevent their extinction.'[114]

Pro-Boer and anti-recruiting sentiment permeated all levels of the separatist debate. In February 1900 Henry McAteer of the Irish Transvaal Committee travelled throughout the south of Ireland, semi-clandestinely distributing 20,000 leaflets in towns where there were military stations and recruitment centres.[115] He appeared in Queen's County and Counties Wexford, Carlow, Clare, Kildare, Cork, Wicklow, the northern reaches of County Tipperary, and in the towns and cities of Waterford, New Ross, Ennis, Clonmel, Limerick, and Tralee.[116] Advantage was taken of reliable I.R.B. members: a thousand leaflets were forwarded to C. J. O'Farrell in Enniscorthy in November 1900, while McAteer came into direct contact with M. J. Furlong in Wexford, a stationer who sold the *United Irishman*. In New Ross pro-Boer leaflets were distributed by three well-placed I.R.B. members: Joseph Roche kept a stationer's shop, Patrick Dinn was a publican, and John Rand was connected

---

[112] *F.J.*, 22 October 1900; *Cork Herald*, 26 October 1900.
[113] C.B.S. Box 18, 23126.
[114] Quoted in Leon Broin, *Revolutionary Underground: The Story of the Irish Republican Brotherhood 1858–1924* (Dublin, 1976), p. 117.
[115] Arrangements were made at a meeting of the Irish Transvaal Committee on 13 February 1900. See Minute Book of the Irish Transvaal Committee (N.L.I., MS 19933).
[116] C.B.S. Box 17, 21334, 24 Feb. 1900; Box 18, 23178, 18 Feb. 1900; Terence Denman, '"The Red Livery of Shame': The Campaign Against Army Recruitment in Ireland, 1899–1914' in *I.H.S.*, xxix, no. 114 (Nov. 1994), p. 213.

to the Commercial Club.[117] There is further evidence of the Irish Transvaal Committee distributing anti-recruiting literature at U.I.L. meetings.[118] An inspector in Gorey worried that the propaganda was proving effective, 'especially at a time when the nationalist portion of the people are excited, and their feelings more or less embittered, by the holding of the '98 demonstration, and the erection of '98 centenary memorials in their midst'. Although he was particularly concerned about the influence of Father Kavanagh who maintained the high profile he had established during the '98 celebrations through the anti-enlistment campaign, overall police observers were unimpressed with the efficacy of the campaign.[119]

Kavanagh mixed a heady cocktail of nationalism and religion, uncompromisingly declaring at the unveiling of a memorial to '98 priest-leader Father Murphy in the Cork east riding: 'But if there be an Irishman who neither fears God nor loves Ireland let him join the British army; his country will be well rid of him.'[120] Yet Kavanagh's reputation was hard to sustain. It collapsed in January 1902 when, as its president, he addressed the Limerick Y.I.S. Not only did he ridicule adherents of physical force, he exacerbated the insult by insisting that the U.I.L. was the only body that could expect to achieve anything for Ireland. His repudiation of physical force might have been tolerated, but in a city where separatist passions ran high, the priest's endorsement of the U.I.L. was unforgivable. Facing expulsion, Kavanagh resigned the presidency.[121]

From the separatist perspective a more convincing contribution to the anti-recruiting campaign was the leaflet reproducing a speech by MacBride's cousin Father Peter Yorke, originally printed in the *San Francisco Nation*, 31 March 1900.[122] Ostensibly a eulogy of Emmet on the anniversary of his birth, the speech, delivered under the auspices of the Knights of the Red Branch, articulated a sophisticated analysis of the Boer War and the effects of imperialism.[123] Yorke posited an increasingly familiar Herderian analysis of national culture that saw the innumerable civilisations of the world as products of the innumerable peoples of the world.[124] Imperialism involved the attempt to suppress the national culture of the colonised, creating a situation at odds with the natural order.

---

[117] C.B.S. Box 18, 23185, c. Nov. 1900.

[118] C.B.S. Box 18, 23303, 15 Nov. 1900.

[119] Denman, '"The Red Livery of Shame"', pp 213–14, 216. The government's decision to allow the Irish regiments to wear the shamrock for St Patrick's Day in 1900 had a pleasing effect on Irish opinion according to the county inspectors.

[120] C.B.S. Box 18, 23141, 22 Oct. 1900.

[121] C.B.S. Precis, Box 3, 20 Jan. 1902.

[122] There is a biography: J. S. Bruscher, *Consecrated Thunderbolt: Father Yorke of San Francisco* (Hawthorne, N. J., 1973).

[123] A copy of the pamphlet is preserved in C.B.S. Box 17, 22441, 29 July 1900. Hereafter Yorke.

[124] Yorke, p. 4.

Imperialism I take to mean that system of government which extends over a large area and which tries to make all the people who live in that area common subjects of a common government. Nationality I take to mean that state of things by which groups of individuals will be permitted to retain their ancient characteristics, to carry out their old ways and to work out their salvation according to the lines on which they have been accustomed to move. . . . the worst government a country could give itself would be better than the best government that could be given to it by any foreign power.[125]

Following some anodyne remarks concerning the indestructible nature of national spirit, Yorke considered the factors that make a nation. He identified clear geographical parameters, a shared language, a government that 'springs' from the people, and an ill-defined conception of race.[126] As Rooney also argued, the rot had set in with O'Connell.[127] His campaign destroyed the Irish language; the dominance of the English language brought English ideas; and the reduction of nationalism to the politics of economic questions facilitated recruitment by the 'English' in Ireland. When nationalism was reduced to a series of campaigns for the amelioration of particular sectional grievances the Irish recruit was left unable to distinguish between patriotic and unpatriotic actions.

Yorke's concluding pages asserted the need for a return to physical force.[128] Although partially based on conventional separatist reasoning – emancipation was achieved owing to the threat of a civil war; disestablishment and Gladstone's first Land Act stemmed from the Fenian rising and the Clerkenwell explosion; Parnell's authority rested on the force of arms he had behind him – Yorke developed the argument as an extension of his analysis of imperialism. Arguing in a Rousseauesque vein, he suggested that the absence of a system of law stemming from the national culture rendered legitimate government impossible. Consequently, just as a man had the right to protect his 'individuality' by force if it was threatened, so too must the nation. Rightful government could only be equated with indigenous and customary systems of organisation; control by an outside force, inevitably on alien lines, could not constitute a legitimate government. Yorke's notion of government legitimacy relied upon the conviction that the nation was an indestructible natural entity and any corruption of this was an illegitimate perversion.

The exceptional quality of Yorke's pamphlet becomes evident if it is contrasted with the more typical anti-recruiting leaflet distributed by the Cork Y.I.S. in July 1900.[129] Scattered from their windows in Great George Street during a U.I.L. parade, the leaflet argued that the Boers proved the ability of

---

[125] Yorke, pp 3, 5.
[126] Yorke, pp 7–9.
[127] Rooney, *Prose Writings*, pp 98–100.
[128] Yorke, pp 12–13.
[129] C.B.S. Box 17, 22478, 30 July 1900.

a small number of farmers to take on the 'English mercenaries'. It quoted Yorke on the instrumental connection between constitutionalism and enlistment, threw in Mitchel's claim that the needs of empire were causing the destruction of Ireland, and, for good measure, quoted Redmond's Cambridge speech.

IV

Parnell died on 6 October 1891; Parnellism heard the last rites in South Mayo in February 1900, and was lowered into a Galway city grave in October 1901. Something of the political clarity 'Clovis' sought in January 1900 was achieved during the by-elections of 1900 and 1901. The home rule party's repudiation of MacBride's candidature and Lynch's rejection by the separatists caused a rupture in Irish nationalist politics, severing what remained of the Redmondite–Fenian nexus.

MacBride and Lynch were heroes of militant Irish separatism owing to their leadership of the Irish Transvaal Brigades. Both were glamorous and popular figures. Great symbolic importance was attached to MacBride's possible election. Not only did the *United Irishman* assert that MacBride's election would demonstrate the Irish people's opposition to empire, but it would 'render inviolable the friendship of the Irish and the Boer nations'.[130] Similarly, following the execution of James Quinlan after Mafeking, a satisfied *United Irishman* declared, 'Ireland now has had her martyrs in South Africa.'[131] This was the orthodox voice of romantic Irish separatism, of a present irreversibly bound by the acts of the past, of the mentality of the anti-Treatyites.

MacBride was defeated by John O'Donnell. O'Donnell was William O'Brien's protégé and the adoptee of the newly reunified Irish parliamentary party; Lynch was approved by a U.I.L. convention and was victorious as the official party candidate. Ultimately, the outcome of these by-elections was the result of this statement of affairs. Yet recent work suggests that these two elections were far from simple contests between respectable and unrespectable candidates.[132] Philip Bull has persuasively argued that in opposing MacBride the parliamentary party missed an opportunity to conciliate Irish separatist opinion. Patrick Maume has countered that the party was driven by the need to assert U.I.L. invincibility in the face of Healyite resistance.[133] By this reading, the by-elections were not a dramatic confrontation between constitutionalist

---

[130] *U.I.*, 17 Feb. 1900.

[131] *U.I.*, 6 Jan. 1900.

[132] The by-elections are not mentioned in F. S. L. Lyons's *John Dillon* (London, 1968) or Frank Callanan's *T. M. Healy* (Cork, 1996).

[133] Philip Bull, 'A Fatal Disjunction, 1898–1905: Sinn Féin and the United Irish League' in Rebecca Pelan (ed.), *Irish–Australian Studies: Papers of the Seventh Irish–Australian Conference* (Sydney, 1994); Maume, *The Long Gestation*, pp 34–5. Maume's position is essentially that of Richard Davis, *Arthur Griffith and Non-violent Sinn Féin*, p. 39.

and separatist nationalisms, but instead were propelled by internal parliamentary party rivalries, specifically the need to affirm the attachment of O'Brien's U.I.L. to the party in the face of Healyite suspicion. Redmond's leadership had been ratified by a party convention barely a month before the contest and his authority owed much to the intervention of Davitt and O'Brien who believed Redmond to be more sympathetic to the U.I.L. than the more popular candidate, Timothy Harrington.[134] The alienation of the separatists then was an unfortunate by-product of intra-party wrangling. Although Maume's explanation of the immediate circumstances is compelling, he is a little too brisk in dispatching Bull's interpretation. This dispute is to some extent rooted in differences in historiographical approach: Maume's assessment is broadly high political, driven by the contingencies of a divided political leadership; Bull seeks to identify the often unintended long-term impact of individual events, constructing bold paradigms that clarify historical trends.[135] If the by-elections are regarded in the context of the destruction of the Redmondite–Fenian nexus then the broader implications of Bull's analysis take on a fresh vitality. Rather than a missed opportunity to embrace the new nationalism, the by-elections provided a propitious opportunity to repudiate the old Fenianism, freeing Redmondism of their taint. Indeed, this retrenchment was mutually beneficial; the Young Turks at the *United Irishman* had no desire to be shackled to the parliamentarians and, as will be discussed in the next section, clear space between the separatists and the constitutionalists was central to the Hungarian policy. At the very least, the failure of the I.P.P. to support MacBride was a symbolic rejection of the politics of the Parnellian gesture: the emergent unified party was novel in its calculated distancing from the separatist tradition. John O'Leary compared the possible election of MacBride to the defiant returns of O'Donovan Rossa and Mitchel in Tipperary in 1869 and 1875,[136] but it might be more profitably contrasted with constitutional acquiescence in the election of John Daly in 1895. Tom Kettle regarded the MacBride candidature as a turning-point, terminating the possibility of separatist co-operation with the unified home rule party: 'But then came South Mayo! and another opportunity of shewing that we have not mastered the great art of politics, the art of forgetting the stupidities of our friends.'[137] Mallon drew similar conclusions at the time, arguing that William O'Brien's behaviour during the campaign ended any possibility of the extremists working with the U.I.L.; if the Cork provocateur was ousted, then 'the most dangerous class

---

[134] Lyons, *John Dillon*, pp 204–6.
[135] Contrast Philip Bull, *Land, Politics and Nationalism: A Study of the Irish Land Question* (Dublin, 1996) with Maume, *The Long Gestation*. See also, Philip Bull, 'The United Irish League and the Reunion of the Irish Parliamentary Party 1898–1900' in *I.H.S.*, xxvi, no. 101 (May 1988), pp 51–78, where it is argued that the nature of the reunification prevented the generational rejuvenation of the I.P.P. hoped for by the I.P.P. leadership.
[136] C.B.S. Box 17, 21353, 6 Mar. 1900.
[137] Kettle, 'Hungarian Policy', p. 322.

. . . would be prepared to back up the League and act as its secret police as they did in former times.'[138] Police observers noted that the catholic clergy played no role in the campaign;[139] their low profile was probably an attempt to conciliate the Parnellites. Only a third of the electorate voted,[140] indicating the grave unease the contest provoked and the small number of voters the separatists could rely upon.

Whereas MacBride's candidature became a transparent contest between separatists and constitutionalists, the nomination of Arthur Lynch provoked much greater confusion. MacBride's uncompromising alignment with physical force nationalism was juxtaposed with Lynch's more ambiguous politics.[141] Arthur Lynch followed a classic Redmondite–Fenian trajectory in the 1890s. He was the defeated Parnellite candidate in Galway in 1892, after which he spent some time in the U.S.A. with Robert Johnston, possibly as an I.N.A. delegate to the Clan na Gael.[142] Back in Ireland, he frequently worked with leading suspects, notably the Amnesty Association stalwarts Thomas O'Gorman and John Crowe. With Mark Ryan's full support Lynch was elected to replace him as the president of the London Irish Political Prisoners Amnesty Association. Lynch delineated his political position in response to accusations of McCarthyism in 1893 (as an enthusiast of the literary revival, he had contributed on literary and scientific subjects to T. P. O'Connor's proto-tabloid *The Sun*).[143] Identifying as 'a thorough believer in the doctrines of Parnell',[144] Lynch continued: 'If I have ever ventured to differ from my friends, the parliamentary representatives of the Parnellite party, it is in the direction of urging a more strenuous and resolute course of action than has recently been pursued.'[145] Only in this way, he suggested, could nationalists tap Irish-American resources. John Crowe and P. N. Fitzgerald were unimpressed by this balancing act and disinclined to trust this English-accented, Australian 'adventurer'.[146] Consequently, the significance attributed to Lynch's leadership of the second Irish Brigade in the Transvaal must be seen in the context of

---

[138] C.B.S. Precis, Box 1, 15 June 1900.

[139] C.B.S. Box 17, 21343, 6 Mar. 1900.

[140] Davis, *Arthur Griffith*, p. 40; *U.I.*, 3 Mar. 1900, claimed the figure was less than a third.

[141] Unless stated otherwise the detail on Lynch's career and the Galway election campaign comes from the large file C.B.S. Box 20, 27053, which was partly comprised of reports made for Major Gosselin on Lynch's movements in the 1890s. See also Mark Ryan, *Fenian Memories*, p. 191: 'Of course he never came near us [the I.R.B.] after he had decided to enter the British parliament.'

[142] Lynch amiably refers to his advanced nationalist connexions in his woolly and self-congratulatory autobiography, *My Life Story* (London, 1924).

[143] See Ian Sheehy, 'T. P. O'Connor and *The Star*, 1886–90' in D. George Boyce and Alan O'Day (ed.), *Ireland in Transition, 1867–1921* (London, 2004), pp 76–91.

[144] *Galway Vindicator*, 9 Dec. 1893.

[145] *United Ireland*, 27 Jan. 1894.

[146] As reported by the south western division, 6 & 12 Feb. 1894. Maume's word, *Long Gestation*, p. 233.

the Redmondite–Fenian nexus. Rather than an aberration, Lynch's involvement in the Boer War was consistent with the peculiar texture of Parnellite politics in the 1890s. Since Lynch was an advanced nationalist rather than an unalloyed separatist, the idea that his candidature in 1901 was a betrayal must rest on the fallacy that the pro-Boer campaign was an exclusively separatist affair. On the contrary, constitutional sympathy for the Boers was widespread,[147] and the complexities of pro-Boer politics was evident when Seamus MacManus urged Terence MacSwiney to set up a Cork branch of the U.I.L. to work in the interests of both the I.R.B. and Lynch's candidature.[148] Moreover, Fenians were not adverse to voting for Lynch and only the most austere separatist felt obliged to obey Dublin's exhortations to abstention.[149] The comments one county inspector made with respect to the 1900 general election were equally applicable to this case:

> The most advanced section of the Irish revolutionists expressed their intention of taking no part whatever in the elections, but the mass of the I.R.B. sympathisers in the county took their share of the excitement and worked and voted for candidates of their choice on no fixed principle whatever.[150]

The Galway campaign further reinforced the sense that these by-elections functioned as an affirmation of the unity of the party. In a letter to John J. Forde (honorary secretary of the U.I.L. and the Galway National Independence Association) Lynch stated: 'I adhere to the general policy of the parliamentary party, and, as its methods are constitutional, it is therefore implied, of course, that I am in accord with that part of its programme.'[151] Forde's position in both organisations was indicative of the home rule party's reconciliation. Lynch's election addresses were anodyne, effortlessly assimilating a bland Irish Ireland agenda with the rhetoric of constitutional nationalism:

> My programme amounts to this: I want to see Ireland's resources and Ireland's industries developed by Irishmen, so that the riches of the country will be sufficient to keep the whole population in comfort, and so that emigration will cease, because Ireland itself will become the promised land. This is not an impossible programme, and I will lend my energies to its realisation.[152]

Lynch's unionist opponent was Horace Plunkett, the target of Redmond's conciliatory policy in the 1890s. Michael Davitt privately claimed that the

---

[147] Terence Denman sees the opposition of the I.P.P. to the Boer War and enlistment as largely passive. Denman, '"The Red Livery of Shame"', pp 214–16, 228–9.
[148] Seumas MacManus to Terence MacSwiney, 12 Oct. 1901 (U.C.D. P48b/316).
[149] U.I., 6 Oct. 1900.
[150] C.B.S. Precis, Box 3, 16 Oct. 1900.
[151] D.I., 14 Oct. 1901.
[152] D.I., 8 Nov. 1901.

party wished to give Plunkett a 'bad beating'. Possibly this was in repudiation of Redmond's earlier rapprochement as well as a flexing of the muscle of the 'Gombeen men', the entrepreneurs who dominated Irish society by running the local pubs and other businesses, monopolising credit availability, and playing a crucial role in local I.P.P. politics, who had been challenged by Plunkett's co-operatist ideas. Redmond appears to have been complicit in this, for along with the M.P.s Mooney, Duffy, Loudon, Joyce, Lurden, and Hayden, he was active in Galway during the campaign. Lynch attracted particular support from William Redmond, who was keen to assert that Lynch was not a carpetbagger.[153] Following Lynch's selection by a U.I.L. convention, Galway county council provided unanimous support.[154]

United Irishman's contempt for Lynch's victory was unconcealed. 'The Galway people think they have done well in electing this man, and that they have vindicated something or another; but I say again that they vindicated nothing but their invincible ignorance and lack of judgement.'[155] This was a voice in the wilderness. For although MacBride's supporters opposed Lynch as a 'traitor' and Galway I.R.B. man Joseph O'Sullivan returned from Dublin with instructions 'to go dead against Lynch', the police reports conclude that most advanced nationalists backed Lynch, partly owing to the advocacy of I.R.B. activist and G.A.A. secretary Frank Dineen, and few saw through their threat to vote for Plunkett.[156]

Michael Davitt's role in both the by-elections reinforced the uncertainties of his position. A somewhat reluctant (and successful) Federationist candidate in 1895, Davitt remained a political maverick, unable to convincingly fashion for himself an appropriate political purpose within conventional home rule politics.[157] He still recognised the necessity of maintaining the close relationship between constitutionalism and militant nationalism and the pro-Boer campaign had brought him closer to the I.R.B. When in the Transvaal in 1899 he corresponded with Fred Allan;[158] back in Dublin he attended the meetings of the Celtic Literary Society.[159] By resigning his South Mayo seat in protest at the war, which provided MacBride's opening, Davitt acted out of personal conviction, and perhaps attempted to better place himself to provide a link between separatism and the I.P.P. From the outset, he worked hard to

---

[153] *D.I.*, 19 Oct. 1901.

[154] *F.J.*, 20 Nov. 1901.

[155] *U.I.*, 30 Nov. 1901.

[156] C.B.S. Box 20, 27053. Yeats reported the possibility that they might to Lady Gregory, cited in R. F. Foster, *W. B. Yeats: A Life. I: The Apprentice Mage* (Oxford, 1997), p. 578, n. 58. For Dineen using his G.A.A. position to recruit for the I.R.B., see report by J. J. Jones, Chief Commissioner, 9 Jan. 1900, Balfour Papers, T.N.A. (P.R.O.), 30/60/28.

[157] See Yeats's penetrating character sketch in *Autobiographies* (London, 1955), pp 356–7.

[158] A small selection of letters are to be found in the Allan Papers, N.L.I. They mainly concern the whereabouts of MacBride.

[159] Foster, *Apprentice Mage*, p. 223.

promote the U.I.L., making near-treasonous speeches calculated to appeal to the 'hillside men'. He approved of William O'Brien's use of the *Irish People* to attract Fenian support,[160] and in the judgement of the D.M.P., 'never fails to do anything he can to attract the extreme party and constitute himself a connecting link between the two parties'.[161] A theme that runs through T. W. Moody's biography of Davitt to 1882 was this attempt to reconcile apparently incompatible tendencies in Irish politics, most particularly Fenianism, Parnellism, and agrarianism. His U.I.L. strategy and the ambiguous response of the I.R.B. both recalled his role in the Land War. Davitt's political instincts were sound, for contrary to the Supreme Council's formal repudiation of the U.I.L.,[162] and the active opposition of the separatists in Dublin,[163] the U.I.L. agitation at the De Freyne estate (County Roscommon) saw, 'the Physical Force men . . . making so little progress with their own movement that, where the U. I. League is active, they feel bound to support it or lay themselves open to the taunt of being traitors.'[164] Indeed, the proclamation of County Longford saw the U.I.L. and the I.R.B. co-operating under the influence of M.P. J. P. Farrell,[165] a precursor of his energising leadership when Longford leapt to the fore of the anti-grazing campaign in 1907.[166] Were it not for his position during the split, Davitt would have been ideally placed to act as under-study to William Redmond, now incapacitated by party propriety. Unfortunately, 'many of the old Parnellites, who embrace some of the staunchest physical force men, are slow to forget the bitterness of his [Davitt's] animosity towards them in the years of the "split" and are slow to trust him again.'[167]

In Galway Davitt attempted to mend the divisions between the separatists and the U.I.L., an earlier attempt to do this through Gonne and MacBride in Paris having failed.[168] But having served two terms of imprisonment for U.I.L. activity, O'Donnell was the obvious popular choice for the constituency. By

---

[160] C.B.S. Box 17, 21065, *c.* 31 Jan. 1900. For Dublin Castle's assessment of the legality of the *Irish People's* articles and its decision that prosecution was politically inexpedient, see C.B.S. Box 20, 26750.

[161] C.B.S. Precis, Box 2, 6 Sept. 1902. Davitt spoke openly of a 'fusion' (police word) between the separatists and the U.I.L. at a public meeting in Belfast, 4 March 1902. At the same time William Redmond and Devlin were on tour in the U.S.A., making speeches reputedly urging the same recombination, once again demonstrating that what was acceptable in the U.S.A. and in Ireland was not always the same. C.B.S. Precis, Box 3, 21 Apr. 1902.

[162] P. T. Daly told Glasgow Fenians excited by the U.I.L. that the Supreme Council was 'opposed to giving it any countenance whatsoever', C.B.S. Precis, Box 3, 1 May 1903.

[163] NA C.B.S. Precis, Box 3, 7 July 1903, also Dec. 1903.

[164] Ibid., 9 Oct. 1902.

[165] Ibid., 5 Nov. 1902.

[166] Bew, *Conflict and Conciliation*, pp 151–8.

[167] C.B.S. Precis, Box 3, 9 Oct. 1902. Cf. Davitt to William O'Brien, 9 March 1899 (Davitt letters, N.L.I., MS 913): 'you are not near as objectionable to Parnellites – or to Priests – as I am.'

[168] C.B.S. Precis, Box 3, 26 May 1902.

contrast, Davitt observed, MacBride could be rejected as having been nominated by 'a few gents in Dublin', who were not in contact with their champion and whose object was to divide the U.I.L. Consequently, he told a Galway crowd, O'Donnell's victory 'was in no sense a defeat for Major MacBride (cheers)'.[169] Davitt's line tallied with the police view that the Supreme Council did not decide to run MacBride until January 1900, making it a last minute gesture.[170]

V

The Hungarian policy was given its most sustained articulation in a series of articles written by Arthur Griffith in *United Irishman* in 1904.[171] Its key ideas were further developed in innumerable articles and Griffith's original articles were published as the best-selling book *The Resurrection of Hungary*. *United Irishman* claimed it sold 25,000 copies in twenty-four hours, an Irish record; Tom Kettle said it had 15,000 readers by February 1905; the second edition went on sale on 18 December 1904.[172] This peculiar mixture of history, prescription, and satire had an immediate impact. Its numerous veiled references to recent political history demanded a knowing, collusive readership. Its attempt to provide legalistic justification for a separatist agenda was profoundly provocative. It was the most ambitious attempt yet to provide a framework for understanding the separatist implications of the Irish Ireland movement and the anticipated industrial revival. *An Claidheamh Soluis*, the Gaelic League newspaper edited by Patrick Pearse, recognised this: '*The Resurrection of Hungary* marks an epoch, because it crystallises into a national policy the doctrines which during the past ten years have been preached in Ireland by the Irish Ireland movement.'[173] The pamphlet also sowed the seeds of

---

[169] *F.J.*, 20 Nov. 1901.

[170] Commissioner John Jones placed the nomination in the context of the defeat of three I.R.B. candidates at the recent Dublin municipal elections, the collapse of a pro-Boer resolution put before Dublin corporation, Allan's apparent desertion of the cause, and Gonne's poor reputation outside of Dublin. Mallon concurred. Jones also reported that Arthur Griffith was trying to get appointed as a county council clerk. C.B.S. Box 17, 21107, 1 Feb. 1900; C.B.S. Precis, Box 2, 21 Feb. 1900.

[171] In addition to Davis, *Arthur Griffith* and Laffan, *Resurrection of Ireland*, recent discussions of Griffith's ideas include Patrick Maume, 'The Ancient Constitution: Arthur Griffith and his Intellectual Legacy to Sinn Féin' in *Irish Political Studies*, 10 (1995), pp 123–37, idem, 'Young Ireland, Arthur Griffith, and Republican Ideology: The Question of Continuity', in *Eire–Ireland*, xxxiv, no. 2 (Summer 1999), pp 155–74, and idem, *Long Gestation*, pp 49–59; and Richard Bourke's excellent analysis in *Peace in Ireland: The War of Ideas* (London, 2003), esp. pp 127–41.

[172] *U.I.*, 26 Nov. 1904, 17 Dec. 1904; Tom Kettle, 'Hungarian Policy', p. 322.

[173] Reproduced in *U.I.*, 3 Dec. 1904; R. Dudley Edwards, *Patrick Pearse: The Triumph of Failure* (Dublin, 1977, 1990), p. 72.

controversy, questioning the relationship between physical force and constitutional nationalisms, between the efficacy of a withdrawal from parliament represented by Deak and the insurrectionary strategy personified by Kossuth.

The themes central to 'the Hungarian policy' – a withdrawal from Westminster, industrial revival, autarky – had been in circulation prior to Griffith's seminal articles. John Sweetman and Sir Thomas Esmonde, respectively maverick members of Meath and Wexford county councils, had both had resolutions passed asserting Ireland's right to a parliament that were based on the resolutions of the Volunteers at Dungannon in 1782.[174] *United Irishman* briefly editorialised on the Hungarian parallel as early as November 1902; Terence MacSwiney, later one of the policy's sternest critics, lectured in the same month:

> Our one true ideal is – sovereign independence – and we will agree to no compromise; but in the meantime we must adopt some attitude towards the parliament to which we are supposed to send representatives and the attitude should be the Hungarian one – that is to send no representatives.[175]

In September 1903 a *United Irishman* correspondent called for 'more light on the Hungarian policy', arguing that without further illumination the National Council could not fulfil its potential as an alternative to the I.P.P.[176] Griffith sought to establish an historical precedent for the strategy of withdrawing from Westminster, suggesting that the policy was less a new departure than an exhumation. O'Connell's aborted Council of the Three Hundred scheme of 1843 was one obvious reference point, the Tithe War of 1831–9 was another: the refusal to purchase confiscated goods was identified as a response to the call to 'Trust in yourselves' and was therefore the 'Sinn Féin policy'.[177]

Griffith has been praised for his practicality and it is certainly true that *United Irishman* fetishised the idea.[178] By focusing on the process of building the nation-state Griffith and the *United Irishman* gave separatist rhetoric a more analytical and functional purpose, supplanting as the dominant mode the Mitchelite model of the 'revolutionary leveller'. In this, the Griffithites were extending the lessons taught by O'Leary and *United Irishman's* early support for Yeats's Irish National Theatre can be understood in this context – Yeats's recent Fenianism made him a logical recipient of Griffith's patronage. Although saturated with mysticism, poetry, and the occult, Yeats spent much of the 1900s in the very practical business of organising an avant-garde theatre company. The paper agreed

---

174 Davis, *Non-violent Sinn Féin*, pp 10–11.
175 *U.I.*, 22 Nov. 1902; MacSwiney Papers (U.C.D., P48b/335).
176 *U.I.*, 26 Sept. 1903.
177 *U.I.*, 30 Sept. 1905.
178 For example, see 'Practical Effort', *U.I.*, 30 Oct. 1900.

with Mr Yeats that nothing save a victory on the battlefield could so strengthen the national spirit as the creation of an Irish Theatre, and though the battle-victory is not yet within our power to achieve, it is within our power to create an Irish Theatre, and we are creating it.[179]

This excited sense of a collective endeavour stemmed from the newspaper's enthusiasm for the creation of national institutions that would form part of the fabric of an Irish nation-state. That Yeats's project soon attracted Griffith's active hostility should not obscure the fact that the Griffithites initially celebrated the theatre company's expected provision of plays to 'rouse every noble emotion and rekindle the fires of patriotism'.[180]

John Sweetman believed that although Ireland could not fight England at the present moment, nationalists could lay the foundations for Irish independence by working to 'create an Irish nation in Ireland'. Developing Irish industry was, therefore, as great a priority as the regeneration of the Irish language and customs.[181] This determination to demonstrate the practical application of Griffithite thinking was exemplified in a series of dry articles exploring Ireland's 'industrial possibilities'. They explained how the country was capable of producing its own supplies of essential goods such as pipes and tobacco, buttons, groceries, bacon, hosiery, leather, machinery, carpets, glass, and silk.[182] One correspondent was concerned that the economic strength of England would lead to the 'practical assimilation of Ireland and England', with the Irish consigned to lower wages.[183] The conviction that Irish producers could not compete with their English counterparts owing to economies of scale provided the basis of Griffith's marshalling of the protectionist ideas of the German economist Fredrick List.

---

[179] *U.I.*, 12 Apr. 1902. In the previous week's edition Yeats had plugged *Kathleen ni Houlihan* in separatist-friendly terms that suggested the play would find its place in the Young Ireland canon: 'My subject is Ireland and her struggle for independence. . . . It is the perpetual struggle of the cause of Ireland and every other ideal cause against private hopes and dreams, against all that we mean when we say the world.' *U.I.*, 5 Apr. 1902. *U.I.* printed a rave review by Griffith of Yeats's *Poems* in April 1901, and published Yeats's essay 'Ireland and the Arts' in August, and the full text of his play *Where there is nothing* in a special supplement. *U.I.*, 27 Apr. 1901, 31 Aug. 1901, 1 Nov. 1902.

[180] *U.I.*, 24 Oct. 1903 was dominated by the controversy provoked by Synge's 1903 play *The Shadow of the Glen*. See also *U.I.*, 28 Nov. 1903 & 12 Dec. 1903, and Foster, *Apprentice Mage*, pp 294–300. The complexities of the Griffith–Yeats symbiosis is a recurring theme in Ben Levitas, *The Theatre of the Nation: Irish Drama and Cultural Nationalism 1890–1916* (Oxford, 2002).

[181] *U.I.*, 10 Jan. 1903.

[182] *U.I.*, 26 Apr., 3 May, 10 May, 17 May, 31 May, 7 June, 14 June, 21 June and 28 June 1902.

[183] *U.I.*, 28 June 1902, cf. James Connelly's fear that English ownership of Irish industry reduced Irish capacity for self-government regardless of Ireland's constitutional status. See his *Labour in Irish History* (1910).

The plan to hold an international exhibition of trade and industry in Dublin provided prime material for the reactive polemic of the Griffithites. In attempting to organise an alternative, however diminutive, they demonstrated their determination to convert antipathy into practical effort. Sweetman, increasingly the respectable face of the National Council, propagated their rival Irish national exhibition at the inevitable public meeting at the Rotunda.[184] He positioned them in opposition to the efforts of the home rule party and the *Daily Independent*. Here again was the urge to establish permanent national institutions and once more the advanced nationalists were drawing battle-lines on the basis of Irish Ireland ideals. As the *Irish Draper* argued, 'an international exhibition is a foreigner's exhibition, while a home or national one realises the healthy maxim of the Gael, "Ourselves Alone".'[185]

Although the Irish national exhibition was supported by the Gaelic League and attracted the support of various boards of guardians and local councils (over a hundred public bodies sent resolutions of support to a Mansion House meeting presided over by the lord mayor),[186] it failed to secure the exclusive support of the Dublin Trades Council, which voted against rescinding its resolution in favour of the international exhibition by fifty-three to twenty-one.[187] There is no evidence that the National Exhibition Provisional Committee came close to selling 100,000 shares at £1 each in order to build a permanent centre dedicated to the promotion of Irish trade and industry.[188] Nonetheless, small locally organised exhibitions took place in Limerick and Cork,[189] providing local businesses with the opportunity to display and advertise their wares and services. Meanwhile, plans continued for a national exhibition on a grander scale. The date was eventually set for 1 May 1907; a Mansion House meeting decided to raise a more modest £25,000 capital through the sale of 10,000 shares at 10 shillings each.[190] Dr Walsh, the archbishop of Dublin, announced his intention to purchase £500 worth of shares,[191] while official endorsement came from the G.A.A., the Irish National Forresters, and Queen's County council.[192] Nonetheless, the plans were soon discreetly dropped and by 1907 Irish separatists were otherwise occupied. The appeal of Sinn Féin to men such as Sweetman was further confirmed by the adherence of the National Society of Great Britain. Its president, Thomas

---

[184] *U.I.*, 26 Mar. 1904.
[185] *U.I.*, 16 Jan. 1904.
[186] *U.I.*, 30 Apr. 1904. The secretary was prominent National Council supporter Alderman Cole.
[187] *U.I.*, 4 June 1904.
[188] *U.I.*, 2 Apr. 1904.
[189] *U.I.*, 9 July & 8 Oct. 1904.
[190] *U.I.*, 29 Oct. 1904.
[191] *U.I.*, 4 Feb. 1905.
[192] *U.I.*, 11 Feb. 1905.

Martin, wrote announcing that the society had aligned with the Hungarian policy owing to the failure of parliamentarianism.[193] Repudiating the 'windy futility of the past', a sure reference to physical force posturing, the society was in favour of 'honest work and practical methods'. Its model was to be the more moderate Hungarian nationalist leader Deak rather than the militant Kossuth; members advocated contesting every electoral vacancy, presenting some kind of ultimatum to the British, and returning to Dublin to devote their energies to developing the industrial resources of Ireland, arresting depopulation, reviving the Irish language, and encouraging Irish art and literature. This letter provides early evidence that Griffith's ideas appealed to disillusioned constitutionalists. Young and influential Fenians were more ambivalent. John MacBride, although praising the Hungarian policy, argued that its promulgation was a hundred years too late: under present conditions it could only work if the people were prepared to back it with force.[194] MacBride argued that if the Irish members withdrew from parliament today the government of Ireland would remain qualitatively the same for collaborators would fill the offices of government. As an example, MacBride cited the farmers' sons who filled the ranks of the R.I.C., but also implied the constitutional politicians and their milieu. A withdrawal in the aftermath of the union would have produced a more genuinely national government owing to its recent experience of independence.

> If the Irish members of the English parliament withdrew from Westminster tomorrow the government of the country would be carried on just as it is today, and it will and must be as long as the people forget that they are Irishmen with a country to free from foreign yoke.

MacBride's subtext was that winning independence through physical force would force the current generation of collaborators to make way for a new generation of authentic Irishmen who would form the nucleus of the new state. This was a version of the orthodox Fenian position that the military defeat of the British would allow the Irish nation to emerge cleansed from the indignity of colonialism. Something akin to this took place during the revolutionary period when the middle-class home rulers, the infrastructure-in-waiting, were supplanted by the emergent revolutionary elite.[195] MacBride's assertion of the specificity of Ireland's case was illustrative of the literalness with which Griffith's ideas were received. 'There should be sufficient brains in Ireland to plan a new movement to meet the requirements and the conditions of our

---

[193] *U.I.*, 14 Feb. 1903.

[194] *U.I.*, 10 Sept. 1904.

[195] See Senia Pašeta, 'Ireland's Last Home Rule Generation: The Decline of Constitutional Nationalism in Ireland, 1916–30' in Mike Cronin and John M. Regan (ed.), *Ireland: The Politics of Independence, 1922–49* (London, 2000), pp 13–31.

country in the twentieth century. Imitations are never successful. An imitation puts one in the mind of the real object, that's all.'

Alice Milligan broadly agreed with MacBride, additionally noting that Ireland differed from Hungary in rejecting any role in the empire. The ethos under which an independent Ireland should be governed had to be created and Milligan went further by rejecting the efficacy of physical force as a means to achieve this transformation. Separation would be premature because the necessary revolution in people's minds was incomplete and the bulk of the population had little sense of what they were fighting for. 'If without grasping any social ideal, and destitute of firmly implanted democratic principles, we were liberated, our country might be tyrannical and grasping and unjust, and have no such perception of injustice as at present.'[196] Thomas O'Looney concurred: 'We must first make our young men and, as it takes twenty years to make a man, long before that time we will have the Hungarian policy well in hand.' This revolution in thinking was also required by the emotional separatism of Terence MacSwiney. Fighting pressure in 1905 from within the Cork Celtic Literary Society to abandon educational work in favour of political organisation, MacSwiney wrote that they were not yet ready and required at least a further five years. Interestingly, his prime concern was that the membership was not 'thoroughly conversant in . . . public administration' which was required if they were 'to succeed in bringing order out of chaos'.[197] MacBride soon moderated his critique, introducing the distinction that the Hungarian policy was an advancement for those allied to constitutional principles, but he would not like it to divert 'young Irish-Irelanders' from the teachings of '98, '48, and '67.[198]

Discussion of the Hungarian policy soon shifted from this initial focus on the efficacy of physical force to the problem of the 1782 constitution and whether this represented true separation. This was a matter of the gravest contention and the insistence on practicality could not indefinitely postpone a debate about ends. The basis of the Hungarian policy lay in the claim that the 1782 constitution reified the right of the Irish to self-government through the aegis of a constitution that guaranteed legislative independence and did not contain any provision for its own dissolution.[199] Ultimately, Sinn Féin's revolution would rest on this legal precedent, on the restitution of illegally withdrawn rights. In recognising the king of England as potentially the king of Ireland, Griffith asserted that under the 1782 constitution it was not necessary for the king of Ireland and the king of England to be the same person. Such thinking was unorthodox but not entirely alien to Fenianism. John O'Leary had written: 'Let England cease to govern Ireland, and then I will

---

[196] U.I., 17 Sept. 1904.
[197] MacSwiney Diary, 18 Sept. 1905 (U.C.D. P48c/99).
[198] U.I., 1 Oct. 1904.
[199] U.I., 11 Mar. 1905.

swear to be true to Ireland and the queen or king of Ireland, even though that queen or king should also happen to be queen or king of England.'[200] Griffith, again on the prowl for an historical precedent, cited the example of the Irish parliament's exclusive offer of the crown to the prince regent when George III went insane. Had the regent accepted George III would have remained the king of England. Unfortunately, the king recovered his sanity before the regent was able to reply. To the claim that the restoration of the constitution of 1782 would mean that catholics would be excluded from government Griffith responded that this was to misunderstand its provisions. The fundamental point was that by granting the Irish self-government the 1782 constitution and the 1783 Renunciation Act gave the Irish the right to decide how they were to be governed. There is more than a passing similarity between this and Michael Collins's claim that the Anglo-Irish treaty of 1921 gave the Irish 'the freedom to achieve freedom'.

As O'Leary had privately admitted regarding the reception of the 1886 home rule bill, he believed that most Irish people wanted a settlement that went beyond home rule, but would accept something short of total separation. He had 'always believed that an absolute repeal of the union would satisfy us'.[201] Despite formulating this policy, Arthur Griffith looked towards a settlement closer to orthodox separatism. Following Sweetman's call for an Irish Deak and suggestion that Griffith should take on this role,[202] Griffith clarified a number of issues. First, he argued that an Irish Deak would have to accept the final settlement between Ireland and England as being the restitution of Ireland's constitutional rights, and this he found insufficient.[203] If he were Hungarian he would have supported Kossuth and his 1849 proclamation of independence. When it was evident that Kossuth could not succeed he would have supported Deak, 'whose wise and brave policy involved the sacrifice of no principle nor loss of self-respect in any Hungarian separatist'. Griffith, however, was adamant that the constitutional and separatist wings of Irish nationalism could cohere around the Hungarian policy. The evident failure of parliamentarianism meant there were many men who could potentially play the role of Deak. Griffith's reply acts as a reminder that, for him, Sinn Féin's departure from the separatist orthodoxy was the product of pragmatism rather than idealism, a tension that troubled the length of Sinn Féin's existence.

Griffith's position was further clarified when he distinguished between constitutional and national rights in his response to the following critique:

---

[200] O'Leary, *Recollections of Fenians and Fenianism* (London, 1896), p. 24.
[201] From O'Leary's hostile comment on John Redmond's infamous Cambridge Union address, reprinted in *U.I.*, 19 Oct. 1901. O'Leary asked where Redmond derived the authority for the address.
[202] *U.I.*, 16 July 1904.
[203] *U.I.*, 23 July 1904.

The constitution of 1782, instead of being the constitutional rights of Ireland, was a usurpation of those rights. If that constitution had never existed, our constitutional rights would be just what they are. They are as old as the Irish race itself. . . . we have been prevented by force from exercising our constitutional rights since the violent abolition of the Brehon laws.[204]

Griffith responded that although in effect he agreed with the writer, 1783 only left the sovereign in common between the two nations. Substantively, the 1782 constitution and the 1783 Renunciation Act granted Ireland the national right to be a 'sovereign, independent state'. In other words, the legislation gave a *constitutional* basis to Ireland's *national* rights. To return to the 1782 constitution would give Ireland the legal authority to exercise its national rights, to transform Irish government in any direction that conserved the sovereign independence enshrined in that constitution. Consequently, to adhere to the Hungarian policy demanded a substantial imaginative leap. Irish separatists had to learn to see that to share a monarch with the British was not to be subservient to the British; constitutionally the monarch would be no more British than he was Irish.

In contrast to the literalness with which MacBride approached the *Resurrection of Hungary*, Tom Kettle regarded the pamphlet as reading

like a fairy tale, or, rather like an epic, spacious and rapid; and by his over-idealisation and dramatisation the author has put himself in this difficulty that he cannot know how many of his fifteen thousand readers have bought the pamphlet for the policy and how many for the style.[205]

Kettle's critique centred on the absence of 'exact designs', of 'details', indeed: 'We are not told clearly enough what it is.'[206] The pamphlet, therefore, should be read primarily as an exciting polemic that had justly generated much comment and enthusiasm, but ultimately was only suggestive of the future direction of Irish nationalism. Although not responding to Kettle by name, Griffith addressed this criticism between March and June 1905 with ten articles under the heading 'Working of the Policy'. Although reiterating the theoretical and constitutional basis of the policy, the articles were largely free of allusion to the Hungarian precedent and any examination of the tension between separatism and constitutional nationalism that suffused the parallel. Rather, the articles were an attempt to delineate a strategy for immediate effect, a prelude for revolution, rather than an urge to revolution itself. Consequently, although monitoring the complexion of local government became an increasingly prominent concern of *United Irishman*, these articles contained little

---

[204] *U.I.*, 13 Aug. 1904.
[205] Tom Kettle, 'Hungarian Policy', p. 322.
[206] Ibid., p. 323.

encouragement towards overt organisation on this basis. A classic Griffith fudge perhaps: apparently full of bold strategies for nation-state building, the 'Working of the Policy' avoided advocating overt engagement, of taking the fight to the ballot box as a means of proving they had won the argument. In this it echoed Griffith's early *United Irishman* article advocating a loose federation of advanced nationalist societies, each with the 'utmost liberty of action';[207] an approach strongly reminiscent of O'Leary's 1885 Y.I.S. speeches. Still, progress was made in September when the Sinn Féin cycling club was founded.[208] More seriously, in London in November the Davis Press Agency was established with the remit of influencing the continental press on the situation in Ireland.[209]

A major preoccupation of the *United Irishman* was the potential of the General Council of the County Councils. Not only could its purchasing power be used to generate the interests of the Irish industrial revival, it also provided the nucleus of a de facto Irish parliament. Using very suggestive language, the paper asserted in September that the 'General Council of the County Councils must develop into the *Supreme Council* of the nation.'[210] Moreover, the 4,000 employees and the 8,000 elected representatives on the Poor Law Unions should direct the £1,500,000 distributed annually exclusively towards the purchase of Irish manufactured goods.[211] Indeed, the *United Irishman* calculated that the total annual expenditure by local government in Ireland, by both elected and charitable bodies was £6,555,979 – all of which should be directed at Irish goods and industries.[212] It was necessary to nationalise the Irish stock exchange and to rid it of pernicious influences that ensured an Irish company only received a quotation on the exchange if it was backed by a powerful influence. At present the small investor could not invest in Irish companies, which turned her into a gambler because she could not direct her investments towards the national interest.[213] Similarly, the banks must be encouraged to lend to Irish businesses, ending the practice of treating them as a higher risk and charging higher rates of interest on loans.[214] The Irish economy needed to be further secured by encouraging the Irish to save in gold; of the £44,000,000 saved, only £4,000,000 was in Ireland in the form of gold; the remainder had been

---

[207] Quoted in Davis, *Non-Violent Sinn Féin*, p. 17; *U.I.*, 3 Mar. 1900.

[208] *U.I.*, 2 Sept. 1905. Cycling was a very fashionable middle-class activity. Myriad features on cycling had filled the pages of the Redmondite press in the 1890s, while it provided the means for MacSwiney's rapturous trips to the country. See the rhapsodic account of a trip to Youghal that closes the second volume of MacSwiney's diaries (U.C.D. P48c/100, 7 Oct. 1905).

[209] *U.I.*, 4 Nov. 1905.

[210] *U.I.*, 2 Sept. 1905, my italics.

[211] *U.I.*, 25 Mar. 1905.

[212] *U.I.*, 3 June 1905.

[213] *U.I.*, 1 Apr. 1905.

[214] *U.I.*, 8 Apr. 1905.

exchanged for paper notes.[215] Evidently, *United Irishman* was impressed with the prestige conferred on Britain by the Gold Standard. Finally, wealthy Irish Americans should be persuaded to invest the £20 million required to tap Irish coal reserves: 174,000,000 tons awaited mining.

A particular concern of the Hungarian policy was the need for Ireland to take its place as an independent state on the international stage. The need for consular representation was frequently voiced, in particular as a means of generating Irish trade, but evidently also as a means for generating international recognition.[216] According to *United Irishman* figures, in 1904 the UK exported £360,000,000 worth of goods; of this one quarter was Irish, indicating Ireland's great potential in foreign markets. More radically, Ireland's role on the world's stage should be 'at the head of a combination of oppressed peoples against British rule'.[217] Among those struggling nations thought ripe for Irish guidance were South Africa, Egypt, India, Malta, the West Indies, and possibly Australasia and Canada – at this point Australia and Canada had dominion status and greater political independence than Ireland.[218] Finally, the judiciary needed urgent reform, ending the current practice of political appointments. 'Men of character', justices of the peace, and 'good' Irish barristers would be appointed judges in the 'national arbitration courts', established to treat matters currently decided under unjust civil law.[219]

The reluctance to fully engage in conventional political activity was evident at the first annual convention of the National Council. It assembled at the Rotunda in November 1905. Edward Martyn took the chair, with John Sweetman, P. T. Daly, J. Wyse Power, Patrick Pearse,[220] Michael Cusack, Oliver St John Gogarty, and W. O'Leary Curtis (president of the Celtic Literary Society) attending. In addition there were six town councillors, ten poor law guardians, and representatives of various branches of the Cumann na nGaedhael, Ingindhe na hÉireann, and other Irish Ireland groups.[221] The

---

[215] *U.I.*, 15 Apr. 1905.

[216] Discussed in Gerard Keown, 'The Ideas and Developments of Irish Foreign Policy from the Origins of Sinn Féin to 1932' (unpublished D.Phil. thesis, Oxford, 1997), pp 20–5.

[217] *U.I.*, 13 May 1905.

[218] *U.I.* boasted that the Australian catholic review *Austral Light* had endorsed the Sinn Féin policy, 15 Sept. 1905.

[219] *U.I.*, 6 May 1905.

[220] In *Triumph of Failure*, pp 72–3, Ruth Dudley Edwards considers Pearse at this stage to be standing 'aloof' from political organisations having adopted a 'non-political' stance. Although any evidence that challenges this is slight, it is worth noting that he was active in the National Council, chairing one of the weekly meetings of the national executive committee in December 1904, which coincided with *An Claidheamh Soluis*'s celebratory reception of the *Resurrection of Hungary*. Nonetheless, in February 1904 the police stated unambiguously that Pearse had no connection with secret societies. *U.I.*, 3 Dec. 1904; C.B.S. Precis, Box 6, Feb. 1904.

[221] *U.I.*, 9 Dec. 1905.

president praised the important work done since the council was founded in 1903, notably its monitoring of pledge-breakers in the Dublin corporation and its handful of successful elections to the Dublin corporation. Their task that day was to establish a basis on which to progress further. Griffith opened the convention with an impassioned speech that argued from first principles in an interesting mix of essentialist and civic nationalism. Their policy must be:

> National self-development through the regulation of the duties and rights of citizenship on the part of the individual, and by the aid and support of all movements originating from within Ireland, instinct with national tradition, and not looking outside Ireland for the accomplishment of their aims.

Alluding to the position of the 1782 constitution in his thought, Griffith argued that the Irish people were a free people and were so until they renounced this freedom, and that it was the intention of the education system in Ireland to make them oblivious to their rights and to disguise the tyranny posturing as government. In other countries the education system provided the middle class, 'the equalising and harmonising element in the population', but in Ireland it steered the middle class towards the English civil service and the 'ranks of struggling clerkdom in Ireland' rather than towards industry. 'University education in Ireland', fumed Griffith, 'is regarded by the classes in Ireland as a means of washing away the original sin of Irish birth.' This would be remedied by taking primary education into their own control; they must withdraw their children from the national schools, entrust them to the Christian Brothers, and set up a national education fund to fund voluntary schools. Griffith acknowledged that this would take time. The speech continued with further exposition of the Hungarian policy. Martyn proposed a general resolution approving Griffith's sermon and Gogarty made an overwrought speech seconding the resolution. Commenting on the effect of British law Gogarty gave way to the anti-Semitism that infected Sinn Féin diatribes (and particularly his personal attitudes) at their most hysterical:

> This is the benign law that depopulated Ireland, refuses to educate it now and turns the country against itself through ignorance and demoralisation, so that we are governed by a force of Constabularymen picked from among our own people, spied on by other fellow countrymen of our own, disgraced in the eyes of the nations of the world by our prowess in the British army, separated and alienated from our educated men, and in a word, made the victims and the tools of the most disgraceful and Jew beridden government in the world (cheers).[222]

Sinn Féin was formed in 1907 of the National Council, the Cumann na nGaedhael, and the Dungannon Clubs. The amalgamation proceeded in two

---

[222] Ibid.

stages. First, the Cumann and the Dungannon Clubs merged as the Sinn Féin League in April at negotiations in Dundalk. Dundalk was roughly equidistant between Dublin and Belfast, the respective centres of the two organisations, and symbolic of the equal status of the two locations. Griffith and the National Council did not join the new organisation, denying its legitimacy by refusing to report its activities. *United Irishman*'s silence indicated the tension and resentment generated on both sides by differences over strategy. By refusing to countenance the Sinn Féin League as the organisational basis of the new separatism, Griffith and the National Council denied it the exposure and legitimacy it needed to make a success of the venture. This controversy has been generally understood as a struggle for the leadership of the new nationalism. Patrick McCartan's regular letters updating Joseph McGarrity on political developments in Ireland are littered with remarks concerning the rivalry between Hobson and Griffith. 'I'm beginning to think Gr. is really jealous of Hobson. It looks very like it.'[223] Michael Laffan has described the defection of C. J. Dolan from the I.P.P. to Griffith's ideas in June 1907 as fortuitous, strengthening Griffith's hand at just the right moment.[224] So, although Dolan's re-election for North Leitrim on a Griffithite platform was never likely, the prominence it gave to Griffith's circle gave it greater leverage on entering negotiations with the Sinn Féin League in September. However, the situation was more complex than this analysis suggests. For as well as strengthening Griffith's hand, Dolan's defection also forced it, pushing the National Council towards a premature engagement with the rigours of national politics. Despite modest successes in local elections, the National Council had refrained from putting up candidates in the 1906 general election and Griffith showed little eagerness to do so in the near future. The demands of the Hungarian parallel provided good reason for resisting formal political engagement. Rather than demanding the creation of a new political party, the policy demanded the conversion of the parliamentary party. I.P.P. members could then act in tandem with the more radical forces that Griffith represented. However, the trickle of I.P.P. defections stymied Griffith's projections; how, then, were the Sinn Féin bodies to respond? Esmonde, Sweetman, and then, in 1907, Dolan and O'Mara, all pushed on the National Council the need for an alternative organisation to the I.P.P. The Hungarian parallel demanded not that the I.P.P. be replaced, but that the I.P.P. adopt the policy of withdrawal. This would then allow the I.R.B., through the Cumann na nGaedhael, to play the role of Kossuth. Fenians could reinforce the new radicalism of the I.P.P., without betraying their political ideals – this would be in line with the I.R.B. constitution. The irony, of course, was that the more orthodox separatists were also pushing for the establishment of a political organisation that drew together the variegated nodules of the new separatism. Griffith was caught

---

[223] McCartan to McGarrity, 2 Feb. 1907, McGarrity Papers (N.L.I., MS 17457/4).
[224] Laffan, *Resurrection of Ireland*, p. 25.

between these two conflicting positions. How could the wishes of the Fenian separatists be reconciled with those of the radicalised constitutionalists?

The private papers of MacSwiney and McCartan clearly show that they did not seek reconciliation, but to ambush the movement from within. In January 1906 McCartan believed that the Dungannon Clubs would support an amalgamation, but that the 'young men will then be able to force the pace',[225] meaning that they would push for the adoption of more extreme ends. At the end of the year he reported:

> Griffith is a newspaper man. Take him out of that & he is useless. Hobson is an organiser and a businessman. I think Griffith would not be jealous of Hobson getting power but he may fear he would go too far and spoil the movement. He wants men whom he can command[,] men who will run to him to see what they will say. This he knows Hobson will not do. He fears the 'immoderate' [. . .] He is a man of unbounded ability and hence all are slow to differ with him. He may be right but I think that he is mistaken. He has the greatest admiration for the Volunteers & considers their triumph the greatest in Irish history. The Nat. Council would be purely another repeal movement only for the Dungannon Clubs.[226]

MacSwiney complained that the National Council was 'taking precautions to prevent themselves . . . being considered separatists. Grattan is the ideal not Tone or Davis or Emmet or Hugh O'Neill.'[227] In October McCartan was more optimistic, anticipating a tripartite amalgamation on the basis of 'the Republic'.[228] By July 1907 MacSwiney hoped that the Cork branches of the Celtic Literary Society and the National Council would draw up a plan for the amalgamation of the Sinn Féin League and the National Council.[229] This attempt to seize the initiative was confused by P. S. O'Hegarty who insisted on proposing that the amalgamation be completed on separatist terms. MacSwiney disagreed; retreating from his earlier orthodoxy he argued that unity could only be achieved on the basis of the Sinn Féin policy. MacSwiney neatly summarised the difficulty the separatists had in defining their aims, demonstrating that constitutionalism's colonisation of advanced nationalist terminology forced separatists into adopting ever more specific demands. The parliamentarians had effectively appropriated 'independence'; the old commitment of the Y.I.S. to 'sovereign independence' had failed to clarify the situation; and this was why the C.L.S. had stated that its objective was an Irish republic, 'as our aim was to make it clear to all that we wanted to break the English connection.'

---

[225] McCartan to McGarrity, 21 Jan. 1906, McGarrity Papers (N.L.I., MS 17457/2).
[226] McCartan to McGarrity, 29 Dec. 1906, McGarrity Papers (N.L.I., MS 17617/1).
[227] MacSwiney Diary, 3 Dec. 1906 (U.C.D. P48c/103).
[228] McCartan to McGarrity, 2 Oct. 1906 (N.L.I., MS 17617/1).
[229] MacSwiney Diary, 3 July 1907, 22 July 1907.

It is evident, therefore, why the controversy over '82 as an alternative to separation had become so acute. For the Hungarian strategy to have any hope of succeeding the Deaks and the Kossuths had to remain organisationally separate. By entering into the Sinn Féin League in September 1907, the National Council effectively abandoned the Hungarian policy. Sinn Féin attempted to impose conformity on the right and the left of the movement and to pose as an alternative to the parliamentary party. Under the precepts of the Hungarian policy neither was necessary. What was necessary was the continued propagation of the plan. Griffith's reluctance to engage in the contests of conventional politics surely stemmed from this vital insight. Sinn Féin's formation was not premature, it was fundamentally the wrong thing to do. As James Doyle of Piltown argued of the impact of the Irish Council Bill: 'It's much to be regretted that men of advanced views are leaving the [home rule] party as they would help very much to drag the laggards on. Extreme men are wanted in every branch and party to give them life.'[230] O'Mara and Dolan reckoned the Council Bill debacle had highlighted the home rule party's inability to affect the decision making process at Westminster. Both regarded Westminster procedural reform and the party's supine posture as rendering attendance on Parnellite principles impossible. To Esmonde, Dolan explained his advocacy of Sinn Féinism and his resignation from the party thus: 'The Irish party went to Westminster, not to legislate, but with the avowed object of making legislation impossible.'[231]

VI

On 5 September 1906 T. W. Rolleston furnished Lady Aberdeen, facing her third term as wife of the Lord Lieutenant of Ireland, with an explanation of the popularity of Sinn Féin. Although a little bruised following *United Irishman*'s harsh criticism of his pamphlet 'Ireland and the Empire', Rolleston admitted that Sinn Féin represented all that was most impressive in Irish politics at the present time. 'It is of course a relic from the old Fenianism,' he began, 'but in a way, it is worse than Fenianism. It does not, for the present at all events, contemplate serious action, as Fenianism did, but it throws itself all the more vigorously into the mission of influencing thought.' Moreover,

> The strength of these people lies in the fact that they have more sincerity, more high-mindedness, more principle, and very much more education and intellect, than any other section of the nationalist party at present possesses. Hence their

---

[230] Quoted in Lavelle, *James O'Mara*, p. 80.
[231] Lavelle, *James O'Mara*, pp 70–88. For Dolan's emergent Sinn Féinism, his attempts to bring the North Leitrim U.I.L. with him, and the by-election in general, see Ciarán Ó Duibhir, *Sinn Féin: The First Election 1908* (Manorhamilton, 1983).

great and growing influence over all the active young minds now coming to maturity in Ireland. Young people are usually impassioned for ideas and reason, when they have education to grasp them. They are getting the education now, in catholic and nationalistic Ireland.

Rolleston predicted that the catholic church was the only force in Irish society likely to prevent Sinn Féin gaining a hold over the young outside of Dublin. However, the most remarkable feature of this letter was the grounds on which Rolleston felt Sinn Féin had to be combated. Suppression by the catholic church could not defeat Sinn Féin thinking; to defeat them fully required 'ideals as high as theirs and more practicable, a logic more in touch with realities. A victory of thought in fact, not a victory of force or authority.'[232] This focus on Sinn Féin's logical and rational outlook indicated the transformation of Irish separatism that it had affected. No conservative, albeit one with Irish Ireland proclivities, would have considered the I.R.B. in the same light. It is easy to be sceptical about Griffith's constitutional theories, his economic projections, and his statistics; it is right to be appalled by *United Irishman's* and *Sinn Féin's* occasional but unquestioning recourse to anti-Semitism;[233] it is hard, however, to deny the impact of Sinn Féin propaganda. Numerically weak, Irish intellectuals and politicians were nonetheless stimulated and slightly alarmed by Sinn Féin. As Tom Kettle had described Sinn Féin, they were 'a small party with a large capacity for getting themselves talked about'.[234] In the *North American Review* of February 1908 Rolleston continued the eulogy:

Young Ireland is now educated as it never was before, and is learning to think. It will not be content with a flabby opportunism in America, imperialism in Australia, agrarianism in Connaught, and a self-reliant nationalism nowhere. Parliamentarianism will be forced back onto first principles. It cannot afford to be nakedly opportunistic and to scoff at principles any longer, as it did in the days when it had indeed *enemies* in Ireland, but no *rivals*.[235]

In 1910 A. G. Wilson, one of Plunkett's close co-workers in the co-operative movement, took up the theme. He gave a wide-ranging lecture at Queen's University, Belfast on the industrial movement in Ireland. This was constructive unionism at its most impressively pluralist. He celebrated as 'the first ripple of a new wave of thought' the foundation of the Gaelic League in 1893, and linked this to the co-operative movement (for which he claimed 900 societies,

---

[232] The letter is reproduced in C. H. Rolleston, *Portrait of an Irishman: A Biographical Sketch of T. W. Rolleston* (London, 1939), pp 117–20.
[233] Griffith was a Zionist who believed the Jews degraded themselves through exploitative practices because there was not a Jewish nation-state.
[234] *W.I.*, 13 Apr. 1907.
[235] Rolleston, *Portrait*, p. 121.

a membership of 100,000, and a turnover in 1909 of £2½ million sterling), and the recently established Local Government Board. What bound these organisations together was the principle of self-help and Wilson claimed as patron saint Belfast's Dr Samuel Smiles, that doyen of mid-Victorian radical respectability. In a neat move that made a mockery of a generation's separatist polemic, Wilson translated self-help into Irish as Sinn Féin, and Sinn Féin, despite its 'comic opera . . . extravagance' on the national question, was congratulated for its 'extremely practical suggestions for the betterment of Ireland'.[236] Such urbane inclusiveness can only have infuriated Sinn Féin.

Political pressures ensured John Redmond was less gracious. In a speech at Battersea responding to the Dolan defection he mocked Sinn Féin's lack of direction. 'I have looked everywhere for any indication of what this new policy is, and I find that after careful study the only new policy which they advocate is the old one – namely the discrediting of the Irish national party (loud cheers).'[237] Redmond could be confident; the party easily won the North Leitrim campaign and it was unclear what Sinn Féin could do next. One solution was offered by the *Weekly Independent*. A cartoon showed a home ruler approaching a Sinn Féiner with his hand outstretched, 'We agree upon the gospel of self-reliance in industrial and social matters, and there is no reason in the world why we should not work hand in hand upon these lines.'[238] An editorial pursued this theme:

> Parnell asked men as advanced as any Sinn Féiner to march along with him as far as their roads lay side by side. It is surely deplorable to see so many young men, who ought to be the backbone of the nationalist movement, standing aside in an attitude of hostility towards the majority of their countrymen. Could not some means be now devised to bring about a better feeling, without humiliation or sacrifice of principle, on either side?

This was not possible. Among Sinn Féin's achievements before the First World War was the fashioning of a nationalist platform, however fragile, which could contain a range of advanced nationalist opinion but was invulnerable to constitutional gesturing. Both constitutionalists and advanced nationalists were inveigled in internal debates concerning aims and aspirations, both embraced a host of political identities, but, thanks in part to the vigilance of Griffith, dallying with the other side ceased to be an acceptable part of Irish nationalist manoeuvring; only defection would do. If Dolan's partial and temporary success in bringing the North Leitrim U.I.L. round to Sinn Féin

[236] A. G. Wilson, 'Recent History of Ireland: With Special Reference to the Industrial Movement' in *The Queen's University of Belfast, University Lectures* no. 2 (Apr., 1910), pp 8–13. For Ireland to ignore England altogether 'would be something like Achill Island "ignoring" Ireland'.
[237] *W.I.*, 13 July 1907.
[238] *W.I.*, 29 Feb. 1908.

thinking indicated the possibility of a Sinn Féin–home rule nexus, the progress of the by-election showed this to be illusory, the final confirmation of the orphaning of Parnellism. Dolan greeted his defeat with defiant prophecy: his result was comparable to the 400 votes John Martin won in 1870 on a home rule platform against the victor's 2,000. A few years later home rule became the dominant political force in Ireland. 'So will it be with Sinn Féin.'[239]

[239] Ibid.

6

Fenian orthodoxies and volunteering, 1910–14

'Not coming believe volunteers will kill home rule'[1]

I

Travelling from Philadelphia to Pomeroy, County Tyrone, in September 1905, Patrick McCartan jotted down his impressions in a letter to Joseph McGarrity.[2] This commenced a lengthy correspondence that ensured the Clan na Gael leader was kept up to date with the progress of advanced nationalism and Fenianism. The familiarity with which McCartan wrote suggested close friendship and something of the relationship between mentor and protégé. McCartan was McGarrity's man in Ireland, providing a record of events that cut through the obfuscation of nationalist propaganda to reveal the manoeuvrings of separatist factions beneath. This opening letter revealed all the impetuous ebullience of youth with a pen in its hand – 'Personally I feel like a fighting cock' – not least in his tendency to extrapolate general conclusions from personal experience. On board the *Umbria* McCartan worked his way through the essential separatist reading of the moment: Arthur Griffith's *The Resurrection of Hungary*, John O'Leary's *Recollections of Fenians and Fenianism*, and a copy of the *Gaelic American*.[3] As was typical of his generation's scepticism for the doings of their Fenian forebears, he was unimpressed by O'Leary's lofty ambivalence. 'I can't see as yet where he did anything himself worth talking of. He thinks a whole lot but as yet he does not seem to put his thoughts into action.' McCartan continued his journey. No copy of *United Irishman* was to be found at any railway station between Cork and Dublin, though in Cork he was offered William O'Brien's *The Irish People*. Fellow travellers were a cause for optimism. A foreign food salesman complained that two-thirds of places

---

[1] Edward Martyn to Roger Casement, 10 Dec. 1913, telegram.

[2] McCartan to McGarrity, 30 Sept. 1905, McGarrity Papers (N.L.I., MS 17457/2).

[3] *Gaelic American*, launched September 1903, edited by John Devoy. Tom Clarke was assistant editor and effectively worked as manager. McCartan and Hobson were at various times its Dublin correspondent. *D.P.B. II*, pp 361–2.

would not take his produce owing to the demand for Irish food. A Presbyterian woman en route from Dublin to Pomeroy told of the scandal among her friends caused by her friendship with a catholic woman. But, she explained, she had been brought up in Killarney where this sort of bigotry was unknown.

It took McCartan a little while to situate himself in the complex topography of Irish nationalist activity. Initially most impressed by the Gaelic League, he sent McGarrity a series of celebratory letters shaped by the literary Fenian perspective:

> I went to the Gaelic League. Could almost cry with joy at what I saw. I found 34 young men & boys and nine girls. They were overswaying with patriotism. . . . They were all beginning to look in the right direction. The dawn is at hand.[4]

> The Gaelic League is the movement at present.[5]

> It is the greatest movement ever started in Ireland. It is not political apparently but it really is political in the worst sense of the word because it does not appear so. It is really doing things as England does them[:] quietly[,] but even more successfully. You see its great power is that it is educational.[6]

Soon McCartan was brought into Hobson's orbit, which saw him establish a branch of the Dungannon Clubs in his 'native locality' – Carrickmore, County Tyrone – on the basis of the Hungarian policy, believing the priests would not object.[7] Simultaneously, he worked through the Dungannon branch at the Royal University in Dublin on plans to issue a manifesto to the students of Ireland.[8] At his first meeting with Arthur Griffith there was no intimation of the troubled relationship that would follow. Griffith seemed unthreatening, diminutive: 'a very quiet man; a regular dreamer apparently'. The die was cast: on meeting Hobson a month later he was impressed by his brains, ideas, and energy.[9] Hobson's visit to the U.S.A. in February 1907 at the behest of Clan na Gael drew high praise from McGarrity: 'a wonderful young man . . . has brains equal to the task'.[10] Encouraged by the initial success of the Dungannon Club in Carrickmore – thirty-one joined at the outset – McCartan planned

---

[4] Patrick McCartan to McGarrity, 9 Oct. 1905, McGarrity Papers (N.L.I., MS 17457/2). The context of these letters appears to have been McGarrity's reluctance to have Clan na Gael continue financing the Gaelic League.

[5] Ibid., 19 Oct. 1905.

[6] Ibid., 24 Mar. 1906 (N.L.I., MS 17457/3).

[7] McCartan to McGarrity, 17 Nov. 1905 (N.L.I., MS 17457/2).

[8] McCartan to McGarrity, 24 Nov. 1905, ibid.

[9] McCartan to McGarrity, 20 & 23 Dec. 1905, ibid. McCartan reported that there were thirty subscribers to *U.I.* in Philadelphia and three in Chicago, while thirty copies of the *Gaelic American* were sold in Dublin each week.

[10] McGarrity to McCartan, 3 Mar. 1907 (N.L.I., MS 17457/4).

to establish a women's branch and a lace-making industry as a means to raise money for a library fund.[11] A month later a local priest, Father Donnelly, condemned the clubs, leaving McCartan furious. 'Wouldn't an act like that make you curse the day you left a free country. One can hardly keep from thinking that Ireland is unworthy of freedom. God knows it is hard to blame the Orangemen for their fear of Rome rule.'[12] Still, Father Short's lace-making class at Carrickmore saw 125 girls attend the opening. McCartan concluded, 'the young are very good everywhere but there is no hope for the old.'[13] Cork activist Liam de Róiste equally disdained the old. He confided his revulsion to his diary:

> Tales, not to their credit, are told about them. There is something repellent to me in all those tales I hear of the remnants of Fenianism: suggestions of treachery, suspicions, cunning 'dodges', [the] absurd air of secrecy. Spies and informers lurk everywhere. No man could trust another. Such is the atmosphere of the 'stories'. Even the private moral character of men who were of some prominence in the Fenian movement is assailed. There are whisperings and shakings-of-the-head. What I think is, that Fenianism: or men connected with it: degenerated. It is not those men who can now lead a movement for the freedom of the banba.[14]

He continued, despondent and brooding, frustrated by the rate of progress:

> Still, after the day, I am tired: tired of the bickerings, the pettinesses, the mean-nesses, that seem to be part of all this 'Irish Ireland' movement. Perhaps the fault lies in myself. I have preached of duty and perseverance: but working for Eire is soul-killing: seems to drag one to mean things.

Alice Milligan similarly warned Hobson off the 'old gang' in Dublin, as did Maud Gonne at the time of Sinn Féin's amalgamation. She 'said her husband [John MacBride] used to attend secret meetings but that it was only an excuse for debauchery & . . . they kept the young men from doing anything.'[15]

At the time of the Dolan defection there was plenty of lively separatist activity to keep McCartan occupied. Meetings under the guise of the National Council, the I.R.B., Sinn Féin, and the G.A.A. took place in December and January across Ireland. Seasonal celebrations took on various forms and Sinn Féin continued to make its presence felt in separatist circles, including the G.A.A. The 1908 G.A.A. annual convention at Thurles decided to hold future

---

[11] McCartan to McGarrity, 29 Dec. 1905 (N.L.I., MS 17457/2).
[12] McCartan to McGarrity, 21 Jan. 1906 (N.L.I., MS 17457/3).
[13] McCartan to McGarrity, 13 Jan. 1906, ibid.
[14] Liam de Róiste Diaries, 11 Dec. 1904 (C.A.I. U271/A/6). Banba: a poetic word for Ireland.
[15] McCartan to McGarrity, 4 May 1907 (N.L.I., MS 17617/1). Letter from Gonne enclosed with 25 May letter to McGarrity from McCartan.

meetings in Dublin, which the police considered would put the convention in the control of the I.R.B.[16]

Police reports over the winter of 1907–8 are striking for the names they bring together. Seumas MacManus, John MacBride, and Denis McCullough, men associated with the revolutionary period and the welter of memoir and history that followed, were under close police surveillance. In the same months Hobson's move to Cushendall, County Antrim, and Tom Clarke's return to Ireland from New York on 5 December and his acquisition of a tobacco shop on Amiens Street, Dublin were monitored.[17] In March notice was taken of Sean MacDermott's presence at a County Antrim Sinn Féin meeting: 120 people attended and he was the guest of Neil J. O'Boyle, member for Ulster on the Supreme Council. According to police sources, O'Boyle believed the I.R.B. had adopted Sinn Féin policy.[18] He was later replaced – willingly according to Hobson – on the Supreme Council by McCullough, who was keen to push the I.R.B. away from this acquiescent attitude to Sinn Féin.[19] A year later Sean MacDermott was based in Tipperary working as official Sinn Féin organiser for the south, associating closely with the local branches of the Gaelic League. When re-establishing the branch of the National Council in Killorglin, County Kerry, he was helped by a number of national school teachers.[20] Ernest Blythe was briefly noted in December 1909 as someone who had come to police attention owing to his association with the '98 movement.[21] He had followed this up with interest in Sinn Féin (he attended several meetings of the central executive) and was known generally for his close association with the most advanced section of Dublin nationalists. Hobson later wrote of the period: 'while Griffith supplied the façade of the policy, the group of men associated with the Dungannon Clubs applied the driving force to organise the country, in so far as it was ever organised.'[22]

It is striking that this activity coincided with the return to Ireland of Tom Clarke, who is traditionally attributed with the organisational rejuvenation

---

[16] C.O. 904/118, pp 3–4, 6, 22, 24, 26–7.

[17] Ibid., p. 21; C.O. 904/11, Dec. 1907, pp 316, 334, 343, 382, 398. Clarke was met by his brother-in-law John Daly at Queenstown with whom he stayed for a few days; on his circuitous route to Dublin he looked up old mates James F. Egan, P. Lavelle, D. Whelan, and James Fitzharris a.k.a. Skin-the-Goat, of Invincibles fame. By June he was established in the shop and had been named sole agent for Colonel Everard's Irish Tobacco; by July he entered into his rightful place on the B list of I.R.B. suspects. P. Lavelle was described by the chief commissioner of the D.M.P. thus: 'He is an associate of the leaders of extreme political movements, and, being a solicitor, is very useful to them professionally. He is fond of drink and consequently not looked up as a man likely to be entrusted with the carrying out of delicate secret society work.' Oct. 1907, p. 299.

[18] Ibid., p. 54.

[19] Bulmer Hobson, *Ireland Yesterday and Tomorrow* (Tralee, 1968), p. 35.

[20] C.O. 904/118, pp 425, 456.

[21] C.O. 904/12, Dec. 1909, p. 171.

[22] Hobson, *Ireland*, p. 22.

of the I.R.B. Clarke's importance, however, can easily be exaggerated. McCartan told McGarrity regarding the later tensions with Sinn Féin, 'Tom Clarke now gets a knock occasionally though poor Tom has not a minute to spare from his business.'[23] Clarke's Dublin shops provided a central headquarters for Dublin Fenianism, functioning rather as Allan's office at the *Irish Independent* did in the 1890s. But he did not travel around Ireland promoting Fenianism and selling the new I.R.B. newspaper *Irish Freedom*. Until his expulsion from the Supreme Council in 1910 for financial irregularities P. T. Daly was the most effective I.R.B. organiser. Sean MacDermott also played a key role, working initially as an official Sinn Féin organiser, but overall the attention paid to Daly invites a questioning of F. S. L. Lyons's grouping of him with the old men seen to be impeding I.R.B. activism.[24] Writing in November 1917, P. S. O'Hegarty remembered Daly and M. J. Crowe as the only men on the I.R.B. Supreme Council of his generation.[25] In Glasgow in November 1907 Daly addressed 100 I.R.B. suspects at the Sinn Féin League rooms, and remarked on how well the organisation was doing in the south of Ireland since the death of an old member, presumably P. N. Fitzgerald. At the same time the police reported a remarkable increase in membership in Cavan from 300 to 800.[26] Daly condemned the Glasgow I.R.B. in May 1909 for its lethargy, urging that any existing member who failed to introduce a new member within three months should be investigated. Such men could 'not [be] keeping the company of the proper class of Irishmen', moreover, 'men with religious scruples were at once [to be] dropped.'[27] Daly boasted that three circles existed in Trinity College (very unlikely), and when one of the students was holidaying in County Leitrim he succeeded in establishing an I.R.B. circle from among members of the A.O.H. MacDermott and MacCartan might have inspired these claims. MacDermott was from Leitrim, and had spent some time in Glasgow, before discovering separatism through the A.O.H. and joining the Dungannon Clubs. McCartan established a branch of the Dungannon at the Royal University, Dublin.[28] Despite this activity, Roger Casement thought advanced nationalism's ability to spread Sinn Féin's ideas in the countryside was inadequate. He told Hobson in September 1907 they needed 'a James Stephens to go round on foot & talk over the firesides to the young men'.[29]

Lyons was surely right to regard Clarke's commitment to a rising in his lifetime and his close links to Clan na Gael as crucial to later events. Clarke's involvement in the bombing campaign of the early 1880s testified to his

---

[23] McCartan to McGarrity, 21 Jan. 1910 (N.L.I., MS 17457/7).
[24] Lyons, *Ireland since the Famine* (London, 1971), p. 318.
[25] P. S. O'Hegarty, 'Recollections of the I.R.B.', manuscript written 7–11 Nov. 1917 preserved in the Casement Papers (N.L.I., MS 36210), pp 1–2.
[26] C.O. 904/11, Nov. 1907, p. 306.
[27] Ibid., p. 421.
[28] Hobson, *Ireland*, pp 8, 21.
[29] Casement to Hobson, 2 Sept. 1907, Hobson Papers (N.L.I., MS 13158/2).

determination, and the years he had spent in prison fortified his vengeful urge. His much-reported single-mindedness chimes with the little evidence there is of him engaging with the Irish Ireland movement and Sinn Féin. Clarke was a throw-back, schooled in the traditions of Fenian conspiracy, who offered little of O'Leary's thoughtful nuance or Pearse's Gaelic mysticism. But he was well connected, with the past and the Clan, which allowed him considerable influence and leverage. He offered certainty freighted with experience and the young men of Hobson's circle, grappling with the dilemmas thrown up by Sinn Féin, found this irresistible. The backdrop to Clarke's ascendancy was the re-emergence of the home rule issue and the consequent decline of Sinn Féin. The organisational work, however, had been long under way thanks to Hobson, MacDermott, and P. T. Daly; they provided the essential foundations of the rejuvenation of the I.R.B. Clarke's status as the leading signatory of the Easter rising has led historians to exaggerate his importance in these early stages. Hobson has been marginalised in the hagiography of the period owing to the compromising attitude he took towards the entry of Redmondites onto the Volunteer executive in the summer of 1914 and his opposition to the 1916 rising.[30]

Later tensions between Hobson and the revolutionaries should not obscure his earlier significance. North Leitrim had filled him with enthusiasm and he believed success would have helped build Sinn Féin's electoral base. He wrote to McGarrity: 'If a good fight is made in Leitrim other M.P.s will resign and once we win a seat the fight will be on and we will rouse the whole country. Four or five others are ready to come over to us and others can be forced presently.'[31] As the later tensions between Redmondite M.P.s and other M.P.s within the home rule party and the overtures of William O'Brien's All-for-Ireland League (discussed below) suggest, Hobson's optimism was not entirely without foundation. A good fight was made, but victory eluded them and Sinn Féin's challenge failed to fructify. Hobson complained of the political leadership the following February:

> They ought to do six times the work they do. Then unless Dublin lead the country won't move. We cannot move Ireland from Belfast how ever hard we work here & I am going to try to move the Dublin men to do some work. Now there are great opportunities for progress if Dublin would only wake up & give the lead. The country is ready and looking for a lead – but has not got it yet.[32]

Provincial resentment of Sinn Féin was characteristic of Hobson's circle. McCartan believed 'the whole aim of the leaders is to centralise everything

---

[30] That his memoirs were published by a minor Tralee publisher at a time when I.R.B. memoirs were a good commercial proposition is also of historiographical interest.
[31] Hobson to McGarrity, 29 June 1907, McGarrity Papers (N.L.I., MS 17612).
[32] Hobson to McGarrity, 17 Feb. 1908, McGarrity Papers (N.L.I., MS 17453).

in Dublin & have all in the hand of Dublin men who will grovel at the feet of Arthur Griffith.'[33] It is striking that the principal separatists of the period and the signatories of the 1916 Proclamation were all, with the exception of Joseph Plunkett and Patrick Pearse, born outside Dublin. Terence MacSwiney and P. S. O'Hegarty were from Cork, Tom Clarke was brought up in Tyrone, Sean MacDermott in County Leitrim, Denis McCullough and Bulmer Hobson in Belfast (albeit of very different backgrounds), Eamonn Ceannt in County Galway, Thomas MacDonagh in Tipperary, John MacBride in County Mayo, James Connolly in Edinburgh, The O'Rahilly in County Kerry, Roger Casement in County Dublin (with family roots in County Antrim), and Constance Markievicz (born in London) in County Sligo. Writing long afterwards Hobson discerned the difference between Sinn Féin and the Dungannon Clubs in terms of spirit rather than policy. Although this underplays the ideological dilemmas provoked by Sinn Féin, it was an acute exercise in self-identification:

> The National Council aimed at building up a political and economic organisation on conventional lines, whereas the Dungannon Clubs sought really to create an intense conviction and a passionate faith among a necessarily small number of people. Griffith looked to local and parliamentary elections, to economic exposition of a logical and hard-headed character, and used satire to great skill and effect. We, in the Club, while advancing much the same arguments, sought to give them an emotional content and force and an intensity of conviction, with the definite aim of creating an unbreakable psychological strength which would compensate for the inevitable material weakness of the Irish movement, as compared with the power of Britain to crush it.[34]

Provincial separatists, then, tended to identify Sinn Féin with the grubby manoeuvrings of Dublin corporation politics, the jettisoning of idealism this required, and an excessive preoccupation with the politics of the home rule party. It is tempting to see these attitudes as anticipating the apolitical culture of the flying columns of the Anglo-Irish war and the pride with which they disdained 'politics'.[35] For example, P. S. O'Hegarty was disturbed by *Daily Sinn Féin*'s pragmatism. Griffith

> has watered down everything as low as he possibly can. In Thursday's issue he proposes an alliance with the Tories! And the only definite idea in the paper seems to be to conciliate the unionists at all hazards. I believe in conciliating them but not at the expense of lowering our own practice or profession of nationalism.[36]

---

[33] McCartan to McGarrity, 18 Sept. 1909, McGarrity Papers (N.L.I., MS 17457/7).
[34] Hobson, *Ireland Yesterday and Tomorrow*, pp 4, 22.
[35] Peter Hart, *The IRA and its Enemies: Violence and Community in County Cork 1916–1923* (Oxford, 1998), pp 236–40.
[36] O'Hegarty to George Gavan Duffy, 15 Sept. 1909, Duffy Papers (N.L.I., MS 5581).

McCartan shared these concerns. Responding to a *Sinn Féin* editorial on the 'balance of power' at Westminster in January 1910, he considered Sinn Féin's policy, 'once a thing to catch the imagination & fire the enthusiasm of Irishmen', had 'become a policy of pointing out the mistakes of Parliamentarianism & indicating the course the advocates of the latter should follow in order to do something for Ireland. Really you can hardly keep from blushing on hearing Sinn Féin mentioned.'[37]

Separatist concern was heightened by Griffith's apparent decision to allow Sinn Féin to co-operate with William O'Brien's All-for-Ireland League (A.F.I.L.). Centred on his support base in Cork and in alliance with Tim Healy, the A.F.I.L. was O'Brien's latest attempt to establish himself as the leader of Irish nationalism. He hoped to link up his Cork supporters with protestant home rulers and advanced men.[38] Claiming support from every section of Cork nationalists, O'Brien looked to a Dublin launch in order to avoid the league taking on 'a certain sectional and provincial aspect'.[39] John Shawe-Taylor was dispatched to Dublin to cut a deal with Griffith. In return for Sinn Féin support, O'Brien would finance Sinn Féin candidates in Dublin and, crucially, a National Council would be established to deliberate on when Irish M.P.s should attend Westminster.[40]

To this end, James Brady – Dublin solicitor, Sinn Féiner, and O'Brienite – offered the Sinn Féiner George Gavan Duffy a Dublin constituency claiming he 'had practically succeeded in getting the Sinn Féin party here to admit to parliamentary representation on certain conditions, viz. subject to control of a national council sitting here.' This was an exaggeration. O'Brien later claimed Griffith was in 'cordial agreement',[41] but in turning down the offer Duffy correctly anticipated Sinn Féin's response.[42] A special meeting of the Sinn Féin executive on 20 December discussed the proposals and the departure from abstentionism was voted unconstitutional. Hobson, Markievicz, and P. T. Daly were among those opposing.[43] O'Hegarty, infuriated by the overtures ('about the worst thing I've come across yet'[44]), printed the Brady letters in a special edition of the *Irish Nation*. He claimed Griffith's co-operation was dictated by a chronic lack of funds and the need to find subsidy for the *Sinn Féin* daily, which folded in January, its sixth month of publication. McCartan wrote to McGarrity, underlining the important role I.R.B. activists, and Hobson in particular, continued to play in maintaining the Fenian ideal:

[37] McCartan to McGarrity, 21 Jan. 1910 (N.L.I., MS 17457/7).
[38] Sally Warwick-Haller, *William O'Brien and the Irish Land War* (Dublin, 1990), pp 259–62.
[39] William O'Brien, *The Irish Revolution* (Dublin, 1923), pp 66–8.
[40] Joseph V. O'Brien, *William O'Brien and the Course of Irish Politics 1881–1918* (Los Angeles, 1976), pp 172–3.
[41] O'Brien, *Irish Revolution*, p. 68.
[42] Brady to Duffy, 9 Dec. 1909, copy of Duffy to Brady, 10 Dec. 1909 (N.L.I., MS 5581).
[43] W. Sears to Duffy, 22 Dec. 1909, Duffy Papers (N.L.I., MS 6681).
[44] O'Hegarty to Duffy, 14 Jan. 1910 (N.L.I., MS 5581).

The men who make movements a success here will not in future have confidence in Griffith on account of his intrigues with O'Brien and the moderates – the decent men of them – will dread him on account of his unscrupulous & malignant attacks on every man who differs with him.

It is amusing to hear sometimes of the explanations for the lack of progress of Sinn Féin, Hobson while he was here was the villain & received most attention but now that he is absent some one else had to be found & Tom Clarke now gets a knock occasionally though poor Tom has not a minute to spare from his business. One member of the executive was told that if he had thrown his influence against Hobson all would be well. They did their best to run Hobson out of being vice-president [of Sinn Féin] and had a great look out for a rival that would beat him. . . .

You see everything was directed to carry off the O'Brien deal & Hobson was supposed to be in the way just as the Dungannon Clubs were in the way of the new Repeal Movement.[45]

At a meeting of the Dundalk Young Ireland Society on 9 February 1910 members who had supported T. M. Healy in the A.F.I.L. interest at the recent North Louth election were expelled.[46]

II

The publication of *Irish Freedom* in November 1910 arose from the need to unambiguously reassert republican virtue. Separatist suspicion of Sinn Féin and Griffith was heightened by the A.F.I.L. controversy, W. P. Ryan's *Peasant* did not strike the right separatist chord ('it has always been more social than national & it could never be popularised'[47]), and Hobson and his associates wished to free themselves from the inertia of the I.R.B. Supreme Council. If the turn of the century had seen advanced nationalism determine upon political independence, the publication of *Irish Freedom* saw the most dynamic clique within the movement bid for the leadership. McCartan's disdain for the direction *Sinn Féin* had taken was revealed in his description of *Irish Freedom* as emulating the advanced nationalist *Gaelic American* and filling the gap left

---

[45] McCartan to McGarrity, 21 Jan. 1910 (N.L.I., MS 17457 (7)).

[46] C.O. 904/119, Feb. 1910, p. 38.

[47] McCartan to McGarrity, 4 Sept. 1910 (N.L.I., MS 17457/8): 'The editor has ideas of his own & they don't entirely coincide with – well those of John Mitchel. He is a nationalist of course but you know of the Gaelic League literary type. Right enough of a kind but not the kind we want.' Also, Casement to Hobson, 23 Dec. 1909, Hobson Papers (N.L.I., MS 13158/6): 'Ryan's socialism exceeds his nationalism almost – altho' I never doubt the depth of the latter. But he takes rather a crabbed view of things often, and it makes one tired week after week.' See also Victoria Glandon, *Arthur Griffith and the Advanced-Nationalist Press, 1900–1922* (New York, 1985), pp 19–23.

by the demise of the *United Irishman*. He thought it on publication 'a huge success'. 'It seems popular in every corner it has reached and I think it got round fairly well. We printed 7,000 of first issue and 6,000 of second issue.'[48] This jubilation stemmed in part from the controversy sparked by the paper's establishment. It was the product of something approaching a *coup d'état* within the I.R.B. Supreme Council and this was not to go unchallenged.

McCullough's famed expulsion of his father from the I.R.B. now seems emblematic of the determination of Hobson's group to reanimate Irish republicanism from within, while at the same time aggressively and openly propagating its message. *Irish Freedom* marked the reassertion of the Fenian ideal. Between November 1910 and its closure the newspaper was successively edited by McCartan, O'Hegarty, Hobson, and after June 1914, O'Hegarty again. Hobson and O'Hegarty wrote the editorials.[49] *Irish Freedom* undoubtedly represented a defeat for Griffith and his attempt to reconfigure advanced nationalism. Promulgating a sophisticated cultural separatism that had absorbed the de-Anglicising agenda of the Gaelic League, *Irish Freedom* was unambiguously republican. Louis Le Roux summarised and simplified the division thus: 'All those who did not find the parliamentarians bold enough but who believed in expediency read Griffith's *Sinn Féin*. Griffith would have accepted concessions, *Irish Freedom* wanted no concessions, but independence – a republic.'[50] Despite its controversial beginnings, the newspaper was financed by the I.R.B., run by the I.R.B., and largely written by members of the I.R.B.[51]

Irish Freedom conclusively ended a partial ideological ceasefire of great complexity and variety. From Isaac Butt's successful attempt to combine tenant right, amnesty, and home rule on the same political platform, through Parnell's domestication of Fenianism and the parliamentary party's reunification, the I.R.B. was in a pragmatic relationship with constitutional nationalism. The irony was that *Irish Freedom*'s reassertion of orthodox Fenianism stemmed from the challenge laid down by Griffith's ideas and journalism. However far the home rule campaign left the I.R.B. embattled and reduced, it did not fundamentally undermine I.R.B. precepts. Again and again the constitutional politicians offered home rule as an efficacious alternative to physical force rather than an unambiguous replacement of it.

The Griffithite subtleties had elicted a less sure-footed response. Not only did Sinn Féin offer a nationalism based upon passive resistance and the '82 paradigm that questioned the achievement of an Irish republic as advanced nationalism's ultimate aim, it also laid down an organisational challenge to the I.R.B.'s primacy within the separatist vanguard. Faced with Griffith's achievement, particularly in Dublin local politics, the I.R.B. Supreme Council

---

[48] McCartan to McGarrity, 4 Sept. 1910, 6 Jan. 1911 (N.L.I., MS 17457/8 & /9).
[49] O'Hegarty, 'Recollections', pp 9–10.
[50] Louis N. Le Roux, *Tom Clarke and the Irish Freedom Movement* (Dublin, 1936), p. 93.
[51] Glandon, *Arthur Griffith*, p. 75.

was largely acquiescent if not openly co-operative. As has been discussed, Daly and MacDermott's organising efforts had been to the benefit of both organisations. This undermined the independence of the I.R.B. and brought into question its exclusive possession of the separatist tradition. Griffith's exact relationship with the I.R.B. is uncertain and a brief sketch of opinion on this matter reveals the shadowy nature of I.R.B. membership. Richard Davis considers the tensions between Griffith and the organisation as easily exaggerated; Leon Ó Broin is inconclusive and although he notes that G. A. Lyons believed Griffith left the I.R.B. he appears to hold that Griffith distanced himself without making a formal break. Patrick O'Keeffe, one-time secretary of Sinn Féin, argued in 1964: 'He was never put out and never went out. There are all kinds of fellows like that.' This somewhat contradicts Hobson's picture of I.R.B. selectivity in this period: numbers may have fallen to around 1,500, but they were 'picked men'.[52] Indeed, Hobson reverses the stress, suggesting that he, O'Hegarty, McCullough, and others ceased to work for Sinn Féin in 1910.[53] Overall Brian Maye's view that there was little contact between Griffith and the I.R.B. in 1910–14 seems close to the truth.[54]

P. S. O'Hegarty's claim in *The Victory of Sinn Féin* that the I.R.B. never quarrelled with Griffith and always worked with him does not help to clarify matters.[55] O'Hegarty had long questioned the legitimacy of Griffith's influence over Sinn Féin. Before the key convention of 1910, when I.R.B. members effectively withdrew from the Sinn Féin executive,[56] O'Hegarty ran his proposed resolutions past George Gavan Duffy. They were highly provocative, saying that Sinn Féin's attention had been diverted away from its principles. The preoccupation with Dublin corporation politics should cease; they should focus on promoting their principles and policy in opposition to all others, 'whether unionist, Redmondite, or O'Brienite'; and, most importantly, the connection with *Sinn Féin* must cease. Given that Sinn Féin exercised no control over the newspaper, Griffith was to cease promoting the paper as the movement's official organ.[57] Both Hobson and O'Hegarty were hostile to the monopolisation of the Sinn Féin executive by Dublin men and were adamant that the best men should be elected despite any organisational inconvenience.[58] Duffy,

---

[52] Hobson, *Ireland*, p. 36.

[53] Richard Davis, *Arthur Griffith and Non-violent Sinn Féin* (Dublin, 1974), p. 67; Leon Ó Broin, *Revolutionary Underground: The Story of the Irish Republican Brotherhood 1858–1924* (Dublin, 1976), pp 135–6, 150; Hobson, *Ireland Yesterday and Tomorrow*, p. 12.

[54] Brian Maye, *Arthur Griffith* (Dublin, 1997), pp 112–16.

[55] P. S. O'Hegarty, *The Victory of Sinn Féin* (Dublin, 1924, 1998), p. 97.

[56] Michael Laffan, *The Resurrection of Ireland* (Cambridge, 1999), p. 31. Hobson, O'Hegarty and Seán T. O'Kelly did not seek re-election to the national executive after they had failed to weaken Griffith's hold on the organisation.

[57] Resolutions preserved in Duffy papers (N.L.I., MS 5581).

[58] McCartan to Devoy, 31 Mar. 1910, *D.P.B. II*, pp 390–4. McCartan's letters to Devoy were more temperate than those to McGarrity.

generally loyal to Griffith, rejected the resolutions on the grounds that they would not stimulate Sinn Féin to more concerted effort: 'if the movement is to live much more radical motions are necessary.' Moreover,

> I will be no party to your open war on Griffith, until I see the man, or men, who are prepared and able to take his place, and, if such a man were visible your motions, or the idea of them, would be carried by acclamation, in spite of the Dublin crowd, but there isn't.[59]

The Victory of Sinn Féin was shaped by the experience of the Irish civil war and questioned the violence which had transformed Ireland *after* the 1916 rising. By underplaying the ideological conflicts of the period before the rising, O'Hegarty strengthened his case that the revolution had been hijacked by brutal men unschooled in the sophisticated separatism of Sinn Féin.[60] His earlier short book *Sinn Féin: An Illumination* was much more obviously a political intervention. Its harsh but balanced characterisation of Griffith formed part of a wider agenda to reclaim the pre-conditions of the rising and the rising itself for the I.R.B.[61] As in *The Victory of Sinn Féin*, O'Hegarty posited the pre-eminent influence of the I.R.B. to Irish nationalist progress. Invigorated by the Gaelic League, the I.R.B. encapsulated the essence of Irish nationalism and contrary to popular perceptions was solely responsible for the Easter rising – 'Sinn Féin had nothing to do with the insurrection.'[62] This erroneous identification of Sinn Féin with the rising 'rehabilitated' the movement following 'their failure to be "out"'. Believing Griffith to have never believed in physical force, O'Hegarty resented the political benefits he accrued from I.R.B. dynamism.[63]

O'Hegarty's assessment was more balanced than this suggests. Griffith was named the most able Irishman since Mitchel, and through his newspapers he was, paradoxically, 'more responsible for the Fenian spirit in Ireland' than any other man. There was 'no epoch of Irish History, no phase of the many-sided Irish problem, that he [could not] elucidate'. But several striking caveats had to be taken into account. O'Hegarty twice highlighted the years 1899–1911 as being those of Griffith's greatest importance, noting that *Irish Freedom* 'more properly represented the Fenian element' from 1911 to 1914. Moreover, Griffith's character flaws were fundamental. He was 'aloof', had 'no real faith in anybody else', and was 'always more or less cold towards anybody who [tried]

---

[59] Duffy to O'Hegarty, 6 Aug. 1910, 10 Aug. 1910 (N.L.I., MS 5581).

[60] O'Hegarty's analysis invites further unpicking. He celebrated Michael Collins and the 'defensive' war of the Volunteers but at the same time condemned the brutality of the 'moral collapse' of the Irish occasioned by the Tan War.

[61] P. S. O'Hegarty, *Sinn Féin: An Illumination* (Dublin, 1919), pp 28–33.

[62] Ibid., pp 52–3.

[63] Cf. *Victory*, pp 96–7 where O'Hegarty celebrates Griffith as a physical force separatist who thought insurrection inefficacious.

to do any political work on his own, in or about his own particular sphere.' O'Hegarty was wholly consistent. At the time of Hobson's 1907 trip to America he described a meeting with Griffith: 'He wouldn't discuss anything, was quite hostile and sneering, and never even smiled.' It was difficult to work with him 'amicably without being a mere echo'.[64] With his harsh instinct for psychological weakness, O'Hegarty identified the death of William Rooney as central to the shaping of Griffith's personality. Left surrounded by lesser men, Griffith became intellectually isolated, which accentuated his authoritarian tendencies. Although O'Hegarty's resentment of Griffith invested this double-edged portrait with a striking polemical force, the pre-war correspondence and diaries of MacSwiney, McCartan, Hobson, and O'Hegarty himself all testify to the accuracy of this characterisation. At the very least, O'Hegarty's were representative of the attitudes of the separatist vanguard.

This confused I.R.B.–Sinn Féin relationship becomes a little clearer if it is remembered that a split with Sinn Féin was not necessary for the I.R.B. to express its dissatisfaction. The amalgamations of 1908 did not involve the I.R.B. formally but were enacted through I.R.B. front organisations, in particular the Dungannon Clubs. Consequently, the I.R.B. retained full autonomy and under pressure from Hobson and his associates expressed this through *Irish Freedom*. Consequently, there remained limited scope for co-operation between Sinn Féin and the Hobsonites, as demonstrated by the controversy over George V's visit of July 1911.

In early 1911 the Supreme Council instructed that resolutions relating to the king's visit should be discouraged or prohibited.[65] McCartan determined on a demonstration similar to those of 1900 and 1903 and put this to the Wolfe Tone Club executive, the latest I.R.B. front organisation.[66] They refused to countenance a resolution at the forthcoming Emmet commemoration at the Rotunda. Believing '[s]omeone has to lead', McCartan put forward a resolution condemning the loyal address proposed by Dublin corporation, which was seconded by Clarke. 'Consternation reigned in the Committee', McCartan sarcastically told McGarrity. 'We introduced politics. We were guilty of a breach of faith etc etc.' John O'Hanlon, Supreme Council member and, owing to his great influence among the Dublin Fenians, Allan's most important ally, resigned as president of the Wolfe Tones, a clear withdrawal of I.R.B. patronage.[67] Sinn Féin, supported by McCartan and Clarke, called a meeting

---

[64] O'Hegarty to Duffy, 9 Apr. 1907 (N.L.I., MS 5581).
[65] Le Roux, *Tom Clarke*, p. 96.
[66] Rather like the Dungannon Clubs, there is very little available evidence of the Wolfe Tone Clubs, from the police or otherwise.
[67] O'Hegarty, 'Recollections'; McCartan to McGarrity, 14 Mar. 1911 (N.L.I., MS 17457/9). McCartan wrote on Wolfe Tone Club notepaper which named the committee as president and trustee John O'Hanlon; honorary treasurers James Stritch and James O'Connor; honorary secretaries S. O'Huadhaigh and Tom Clarke; committee members Michael O'Maolin, P. J. Devlin, T. O'Flanagain, James J. Buggy, and J. McGrane.

of all nationalists and sent a circular to all members of the corporation signed by Griffith, John Nugent (of the A.O.H.), Lorcan Sherlock (leader of the U.I.L. in Dublin and the city's sometime lord mayor), and Jennie Wyse Power (representing 'nationalist women'). Allan was vilified in Hobsonite circles and McCartan hoped that if forced to resign from the Supreme Council Allan would go with him.[68] The police reported in April that Sinn Féin had little success in generating opposition to the loyal address, although McCartan reported a crowd of 20,000 at the public meeting of 22 June where MacBride put the resolutions. As he cynically commented: 'The King of England is here at present. There were big crowds out to see him apparently. . . . The people go to see him as they would go to see a circus.'[69]

O'Hegarty again provides indirect clarification of the issue at stake in these I.R.B. disputes. In *Sinn Féin: An Illumination* he describes the pattern by which separatism could take on a more popular membership base.

> The question, then, of the adhesion of any given generation to a separatist movement resolves itself practically into the question of the formation, at the right time, of a separatist movement with an open policy; and practically any generation of Irishmen is liable to be drawn from a moderate movement to a separatist movement if the separatists should develop a sufficiently attractive and workable open policy.[70]

In O'Hegarty's view the post-rising republicanism of Sinn Féin provided just such a combination of practical strategy with separatist ends. The I.R.B. had raised separatist consciousness; the 1916 executions rendered the heinous reality of Anglo-Irish relations transparent, making it time to put Sinn Féin's strategy of passive resistance into action. However, as O'Hegarty's resolutions of 1910 suggest, he believed that Sinn Féin's strategy was feasible without a consciousness-raising insurrection. Propaganda work was the key to separatist success. Passive resistance provided the strategic basis for an open advanced nationalist movement, but to be adopted by the I.R.B. it had to be unambiguously separatist. Growing disillusionment with Griffith's compromises made *Irish Freedom* necessary and it was to be the I.R.B.'s most sustained promotion of the Fenian ideal since the turn of the century uncertainties if not the 1860s. It seems the Supreme Council's opposition to 'politics' was the old opposition to open activity, suggesting that Allan and O'Hanlon remained committed to the policy of insurrection and co-operated with Sinn Féin rather as they had co-operated with Parnellism. Vampirically increasing I.R.B. membership

---

[68] McCartan to McGarrity, 2 June 1911 (N.L.I., MS 17457/9).
[69] C.O. 904/84, Apr. & June 1911; McCartan to McGarrity, 23 June 1911, 9 July 1911 (N.L.I., MS 17457/9). John Daly welcomed the king by flying two black flags from his house, C.O. 904 119, June 1911.
[70] O'Hegarty, *Sinn Féin: An Illumination*, p. 13.

through non-Fenian organisations remained wholly legitimate, but any movement to an open separatist movement was unacceptable. This was the same tension that characterised the I.R.B.'s interactions with cultural nationalist groups in the 1880s and 1890s. O'Leary's disregard for the separatist orthodoxy of secrecy was mirrored in Hobson's Dungannon Clubs and his newspaper the *Republic*. With the advent of *Irish Freedom* this tendency was now at work in the Supreme Council itself. The Supreme Council's toleration of Griffithite Sinn Féin was permitted by its determination to restore the 1782/3 constitutional settlement. Had Griffith advocated a republic he would have trespassed onto I.R.B. turf, undoing the linkage between orthodox separatism and the traditions of the I.R.B. As it was, Griffith offered another compromise with which the I.R.B. could co-operate without undermining their wider objectives. Finally, this perspective helps clarify the problematic relationship of Hobson's *Defensive Warfare* to the development of Irish separatism. Although unambiguously republican, Hobson's ideas permitted an open movement that queried the necessity of insurrection.

Reflective of the ascendancy of the Hobsonites within the I.R.B. and the marginalisation of Allan was the progress of McGarrity's tour of Ireland in August 1911. McCartan warned him he would see:

> some green flags & green flaggery and green nationalism. Still the driving force behind it all is real nationalism though not 1 per cent of those present realise what nationalism is. Their tomfoolery is but a misdirected outburst of nationalism which we could all admire if the vulgar veneer were removed from it.[71]

From late 1910 Allan found that his letters to the Clan leadership were going unanswered and he complained to John Devoy. Allan's reputation among Fenians in the U.S.A. had been damaged by his association with Lord Mayor Pile and Queen Victoria's welcoming reception of 1900, while Allan believed dislike of him in Ireland could be traced back to the I.R.B.–I.N.A. split.[72] It was clear, however, where Clan na Gael loyalties lay. On tour in Ireland during August 1911, McGarrity visited R. C. Bonner in Donegal before staying for two weeks in his home town of Carrickmore with Bernard McCartan. In Belfast he visited McCullough, then Hobson and O'Hegarty (home from London on his holidays), before a final meeting in the *Irish Freedom* offices with McCartan, Hobson, and Con Collins.[73] The I.R.B.'s internal rivalries reached a climax in the *Irish Freedom* confrontations of November and December 1911, and McGarrity's intervention proved crucial in shoring up the Hobsonite position.

---

[71] McCartan to McGarrity, 12 Aug. 1911 (N.L.I., MS 17457/9).
[72] Allan to Devoy, 4 Mar. 1912, *D.P.B. II*, pp 401–2; Ó Broin, *Revolutionary Underground*, pp 134–5. According to Allan his renewed activity as an I.R.B. organiser in 1910 was prompted by invitation following the exposure of P. T. Daly's embezzlement of Clan na Gael funds. Clarke was co-opted onto the Supreme Council in Daly's place.
[73] C.O. 904/119, Aug. 1911.

In early December McCartan reported that Clarke had been asked to resign from the Supreme Council and threatened with a trial when he refused to do so. Allan led this move and was apparently motivated by his desire to 'kill the paper'.[74] It is not clear what were the exact charges levelled against Clarke but it is clear that in forcing them Allan overestimated his personal influence. The executive of the Wolfe Tone Clubs suspended the newspaper committee and, facing Hobsonite defiance, raided the office, seizing the half-printed issue of December 1911. McCartan felt far from confident at this stage:

> The whole business is thrown on B.[ulmer Hobson,] myself & Father Tom [Clarke]. We may not secure the desired reforms but at least we did our part in trying. If we lose there is no hope for years. If we win ___. There is too much smoke around at present to get anything like a clear view of the outlook. Perhaps you'll say I'm a damned fool & perhaps I am. I'm sorry I did not run away now. They saw their power slipping away & they had to strike to try and hold on. Else Windows [Allan] deliberately planned the whole thing for it is very far reaching.[75]

Alternative printers were found – Devereux and Neuth of Omagh – but they were afraid of legal action and insisted on a £100 deposit. Clarke stumped up the cash from I.R.B. sources and McGarrity reimbursed him:[76] 'It was the means of winning the day for us', wrote McCartan in thanks. 'The outlook is very bright.'[77] December 1911 saw two rival issues of *Irish Freedom*, one proclaiming Dr Patrick McCartan its editor. The rebels emerged from the conflict strengthened. McCartan and Allan were removed from the committee and MacDermott was put on. Hobson was made editor of the newspaper and, as the smoke cleared, McCartan wrote triumphantly:

> This is a score for us. . . . The combination has been practically smashed. Windows needs just another kick but apparently he'll not wait for it as he is running away & his man Friday [O'Hanlon] is running with him as they'll not accept defeat. It is sufficient at the present to say that we are all surprised at our muscles.[78]

The resignations left Clarke practically in control of the I.R.B. and Allan resigned from the I.R.B. altogether in March 1912.[79] In September 1912

---

[74] McCartan to McGarrity, 2 Dec. 1911 (N.L.I., MS 17457/9).

[75] McCartan to McGarrity, 12 Dec. 1911, ibid.

[76] In 1960 Denis McCullough was unable to remember the immediate cause of the seizure of the issue but it was motivated fundamentally by the struggle over control of the I.R.B. As treasurer of the Supreme Council, Clarke was at liberty to supply the cash given the majority in favour (McCullough, McDermott, Hobson, and P. S. O'Hegarty). D. McColla to Pádraig Ó Mardin, 2 Aug. 1960, Leon Ó Broin Papers (N.L.I., MS 31696).

[77] McCartan to McGarrity, 2 Jan. 1911 (*recte* 1912).

[78] Ibid.

[79] McCartan to Ó Mardin, 10 May 1960, Ó Broin Papers (N.L.I., MS 31696); McGee, 'Frederick James Allan', p. 32.

MacDermott attended the annual Clan na Gael convention on behalf of the I.R.B., clear evidence of the new ascendancy. 'By gum', said Clarke, 'now if we don't get something done it'll be our own fault.'[80]

III

The first edition of *Irish Freedom* contained a memorial to William Rooney by 'Lucan'. In a now familiar historicising mode it recalled the halcyon days of the *United Irishman's* first publication:

> Personally, I can vividly remember how the advent of the *United Irishman* came to me with the headiness and bewilderingness of wine, with the sense of comradeship, with hope and confidence, with the dawn of a new interest in life; the certainty, at the end, the dazzling certainty that there were still in the country men who worked away at the old ideal of Tone and Mitchel, who would neither compromise or bend, men who preached the old faith in tones that bespoke sincerity and confidence, knowledge and determination. That it was the publication of the *United Irishman* which rendered the present movement possible, for it at once organised and concentrated, educated and invigorated, the isolated separatists who till then had neither knowledge of each other's existence nor means of testing their faith in the light of the general faith of the nation.[81]

In an important editorial of October 1913, *Irish Freedom* had posited the degenerating impact of centralised political organisation and direction, presenting it as a betrayal of the communal traditions of Irish society. This was equally a critique of Sinn Féin and the parliamentary party and anticipated later argument advocating the volunteering principle:

> The Irish co-operative instinct, which was the inspiring force of early Irish civilisation, is exemplified in later times chiefly in our capacity for organisation. In that capacity it has done excellent work for the nation. . . . But that direction of the national co-operative instinct is really a perversion of it, a perversion which has become more perverted as the [nineteenth] century dragged on. In the high tide of Irish virility the national co-operative instinct was primarily a working instinct. Men and women worked together and the sum total of their work was great. . . . But in modern times that instinct has been perverted into half-a-dozen or a dozen men doing the nation's thinking, while the mass of the people merely gave adhesion to acts of whose general purport they had only the vaguest general perception. That is the weakness of all current Irish organisations and leagues, that they are not directed, as the ancient Irish would have directed them, to increased individual

---

[80] Quoted in O'Hegarty, 'Recollections', p. 14.
[81] *Irish Freedom*, Nov. 1910. The same account of *United Irishman's* significance is given in O'Hegarty, *Sinn Féin: An Illumination*, p. 16.

effectiveness, but to increased effectiveness in masses; and the masses have grown up in the tradition that all they need do is pass needful resolutions, subscribe needful money, and let the dozen or so at their head do their thinking and command their movements.[82]

The Dungannon Clubs, on the other hand, had suggested an Irish separatism energised by the Gaelic League, grass-roots dynamism, and idealism, an atmosphere imported to *Irish Freedom*. The course of Terence MacSwiney's political career illustrates the new newspaper's significance. His activist career in Cork was turbulent because he was convinced any dilution of ideals would inhibit rather then fuel 'progress'. He had grown frustrated by the Cork Young Ireland Society's preoccupation with erecting monuments rather than promoting the ideals of '98 and had withdrawn with a dozen others in 1905.[83] He founded a branch of the Celtic Literary Society and it affiliated to Cumann na nGaelhael but the society soon ran into trouble when it embraced Griffith's *Resurrection of Hungary* and showed its determination to prioritise political agitation rather than education. MacSwiney rejected such short-termism along with all forms of political pragmatism. Sceptical of the Hungarian parallel from the outset, MacSwiney noted in his diary his own and Alice Milligan's intention to publish a pamphlet that would consider alternative approaches including Fenianism, although he did not favour secret societies in principle.[84] Initially, however, MacSwiney believed that it would be possible for the Griffithites and orthodox separatists to co-operate in the same organisation. 'Our path[s] lie together, only one goes further; and that one the C.L.S. under possible new arrangement would declare for.[85] But disappointment with the subsequent ideological inconstancy of the C.L.S. and the ascendancy of the Griffithite line provoked a second withdrawal. P. S. O'Hegarty sent imploring letters urging he reconsider: Sinn Féin needed MacSwiney, it was 'rotting from want of a man with passion in him, a man with the idealistic touch', and he was 'the ablest man in the movement in Cork'. O'Hegarty admitted that Griffith was no longer as inspiring as when he had published *United Irishman* and that Sinn Féin was in danger of degenerating from a 'national faith' to a 'party faith', with all the self-interest and low politicking this suggested. It was all the more urgent, therefore, that MacSwiney work with the movement, saving it from domination by the 'cranks', the 'politicians', and the 'petty'. Appealing to MacSwiney's particular sensibilities, O'Hegarty dismissed Cork man D. D. Sheehan as an incoherent thinker and a 'materialist'.[86] He was met with a lengthy reply. The amalgamation of Sinn

---

[82] *I.F.*, Oct. 1913.
[83] MacSwiney Diary, 28 Oct. 1905 (U.C.D. P48c/101).
[84] MacSwiney Diary, 22 Apr. 1905 (U.C.D. P48c/100).
[85] MacSwiney Diary, 20 Jan. 1907, ibid.
[86] P. S. O'Hegarty to MacSwiney, 27 Feb. [?] 1908 [?] (U.C.D. P48b/377–8).

Féin was a mistake, and they had been duped into recognising the king against reassurances that this would not happen; compromise, rather than advancing the cause, was rejected as 'backsliding', which reinforced the need to clearly establish their principles and propagate on that basis. MacSwiney did not impugn O'Hegarty's stance but argued that O'Hegarty's high profile at the amalgamation conventions meant that he could make his position clear even if his amendments fell. MacSwiney's involvement at the local level did not allow this, leaving him personally compromised. The full extent of his disillusionment was expressed through two convictions. First,

> there was more real value to the nation in the existence of a dozen men in a small room holding a true and vigorous faith and keeping to it in the face of every difficulty than in a whole country unified in professions that would inspire nobody.

Second, each man was obliged to 'make his life consistent with what he believes'.[87] MacSwiney immediately approved of *Irish Freedom*, seeing it as a possible recipient of a long article on separatism 'to show how the idea affects us and is justified by all it implies in every walk of life'.[88] In 'The Basis of Freedom' he wrote:

> A spiritual necessity makes the true significance of our claim to freedom. The material aspect is only a secondary consideration. A man facing life is gifted with certain powers of soul and body. It is of vital importance to himself and the community that he be given a full opportunity to develop his powers, and to fill his place worthily. In a free state he is in a natural environment for full self-development. In an enslaved state it is the reverse. When one country holds another in subjection that other suffers materially and morally. It suffers materially, being a prey to plunder. It suffers morally because of the corrupt influences the bigger nation sets to work to maintain its ascendancy.[89]

MacSwiney developed these ideas in his series 'Principles of Freedom' between March 1911 and February 1912.[90] By focusing on the idea of 'freedom' he worked to remind Ireland that it was in a state of subjection. Hobson was very encouraging. Thanking him for his contributions, he commented in a number of letters:

---

[87] MacSwiney to O'Hegarty, 21 Dec. 1908 (U.C.D. P48c/299). Although preserved in the MacSwiney Papers there seems no reason to doubt a copy of this letter was sent.
[88] MacSwiney Diary, 4 Dec. 1910 (U.C.D. P48c/103).
[89] *Irish Freedom*, Jan. 1911.
[90] The articles were March 1911 'Separatism', May 1911 'Moral Force', June 1911 'Brothers and Enemies', August 1911 'The Secret of Strength', September 1911 'Principle in Action', October 1911 'Loyalty', November 1911 'Womanhood', December 1911 'The Frontier', February 1912 'Literature and Freedom'. Published in book form in 1921.

I like your article & agree with you. There are so few people who see that nationality is really a spiritual thing.

I feel specially that we want our younger readers to understand the underlying principles of nationality – & you & I are possibly the only two writers who are much concerned with that side of it.

In Ireland we don't suffer from bad morals but lack of morals & the application of a moral outlook to our political questions is a very great necessity.[91]

In 1908 MacSwiney had founded with Daniel Corkery the Cork Dramatic Society ('An Dún') based at the Gaelic League hall in Cork.[92] This occupied his spare time until he become involved in the Irish Volunteers in 1913. It seems certain that *Irish Freedom* was central to MacSwiney's re-engagement with Irish separatist activism. It provided an unambiguously sympathetic forum for his political convictions and, according to Diarmund Lynch (Munster representative on the Supreme Council), brought him to the attention of the I.R.B., although they decided against inviting him to join.[93]

The *Irish Freedom* editorial of October 1913 continued:

We, on our side of the question, have wakened up to the fact that the danger to the nation was mental rather than physical: that we were threatened far more effectively by the permanent forces of Anglicisation, the English language and English ideas and English outlook, than by its temporary physical force: that all the agitation of the nineteenth century has harmed Ireland far more than it has helped her, for it killed her dependence on herself, turned her thoughts away from her own civilisation, her own traditions, and hindered Anglicisation very little.

This was an effective separatist expression of the vital importance attached to the Gaelic League agenda. It reversed the usual priority of political status over culture and provided a subtle analysis of the nature of British government in Ireland. It was not Castle-orientated, dominated by concerns over democracy, the army, police, and expenditure. Rather, it identified imperialism as an enterprise of cultural penetration and domination, a reading descended from Mitchel's identification of the 'Thing', and filtered through the thinking of Young Ireland, Yeats, Hyde, Rooney, Milligan, and Moran. It provided an alternative analysis to the belief supposedly held by the British that their presence in Ireland was benign, engendering stability and prosperity, all the more so given the concessions generated over land, local government, and education. *Irish Freedom* challenged this interpretation and, by implication,

---

[91] Hobson to MacSwiney, 7 Nov. 1910, 26 Dec. 1910, 28 April 1911 (U.C.D. P48b/318, /319, /321).
[92] For 'An Dún' and MacSwiney's plays, see Patrick Maume, *Life that is Exile: Daniel Corkery and the Search for Irish Ireland* (Belfast, 1993), pp 29–33.
[93] Diarmund Lynch, *The I.R.B. and the 1916 Rising* (Cork, 1951).

the legitimacy of imperial home rule. Separatists perceived in 'English' official discourse unquestioned assumptions regarding the congruence between the English liberal political system, English culture, and progress. From this perspective, the English presence in Ireland could not, ultimately, be contrary to the advance of civilisation. The cultural nationalism of the separatists developed in response to what they perceived as the unconscious English imperial drive for cultural hegemony. Over the previous forty years a narrative of Irish deracination had evolved that explained the *sense*, Thomas Davis's 'felt history' perhaps, that the pernicious effect of English government could not be satisfactorily accounted for exclusively in terms of the imposition of a governing apparatus centred on Dublin Castle. The Anglophobia generated by British misgovernment had developed a more positive foundation that looked to the restoration of 'Irishness'.

Thus the education of children in the ways of nation, the principal concern of Young Ireland Societies of the 1880s, remained central to the separatist agenda. At first glance it looks as if circumstances ensured that talk of insurrection, of alliance with the Germans, and the need to import arms were relegated to secondary importance, but, as the following extract suggests, in the idealised priorities of the vanguard they were of secondary importance in an absolute sense too:

> The problem of the Irish nation may be said to be, roughly speaking, the problem of children, the problem of establishing conditions in Ireland such that each generation of children shall form up naturally, and without special propaganda, nationalists, as they do in other countries. And the root of that problem lies in education and in the national language, which are one problem and not two. There can be no Irish education in Ireland without the language.[94]

The decline of the language provided the strongest example of the negative impact of English on Ireland and the strongest reason for ending the connection. With remarkable frankness *Irish Freedom* admitted the fragility of Irish nationalism rather than its strength:

> That has meant that, instead of Irish nationalism being a natural portion of the growth of the Irish children, it has been to a large extent an instinct, almost submerged, struggling against enormous odds, and having to emancipate itself from the effects of years and years of careful 'education'. Does Ireland, in the conscious national sense, begin to mean anything to any of us until we have done with what passes for education and, in order to face and find life, have to throw it off and get at reality? It has meant an enormous waste of time and energy. Every generation has had to educate itself into the truths of Irish nationality, educate itself slowly and laboriously, by debating societies, agitating societies, much talk and speculation

---

[94] *I.F.*, June 1913.

and argument, into a conception of and an acceptance of the Irish nation and its duties towards it. And by the time a generation, or a small portion of it rather, has got itself pulled over into conscious nationalism, it is almost at its passing, and the younger generation, the Future, has grown up, blind and helpless, struggling, chaotic, even as the older. For while each adult generation has had to find salvation for itself, slowly and painfully, the enemy has had practically a free hand with the children. And so the nation is in continuous rebirth and decay, phoenix-like it rises from its ashes every generation, but it always goes back again: and the work is always doing, always beginning, and never quite ending. . . .

And so even a virile and nationalist generation, like the Fenian generation – the generation of the last century which came into its national birthright quickest – gave no permanency to the nation. Each generation has to begin afresh.[95]

The agenda *Irish Freedom* shared with the Young Ireland Societies was not limited to the priority given to nationalist education. It also sought to clarify the role separatists could play in a home rule Ireland, sharing the pragmatism of the earlier generation. The talk of alliances with Germany and of importing arms that worried the police should be balanced against the more restrained tone of *Irish Freedom*'s editorials.[96] The newspaper's response to the published home rule bill was pithy: it was the means 'by which England planned to change the manner, but not the extent of its control over Ireland'.[97] The separatists thought the progress of the home rule debate demonstrated the marginality of the home rulers to the Westminster process and the battles within the I.R.B. in late 1911 take on a broader significance given the apparent imminence of home rule. McCartan looked for reasons to remain optimistic, but the overall weight of his commentary was pessimistic.

> Things are pretty rotten politically. Everybody is cock sure home rule is a dead certainty but it is evident that there is many a hidden rock before it. . . . There is no alternative apparent but if home rule does not come I believe parliamentarianism is dead & damned – and so much the better.[98]

He believed Irish nationalists, disillusioned by the political process, were beginning to look to the Wolfe Tone Clubs for leadership and this accentuated the need to release Allan's grip on the organisation. Over the crucial summer of 1912 the vanguard's position gradually hardened in response to the emergence of the idea of county exclusion as a means to placate the increasing militancy of Ulster unionism. Separatist responses to the Agar-Robartes amendment of June 1912 – the parliamentary debut of county exclusion – intimated a wholly new strategy. Facing the prospect of 'a kind of nationalist

---

[95] Ibid.
[96] C.O. 904/88, Sept. 1912, p. 22, Oct. 1912, p. 214.
[97] I.F., May 1912.
[98] McCartan to McGarrity, 28 Nov. 1911 (N.L.I., MS 17457/9).

imperialist party' descending from the home rule party and seeking Irish votes in a home rule Ireland it was necessary to establish a new party to counter this threat:

> [This new party could not] go to the Irish people with the vague or ill-defined political ideal, and it will have even at the beginning sufficient strength to be able to afford to disregard the possible alienation of support in certain quarters because of its 'extreme' principle. It must therefore be either an '82 party or a republican party, and an '82 party will have no justification now save as a monarchist party; we think that the only possible basis is a definite republican basis. If there is anything to be gained by a platform of 'independence' or 'separatism' without specifying monarchy or republic we have no objection to it, but at present we do not see what is to be gained. A republican party would have no limitations in dealing with the situation, and would be able to take full advantage of every power in the nation.[99]

This extraordinary statement suggested another new departure that would see separatists engage with the political process in a home rule Ireland. It might be contrasted with Fianna Fail's non-engagement with the Free State in the years immediately after the civil war. The home rule bill promised another rending of the veil. Just as the Parnell split was seen as caused by the iniquity of the 'union of hearts' and prompted a natural recourse to Fenianism, the publication of the third home rule bill would jolt Irish nationalism out of its complacency. This almost mystical sense of those moments of national realisation rested upon the belief that the bulk of nationalist Ireland failed to comprehend the reality of the home rule position. Through fixing home rule in a legislative form and through the protracted wrangling over its provisions that would follow, the prosaic reality of this political compromise would become evident. The separatists believed that in the end of the home rule campaign and in the beginning of legislative process might be found their opportunity, not to mount an insurrection, but to ride the anti-climax. Their optimism chimed with the widespread lack of enthusiasm that met the publication of the bill.[100] That this schema was shown to be an illusion at the crucial intersections of the Parnell split and the treaty debates, should not divert attention from its essential role in the separatist belief system.[101] It was this

---

[99] *I.F.*, July 1912.
[100] Michael Wheatley, '"These Quiet Days of Peace": Nationalist Opinion before the Home Rule Crisis, 1909–13' in D. George Boyce and Alan O'Day (ed.), *Ireland in Transition, 1867–1921* (London, 2004), pp 63–7.
[101] This analysis provides strong evidence for explanations of the Easter rising that identify its chief purpose as propagandic. Again this can be clarified through recourse to O'Hegarty. His denial of legitimacy to political violence after the Easter rising reflected his identification of the rising as the essential lifting of the veil, the catalyst needed to awaken national consciousness. With this process complete the work of Sinn Féin on the passive resistance model (albeit with republican aspirations) could be pursued. Consequently, the rising fits

reading of the political situation that led the separatists to celebrate the mobilisation of the unionist Volunteers. Despite the connivance of the Tories, it was a 'goodly thing to see arms in Irish hands'[102] because it was a moment when Irishmen took control of their own destiny and acted with autonomy.

In 1912 the position was further complicated by the Parliament Act. It may seem surprising that the house of lords was rarely identified as the major stumbling block to home rule, particularly given the commons majority in favour of Gladstone's 1893 home rule bill. But to take account of this would impact negatively on separatist narratives of English suppression and non-recognition of Irish national identity. Mitchel's structuralist analysis of the 'Thing' provided the essential foundation on which this discourse was built. To begin to deconstruct it, to isolate individual components, such as the house of lords, would weaken the overall edifice on which romantic separatism was built. Nonetheless, the above *Irish Freedom* editorial represented a profound departure for Fenianism. It anticipated Irish republicans engaging in organised electoral politics in an arena subservient to Westminster and the crown. It may have firmly refuted the specifics of the Griffithite agenda, openly rejecting its apparent inadequacies in the light of these new realities, but the party-political and electoral urge was a partial vindication of Sinn Féin. After all, Griffith's '82ism had always had a provisional air about it; in the debates that greeted the publication of the *Resurrection of Hungary* in the *United Irishman* he had made this clear, identifying Repeal as a possible route to separation. So although Griffith's attachment to the 'dual monarchy' ideal helps makes sense of his later support for the Anglo-Irish treaty, great care must be taken in discerning too great a difference between his position and Michael Collins's argument that the treaty was a 'stepping-stone' to separation.

The apparent tardiness in responding to the Ulster Volunteer Force with a nationalist force stemmed from two basic assumptions: first, the belief that home rule would go through, and second, that the unionist mobilisation was little more than political theatre, an attempt to consolidate the unionist bloc rather than a departure from constitutional methods. These insights featured in *Irish Freedom* commentary in the late summer of 1912. Moreover, they grasped the fundamental irony the possibility of home rule raised, namely the pressure on Irish nationalists to go to extraordinary lengths to demonstrate their loyalty and the need for unionists to resort to the threat of illegality to express theirs:

> There has been a revolution – so curious – so sudden that many of us have not got the measure of it yet. The party of loyalty to England – the virtual English garrison

into a powerful strand of separatist thinking, one of a series of moments that should cause a communal epiphany. O'Hegarty, *Victory*, pp 120–1.

[102] Pearse's famous phrase, quoted in R. Dudley Edwards, *Patrick Pearse: The Triumph of Failure* (Dublin, 1977, 1990), p. 179.

– is threatening an insurrection while on the other hand the nominal nationalists are protesting their unflinching loyalty to the British empire. . . . We can, however, sum it up briefly by saying that Ulster *won't* fight and the rest of Ireland *won't* be loyal to the English interest, at least not for any length of time.[103]

The clarity separatists had sought since the turn of the century was finally provided by the first reading of the home rule bill. The multiple confusions over the implications of the Irish Ireland agenda, the Irish language movement, the '82 paradigm, and the All-for-Ireland League overtures, were erased by the revelation of the bill. No longer could there be any uncertainty regarding the limited ambitions of the home rule party and the separatists asserted their specific agenda with conviction. This conviction had not been absent in the past but the publication of the bill saw separatist certainties enflamed by vindication:

> One of the English speakers asked, and asked in vain, where now was the separatist element in the Irish parliamentary party. There is none; it has got corrupted into imperialism, an imperialism which not alone is imperialism but is almost pro-English. The situation in Ireland in the past has been complicated by the fact that the party which claimed to carry on the work of Emmet and Mitchel was actually an imperialist party, attending the imperialist parliament, swearing allegiance to the English crown and constitution, and helping England to govern this country. That, at least, will now disappear, and there will be a clear line of demarcation in the future between the nationalist and the imperialist, between the traditions of Tone and the traditions of Grattan. We have often wished, in the years gone by, that Mr Redmond and his party would come out nakedly as imperialists, would do something that would enable everyone to see what their nationalism consisted of; and it is a relief at last to see that they have done it, even although it is in a fashion which will take some time yet to be clear to the majority of the people.[104]

The 28 September 1912 changed everything. A total of 237,368 men signed the Ulster Convenant pledging to use 'all means which may be found necessary to defeat the present conspiracy to set up a home rule parliament in Ireland'.[105] *Irish Freedom* dropped the constructive and conciliatory air and responded in kind. The possible defeat of home rule would mean the end of parliamentarianism and nationalists had to be ready to fill the gap:

> In such an event it will be necessary to proclaim insurrectionary doctrines openly and boldly in every part of the country – and that without the loss of a moment. The nationalists throughout Ireland – and they are a much larger body than is

---

[103] *I.F.*, Sept. 1912.
[104] *I.F.*, Aug. 1912.
[105] Quoted in Paul Bew, *Ideology and the Irish Question: Ulster Unionism and Irish Nationalism 1912–1916* (Oxford, 1994), p. 68.

commonly supposed – must be ready to take concerted action. To that end we advise them to organise *now.* . . .

To conclude: if home rule passes our work will be constructive; it will be the utilising of new conditions for the advancement and strengthening of the Irish nation considered as a whole. If, on the other hand, it does not pass, our work will be destructive, and will be an attack all along the line on every English institution in Ireland. For that we must work – perhaps alone – but if possible in league with England's enemies within and without the empire, but whether alone or with outside aid the work will be undertaken and it will be carried through.[106]

In the event the facts did not quite fit the prescription. Home rule was passed, but immediately suspended; some form of partition remained likely: 'Ireland considered as a whole' was slipping down many political agendas. McCartan, furious to see William Redmond sharing platforms with Liberal politicians, perhaps dashing any hopes that this most strenuous advocate of independent opposition would yet work with the separatists, fell back on easy assumptions.

There is or was a rumour that home rule is to be shelved. If that be so the fat will be in the fire. The real spirit will be speedily seen through Redmond's veneer of loyalism which is as spurious as Carson's disloyalty. Still Ireland's eyes will be opened some of these days no matter how the cat jumps. Home rule or no home rule will have much the same effect.[107]

McCartan become a Fellow of the Royal College of Surgeons in the same month and put his celebrations to good use. He and four girls, three of whom were sisters and protestants,[108] tried 'to get in touch with spirits and had a thrilling experience'.[109] Finding a spirit that knew McCartan (it had met him in the U.S.A. with Devoy) they prospected Ireland's future. McCartan would live to see an Irish republic but Devoy would not. When England and Germany went to war the Irish would have to defend Ireland against the invading Germans. Temperament would ensure that McCartan and three of the girls would fight for the republic. Clarke, Hobson, McCullough, Griffith, Gonne, and Connolly would join them; Markievicz would not owing to her 'confusion of thought'. George Russell would not, although 'he was sometimes a separatist', F. J. Bigger would not and the spirit 'did not like him'. 'Would young William Redmond fight for the Republic[?] No.' McGarrity or Larkin were unknown to the spirit, but it could confirm that no other nation would fight with Ireland and the first president of the Irish republic would live in Dublin and be 'Ulic Ward'.

Tom Clarke tried to find a rational explanation.

---

[106] *I.F.*, Oct. 1912.
[107] McCartan to McGarrity, 9 Nov. 1912 (N.L.I., MS 17457/10).
[108] Probably the Gifford sisters.
[109] McCartan to McGarrity, 30 Nov. 1912 (N.L.I., MS 17457/10).

IV

Much has been written on the history of the Irish Volunteers between the establishment of the organisation in November 1913 and the outbreak of war in 1914.[110] Argument over who originated the idea has exercised biographers to a great degree. Compare the prominence Charles Townshend gives to spontaneous drilling in the provinces to Michael Tierney's scholarly advocacy of Eoin MacNeill and Aodogán O'Rahilly's championing of his father.[111] Both authors question the assumed influence of the I.R.B. (neither of their subjects were Brothers), Tierney in particular characterising the Volunteers in the image of his subject: a complex amalgam of constitutional and advanced nationalist tendencies generally hostile to insurrection. To a great extent this is justified. Preoccupied with attempts to create an alliance with the I.P.P. that would not compromise the non-political principles of the Volunteers, MacNeill wrote to Darrell Figgis in May 1914:

> In launching such a movement one had only to hold up a finger & naturally every physical force man & every Sinn Féiner would come in. At the same time, in the absence of a lead from the Irish party at the time when no such lead would be expected, it was very difficult to attract men of standing from among the party's adherents. . . . I did all I could to persuade people, telling them Mr Redmond could not possibly become responsible for the movement at the initial stage, & that therefore it could never be initiated if it were left to Mr Redmond. It was hard to persuade even a few, & we had to start with a committee on which the majority in the country were represented by a minority.[112]

MacNeill was adamant that they should do nothing to endanger Redmond's position at Westminster or in Ireland.[113] One recent commentator has calculated that the I.R.B. was the largest single group on the provisional committee, with twelve of the thirty representatives. They were bolstered by

---

[110] The best general account of the progress of the Volunteers in 1913–14, with particular focus on the negotiations between the provisional committee and the leadership of the I.P.P., can be found in Michael Tierney, *Eoin MacNeill: Scholar and Man of Action, 1867–1945* (Oxford, 1980), pp 97–166. Also, Charles Townshend, *Political Violence in Ireland: Government and Resistance since 1848* (Oxford, 1983), pp 256–61, 278–9; F. S. L. Lyons, *Ireland since the Famine* (London, 1971), and the opening chapter of Joost Augusteijn, *From Public Defiance to Guerrilla Warfare: The Experience of Ordinary Volunteers in the Irish War of Independence* (Dublin, 1996). For a full account of the Howth gun-running episode see Bulmer Hobson, *A Short History of the Irish Volunteers* (Dublin, 1918), pp 148–67. Cf. report of the 'Royal Commission on the circumstances connected with the landing of arms at Howth on July 26th, 1914', copy preserved in Hobson Papers (N.L.I., MS 13174/9).

[111] Tierney identified in order of importance MacNeill, Hobson, and O'Rahilly. Aodogán O'Rahilly, *Winding the Clock: O'Rahilly and the 1916 Rising* (Dublin, 1991), pp 92–7.

[112] MacNeill to Figgis, 12 May 1914, Hobson Papers (N.L.I., MS 13171/3).

[113] MacNeill to Casement, 27 Nov. 1913, Casement Papers (N.L.I., MS 36203/2).

men of more ambiguous political identity like MacNeill and O'Rahilly, while six further men identified as 'advanced nationalists', including Casement, Michael J. Judge of the A.O.H., and Colm O'Lochlainn, assistant master at Patrick Pearse's school, St Enda's.[114] Shortly after the meeting, MacNeill told Casement that of the various groups the Sinn Féiners were the most determined on making the committee 'representative'.[115] Pearse later identified six of the members with the A.O.H.[116]

In seeking a basis of co-operation with the I.P.P. the uncertainties within the leadership of the Volunteers regarding its role and character became evident. As David Fitzpatrick has commented, 'no simple definition can do justice either to the richness or to the amorphousness of the new force.'[117] This was reflected in the different emphases in contemporary and retrospective responses. For example, Tom Clarke was ecstatic ("Tis good to be alive in these times'), detecting a transformation in 'the young men' reminiscent of McCartan's first encounters with the Gaelic League.[118] William O'Brien, completing a process that began with his opposition to Redmondism and ended with him identifying with Sinn Féin after 1916,[119] retrospectively identified the Volunteers with the desire to throw off the influence of the A.O.H.[120] Paradoxically, as will be shown, the A.O.H. was the largest source of Volunteer recruits throughout 1914.

A range of attitudes characterised the leading separatists involved in the Volunteers. Their strategies ranged from the insurrectionism of the professional revolutionaries (Clarke, MacDermott, and the I.R.B.), through the passive resistance republicanism of Hobson (who in opposing the 1916 rising showed himself loyal to the democratic exactitudes of the I.R.B. constitution), to the cultural separatism of MacNeill, Gaelic League leader and opponent of I.R.B. insurrectionism.[121] One recent commentator has distinguished between those separatists in pursuit of a defensive strategy, personified by MacNeill, and the offensive strategists of the I.R.B. By this reading, when planning the rising

---

[114] C. Desmond Greaves, *Liam Mellows and the Irish Revolution* (London, 1971), pp 58–9. In this I.R.B. head-count Pearse, Thomas MacDonagh, and Joseph Plunkett are included, although in November 1913 they had not yet been sworn into the Brotherhood.

[115] MacNeill to Casement, 25 Nov. 1913, Casement Papers (N.L.I., MS 36203/2).

[116] Namely, Laurence Kettle, John Gore, Tom Kettle, Michael Judge, John Walsh, and James Lenehan. Pearse to Devoy, 12 May 1914, *D.P.B. II*, pp 440–1.

[117] David Fitzpatrick, *Politics and Irish Life 1913–1921: Provincial Experience of War and Revolution* (Cork, 1977, 1998), p. 86.

[118] Clarke to Devoy, 14 May 1914, *D.P.B. II*, pp 444–6; Devoy, *Recollections*, pp 394–6.

[119] Patrick Maume, *The Long Gestation* (Dublin, 1999), pp 181, 205.

[120] O'Brien, *Irish Revolution*, p. 223.

[121] MacNeill to Father Convery, 2 July 1904, 'In theory I suppose I am a separatist, in practice I would accept any settlement that would enable Irishmen to freely control their own affairs, and I would object to any theoretical upsetting of such a settlement. If the truth were to be known, I think that this represents the political views of 99 out of every hundred nationalists.' Quoted in Tierney, *Eoin MacNeill*, pp 104–5.

the Irish Volunteers provided the I.R.B. with a revolutionary vehicle.[122] Conversely, in volunteering the Redmondite Tom Kettle sought salvation for the dignity of Irish manhood, while Colonel Maurice Moore (brother of George, son of a catholic landowner and Volunteer inspector-general), regarded volunteering as a necessary extension of his commitment to the Gaelic League. Amorphous yes, but the force was undoubtedly 'advanced'. For regardless of how numerous were Volunteers who retained membership of constitutional nationalist organisations, and regardless of how carefully described and delimited their Volunteer allegiance was, adherence to the Volunteers inescapably bespoke a critique of Redmond's strategy and constitutional nationalism more generally. As Edward Martyn brusquely telegrammed Casement when invited to attend the Galway meetings of December 1913: 'Not coming believe volunteers will kill home rule.'[123]

The well-honed separatist critique of the parliamentary strategy that had developed since the advent of the home rule campaign had changed little in its essentials. This discourse came readily to hand for those attempting to explain the situation that necessitated the Volunteers. It is an historical cliché to say that events outstripped Redmondism and, as has been suggested, the roots of this failure lay in the ideological retrenchment of the early 1900s. As significant was the way in which this retrenchment partially disguised more uncertain divisions within the home rule party itself. In many parts of Ireland the Volunteer organisation was carried out by U.I.L. and A.O.H. leaders, sometimes with the support of their local M.P., which testifies to the weakness of Redmondism within the party. Any analysis of popular activism in this period must be alert to the extent to which to classify any individual or organisation as Redmondite is to posit a particular loyalty to the vision and leadership of a clique within the party. Just how Redmondite the home rule party and its associated organisations actually were is a question that is increasingly shaping historical analysis of this period. In short, the home rule movement led by Redmond was not Redmondite in the impassioned way it had been Parnellite in the 1880s. One elderly autobiographer saw the problem in terms that chime with the analysis pursued here:

> Young men of promise in his [Parnell's] day might hope to be welcomed into the ranks of his party, even if their ideas were a little wild. Within the party they might learn sense. Dillon however had closed the party against all but his personal adherents, and he failed to attract representatives of the younger generation.[124]

Clearly then, the nationalist militia had identity problems. Were they the National Volunteers, the Irish Volunteers, or the Irish National Volunteers?

---

[122] Peter Hart, 'Republican Paramilitarism, 1912–1922' (unpublished paper).

[123] Martyn to Casement, 10 Dec. 1913, Casement Papers (N.L.I., MS 13073/11).

[124] A. M. Sullivan, *Old Ireland: Reminiscences of an Irish K.C.* (London, 1927), p. 150.

Casement recognised the importance of these differences. To be a member of either the National Volunteers or the Irish National Volunteers was to align with a particular section of the Irish population. To be an Irish Volunteer was to believe in an Irish nation that transcended the political divisions not just within Irish nationalism, but also between Irish nationalists and unionists. To be a National Volunteer implied a loyalty to the sectional political identity of the I.P.P. Casement reminded Moore in June 1914: 'Please always bear in mind the correct title of Irish Volunteers not "National" or "Nationalist" Volunteers (the latter wholly damnable).'[125] Following the split in September 1914 it was clear they were the Irish Volunteers and the National Volunteers. The I.V. seceded from the main body, now the N.V., in response to Redmond's infamous 'twofold' commitment of the force to the defence of Ireland and the empire.[126] Led by MacNeill but largely controlled by the I.R.B., the I.V. numbered 12,000 of a total of 170,000. The majority remained loyal to the home rule brand, a large proportion of whom had joined the organisation in the months following Redmond's successful imposition of his representatives onto the Volunteer executive committee in June 1914. Redmond's justification for this incursion was that the executive committee was 'unrepresentative'. This was a transparent attempt to take control of an organisation that increasingly questioned the exclusive right of the home rule party to negotiate on behalf of nationalist Ireland. In order to grasp the extraordinary change in separatist fortunes that took place over 1913-14 there is no need either to exaggerate the influence of the I.R.B. or to underplay the predominance of Redmondism. Rather, it was a period in which fundamental separatist precepts appeared vindicated and in the subsequent course of events this feeling took on an ever more concrete reality. The benefit of 1913–14 to Irish separatism rested as much on the dividends paid in the battle of ideas as it did on the improved organisational capacity of the I.R.B.

V

Since the passage of the Parliament Act, the failure of the Agar-Robartes amendment in June 1912, and the mobilisation of the U.V.F. in January 1913, the chief problem exercising the home rule party had not been securing the passage of a home rule bill but the reconciliation of the unionist population of the north to this settlement. The likelihood of some form of separate treatment of a number of Ulster counties had met with strong opposition from the I.R.B. *Irish Freedom* fulminated against partition in an editorial headed 'The Lowest Depths'.

---

[125] Casement to Moore, 2 June 1914, Moore Papers (N.L.I., MS 10561).
[126] For an analysis of Redmond's strategy and his freedom of manoeuvre see Bew, *Ideology and the Irish Question*, pp 118–24.

It is a fundamental principle of all national effort, and national polity, in Ireland that the nation is one and indivisible, from the Fair Head to Cape Clear, and from Beann Edair to Gallimh, Gael, Dane, Norman, Scot, Cromwellian, Williamite, all have been taken to Ireland's bosom, and all are of her children. We deny the right of any party in Ireland to give allegiance to any power outside of Ireland, we deny the right of any party to alienate itself or any of the Irish soil it holds from the main body of the nation, and we deny the right of any party in Ireland to consider any dismemberment proposal, much less accept it.[127]

This non-sectarian, pluralist Irishness, with its American republican overtones, did not include an opt-out clause. Here the United Irishmen civic republican tradition merged with the revivalist search for an Irish identity rooted not in inherited confessional identities but in the atemporalities of landscape. Where D. P. Moran argued that the 'Gael must be the element that absorbs',[128] *Irish Freedom* identified a succession of equally favoured children. 'Party' was condemned as subversive of nationality, and the warning to the home rule party was blunt: 'if any party in Ireland does accept such a proposal' – the severing of the body of the nation – 'the young men of Ireland will make it hot for that Party.' The message to Ulster was equally clear and uncompromising. 'As for Ulster, Ulster is Ireland's and shall remain Ireland's. Though the Irish nation, in its political and corporate capacity, were gall and wormwood to every unionist in Ulster, yet they shall swallow it.' The message was strangely paradoxical: 'We will fight them, if they want fighting but we shall never let them go, never.' Following the Curragh incident *Irish Volunteer*, the official weekly newspaper of the movement,[129] warned that the Volunteers would be used to enforce the decisions of Westminster, strongly implying this would involve coercing Ulster.[130] Where *Irish Freedom* dealt in the muscularities of separatist certainty, the more ambivalent constituency of the *Irish Volunteer* demanded allusion, the sinewy provocations of the perennial fence-sitter.

With some perspicuity George Dangerfield described the situation thus:

No matter what happened in parliament, however decisively, nor what schemes were advanced, however subtle, neither the Orangemen nor the nationalists intended to pay the smallest attention. The quarrel was beyond the control of the English electorate; it was also – though he did not realise it as yet – beyond the control of Mr Redmond.[131]

---

[127] *I.F.*, Apr. 1914.
[128] D. P. Moran, *The Philosophy of Irish Ireland* (Dublin, 1905), p. 37.
[129] The *Irish Volunteer* was printed by the North Wexford Printing and Publishing Company Ltd and police estimated 7,000 of the August 1914 edition were produced, C.O. 904/197.
[130] *I.V.*, 4 Apr. 1914.
[131] George Dangerfield, *The Strange Death of Liberal England* (1935, Stanford, 1997), pp 273–4.

Unwittingly perhaps, Dangerfield described what Sinn Féin wanted: the Irish question becoming a problem the Irish, protestant and catholic, nationalist and unionist, would settle in Ireland on the basis of their specific indigenous agendas.[132] Although the anti-Redmondite cohort of October 1914 was stronger than anything the separatists could have mobilised a year earlier, the influence of home rule organisations on the Volunteers was strong throughout 1914. Dangerfield's Delphic utterances contain clear teleological dangers, for although a source of Redmond's failure depended in part on his loss of influence at Westminster (the patriotic unity engendered by the outbreak of war ended the conditions that had allowed home rule M.P.s leverage after 1910), the intervention of the First World War allowed him temporarily to reassert his authority in Ireland. In the meantime, the rejuvenation of the I.R.B. and the emergence of the militant socialism of Larkin and Connolly strengthened political forces that were ideologically incompatible with the home rule party. In contrast to the Liberal party, the home rulers were ideologically ill-equipped to build constructive relationships with organised labour. The labour interests of an M.P. like William Field were sidelined by the national platform, as the progress of the party since reunification indicated, a tendency decisively compounded by the Dublin lock-out of 1913, which left a lasting bitterness among substantial sections of the Dublin working class. Redmondite manipulation of the Irish party system of conventions (regional bodies dominated by the U.I.L. constituted to select Irish M.P.s) protected the party against the destructive factionalism of local politics and was indicative of a strategy focused exclusively on winning the Westminster campaign. The concomitant inactivity and decline of U.I.L. branches outside the areas of continuing agrarian conflict and the party's increasing dependence on Irish-American sources of funding were further indices of this trend.[133] It was on this – to some extent O'Brienite – analysis that constitutional support for the Volunteers was based. Owing to the subordination of all other political issues to the home rule problem an inherently conservative political party had evolved that sat uneasily with all forms of political radicalism. Particularly troubling, for example, was Laurence Ginnell's campaign against the graziers which resulted in political tensions that helped generate his flirtation with Sinn Féin.[134]

Consequently, much Volunteer polemic celebrated dissent, recognising it as characteristic of a mature political democracy. But the promotion of the

[132] Richard Bourke, *Peace in Ireland: The War of Ideas* (London, 2003), p. 133, considers Griffith's insinuation that if 'only Britain would stand aside . . . [sectarian] intransigence would be eased and hostility assuaged'.

[133] See James McConnel, 'The View from the Backbench: Irish Nationalist MPs and their Work, 1910–1914', Ph.D., Durham, 2002.

[134] For Ginnell see Bew, *Conflict and Conciliation*, Patrick Maume, *Long Gestation*, and Fergus Campbell, *Land and Revolution: Nationalist Politics in the West of Ireland 1891–1921* (Oxford, 2005). Although Griffith was socially conservative, Sinn Féin's collective attitudes were more complex, as suggested by the close relationship with W. P. Ryan's *Irish Peasant*.

Volunteers as a 'national' rather than a 'political' body actualised a distinction dear to advanced nationalist thinking and exposed its political conservatism. This analysis found its clearest and most forceful exposition in an article on 'Politics and Patriotism' in *Irish Volunteer* by Peter Macken, ex-alderman, Labour leader, and member of the Gaelic League and Sinn Féin. Macken considered politics in 'a self-governing country' to be shaped by class and economic rivalries filtered through personality. He argued that the Gaelic League taught nationalists to distinguish between 'nationality', that is Irish identity, and 'party politics', the machinations of the political process. Political disagreement should not impugn the claim of an individual to her Irishness. According to Macken, the Volunteers developed these distinctions further, teaching the difference between 'patriotism' and 'party politics'. Threats to home rule identified a clear patriotic agenda that provided common ground for all nationalists. Until this they had faced,

> a desperate attempt to keep within one political party a number of conflicting elements whose natural instinct is to fly asunder rather than combine. When the natural tendency prevails over the discipline necessarily imposed for the purpose of gaining our legislative independence, we are treated to the usual comments on the Irish inability to unite and the Irish tendency to split up into factions, as if the councils of all the peoples on earth were like so many tea parties, whose outstanding characteristic is a desire to be agreeable.[135]

When Ireland finally experienced 'real politics' as a 'free country' nationalists would discover that the system of two parties, nationalist and unionist, was unsustainable and would fragment along other lines. Embedded in this was the socialist thesis that the advent of normal politics would ensure the replacement of sectarian with class divisions. Vertical class integration would crumble as politics matured, bringing Ireland into the European mainstream. Consequently, the principal function of a permanent Volunteer force would be the maintenance of patriotic unity. 'An army is not a political organisation. We can in a Volunteer corps drill and march and learn to shoot without forfeiting our individual views and without giving offence to or showing intolerance for the man who drills beside us.' Macken closed by suggesting that patriotism may even be 'the privilege of the man who is of no party, who is simply a Volunteer'. Again, evident here are intimations of the apolitical culture of the flying columns, but as striking is what this argument suggests about the troubled relationship between Irish nationalism and socialism. This celebration of volunteering denuded Macken's politics of any revolutionary socialist potential, pointing towards an Irish polity with a reformist labour movement and a potentially counter-revolutionary Volunteer force. Sinn Féin's decision

---

[135] On the 'legend' of Ireland's 'preternatural tendency to disunion and fratricidal strife' see also, for example, Hugh A. MacCarten, 'Comrades All!', *I.V.*, 4 July 1914.

at the 1917 ard-fheis to postpone consideration of what kind of state they wanted to create until after the establishment of an Irish democratic republic embodied a similarly conservative dynamic. In essence, Irish independence could be achieved within the socio-economic status quo. John O'Leary would have been pleased that the doctrine of nationalist tolerance he had preached at the Y.I.S. meetings was shaping advanced nationalist politics in this direction.

1914 did, however, see the partial breakdown of the political categories that had been established in the aftermath of the reunification of the parliamentary party. On the parade grounds of the Volunteers clear barriers collapsed with men and women closely associated with the home rule party, very often through the A.O.H., coming into the orbit of the separatists and ideas that marked a radicalisation of the home rule agenda. Although an association with the Volunteers clearly did not signify an adherence to the insurrectionism of the I.R.B., by highlighting the shortcomings of home rule it did subvert the Redmondite strategy. To reduce the destabilising threat the organisation posed Redmond precipitated a split, forcing an orthodox home rule character on the bulk of the Volunteers and reasserting the political categories of 1900. As a result, the Volunteers effectively ceased to be a popular organisation. The National Volunteers declined, partly depleted by enlistment in the British army,[136] partly left redundant by the government's refusal to integrate them into the war effort. The Irish Volunteers, with the Irish Citizen Army, became unambiguously revolutionary and contained an influential faction intent upon insurrection. This completed the process begun with the reorganisation of the I.R.B. under Hobson, MacDermott, and Clarke. Open drilling and rifle practice strengthened the organisation and provided a patina of legality after the split. Ostensibly committed to the manifesto of November 1913, the Volunteers provided a cover for revolutionary activity, dodging legal censure.

Before September 1914, then, volunteering failed to produce an alternative Irish nationalist polity. Little clarification of how it would fulfil the maxim of the Irish Volunteer's first editorial was achieved: 'Belief must always translate itself into action or that belief will die.'[137] In its complex of constitutionalist, separatist, physical force, and moral force nationalisms, volunteering shared some of the qualities of Parnellism – although powered by a more overt threat of violence – but, crucially, it lacked a charismatic centre.

One person obliged to make sense of the Irish Volunteers was Augustine Birrell, chief secretary of Ireland. In April 1914 he provided his cabinet colleagues with a confidential memorandum on these Irish organisations. Although consisting of 'somewhat ragged regiments, ill-equipped as yet and not particularly well disciplined', the Irish Volunteers were 'daily increasing

---

[136] Of the 40,000 Irishmen who enlisted in the first four months of the Great War 16,000 were National Volunteers.
[137] I.V., 7 Feb. 1914.

in number and may become a formidable force in the future'.[138] By contrast, it had been communicated to the county inspector for Antrim that in the event of the implementation of home rule and the establishment of a provisional government by the Ulster Unionist Council, the U.V.F. would co-operate with the R.I.C. provided it was 'confined to the duty of protecting life and property'. However, the R.I.C. would meet 'determined resistance' if used 'for purely combatant purposes': 'they will be treated as hostile, and dealt with accordingly.' The Ulster Unionist Council made it clear that the U.V.F. would be mobilised against the forces of the crown to prevent the implementation of the policy of His Majesty's government. This possible recourse to illegality was central to unionist rhetoric throughout the crisis. Even if the threat of rebellion and civil war was the bluff suggested by *Irish Freedom*, it remained the case that the Ulster unionists consistently voiced their readiness to resort to unconstitutional means.

By contrast, the purpose of the Irish Volunteers was more perplexing. Birrell, sensitive to the subtle nuances of Irish nationalist discourse, noted that the 'word "Volunteer" in Ireland is full of historical significance, and touches the national sentiment in all parts of the country'.[139] In the advanced nationalist milieu of the 1900s the historic Volunteers were of particular importance. Griffith regarded their disbanding as the essential precursor to the passage of the Act of Union, denuding Grattan's parliament of the essential source of its patriotic defence.[140] MacNeill made the same argument in 'The North Began',[141] and on a fundraising tour in the U.S.A., Pearse told a Philadelphia crowd in March: 'Had the Volunteers not handed back their arms, the horrors of '98 would never have come. The union would never have been accomplished. The sacrifice of Emmet would not have been needed.'[142] The call in 1782 by the Volunteer convention at Dungannon for the repeal of constitutionally limiting legislation was memorialised in Hobson's Dungannon Clubs. In separatist historiography the Dungannon Convention was the moment *par excellence* when popular pressure reinforced the demands of the politicians. The achievement of legislative independence was directly attributed to the existence of this armed body of patriotic Irishmen and although in reality they had little in common with Fenianism and were motivated by a very particular form of Ascendancy patriotism, twentieth-century advanced nationalists saw in them the martial spirit to which they aspired. The Dungannon Convention suggested the battle could be won by

---

[138] C.A.B. 37/119/51, 2 Apr. 1912. Cf. the Royal Commission on the Howth gun-running incidents which described the Volunteers as 'composed of respectable citizens, and all its operations had been conducted without disorder.' See above, note 110.
[139] Ibid.
[140] Arthur Griffith, 'National Unity: Back to the Base' in *IV*, 14 Feb. 1914.
[141] Tierney, *Eoin MacNeill*, pp 107–9.
[142] Transcript sent by William Maloney to Bulmer Hobson, 25 Oct. 1938, McGarrity Papers (N.L.I., MS 17453).

taking a determined stance on a series of well-articulated demands. It was the ambiguous legacy of the eighteenth-century Volunteers that provided much of the historical justification for Sinn Féin's nimble quickstep between constitutionalism and Fenianism. Unlike the republican abstractions of Fenianism, the eighteenth-century Volunteers suggested solutions rooted in the specificities of England and Ireland's constitutional relationship.

A close reading of the manifesto approved at the inaugural meeting of the Irish Volunteers on 25 November 1913[143] – the benchmark against which all future developments of the movement were measured[144] – indicates, however, that volunteering was not the mirror image of the U.V.F. because it was not simply the means to enforce home rule. Rather, its stated purpose was to defend the 'semblance of civil government' that the Ulster unionist–conservative nexus threatened. The overarching danger was the sacrifice of 'the future control of all our national affairs' to popular agitation. Despoiled by these developments, Westminster could no longer be even partially relied upon and Irish nationalists were forced to consider whether they were to 'rest inactive in the hope that the course of politics in Great Britain may save us from the degradation openly threatened against us?' 'British politics', after all, was 'controlled by British interests' and the British would not help the Irish if they were 'quiescent' or 'unworthy of defence'.

'But the Volunteers, once they have been enrolled', continued the manifesto, 'will form a prominent element in the national life under a national government. The nation will maintain its Volunteer organisation as a guarantee of the liberties which the Irish people shall have secured.' To insist on the force providing Ireland with a permanent and independent defensive capacity was incompatible with the claim that home rule would reconfigure the union in a manner that would restore the legitimacy of Westminster, the crown, and its agencies as the ultimate source of authority in Ireland. Constitutionalist support for this aspect of the volunteering agenda represented a radicalisation of the Redmondite project. It partially acknowledged the legitimacy of Sinn Féin's insistence on Ireland acquiring the means to pursue an independent foreign policy and highlighted just how far home rule fell short of this.[145] And if Irish receptiveness to advanced nationalist rhetoric generated wider adherence only when allied to specific grievances, unionist obstructionism generated just such a grievance, and the claim that to bear arms for the

---

[143] Reproduced in Dorothy MacArdle, *The Irish Republic* (4th ed., Dublin, 1951), pp 909–11.
[144] For example, see the statement by MacNeill and Laurence Kettle, 4 September 1914, demanding the transfer from the government of the material means to defend Ireland as a fulfilment of the manifesto. Also, the circular of 24 September 1914 announcing that Redmond's nominees were no longer members of the committee on the grounds that his Woodenbridge speech was incompatible with the manifesto. Hobson Papers (N.L.I., MS 13173/1 & /10).
[145] A modicum of autonomy in the foreign arena was among the major advances the form of dominion status allowed by the Anglo-Irish Treaty of 1921 represented over home rule.

protection of the 'rights and liberties common to all the people of Ireland' was a civic duty had a widespread resonance.

In the specific circumstances of 1912–14, these aims make perfect sense. Through the U.V.F. the Tories had inhibited Westminster's ability to devolve political rights to Dublin and for Liberals to submit to unionist obstructionism was to renege on the understanding established between Gladstone and Parnell in 1882. If Westminster ceased to be the principal forum for the determination of the great political questions then loyalty to the parliamentary party was predicated on false assumptions. After the Curragh incident of March 1914 a front-page commentary in the *Irish Volunteer* starkly delineated the implications of this analysis, strongly implying an affinity between the organisation and Fenianism. 'We sacrificed "unconstitutional" methods for constitutional, and if at the last minute England tells us that her constitution is a sham we must take her words and take back the arms we dropped.'[146] This was pure Parnellism. The inverted commas problematised the legitimacy of British political categories; the 'we' signified that now familiar Irish nationalist narrative that traced the collective shift from Fenianism to constitutionalism; and the 'if' hinted that the moment of rupture that would reverse this shift had not yet arrived. At issue was not whether home rule would get onto the statute book, but whether England was sufficiently determined to enforce its provisions. It was to ensure implementation of the law that the Volunteers, armed and drilled, were essential.

> The time for mere empty talk is past, and on behalf of an armed Irish nation leaders will speak with the consciousness of power that will make their voices of the utmost weight. Behind the ballot box is the rifle, behind the Irish parliamentary party must be the army.[147]

Paradoxically, a partial recourse to Fenianism would be the saving of constitutionalism.

Parnellism, however, was dead. Advanced and constitutionalist agitations had cohered around agrarian agitation, which, as already noted, provided a series of prescribed enemies and broad policy agendas. The crisis of 1914 and the resultant agitation had entirely different causes. Parnellism had never been predicated on the possibility of an Irish civil war or direct attacks on the British state. As the Parnell split appeared to demonstrate, however, if home rule was categorically seen to have failed, Irish nationalists would return to Fenianism. In March 1914 Casement discarded Volunteer propriety, giving full expression to the implications of this scenario.

---

[146] *I.V.*, 4 Apr. 1914.
[147] Cf. Danny Morrison's notorious summary of Sinn Féin's approach to electoral politics in the 1980s, with 'ballot paper in this hand and an Armalite in this hand'.

The freedom of Ireland was not going to be won at Westminster. If the people of Ireland wanted it as much as the people of Ulster did not want it they must be prepared to fight for it. They must put revolution in the place of resolution as they had enough resolutions already. If they meant to have home rule they should be prepared to shed their blood for it. No nation could ever win its freedom without fighting for it. Unless they fought for it they would not get it.[148]

Casement's words could not go unchallenged. Moore worried he was 'drifting into cloudland' and reminded him Ireland had to build itself up gradually, 'not attempting too much at a time, not more than its strength will permit'.[149] Casement was not entirely reassuring: 'I am not a "revolutionary"[,] an "idealist" – beyond the limit of most of my countrymen – or anxious for "rebellion".'[150] But the threat of partition permitted further departures from orthodox Volunteer rhetoric. In Tullamore Casement was adamant: the Volunteers stood for 'a united Ireland, and in the end for a free Ireland'. By ratcheting up his rhetoric, Casement grabbed the opportunity to assert separatist orthodoxy. Voices urging restraint came from unexpected quarters. In early June Erskine Childers warned Casement that they must not alienate the Liberals or undermine Volunteer discipline by heightening expectations. Childers was afraid the rank and file had not comprehended the belt-tightening that 'genuine home rule' would demand. Volunteering, it seems, might become a means to discipline a potentially restless population.[151]

In May 1914 the R.I.C. inspector-general discerned a rather different challenge in the Volunteers. Rather than perceiving a revolutionary force, he foresaw the gradual diminution of Dublin Castle's ability to govern Ireland.

In Ireland the training and drilling for the use of arms of a great part of the male populations is a new departure which is bound in the not distant future to profoundly alter all the existing conditions of life. Obedience to the law has never been a prominent characteristic of the people. In times of passion or excitement the law has ever been maintained by force, and this has been rendered practicable owing to the want of cohesion among crowds hostile to the police. If the people become armed and drilled effective police control will vanish. Unless the population which is now being drilled and armed is placed under some responsible leadership or control, these trained bands of men will be used for cattle-driving, or other similar

---

[148] C.O. 904/194/46, 5 Mar. 1914.

[149] Moore to Casement, 8 Apr. 1914, Casement Papers (N.L.I., MS 36203/3).

[150] Casement to Moore, 9 Apr. 1914, Moore Papers (N.L.I., MS 10561). MacNeill mollified: 'Casement is all right. In conversation, he is the deadly enemy of the existing order, as we all are, only that we do not let ourselves go to the same extent. In all matters of action, he is wise and careful, and worthy of the fullest confidence.' MacNeill to Moore, 13 Apr. 1914, Moore Papers (N.L.I., MS 10561).

[151] Erskine Childers to Roger Casement, 8 June 1914, Casement Papers (N.L.I., MS 36203/3).

illegalities, which may find favour in the localities where they carry out their military drill.

Events are moving. Each county will soon have a trained army far outnumbering the police, and those who control the Volunteers will be in a position to dictate to what extent the law of the land may be carried into effect. In Ulster, where party disturbances are numerous; in Cork, where there are acute political disagreements; and in Galway and Clare, which are permeated by dangerous secret societies,[152] the general arming and drilling of the population will be a recurring menace to the peace.[153]

Although there is some congruity between these almost Hobsonian expectations of a revolution by attrition, an un-ideological whittling away of British authority, and the exalted yet nebulous aims of the Volunteers, it is equally striking that the policeman feared the agrarian implications of this process more than any advanced nationalist dangers.

VI

As Charles Townshend has shown, although the legality of the volunteering movement was dubious, drilling in defence of 'rights and liberties' was permitted.[154] The constitutional position of the Volunteer force was particularly complicated because the 'rights and liberties' they proposed to defend had yet to be granted. Moreover, as suggested, the permanency claimed for the force surpassed these anticipated 'rights and liberties'. Tom Kettle contributed an essay to the *Irish Volunteer* suffused with this paradox. Consistently loyal to Redmond, Kettle would emerge as one of the firmest advocates of full Irish involvement in the war against 'Prussian tyranny'.[155] Alongside his brother Lawrence he was a member of the Volunteer 'provisional committee', giving credence to its non-partisan identity. Later his involvement caused antagonism – even MacNeill agreed this troubled individual was using the Volunteers to ingratiate himself to the parliamentary party.[156]

By thinking about the Irish question in an international context Kettle related volunteering to 'the strange' worldwide 'reversion to the gospel of the

---

[152] A reference to the Galway agrarian agitation led and inspired by the revolutionary Tom Kenny.

[153] C.O. 904/93, May 1914, pp 235–6.

[154] Townshend, *Political Violence*, pp 248–9.

[155] Senia Pašeta, 'Thomas Kettle: "An Irish Soldier in the Army of Europe"?' in Adrian Gregory and Senia Pašeta (ed.), *Ireland and the Great War: 'A War to Unite us all'?* (Manchester, 2002), p. 16.

[156] MacNeill to Darrell Figgis, 12 May 1914, Hobson Papers (N.L.I., MS 13171/3). MacNeill suspected Kettle's method was to raise I.P.P. suspicions regarding the provisional committee and then to pose as the guardian of the party's interests.

force'.[157] This applied equally to the international arms race and the violence of class conflict (the 'prologue to passionately desired rebellion'). Fenian expectations that disappointment with home rule would purify national sentiment were to some extent affirmed by Kettle's assertion that the programme of the Volunteers was the product not of 'logic' but of a 'sudden illumination'. Liam de Roiste also identified a mystical group psychology: 'The idea of the Irish National Volunteers came as an inspiration. It struck not one mind, but many. That idea was one of those psychic forces whose origin is unknown but whose effects are seen in the action of multitudes.'[158]

Kettle's constitutional credentials were further undermined by his distrust of the forces of the crown. He deemed the modern practice of delegating responsibility of defence to a professional army unmanly and, in Ireland's particular case, not 'safe'. The 'Castle-controlled policeman' or the 'London-controlled soldier', the officials responsible for the maintenance of law and order, could not be relied upon to arbitrate on the competing claims on their authority. Kettle's fear that it was 'something too much of a gamble whether the baton . . . will crack the right skull or the wrong one' recalls Pearse's notorious (if ironic) apologia of November 1913 ('we may make mistakes in the beginning and shoot the wrong people; but bloodshed is a cleansing and sanctifying thing'), demonstrating the ambiguous rhetorical currency images can gain.[159] Kettle's explanation strongly echoed the language of 'perfidious Albion': military organisation in Ireland was 'created not to defend the nation against invaders, but to defend the government against the nation'. The fraught circumstances of 1914, compounded by the Curragh incident, saw Kettle tell a Tullamore crowd that they 'were not going to rely . . . for their national security upon the whims or the fancies of some old fellow with gold braid down the seams of his breeches (laughter). Irishmen were going to take care of themselves, and they meant to do it (cheers).'[160] Above all, the movement radicalised the home rule demand. 'Whoever is responsible for the government of the country will be forced to regularise and adopt' the Volunteers. The home rule bill contained no provision for an Irish defence or military capacity, yet Kettle regarded the Volunteer opportunity as restoring to him his 'self-respect as a citizen' by enabling him to efficiently fulfil those attendant obligations, rather than relying on 'inadequate proxies'.

Kettle's preoccupation with the restoration of self-respect in part stemmed from particular personal necessities – he was battling a serious drink problem – but this was a central theme of Volunteer polemic that drew on the Fenian

---

[157] I.V., 25 Apr. 1914.
[158] I.V., 14 Feb. 1914.
[159] I.V., 25 Apr. 1914; R. F. Foster, *Modern Ireland 1600–1972* (London, 1988), p. 477.
[160] Kettle continued: 'The objective of this movement is a force of 50,000 or 60,000 trained men, armed with modern rifles, and capable of resisting any attack upon the common liberties of this country.'

discourse linking revolution with the restoration of Irish manliness.[161] For if the experience of colonial subjugation had rendered Irish manhood feminised, subservient, and dependent, this was enhanced by the secondary dependency on the parliamentary party. Volunteering partially answered the Fenian complaint that the role of ordinary Irishmen had been reduced to voting pointless resolutions and paying subscriptions. Griffith's doctrine of self-reliance had provided one such means of emancipation from this emasculating political culture, volunteering's martial spirit another.

Inseparable from the restoration of Irish autonomous action was the firearm. *Irish Volunteer* readers may have been assured that 'however well a signed article may sum up any or all phases of the movement . . . it does not officially speak for the National Volunteer', but on the linkage of arms and masculinity there was a wholly consistent line. Every Volunteer 'loves a rifle' claimed the paper, and a number of writers of greatly differing temperaments addressed this theme. Casement, advocating the celebration of the 900th anniversary of the Battle of Clontarf, argued that 'to be a good Irishman means also to be a good Christian, and that it is only the strong man armed who keepeth his own house and Church.'[162] Joseph Plunkett used similar muscular Christianity arguments: 'it is at once the duty and the dignity of Christian manhood to bear arms, even if only for their symbolism, and if there were to be no likelihood of the necessity for their use.'[163] This chimes with Michael Laffan's observation that Pearse's claim that 'nationhood is not achieved otherwise than in arms' was qualitatively distinct from Lyons's paraphrase 'Nationhood could not be achieved other than by arms.'[164] Again, the shortcomings of the home rule bill were indicated. By failing to extend to Ireland the power of self-defence it failed to render 'Ireland a nation' and to restore to Irishmen their masculinity:

> A man is not fully a man, nor is a nation a nation without the power to direct a policy and to ensure civil and religious liberty to those who demand those blessings. For this reason conscription is the prevailing military policy among the powers of Europe. The whole nation must bear arms.

---

[161] There was no room for feebleness in the Volunteers. William Royce made the case for the adoption of the kilt as their uniform: 'The only objections that can be made to its adoption as a uniform for Volunteers are those which will come from the skinny-legged, knick-kneed type for whose faulty or undeveloped "understandings" the pants as a covering are a veritable Godsend.' *I.V.*, 14 Feb. 1914.

[162] Cf. Casement to Hobson, 7 Sept. 1909 (N.L.I., MS 13158/6): 'The Irish catholic, man for man is a poor crawling coward as a rule. Afraid of his miserable soul and fearing the priest like a devil. No country was ever freed by men afraid of bogies. Freedom to Ireland can come *only* through protestants because they are not afraid of any bogey (except the Pope, and their fear of him is after all a bit of play acting – he'd have a damned bad time of it in Lurgan if he showed up there!).'

[163] *I.V.*, 7 Feb. 1914.

[164] Michael Laffan, 'In Search of Patrick Pearse' in Máirín Ní Dhonnchadha and Theo Dorgan (ed.), *Revising the Rising* (Derry, 1991), p. 128.

This argument challenged the cultural nationalist conception of the nation as the embodiment of a culture rooted in an ethno-linguistic specificity with one in which the nation could only be realised through political activism. Without the capacity to conduct an independent defence of its liberties the nation and its manhood were a sham, a prospect Plunkett anticipated in home rule. Like Kettle, his justification of the Volunteers offered a fundamental critique of the likely achievement of the constitutionalists.

After the Curragh incident and the Larne gun-running this discourse became more strident. In May the *Irish Volunteer* proclaimed the 'man who has once handled a rifle and is not smitten with a desire to own one is not an Irishman'.[165] In defiance of the acceptance of Redmondites onto the executive committee, the paper made its priorities clear in July. 'We must have rifles. Whether the proclamation [against importing arms] is torn up or not the rifles must come. . . . All the rest, uniforms, equipment, standards, could be dispensed with, but the rifle is the soldier's arm.'[166] A subsidiary dimension to the talk of arms was their role in tempting young men into the movement. How effective this was as a recruiting strategy is difficult to determine, but there is evidence that young men coveted rifles and revolvers. Moreover, the increase in the circulation of arms and the incidence of gun-related crime further conditioned the reception given to the Volunteers.

By the government allowing the Peace Preservation Act of 1881 to lapse in 1906 the limited legal restrictions on the importation of arms to Ireland were removed.[167] One melodramatic witness suggested a clear causal link between this liberal move and future events: 'The Arms Act was dropped. The Irish party and their cause were swept into oblivion in consequence.'[168] The remaining 1870 Gun Licence Act provided a narrow legal basis on which to control the circulation of arms. The police could bring before the resident magistrate or justice of the peace 'all persons of bad, doubtful, or indifferent character whom they may detect in the possession of arms, especially revolvers, with a view to requiring them as "persons of influence" to find sureties to be of good behaviour'. Concern was particularly acute in County Clare, especially following the sale of between eighty and ninety firearms by Limerick dealers to County Clare people between July 1907 and October 1908. Moreover, a shipment of sixty revolvers was reportedly distributed in October 1908 among Clare U.I.L. members and at a cattle drive of 4 October at Lamanagh numerous shots were fired.[169] The *Irish Catholic* shared this concern, lamenting

---

[165] I.V., 2 May 1914.

[166] I.V., 4 July 1914; Liam de Roiste to Casement, 22 June 1914, Casement Papers (N.L.I., MS 36203/3). Arms were prohibited from import by Royal Proclamation of December 1913, but this was mysteriously rescinded on 5 August 1914. Between times the Volunteers pressured the I.P.P. to lobby for the lifting of the ban before defying it altogether in July at Howth.

[167] Townshend, *Political Violence*, p. 264.

[168] Sullivan, *Old Ireland*, p. 150.

[169] C.O. 904/23, 'Possession & carrying of Arms specially Revolvers – corres. 1907–12'.

the foolish and irresponsible farmers' boys and village youths to whom the prospect of acquiring revolvers in payment of a shilling a week has been an irresistible temptation. We unhesitatingly say that the policy or legislation which rendered possible the creation of such a situation as this is simply immoral.

A 'home rule administration', the newspaper argued, would not have allowed this to happen.[170] Of the many examples of newspaper advertisements for firearms in this period a typical example was carried by the *Weekly Freeman* for a Birmingham company offering the aptly named Davis's Original & Genuine 'Defiance' Gun for 50 shillings.[171]

After 1906 there was a marked rise in the number of offences committed with firearms. Historically, times of political unrest brought an increase in indictable offences. This becomes clear if a series of five-year periods are examined (see Table 6.1).[172] Moreover, the immediate context was a period of relatively low incidence. The lowest figure in the 1848–1914 period was 1901 with twenty 'firing outrages' while the annual average for 1902–1906 was thirty-eight. Thereafter the annual figures were: 1907: 87, 1908: 131, 1909: 84, 1910: 86, 1911: 73, 1912: 80, 1913: 83, 1914: 93. The majority of firing offences were classified by the police as non-agrarian: in 1907 there were eighteen examples of the indictable offence of firing at the person in a non-agrarian context and nine in an agrarian context. In both categories there was an increase in the years after the repeal of the Peace Preservation Act but it was proportionately bigger in the agrarian context.[173] Between 1900 and 1906 there were 13 indictable agrarian cases and 88 indictable non-agrarian cases. Between 1907 and 1913 there were 76 agrarian cases and 183 non-agrarian cases. This amounted to a near nine-fold increase in the agrarian crime compared to something over a two-fold increase in the non-agrarian. This trend was more marked for the crime of 'firing into dwellings'. Using the same time-spans and classifications, from a position of near-parity (1900–1906: 53 agrarian, 47 non-agrarian) a three-fold increase was evident in the non-agrarian crime and a four-fold increase in the agrarian crime (1907–1913: 212 agrarian, 149 non-agrarian). However, the incidence of both these crimes suggests a downturn in the agrarian crime from 1912 and little change, if not an increase, in the non-agrarian category (firing at the person, non-agrarian: 1912: 34, 1913: 33, 1914: 42, agrarian: 1912: 5, 1913: 7, 1914: 5; firing into dwellings, non-agrarian: 1912: 21, 1913: 31, 1914: 35, agrarian: 1912: 20, 1913: 12, 1914: 11).

---

[170] *The Irish Catholic*, 7 Nov. 1908.

[171] *W.F.*, 24 Oct. 1908.

[172] C.O. 903/18, 'Firing Outrages in Ireland since the 1st January, 1848', p. 68. Re. analysis of crime statistics cf. Augusteijn, *From Defiance to Guerrilla Warfare*, pp 14–19.

[173] C.O. 903/18, 'Indictable Offences for the Past Fifteen Years', pp 74–5.

Table 6.1 Increase in indictable offences at times of political unrest

Five year period	Annual average
1848–1852	139
1858–1862	55
1868–1872	58[a]
1878–1882	157
1888–1892	72
1908–1912	90[b]

Notes

(a) It appears that the police did not include any shots fired as part of the Fenian rising of 1867 when only twenty-eight indictable offences are recorded, higher only than 1866 in that decade.
(b) The only other period when the annual total topped 100 was 1886–1888, coinciding with the Plan of Campaign: respectively 135, 120, 103.

The conclusions that can be drawn from these trends are limited but significant speculations can be made. First, there is a strong correlation between the lifting of the restrictions on the purchase of arms and the increase in the incidence of gun-related crime. Second, from 1848 the increases and decreases in agrarian and non-agrarian crime tended to coincide, suggesting that there was a general increase in lawlessness at times of agrarian agitation. That said, during the Land War agrarian gun crime far outstripped the non-agrarian equivalent.[174] The signs of a trend away from agrarian gun crime after 1912 suggests that with the decline in U.I.L. agitation (for example, in 1914 settlement of the Clanricarde estates in County Galway was finally reached) there was a general decline in rural lawlessness. On the other hand, the increase in non-agrarian gun crime continued and it seems likely this both conditioned the emergence of the Volunteers and was symptomatic of this development. Indeed, recognition of this seems congruent with the inspector-general's characterisation of the Volunteer threat as chiefly one to law and order. Pearse's notorious demand of November 1913 that 'We [the Irish] must accustom ourselves to the thought of arms, to the sight of arms, to the use of arms'[175] gave an ideological gloss to a process already at work. The existence of a section of nationalist Ireland predisposed to the ownership and use of firearms in an apolitical arena must provide part of the explanation for the spontaneous drilling of 1913. The Ulster Volunteer Force may have returned the gun to Irish politics, but it certainly was not responsible for bringing it to Irish society.

Bulmer Hobson and Countess Markievicz's Fianna Éireann (boy scouts) was the first avowedly nationalist organisation to impose some discipline on these

---

[174] 1880–1882 firing at the person, agrarian: 146, non-agrarian: 126. Firing into dwelling, agrarian: 325, non-agrarian: 89.
[175] P. H. Pearse, 'The Coming Revolution' in *Political Writings and Speeches* (Dublin, 1966), pp 98–9.

militaristic trends. Among the 2,000 (Clarke claimed 5,000) communicants that gathered at Bodenstown in June 1913 were twenty-five Fianna standing guard at the graveside armed with guns and bayonets.[176] Pearse made a moder-ately successful speech that celebrated Tone's ardour, valour, purity, tenderness, and gaiety, and repudiated the divisions within Irish nationalism;[177] Sinn Féin distributed anti-enlistment pamphlets;[178] and J. T. Jameson made a film of the proceedings which was later shown two or three times a day at the Rotunda and in Rathmines. Clarke was greatly enthused. The film was due to be shown in Galway, Tralee, Queenstown, Cork, and the Curragh and he was 'feeling ten years younger since Sunday'. 'At last we see tangible results from the patient, plodding work of sowing the seed', he told Devoy. 'The tide is running strongly in our direction. *We have the rising generation.*'[179] The Fianna display was repeated at the successful Manchester Martyrs commemoration in November.[180] 'John Clancy's boys', shouldering camans, had guarded Parnell's coffin as it moved through Dublin. It was fitting that the 'uncrowned King of Ireland' should receive the martial trappings of a state funeral. But at the grave of an insurrectionist, young boys, old guns, and the exaltant exhortations of a school teacher were of an entirely different quality. Where the G.A.A. presence had reinforced the dignity of the occasion, emblematising the nation in mourning, the Fianna spoke intention, a renewed commitment to armed rebellion.

Against the background of the mass mobilisation of the U.V.F. small groups of boys were of little significance, but the Bodenstown and Manchester Martyrs displays were indicative of the changing flavour of Fenian memorial. Indeed, the I.R.B. in Armagh was reportedly pleased with the mobilisation of the U.V.F. – Carson was only doing what they'd be doing in a couple of years – and new members entering I.R.B. circles in Newry were greeted enthusiastically. Despite

---

[176] In Limerick John Daly oversaw 210 Fianna; they were addressed by James MacCarthy of Clan na Gael on 26 May 1912. C.O. 904/86, June 1912, p. 16. For a photograph of O'Rahilly's sons and nephew in their Fianna uniform, see O'Rahilly, *O'Rahilly and the 1916 Rising*, facing p. 111.

[177] Dudley Edwards, *Patrick Pearse*, p. 174, 'we agree to accept as fellow-nationalists all who specifically or virtually recognise this Irish nation as an entity and, being part of it, owe it and give it their service.'

[178] C.O. 904/14 Part 1, June, Sept. & Oct. 1913, pp 57, 124, 188–9, 191. Liam Mellows, following his appointment as national organiser at the Fianna annual convention in July, was in Tuam in September drilling forty local Fianna boys and lecturing on the life of Mitchel. For more on Mellows and the expansion of Fianna organisation, see C. Desmond Greaves, *Liam Mellows and the Irish Revolution* (London, 1971), pp 47–52.

[179] Clarke to Devoy, 25 June 1913, *D.P.B. II*, pp 410–12.

[180] Eoin McGee, '"God Save Ireland": Manchester Martyr Demonstrations in Dublin 1867–1916' in *Eire–Ireland* (Fall–Winter 2001), pp 6–7. The police reported an attendance of 12,000, making it the largest meeting since 1879. Clarke and the Sinn Féin councillors Sean T. O'Kelly and Richard O'Carroll acted as marshals, and the proceedings were filmed. C.O. 904/14, pp 207–8.

this, overall the intimidating atmosphere created by the U.V.F. left northern nationalists apprehensive: 'throughout Ulster [nationalists] are keeping extremely quiet.'[181]

An atmosphere conducive to the organisation of gun clubs compounded the readiness of pre-existing political organisations to transform themselves into Volunteer branches. As with the growth of the '98 centenary organisations, this resurgent popular activism ended a period of political quiet. As the police observed: 'The introduction of the home rule bill has evoked little or no enthusiasm throughout the country. In connection with the measure there seems to be considerable dread of extra taxation.'[182] Outside Ulster the response to the second reading of the home rule bill was muted.[183] By contrast, 25,000 attended meetings in Cavan, Londonderry, and Monaghan addressed by Robert Harcourt, Joe Devlin, and William Redmond.[184] Things were livelier by August, when 15,000 attended a U.I.L. meeting in Enniscorthy to hear the lord mayor of Dublin and the M.P.s French and Esmonde discuss the bill.[185] In November 1912 the R.I.C. inspector-general observed:

> In rural Ireland generally, political enthusiasm is not very marked. Purchased tenants are contentedly improving their farms, while those who have not yet bought their holdings appear to devote all their energies to expediting land purchase. However, in a few places some activity is observed amongst the extreme party, who are making efforts to gain support by denouncing the home rule bill as totally inadequate, and in the columns of a seditious newspaper called 'Irish Freedom', which circulates monthly in country towns, the policy of insurrection when a favourable opportunity occurs is freely discussed and advocated.[186]

The Irish nationalist response to the home rule bill has been described as 'apathetic', which might be glossed a little.[187] Although political participation *was* at a low ebb, the introduction of the home rule bill had clearly shifted the initiative to the Westminster arena, leaving Irish nationalists with little choice but to observe from afar the parliamentary process. Redmond's insistence that the 'two nations' theory of Ireland was 'an abomination and a blasphemy' provided further reassurance.[188] Indeed, the foundation of the Volunteers

---

[181] C.O. 904/14 Part 1, June, July & Aug. 1913, pp 60, 101–2; C.O. 904/91, Nov. 1913, p. 415. According to an informant in Armagh the I.R.B. numbered 350, structured around 24 circles, 23 centres, and 5 or 6 district centres.
[182] C.O. 904/86, Apr. 1912, p. 688.
[183] C.O. 904/87, June 1912, pp 17, 50.
[184] C.O. 904/87, June 1912, pp 196.
[185] C.O. 904/87, Aug. 1912, p. 595.
[186] C.O. 904/88, Nov. 1912, p. 408.
[187] Wheatley, "'These Quiet Days of Peace'", p. 74.
[188] Michael Wheatley, *Nationalism and the Irish Party: Provincial Ireland 1910–1916* (Oxford, 2005), p. 179.

was only indirectly triggered by the unionist mobilisation. In the aftermath of Carson's declaration of a provisional government Liberal parliamentary moves in the autumn of 1913 towards some form of separate treatment for a number of northern counties suggested that the unionist mobilisation had finally endangered the home rule bill. In response, Michael McDermott-Hayes, secretary of the South Westmeath U.I.L. and editor of the *Westmeath Independent*, concocted a story of 5,000 men parading, with buglers, drums, and cavalry, and formed into twenty companies.[189] The story was picked up by the Dublin press and J. P. Farrell (nationalist M.P. for Longford) airily encouraged drilling in a series of speeches.[190] I.R.B. restlessness during the foregoing month or two added to the mounting unease. By the summer of 1914 the county inspector for Tyrone noted the evident fillip given to the advanced men.

> The impunity with which the Ulster army of 100,000 men enrolled, drilled, and armed themselves, has given an immense stimulus to the physical force party. They say it is proof of what they always asserted, that England will yield everything to force, and nothing to other considerations.[191]

The Irish Volunteers did not, however, become a large body until the summer of 1914 when the Redmondites forced themselves onto the controlling committee. According to police figures, the total membership in March was 10,489; by late April it had reached 19,206, and in May 25,000.[192] O'Rahilly, appealing to Devoy for money for rifles, claimed there were 25,000 members by the beginning of April with the potential to build a force of 200,000.[193] Moore, the Volunteer inspector-general, imagined this eventual force defending Ireland against a German invasion force of 20,000.[194] The detailed police figures available for March 1914 report the following. There were 4,390 Volunteers in Ulster organised into 18 branches; about 993 in Leinster with 8 branches; approximately 2,333 organised into 11 branches in Munster; 1,638 in Connaught in 11 branches; and 1,140 and 9 branches in the D.M.P. area.[195] To achieve these modest figures had not been easy. A early meeting broke up in Cork and little initial success was observed, for example, in Limerick,[196]

---

[189] Joseph Brennan noted the scorn in official circles for reports of drilling in autumn 1913. See Leon Ó Broin, *No Man's Man: A Biographical Memoir of Joseph Brennan – Civil Servant and First Governor of the Central Bank* (Dublin, 1982), p. 20.

[190] Farrell soon adopted the orthodox Redmondite line, arguing in May 1914 that 'the time is not opportune'. Bew, *Ideology and the Irish Question*, p. 113.

[191] C.O. 904/93, June 1914, p. 496.

[192] C.A.B. 37/119/51, C.O. 904/93, Apr. 1914, p. 19. Hobson argued the official figures underestimated membership, see *History Irish Volunteers*, p.93.

[193] O'Rahilly to Devoy, 6 Apr. 1914, *D.P.B. II*, pp 425–7.

[194] *I.V.*, 7 Feb. 1914.

[195] These figures were evidently collated from police reports.

[196] By March the inevitable struggle for control between the U.I.L. and Daly had been noticed. C.O. 904/14, Mar. 1914, pp 28–9.

Galway, Kerry, and Wicklow. In East Limerick the local M.P. Thomas Lundun explained at a U.I.L. meeting that the Volunteers were not yet necessary and they should await the instructions of the party leadership. Richard Hazelton told his Galway constituents the same.[197] Nonetheless, February saw rapid proliferation, with branches soon reported in seventeen counties. However, this did not compare favourably with the extraordinarily rapid growth of the Ulster Volunteer Force (reported at 100,000 in June 1913).[198] A renewed nationalist 'vitality' was widely noted and although all county inspectors agreed that the movement would only grow rapidly if it were supported by the I.P.P., nationalist Ireland was in 'general sympathy'.[199]

Such indicators as there are of the social complexion of the Volunteers suggest the bulk of the membership was of the lower middle classes and the labouring class. However, nationalists from across the social spectrum associated with the movement, particularly from the end of May:

> The rank and file consist so far of farmers' sons, shop assistants, and servant boys, but the Roman Catholic clergy, professional men, county and district councillors, magistrates, . . . and a very few ex-military officers, have identified themselves with the movement.[200]

Social divisions were felt in the Volunteer ranks and in some areas these overlapped with sectarian tensions. Class tension was reported in Carlow where the 'labour and corner boy element' was resented by the shop assistants and the farmers' sons. Class and sectarian divisions combined in Donegal: while 'farmers and their sons drill in the unionist hall their labourers drill in the opposite camp'. In Armagh, where 3,000 had joined, it was noted that 'the better class of nationalists' had kept their distance, whereas in Mayo not only did the Volunteers attract support from across the class spectrum but they were also supported by persons who were not known to have joined nationalist organisations before. In Westmeath no nationalist section opposed; in Waterford the O'Brienites held aloof.[201] In Galway college students joined up, possibly reflecting the strong Gaelic Athletic Association and secret society presence. Casement reported that they could barely cope with the initial rush of 4–500 recruits: 'every section of the populace was there (but no gentry) of the town and all parties' he wrote to Maurice Moore. 'If one resolute,

---

[197] C.O. 904/91 & 93, Dec. 1913, pp 613–14, 627, Apr. 1914, p. 19.

[198] Tierney, *Eoin MacNeill*, p. 110. Promoting the organisation made heavy demands on the activists. To take one example, Casement was in Limerick 25 January, Kilkenny 5 March, Tullamore, King's County, 19 April, Galway in April, Cushendall, Omagh, Londonderry, and Dundalk in May, Belfast and Dungannon in June. C.O. 904/195, pp 326, 331, 334–7, 339–44, 347, 347–53, 358–9, 361–5, 366, 389–71, 374–7, 380–95.

[199] C.O. 904/92, Feb. 1914, pp 216, 219, 222–3, 228.

[200] C.O. 904/93, May 1914, pp 222–34.

[201] Ibid., pp 222–30.

clearheaded Irishman who cared for Ireland, as an Irish gentleman should, lived here and took the boys up he could have a splendid national corps in six months. So far I can see no man.'[202]

Moore was receptive to this patrician attitude. Colonel and veteran of the Connaught Rangers, he had been drawn into Irish nationalist activism through extensive work for the Gaelic League and was a friend of MacNeill and Hyde.[203] His class status strongly conditioned his nationalism as was shown when he was approached by a group of protestant landlords in September 1912 who had been persuaded of the necessity of home rule. Their draft resolution required certain conditions be attached to home rule, including the address of the problems with the financial clauses and a guarantee that the scheme of land purchase be completed (to remove the danger of expropriation). They strongly repudiated any notion that home rule would bring 'religious persecution or intolerance' and hoped the sectarian divide could be overcome by a conference of 'moderate men'.[204] Moore replied sympathetically, suggesting that Irish landlord opposition to home rule had been consolidated by government acquiescence in their 'plunder'. Home rule, they feared, would bring a more threatening agitation and moderate men must persuade the government to offer the landlords fairer terms. Moore made it clear that he did not regard his patrician moderation on these issues as incompatible with his wider nationalist convictions: 'I have been a nationalist (even an extreme one) all my life.'[205] Later a Redmondite Volunteer, Moore provides an example of another combination of interests that amounted to 'extreme' nationalism.

In Galway the police identified an important social phenomenon. 'There is a tendency recently of persons who were heretofore regarded as strong catholic unionists to support the movement. They have not come forward in public, but doing so is only a matter of time.'[206] Although speculative, the apparently apolitical stance of the Volunteers when combined with an emphasis on discipline might have appealed to those who identified with the landowning class and had unionist leanings. Volunteering invited retired soldiers to take a leadership role, appealing to a patrician instinct otherwise denied expression.[207] In Galway Volunteers were drilled by pensioner Stephen

---

[202] Casement to Moore, 11 Dec. 1913, Moore Papers (N.L.I., MS 10561/3).

[203] For Hyde's letters to Moore, 1899–1910, see Moore Papers (N.L.I., MS 10561/21).

[204] Dunraven, MacDonnell, and Hutcheson Poe to Moore, 19 Sept. 1912, including draft declaration, Moore Papers (N.L.I., MS 10561/10).

[205] Moore to Dunraven, MacDonnell, and Hutcheson Poe, 27 Sept. 1912 (N.L.I., MS 10561/10).

[206] C.O. 904/93, June 1914, p. 496.

[207] This was much more common after the Redmondite takeover. Cf. Bryan Ricco Cooper, protestant landowner from Sligo, who was frustrated that he could not take the leadership role in the community traditionally assumed by his class. In the communal forge of the Gallipoli campaign he made his migration from the Irish Unionist Alliance to Irish nationalism. See Lennox Robinson, *Bryan Ricco Cooper* (Dublin, 1931) and my *New D.N.B.* entry.

Shaughnessy, formerly of the Irish Guards; others of his ilk included two ex-sergeants of the Connaught Rangers, Charles Phillips and C. Flynn. William Devine, ex-corporal of the Connaught Rangers, drilled Tralee Volunteers. Similar roles were taken by Edward Leen, ex-sergeant of the Royal Munster Fusiliers; John Holland of Limerick, ex-lieutenant A.S.C. and H.M.V.; O'Brien of the Imperial Yeomanry; and James McGlinchery, ex-corporal of Royal Inniskilling Fusiliers.[208] Hobson later joked of his embarrassment at having attracted 'as many members of the House of Lords as the Ulster Volunteers'.[209] Particularly in Galway, where the campaign against the graziers had been especially 'advanced', the advent of the Volunteers fulfilled these patrician needs. That said, this tendency had limited effect: 'the Riding cannot be described as peaceable as it is in the grip of the Volunteers who are recruited in nearly every branch by moonlighters and other seditious and undesirable characters.'[210]

The numerical strength of Volunteers in Ulster owed much to the involvement of the Ancient Order of Hibernians. They dominated the five branches in County Tyrone, the largest of which comprised the 750 members in Strabane; they were similarly prominent in Fintown, Donegal. It is probable that the A.O.H. presence was as marked where branches were identified as run by 'local' and 'prominent' nationalists, notably the 960 Volunteers of Ballyshannon, County Donegal and the 935 of Derry, County Londonderry. Strikingly, the 100 members of the Falls Road, Belfast, practising 'simple drill indoors' were identified with the I.R.B., evoking Hobson's memory of nervously promoting the Dungannon Clubs on Falls street corners with MacDermott.[211]

Pearse may have hoped that he might one day see arms in the hands of the A.O.H.,[212] but many separatists bitterly resented their presence in the Volunteers. Thomas Ashe was enraged that the organisation was 'practically ruled today by the A.O.H. Board of Erin', believing the high profile of the A.O.H. threw the whole Volunteer project into doubt.[213] His anger slightly predated the instruction of 9 May issued by the national secretary of the A.O.H. that local organisers draft their members into the Volunteers.[214] MacDermott, Ceannt, and the 'Dublin boys' were attempting to keep them 'straight', Ashe told Devoy, 'but their efforts will be to no avail as the preponderating majority are U.I. League and Hibs.' Devoy was equally concerned and O'Rahilly, hoping the Clan would help with the provision of rifles, addressed

[208] C.O. 904/120, Apr. 1914, pp 71–2.
[209] Hobson, History Irish Volunteers, p. 183.
[210] C.O. 904/94, July 1914, p. 6.
[211] Hobson, Ireland Yesterday and Tomorrow, p. 9.
[212] Dudley Edwards, Patrick Pearse, p. 179.
[213] Ashe to Devoy, 27 Apr. 1914, D.P.B. II, pp 427–9.
[214] Fitzpatrick, Politics and Irish Life, p. 88. 'If the Volunteers have already been organised in your parish or district you should co-operate in the movement. If on the other hand no company exists you should at once establish a company.'

his gravest concerns in April: 'The men at the wheel are straight thinkers and include all the advanced and sincere who are interested in real nationality.'[215] The separatists clearly needed Devoy's full support and patronage if they were to exploit the revolutionary potential of the new force. 'In order to be representative', he explained to Devoy, 'we include the inevitable proportion of jelly fish and of compromisers besides a crank or two, but they are keeping fairly well in line.' Ultimately, the 'objects of the men *who are running this movement* are exactly the same as yours.'

Relations between the I.R.B. and the Ancient Order of Hibernians had been transformed since the factional fights of the 1890s. Of obscure origins, caught somewhere between a communal catholic response to the Orange Order, a development from Ribbonism, and a friendly society, the A.O.H. had developed into the principal nationalist organisation in the north of Ireland. Under the provisions of 'new' Liberal social legislation, it was recognised as an 'approved society' and grew rapidly after 1909.[216] Though hardly the jack-booted *squadristi* of O'Brienite lore, the 'Mollies'' reputation for political rowdiness was confirmed by the notorious 'baton' convention of 1909: William O'Brien's supporters were driven from a party convention by Joe Devlin's boys, earning O'Brien's unstinting opprobrium.[217] O'Brien later condemned the 'narrow sectarian intolerance' of the A.O.H., claiming the Volunteers reflected the 'longing of the youth of Ireland for some escape from the corrupt atmosphere of the Hibernian tyranny to a higher and more generous plane'.[218] Separatists viewed the A.O.H. as representative of all that was most retrograde about nationalist politics in the north, regarding it as particularly threatening to the links they hoped to build with sympathetic protestants. In 1909 McCartan had written: 'The A.O.H. in any shape or form is a barrier to the progress of real nationalism as it fosters distrust and bigotry.'[219] The civic republicanism of Volunteer discourse was a response to the rancid sectarianism of the Ulster Crisis by activists determined to resist the northern-isation of Irish nationalism.

---

[215] O'Rahilly to Devoy, 6 Apr. 1914, *D.P.B. II*, pp 425–7.

[216] Maume, *Long Gestation*, pp 94–5, 125. Fifteen new branches of the Board of Erin A.O.H. were identified in February 1912 alone, C.O. 904/86, Feb. 1912, p. 293. For a lurid account of the origins of the A.O.H. see H. B. C. Pollard, *The Secret Societies of Ireland: Their Rise and Progress* (London, 1922, Kilkenny, 1998).

[217] Joseph V. O'Brien, *William O'Brien and the Course of Irish Politics 1881–1918* (Los Angeles, 1976), pp 187–8.

[218] O'Brien, *Irish Revolution*, p. 223. This is an essential text of the revolution, an attempt to demonstrate the possibility of a non-violent and non-sectarian route to Irish independence. With its Cork orientation it provides a genuinely alternative polemic to the Dublin-orientated separatist and parliamentarian dichotomies. In print O'Brien was highly intelligent, deeply one-sided, always provocative, and never boring.

[219] McCartan to Devoy, 20 Feb. 1909, *D.P.B. II*, pp 376–7.

Separatist hostility against the A.O.H. also stemmed from the politics of its sibling organisation in the U.S.A. In this case, Ireland followed where Irish-America led. The bulk of the American organisation had broken with Clan na Gael, provoking a split between the Clan and the organisation in Ireland. The 1902 Dublin conference, intended to heal this break, triggered a split within the organisation in Ireland. The new minority faction, known variously as the Irish-American Alliance or the Scottish Section, aligned with the I.R.B. and the Clan na Gael. In the meantime, Devlin had identified the A.O.H. as the more effective vehicle for political mobilisation in the north than the U.I.L. In close cahoots with Bishop Patrick O'Donnell of Raphoe, Devlin succeeded in having the clerical ban on the organisation lifted. Although this move did not entirely end clerical hostility, it did end any pretensions the organisation had to being a secret society and was the necessary precursor to its successful integration into the party machine at the Dublin convention of July 1905.[220] This process rendered explicit what had always been implicit: the support of the majority of its members for the home rule party. Catholic benefit societies such as the Irish National Forresters and the Catholic Young Men's Societies had always dabbled at the fringes of separatism, being a presence at commemorative marches and contributing to the various monument funds.[221] In important work, Joost Augusteijn has argued that I.R.B. factions within the A.O.H. helped radicalise its nationalism, which was an important precondition of the expansion of the Volunteers.[222]

Devlin's opposite number in the Scottish Section was Seumas MacManus. A Donegal littérateur and separatist, he was backed by Henry Dobbyn, Robert Johnston, M. J. O'Farrell, and M. J. Pender. Leaders of Belfast Fenianism in the 1890s, but marginalised by the separatist developments of the 1900s, they retained some influence through the communal catholic politics of Belfast and the north. The attempt to unify the two sections intensified the Irish-American dimension of the problem.[223] The strength of the U.I.L. in the U.S.A. had significantly weakened the Clan na Gael and although Devoy continued to churn out the *Gaelic American* the Clan had ceased to be the dominant Irish political force in America. Following Johnston's appeal for Clan recognition,[224] the Irish-American organisation hoped this would be an opportunity to strengthen its position in Ireland and the U.S.A. by engineering the reunion

---

[220] Eamon Phoenix, *Northern Nationalism: Nationalist Politics, Partition and the Catholic Minority in Northern Ireland 1890–1940* (Belfast, 1994), pp 4–5.

[221] Irish National Forresters, established Dublin 1877, was a friendly society providing food and board for members travelling in search of employment. Membership was open to people who were Irish by birth or descent and although 'moderately non-political and respectable . . . some members who hold office in the society use the society as a cover for criminal societies', in particular the I.R.B. Pollard, *Secret Societies of Ireland*, pp 215–16.

[222] Augusteijn, *From Public Defiance to Guerrilla Warfare*, pp 32–6, 40–2.

[223] C.O. 904/78, May 1909, pp 19–20. Cf. Pollard, *Secret Societies of Ireland*, pp 86–90.

[224] Robert Johnston to Devoy, 5 Feb. 1907, *D.P.B. II*, pp 357–8.

of the two factions on its terms. To this end, in April 1909 Matthew Cummings, A.O.H. president in the U.S.A., General John McCarthy of the Hibernian Rifles, and Rev. P. O'Connell, a chaplain to the A.O.H. in the U.S.A., were despatched to Ireland. A conference at the Gresham Hotel saw Cummings in confrontational mood: the only people who could style themselves Hibernians, he asserted, were those under the leadership of Dobbyn and Ferguson. Moreover, the A.O.H. should cut adrift from the U.I.L., declare itself separatist, and transform itself into a revolutionary party. Devlin was contemptuous. He demanded to see the books of the Scottish Section, as the Fenian A.O.H. group was known, claimed the Board of Erin had 60,000 members, and argued that access to nationalist Ireland could only be negotiated through the A.O.H. and the U.I.L. He was unimpressed by Cummings's promise of access to the resources of the Clan.[225]

The visit ended with the divisions enhanced and the links between the Scottish Section and the Clan strengthened through federation. This allowed simple transference of membership from the Scottish Section to the American order, while a member of the A.O.H. Board of Erin would have to rejoin that American order. The police believed that this might strengthen the Scottish Section among those considering emigration to the U.S.A.[226] The Scottish Section gathered 200 supporters at the Antient Concert Rooms on 23 May 1909 and escorted their guests to the Kingsbridge terminus en route to Queenstown.[227]

A series of demonstrations and counter-demonstrations followed and it was evident the A.O.H. Board of Erin had little to fear from the separatists. Devlin and Matthew Keating M.P. addressed 5,000 supporters at a 15 August demonstration in MacManus's home town of Mountcharles, Donegal.[228] In the county as a whole in August 1913 the Board of Erin boasted seventy-four divisions and 5,400 members. MacManus's Irish-American Association countered with nine divisions and four hundred members.[229] Devlin ably merged the Sinn Féin agenda with the constitutionalism of the home rule party. He talked advanced nationalism but showed that his disloyalty was conditional:

One of the arguments used against home rule in England was that the Irish were disloyal. For his part he never denied that. On the contrary he gloried in the fact (cheers). If the Irish people were loyal to British rule in Ireland as it exists at present, they would be a nation of soulless slaves unworthy of respect or sympathy (hear hear). And if being disloyal they were afraid to avow it, they would be a nation of

---

[225] C.O. 904/12, Apr. 1909, pp 25, 35–9.
[226] C.O. 904/78, May 1909, pp 19–20.
[227] C.O. 904/12, May 1909, p. 61.
[228] C.O. 904/118, Aug. 1909, p. 392; C.O. 904/78, Aug. 1909, pp 652–3.
[229] C.O. 904/90, Aug. 1913, p. 649.

cowards and hypocrites. Now the Irish were neither cowards, slaves, nor hypocrites. They repudiated the Act of Union as having no moral or binding force whatever upon them (cheers). They claimed the right of self-government and so long as that was withheld from them they were, and would continue to be, disloyal (hear hear).

So, although repelled by the high profile of the A.O.H. in the Volunteers, the I.R.B. had little choice but to tolerate them. To prevent the organisation from becoming merely an adjunct of the parliamentary party the original Volunteer manifesto had prohibited individual branches being based on individual organisations. Volunteer identity was to be regional.[230] In practice, through sheer weight of numbers the A.O.H. undermined the influence of the separatist minority in nominal command. Hobson's acceptance of Redmond's demand that twenty-five of his nominees were invited onto the Volunteer committee acknowledged this reality. O'Hegarty later attributed Hobson's 'surrender' to Casement's influence, saying Casement had threatened to withdraw from activity if there was a split – an irony given Casement's disregard for constitutional nationalist sensitivities.[231]

But to regard this as a betrayal of all Hobson had worked for since the 1900s would be to take a very narrow view of I.R.B. strategy. Certainly Hobson gave in to immediate political pressures, but he also ensured the organisation remained one the I.R.B. could work through rather than against. A bastardised New Departure perhaps, but one approved by a majority of the committee later formed by the break-away separatist faction.

VII

Shortly before the Volunteer split of September, official figures suggested the organisation to be 181,732 strong (one set of published figures suggested a total of 153,000).[232] Enrolment remained highest in Ulster (59,892 members, 442 branches), followed by Leinster (47,103/441), Munster (42,750/412), and finally Connaught (31,987 / 318). The totals for each county are detailed in Table 6.2.[233]

---

[230] MacNeill to Casement, 27 Nov. 1913, Casement Papers (N.L.I., MS 36203/2).

[231] O'Hegarty, 'Recollections', p. 16.

[232] *Round Table*, 16 (Sept. 1914), p. 715.

[233] The data for Table 6.2 were compiled from three Colonial Office reports 'Return setting forth the strength of the Volunteers in September, 1914, before the division of the two bodies subsequently known as the National Volunteers and the Irish Volunteers', 'Return setting forth the strength of the Irish Volunteers and the quantity of arms in their hands in the month of December, 1914', and 'Arms in the possession of the National Volunteers on the 10th December, 1914'. C.O. 903/18, pp 51, 54. Regarding arms the police identify rifles of various kinds (Italian, Mauser, Martini, Lee-Metford, and Lee-Enfield) and consider levels of ammunition available as between 'None', 'Not much', 'A little', or 'Some'. Belfast City, Tyrone and Kilkenny were considered to have 'Some'.

Table 6.2 Number of Volunteers in late 1914

County	Number of branches before split	Number of members before split	Number of Irish Volunteers, 10 December 1914	Arms in possession Irish Volunteers, 10 December 1914 (National Volunteers)
Ulster				
Antrim	20	3,200	211	5 (435)
Armagh	36	4,872	181	– (275)
Belfast City	1	3,250	200	87 (1,100)
Cavan	52	4,142	295	62 (166)
Donegal	74	10,661	234	5 (444)
Down	50	7,713	90	– (860)
Fermanagh	28	3,933	201	– (146)
Londonderry	46	7,405	305	15 (845)
Monaghan	43	5,764	48	40 (202)
Tyrone	92	8,952	517	116 (667)
Total	442	59,892	2,282	330 (5,140)
Leinster				
Carlow	21	2,586	21	– (13)
Dublin	33	3,949	260	78 (248)
Kildare	32	4,492	344	24 (162)
Kilkenny	53	4,479	187	3 (133)
King's	33	3,017	211	9 (18)
Longford	23	2,504	150	– (6)
Louth	26	4,862	149	– (196)
Meath	62	5,641	220	11 (34)
Queen's	36	3,978	166	– (55)
Westmeath	40	3,993	194	21 (106)
Wexford	54	5,043	438	94 (332)
Wicklow	28	2,559	–	– (427)
Total	441	47,103	2,340	240 (1,730)
Connaught				
Galway, E.R.	56	4,814	279	27 (134)
Galway, W.R.	57	5,117	534	5 (32)
Leitrim	41	4,216	95	– (53)
Mayo	65	7,406	661	– (127)
Roscommon	55	5,483	122	– (7)
Sligo	44	2,559	274	12 (1)
Total	318	29,595	1,965	44 (354)
Munster				
Clare	64	5,156	394	29 (121)
Cork, E.R.	51	7,447	329	161 (218)
Cork, W.R.	33	2,996	493	– (38)
Kerry	48	4,437	1,062	383 (162)
Limerick	80	8,235	437	176 (65)
Tipperary, N.R.	35	3,738	190	– (140)
Tipperary, S.R.	64	6,747	198	48 (364)
Waterford	37	3,994	173	4 (275)
Total	412	42,750	3,276	820 (1,383)
Grand total	1,613	179,340	9,863	1,415 (8,607) (inc. D.M.P. 8,947)

By December 1914 the police estimated Irish Volunteer membership to be at 9,971, a figure calculated from the county inspectors' returns. As with all such statistics these are problematic, but they bring into question the revisionist analysis that follows Hobson's claim that between two and three thousand stayed with the Irish Volunteers as opposed to the traditional figure of 11–12,000.[234] In October/November 1914 the police identified 11,000 as loyal to the provisional committee and Sinn Féin, but added the important caveat that numbers were sufficient to form separate corps only in Cork, Belfast, Limerick, Athenry, and Enniscorthy.[235] This ready association of the Irish Volunteers with Sinn Féin (S.F.) was significant. Further examples from October 1914 included the 120 S.F. Volunteers addressed by McCullough in Belfast,[236] the 160 Dublin S.F. Volunteers who marched to Tallaght, the thirty S.F. and 320 Redmondite Volunteers in Queen's County, the forty S.F. Volunteers out of a total of four hundred in Enniscorthy (the numbers volunteering in late 1914 were fifty and 350 respectively), and the 130 S.F. Volunteers who marched past a Kerry meeting as John O'Donnell M.P. established a Redmondite branch and enrolled 400.[237] These were just some of the innumerable figures bandied about in the reports and they suggest the caution with which any should be taken, including those tabulated in Table 6.2.[238] However, given the later ready association of the Easter Rising with Sinn Féin, it is striking that at this stage opposition to the parliamentary party was consistently labelled as Sinn Féin. This suggests that despite the organisation's decline since 1910 and the reassertion of orthodox Fenianism through *Irish Freedom*, Griffith's journalism retained possession of the official ear, and as a result succeeded in establishing an almost exclusive association between Sinn Féin and advanced nationalism. Despite Griffith's ideological subtleties or O'Hegarty's attempts to disassociate Sinn Féin from *Sinn Féin*, by this stage 'Sinn Féin' had become analogous with advanced nationalism in all its ideological variety. It was not until the Military Council (nominally part of the I.R.B., but effectively the tool of a section within the organisation) had completed its revolutionary preparations that the subtle gradations that existed within the Sinn Féin bloc consolidated into distinct political positions – and then only temporarily. The post-1916 reconstruction of Irish politics saw Sinn

[234] The traditionalists include Lyons, *Ireland since the Famine*, p. 330 and Alvin Jackson, *Ireland 1798–1998* (Oxford, 1999), p. 198 and the revisionists Tierney, *Eoin MacNeill*, p. 154 and Townshend, *Political Violence*, p. 279.

[235] C.O. 904/120, Oct. 1914, p. 114; C.O. 904/95, Nov. 1914, p. 222.

[236] On 4 October Devlin addressed 2,000 Volunteers at St Mary's Hall, Belfast and McCullough was shouted down.

[237] C.O. 904/120, Oct. 1914, pp 114–18.

[238] For example, it seems more likely that the gaps in the column regarding arms in possession of Irish Volunteers were caused by the police not recording their estimates rather than a complete absence.

Féin consolidated as Irish nationalism's strongest brand, to the chagrin of O'Hegarty and others.

In contrast to the National Volunteers, the early months of war saw the 'Sinn Féin Section' importing rifles and showing signs of determined activity. McCullough and A. Heron oversaw the rifle practice of thirty Volunteers in Belfast on 14 November; on 22 November when eighty-five Sinn Féiners marched to a meeting at St Mary's Hall, thirty-five of them carried loaded rifles with fixed bayonets. While fourteen Sinn Féiners had rifle practice on 8 November in Donegal, 850 mostly armed S.F. Volunteers marched from Dublin to Swords, where they met sixty local Volunteers and conducted a mock battle. In Galway, O'Neill and Judge inspected 300 S.F. Volunteers; thirty-six were armed, although only twenty turned out to hear MacBride lecture at Tuam on 22 November. In Tralee a disorderly march ended with two men being charged for firing shots; in Castleisland (County Kerry) twenty-four rifles were delivered from a Dublin dealer. Near Listowel a 'skirmishing drill' was practised on 8 November and 160 Limerick S.F. Volunteers attended rifle practice at Woodcock Hall, County Clare.[239] These were extraordinary scenes. London and Dublin Castle looked on, reluctant to intervene, while an avowedly revolutionary organisation, hostile to the British government and empire, conducted armed drills in preparation of rebellion. Much of the explanation of this must lie in the close study of the British 'Thing', of the tensions between the immediate political dangers, both in Ireland, at home, and on the continent, and its underlying liberal assumptions. Equally important, however, was the nature of the threat. With good reason the military authorities devoted far more energy to tracking the importation of arms by the Ulster Volunteer Force. In November–December 1914 the total number of arms in the possession of Volunteer forces in Ireland was judged to be 66,386. The U.V.F. held 55,166, the National Volunteers 8,947, and the Irish Volunteers 2,275.[240] That same month, the R.I.C. county inspector for Tyrone reported: 'Information has been received that a meeting of sixteen local I.R.B. members was held in a field at Mullaghmore near Dungannon on 9 December, with the object of encouraging the growth of the association.'[241] Marginal concern at the rate of catholic enlistment can have been little enhanced by sixteen men in a field, stamping their feet, rubbing their hands and, amid frosty breath, plotting revolution.

As the Redmondite project began to unravel, the principal dynamic at work was the increasingly shrill cold war between unionism and nationalism. On the nationalist side this process began in the medium term with the ideological retrenchment resulting from the death of Parnellism. Redmond's ultimate

---

[239] C.O. 904/95, Nov. 1914, pp 231–3.
[240] For U.V.F. arms importing see C.O. 904/28/1–2; overall figures in C.O. 904/29.
[241] C.O. 904/95, Dec. 1914, p. 431.

failure was rooted in this process. When his parliamentary strategy began to fail, when it became clear that some form of separate treatment for Ulster was inevitable, when, essentially, it became obvious Westminster would not deliver its side of the bargain and Ulster unionism was not open to conversion, Redmond proved unable to hold together a strong nationalist coalition. His political discourse – his advocacy of imperial home rule – was too fixed and too limited to permit the defiance necessary to rally Irish nationalism. The events of 1912–14 were a partial vindication of the separatist critique of the parliamentary strategy: the passage of the parliament bill disrupted the equilibrium that had sustained moderate unionism and nationalism. The comfortable collusiveness of Irish politics was disturbed in a manner favourable to the logics of irreconcilable Orangeism and radical separatism.

Epilogue

Fenian song and economic history

I

This Volunteer movement is the greatest shakeup [*sic*] we have had for a century: language, and all you can say for it does not appeal to all the sleeping instincts of our race with anything like the power of the tramp of marching men – our very own, not our own in the hire of the stranger.[1]

So wrote John O'Leary to F. J. Bigger in May 1915. Not a voice from the grave but, according to his headed notepaper, the 'Baker, Confectioner and Grocer, Stationer and Newsagent' of Graignamanagh, Co. Kilkenny. He supplied, from his 'General Fancy Warehouse', earthenware, wickerware, china, and glass. He was also an artist, was active in the Catholic Truth Society, and his letters touched on the ecclesiastical antiquities of Counties Carlow and Kilkenny. Bigger had commissioned a painting of mass being held at St Mullins in the penal times. Conscious of the ironies of his own days, O'Leary observed that near the mass rock Henry Hammond was buried, a local blacksmith hung for making pikes in '98 and 'seducing the king's soldiers from their allegiance'. What would Edward Carson's fate have been then?[2]

Volunteering was a cathartic experience. Here was a generation of young men granted a taste of the possibilities of mass mobilisation. Their activity brought Fenianism and the United Irishmen to life, a living embodiment of the spirit of an empowered comradeship evoked in countless addresses and speeches. Volunteering was an act of reappropriation, restoring political agency to the ordinary man and woman, liberating it from the suffocating and narrow strictures of the increasingly distant home rule campaign at Westminster. This was the spirit of Fenianism, a brief moment when full expression was given to an Irish national identity otherwise suppressed by pragmatism and opportunism.

---

[1] John O'Leary to F. J. Bigger, 1 May 1914 (Bigger Collection, OL5, Belfast Central Library).
[2] Ibid., 4 Aug. 1913, 28 & 29 Apr., 5 & 12 May, 10 June 1914.

This, at least, was the experience promoted by the *Irish Volunteer* and *Irish Freedom*. And as the O'Leary letter suggests, this discourse provided the framework within which the emotional experience of volunteering could be understood, granting it great political significance and meaning. But the political implications of this experience remained obscure. Police contempt for the ineffectiveness of the force provided one indicator of the uncertainty at the heart of volunteering, the recourse to secret plotting by the I.R.B. another. In part, volunteering was another example of, in R. V. Comerford's influential formulation, 'patriotism as pastime'.[3] This was expressed well by Colonel J. J. O'Connell in his manuscript history of the Volunteers. He testified to the ideological intensity of the Fianna in contrast to the more comradely atmosphere of the Volunteers:

> the boys selected boys with a touch of iron essential for leadership; whereas the men commonly selected someone because he was popular or distinguished in some sphere or other. The Fianna in short were primarily soldiers: the raw Volunteers were primarily friends and neighbours.[4]

And although the texture of this patriotic conviviality was moulded by a generation of Irish Ireland and cultural separatist polemicists, as the O'Leary commentary suggests, volunteering provided a sense of political immediacy that earnest cultural pursuits could not match.

Britain's declaration of war on Germany influenced Irish politics profoundly. For a short while, volunteering had papered over the ideological cleavages that had opened up in Irish nationalism since 1900, but Redmond's Woodenbridge intervention destroyed the ambiguity that had allowed the Volunteers to enjoy the support of nearly all nationalists. The Volunteer split made the distinction between separatist and constitutionalist fundamental once again. It is indisputable that Redmond's commitment of the Irish Volunteers to the war effort violated the organisation's constitution and, as such, he precipitated the split. Whether Redmond hastened the formation of the I.R.B. Military Council is another matter, but his action undoubtedly focused the activities of the revolutionary elite within the movement. Although all historical periodisation is artificial, and to halt a study of Irish separatism at this decisive moment might seem wilfully perverse, this act of periodisation functions to enforce a pause before the rush of events selects that which posterity will regard as most significant. Easter 1916 was the culmination of a particular strand of Irish separatist commitment and one of the aims of the later chapters in this book has been to delineate the emergence of a core group of activists determined on insurrection in the Fenian tradition.

[3] R. V. Comerford, 'Patriotism as Pastime: The Appeal of Fenianism in the mid-1860s' in *I.H.S.*, xxii (1981), pp 239–50.
[4] J. J. O'Connell, 'History of the Irish Volunteers', unpublished manuscript, p. 3, preserved in Hobson Papers (N.L.I. Ms. 15168).

But the I.R.B. was not all, and to reduce the totality of the separatist activity described here to a sublimated Fenianism would be deceptive. Rather, by tracing the fortunes of an idea – of the separation of Ireland from Britain – it has become clear how misleading simplistic conceptions of constitutionalism and separatism can be. By drawing attention to some of the ambiguities associated with home rule, by examining the temporising discourse of John O'Leary, the cultural separatism of some aspects of the literary revival, and the ideological experiments of Arthur Griffith and the dilemmas provoked by Sinn Féin, and, finally, by looking at the political complexion of the Irish Volunteers, it becomes clear that the history of separatism should not be reduced to the history of the I.R.B.'s dilapidated revolutionary organisation. Instead, Fenianism emerges as the central influence in an Irish nationalist culture that was deeply embedded in the texture of Irish identity. It was a source of emotional energy, a storehouse of memory and example, and, above all, the basis upon which the Irish nationalist passions were comprehended. And although some Irish nationalists dismissed Fenian and separatist ideals as archaic and foolish, home rule did not achieve the same level of emotional resonance with the Irish people. As a political strategy, however, the practical application of separatist ideas was highly limited. The I.R.B. Military Council offered insurrection; the Hobsonites guerrilla warfare; Griffith advocated shopping for Ireland; and MacNeill urged the patriotic defence of the motherland, earnestly believing that this would generate a non-sectarian Irish nationalism rooted in traditional republican principles. Whether promising a republic or a dual monarchy, only insurrectionism had tactical immediacy.

The most sophisticated of these options was Griffith's state building. He queried the lack of forward planning in Fenianism, exposing the weakness of an ideal that left all the hard decisions until after independence was won. Griffithite ideas, however, formed part of a fashionable self-help conversation, with unionist as well as nationalist advocates, that was all too easily appropriated by the home rulers and bowdlerised into a matter-of-fact patriotic rhetoric. And despite Griffith's optimistic advocacy of a consumer-led revolution, it is hard to imagine how Ireland could have fulfilled his vision without access to the levers of state. There is an interesting parallel here in the development of Indian nationalism. Partha Chatterjee has argued that Indian nationalism only 'arrived' with Jawaharlal Nehru's realisation that a worthwhile nationalism was inseparable from the pursuit of social justice, which could only be achieved through state intervention and was not in the interest of the colonial state.[5] The return of home rule to the political centre-stage reduced Griffith to impotence, upsetting the delicate balance he had kept between biting satire and constructive argument.

[5] Partha Chatterjee, *Nationalist Thought and the Colonial World: A Derivative Discourse?* (London, 1986), pp 131–67.

MacNeill's vision was perhaps the least satisfactory of all. The ideal of an Irish nationalism predicated on the inclusivist eighteenth-century republican ideals of an armed citizenry rather than a mass catholic democracy was a noble one, and attractive when compared to the aggressive imperial nationalism of a militarised Europe. But as a solution to the problems raised by Irish politics in 1913–14 it was terribly naïve. By contrast, although the democratic exactitudes of the I.R.B. constitution made their ideals politically feasible, the Irish people's failure to grasp that 'Ireland's opportunity' had arrived saw the new leadership embrace insurrectionism. Redemptive failure was not new to Fenian polemic, but again it is clear that the impassioned cultural politics generated by revivalism enhanced its appeal. That said, it has become more common, contra the established historiography, to assert that the efforts to secure German intervention before 1916 were evidence of the serious military ambition at work.[6] Maybe so, for the meaning of 1916 should not be reduced to the blood sacrifice writings of Patrick Pearse. His sacral nationalism was only one of several perspectives shaping 1916. Faced with 'Ireland's opportunity', another was the I.R.B.'s need to fulfil the promise and sustain the dignity of the Fenian tradition. O'Hegarty remembered Sean MacDermott putting this simply: 'If this thing [the war] passed off without us making a fight I don't want to live. And Tom feels the same.'[7] The marginalisation of more cautious men like Bulmer Hobson is evidence of this determination to rise come what may, a determination that gave the insurrectionists the initiative, allowing them to dominate the separatist agenda. A further variation on the Pearsean ethic was the more mechanistic hope of provoking an epiphanic exposé of the oppression at the heart of British government in Ireland. The executions following the rising and the consequent outpouring of grief and anger fulfilled insurrectionist expectations. Despite the fact that political developments subsequent to 1916 did not conform fully to separatist wishes, the transformation in Irish public opinion broadly did. James Connolly's 'conversion' to insurrectionism has generated the closest scrutiny of all, with much of the focus falling on his apparent privileging of national over class interests. Much of the discussion is driven by contemporary political debate rather than strictly historical analysis.[8] As O'Hegarty recorded, during 1915

[6] For example, Margaret O'Callaghan, '"With the Eyes of Another Race, of a People Once Hunted Themselves": Casement, Colonialism and a Remembered Past' in D. George Boyce and Alan O'Day, *Ireland in Transition, 1867–1921* (London, 2004), p. 174.

[7] P. S. O'Hegarty, 'Recollections of the I.R.B.', manuscript written 7–11 Nov. 1917 preserved in the Casement Papers (N.L.I. MS 36210) p. 20.

[8] The closest reading is W. K. Anderson, *James Connolly and the Irish Left* (Blackrock, 1994), pp 41–75; a good assessment is Owen Dudley Edwards, *The Mind of an Activist: James Connolly* (Dublin, 1971), pp 65–83; C. Desmond Greaves, *The Life and Times of James Connolly* (London, 1972), pp 351–431, esp. pp 425–31 provides the most ideologically committed analysis; Brendan Clifford, *James Connolly: An Adventurous Socialist* (Cork, 1984), pp 7–12 contains some very suggestive but undeveloped ideas, particularly the

he was impatient for action and the I.R.B. took him on board in order to bring his Irish Citizen Army under control thereby avoiding any premature outbreaks;[9] this was perhaps also an attempt to prevent him from seizing the ideological initiative. Connolly himself, like his co-conspirators, seems to have embraced Leninist revolution, arguing 'It is not the will of the majority which ultimately prevails; that which ultimately prevails is the ideal of the noblest of each generation.'[10] Such words echoed the more messianic appraisals of Parnell's significance as well as the Toneology of 1898, providing further evidence of the emulative individualism of the Irish separatist imagination.

Despite the foregoing, historical analysis of the 1914–16 period should not be reduced to the intricacies of I.R.B. and Connollyite plotting. Broader shifts in attitude shaped the confused reception of the rebellion and its aftermath. In 1914 Irish political commitment was dramatically changed as the war became the decisive political question, pushing the problem of the North down the scale. This was not an atomised society. Collective experiences reinforced self-interested calculations and the communal experience of war was textured by specifically Irish perspectives which invested it with tremendous political significance. Most importantly, the war made real to men and women not driven by abstract political ideas the implications of Redmondism. One Redmondite strain of thought judged the magnitude of the European struggle to render Irish anti-Englishness the luxury of a more innocent age. Linked to this was popular anger at Irish pro-Germanism, which was informed by sentiments similar to those shaping Tom Kettle's internationalism. That this feeling can be attributed to British and Redmondite propaganda, that it might, as the separatists argued, be considered a form of false consciousness, does not alter its significance. The separatist conviction that Irish interests were necessarily at variance with English interests was not immediately obvious to many Irish nationalists. For if one believed, as many home rulers did, that Britain and its liberal empire was standing up to continental abuses, then the war reinforced the argument for sustaining Ireland's British link. Indeed, since Isaac Butt's pioneering advocacy of home rule, imperialism had been central to its conception and pre-war debates throughout the Empire concerning the Empire's evolution idealised its future as a family of nations, bound by shared values reconcilable to national ideals. In the late 1880s the Buttite lawyer W. D. Seymour – son of a Roscommon vicar – captured this Redmondite idealism in his half-jesting anticipation of the time of Victoria, 'Empress-Queen

---

comparison between Connolly and the Polish 'social patriot' Pilsudski; Austen Morgan, *James Connolly: A Political Biography* (Manchester, 1988) is useful, especially on labour activism in 1914–16; Desmond Ryan, *James Connolly: His Life Work and Writings* (Dublin, 1924) is much the most engaging account and, given copious quotation from Connolly's writings, in some ways the most useful.

[9] O'Hegarty, *Recollections*, p. 26.
[10] Quoted in Pádraig Yeates, *Lockout Dublin 1913* (Dublin, 2000), p. 581.

of the British Dominions'.[11] The problem Ireland faced, Seymour believed, was the unionist failure to distinguish between, in Dicey's phrase, 'colonial independence' and the reality of the home rule aspiration, namely 'federal union between Great Britain and Ireland'.[12]

The 'Sinn Féiners', of course, rejected this analysis as so much self-interested delusion and although commanding only a small force in 1914–16, determined activity ensured their influence far exceeded their numbers. Redmondite encouragement of enlistment prompted a 'Sinn Féin' anti-enlistment campaign. Apparently effective, the police noted 'Sinn Féin' possessed 'greater influence than is warranted by their numbers and position', but the positive reaction to their arguments was regarded less as ideological conviction than an opportunistic alignment by those 'naturally disinclined to enlist'.[13] Indeed, the authorities quickly noted that the wartime agricultural boom undermined the readiness of the young men of rural Ireland to enlist, particularly in the west. Undoubtedly fearful for their sons' prospects in the trenches, parents were also reluctant to lose such a valuable part of their workforce. Paradoxically then, the economic boon of war generated behaviour that was construed as disloyal. A more sensitive analysis would have recognised that it is just such inclinations that generate political allegiance: opportunistic Sinn Féinism in response to the war hardened over time into convinced disloyalty.

Nonetheless, this assessment suggests different implications from those put forward in recent historical research which demonstrates that Irish enlistment, protestant and catholic, was broadly in line with wider British patterns, and that the rate of Irish catholic enlistment was not proportionately low.[14] It is revealing that the police got the impression that rates were low, suggesting an assessment shaped by the atmosphere of disloyalty that increasingly suffused Irish society. With or without the Ulster Crisis, a significant proportion of the Irish population was immune to the cultures of deference, patriotism, and obligation that were believed to characterise the British working class. Moreover, few Irish M.P.s were willing to promote recruitment (those that did were most closely associated with John Redmond) and where they did there is little evidence of a local recruiting surge.[15] As David Fitzpatrick has argued, individuals enlisted for social (unemployment, camaraderie, adventure) rather than ideological reasons.[16] Few went to the front to speed the enactment of home rule. In effect, taxation was considered a necessary evil; the demands

---

[11] William Digby Seymour, *Home Rule and State Supremacy; or Nationalism Reconciled with Empire* (London, 1888), p. 49.

[12] Ibid., p. 35.

[13] C.O. 904/95, Oct. 1914, p. 10.

[14] David Fitzpatrick, 'Militarism in Ireland, 1900–1922' in Thomas Bartlett and Keith Jeffery (ed.), *A Military History of Ireland* (Cambridge, 1996), pp 386–90.

[15] See forthcoming work by James McConnel.

[16] Fitzpatrick, 'Militarism in Ireland'.

of the recruiting officer were of an altogether different order – the police observed in October 1914 that the chance the government would enforce the Militia Ballot Act 'caused hundreds to rush off to America'.[17] As O'Hegarty later argued, it was 'the spirit, the viewpoint, which made the difference, and not the respective contributions of man-power'.[18]

In the same October 1914 report some observers regarded the exodus as reflecting a more general shift in attitude: 'while the number of persons who are pro-German remains small, there is now a much greater anti-English feeling abroad than was the case at the beginning of August [1914] . . . and [it] is no doubt largely due to the Sinn Féin propaganda.'[19] Although the police inspector-general argued in November that Sinn Féin's pro-Germanism was no more than a means to embarrass Redmond, Casement's mission to Germany and Clan na Gael's German contacts bespoke the possibility of a high profile German intervention in Ireland. This, he felt, would attract little support;[20] 'bitterly disloyal' extremists might 'rejoice to see England beaten and humiliated' but few would welcome German troops onto Irish soil.[21] As Casement put it, 'I didn't choose the Germans – it was England. If she had attacked France – I'd have gone to France.'[22] This chimes with Ben Novick's analysis of advanced nationalist propaganda. Early in the war there was little overt pro-Germanism and MacNeill and others were angered when so accused. Nonetheless, in the years before the rising fantasies that Germany, apparently a higher Christian civilisation than England, would defeat Britain and liberate Ireland were common. After the rising such dreams had less purchase.[23]

On balance then, police evidence confirms that the climate of opinion was not favourable to the separatists.[24] Anti-recruiting activity and opposition to conscription clearly paid some dividends – between 1914 and 1916 separatist organisations grew steadily but slowly – but among the factors limiting their advance was the hostility 'disloyalty' provoked among those whose sons, brothers, husbands, and fathers had enlisted. Just as the deaths of Irish soldiers led some to question whether the war was in Irish interests, solidarity with the soldiery could equally strengthen home rule and imperial sentiment. The

---

[17] C.O. 904/95, Oct. 1914, p. 11.

[18] P. S. O'Hegarty, *The Victory of Sinn Féin* (Dublin, 1924), p. 35.

[19] C.O. 904/95, Oct. 1914, p. 11.

[20] C.O. 904/95, Nov. 1914.

[21] C.O. 904/97, June 1915.

[22] From an undated manuscript 'Professor MacNeill's Connection With Me' by Roger Casement, the main aim of which is to demonstrate that MacNeill was not privy to the German plans. Copy in the Casement Papers (N.L.I. MS 35,203/1).

[23] Ben Novick, *Conceiving Revolution: Irish Nationalist Propaganda during the First World War* (Dublin, 2001), pp 120–31.

[24] The following discussion might be read in conjunction with D. George Boyce, 'A First World War Transition: State and Citizen in Ireland, 1914–19', in D. George Boyce and Alan O'Day (ed.), *Ireland in Transition, 1867–1921* (London, 2004), p. 104.

commitment of Irish troops to the British cause made that cause an Irish one: war repoliticised and reanimated home rule, imbuing a tired cry with new vitality. Just as unionists believed the Somme coagulated the union into permanence, for the first time home rule could be died for. Yet if fighting the war partially rejuvenated Redmondism's moral authority, its new rhetoric of blood sacrifice carried its own risks. Such exalted notions seemed at odds with political realities. For, given that Redmondite support for the war was not a temporary expediency driven by the need to conciliate British opinion, but reflected fundamental imperial loyalties, Redmondism faced a two-fold political problem. First, the British government's failure to achieve a home rule settlement inevitably created the sense that dying on the western front was the price that had to be paid for home rule: an absurd mark-up. The self-sacrifice of 1916 for a more exalted national ideal seems less extreme in this context. Second, the war exposed – like no other crisis could – the limitations of home rule. Indeed, so scant a trace of Parnellite defiance remained in Redmondism that Pearse could marshal the uncrowned king in 'The Separatist Idea', his powerful evocation of the apostolic succession of Irish separatist martyrs.[25] Home rule would achieve limited self-government not independence, nor, in the increasingly fashionable phrase, self-determination. With or without home rule, the war demonstrated that the young catholic men of Ireland were not reliably British; ultimately, home rule could not be reconciled to the realities of Irish (dis)loyalty.

All of this created a terrible dilemma for the home rule party. Persuading men to voluntarily enlist was essential to staving off the political disaster conscription threatened, yet home rule M.P.s were reluctant to identify with the recruiting sergeant, well aware of the destabilising threat the issue posed. Adding martial ardour to Redmond's political armour carried grave political dangers.

The Redmondites' support for the war did not protect them from ignominious treatment by the authorities. Redmond's diminished influence and humiliations at Westminster after September 1914 have been well documented; similar treatment at the hands of the Irish authorities testified to their suspicion. A good example of this was the galling pettiness with which high officialdom treated Redmondite attempts to arm the National Volunteers.[26] While the Irish Volunteers imported arms through various illegal channels (a raid on the Dublin arms dealer J. Lawler & Son on 2 December 1915 yielded the largest single cache before the rising),[27] Laurence Kettle, working for the

---

[25] Patrick Pearse, 'The Separatist Idea' in *Tracts for the Times*, no. 11 (Dublin, 1916), pp 1–20.

[26] In general, see Ben Novick, 'The Arming of Ireland: Gun-running and the Great War, 1914–16' in Adrian Gregory and Senia Pašeta, *Ireland and the Great War: 'A War to Unite Us All'?* (Manchester, 2002), pp 73–93.

[27] C.O. 904/28/4.

National Volunteers, sought from the military authorities the necessary permits. As an increasingly comic correspondence demonstrated, Kettle's claim that the National Volunteers were taking up guard duties to relieve the military was not treated seriously.[28] Meanwhile, Redmond's personal attempt to import a hundred rifles he had bought in London came up against military obstruction. A letter he addressed to Asquith seeking the prime minister's intervention was soon circulating in Dublin Castle. Exasperated, Matthew Nathan, the under-secretary, wrote to Major-General Friend on 12 May 1915, revealing not merely the administrative mess but the many attempts Redmond had made to get satisfaction:

> The machinery for letting Mr Redmond purchase a small consignment of arms seems somewhat imperfect if it requires as intermediaries –
> (1) the Prime Minister,
> (2) the Under-Secretary of State for War,
> (3) the Master-General of the Ordnance,
> (4) the General Officer Commissioning London District,
> (5) the Chief Secretary for Ireland,
> (6) the Under-Secretary for Ireland, and
> (7) the General Officer Commanding-in-Chief the Forces in Ireland.
> Will you kindly do what you can to hasten the fulfilment of Mr Redmond's desire in this particular case, and we must concert some method for simplifying the procedure in the future.[29]

Friend replied that all Redmond had to do was follow procedure and, anyway, Laurence Kettle had an unused permit for the import of 350 rifles. Nathan put all of this to Redmond, repeating the list of intermediaries, and Redmond apologised for the confusion. Five months later the problem still festered because the North Western Railway Company refused to carry the goods to port despite having done the same for other U.K. volunteer corps.

Redmond's humiliation, Nathan's condescending exasperation, and Friend's suspicious obstruction were the grim background to the proud display by the home rule press of constitutional nationalism's military credentials. For example, coverage of a recruiting meeting in Killarney in June 1915 addressed by Lieutenant Stephen Gwynn M.P. included photographs showing a moder-ately sized crowd and a banner reading 'Boys come and join to fight for Ireland. God save Ireland and the King.'[30] Improvements in technology and lower costs had seen photography become the dominant form of newspaper illustration. Gone were the Victorian line drawings of nationalist politicians and dramatic incidents, such as those that so vividly fashioned perceptions of the Parnell

---

[28] This correspondence can be found in C.O. 904/29.
[29] Ibid.
[30] *D.I.*, 15 June 1915.

split. Photography brought images of the war from distant locations and kept pictures of Irish men in uniform continually before the Irish people. Advanced nationalist propaganda responded to this as delicately as possible. Initially scornful of men who signed up, faced with chilling casualty figures, their scorn soon developed into pity, with the accusative spotlight shining on the murderous recruiting officer and the stooge-like home rule leadership.[31]

Nonetheless, anti-recruiting activity, especially when tinged with pro-Germanism, could seem grotesquely insensitive. In small town Ireland it provoked the kind of street violence reminiscent of earlier lower class reaction to protestant street preaching.[32] In May 1915 Pearse led 900 Volunteers through Limerick. According to press reports they were booed and stoned. Pearse's men fired blank shots in warning – extraordinary in itself – but in the end they were protected by the police and the Royal Munster Fusiliers.[33] To note that such antagonism between separatists and home rulers was unprecedented hardly registers the emotional intensity of this conflict. From the beginning of the war, division in Irish politics rendered the traditional political labels used throughout this book inadequate. Political affiliation had, of course, always stemmed from a concatenation of emotion and self-interest that was only loosely embodied in party political agendas. The emotional demands of war enhanced these loyalties, rendering allegiances more sentimental and further divorced from policy platforms.[34] Initially then, the backlash provoked by anti-war activity enhanced the conflict between separatists and home rulers with a novel physicality. Over the longer term, however, this new emotionalism worked to Sinn Féin's advantage by simultaneously intensifying and destabilising popular political loyalties. With talk of the war being over by Christmas, the Woodenbridge speech must have seemed a bold but sensible political gesture, explosive only in the short term. Instead, as Christmas came and went, it was clear that Woodenbridge had immeasurably raised the stakes, creating expectations that the home rule leadership could not meet.

II

The realities exposed by war generated shifts in Irish nationalist politics that preceded the shock and aftermath of the 1916 rising. The two by-elections of June 1915 provide an effective illustration of how the popular foundations of Redmondism were in jeopardy. Vacancies occurred in North Tipperary and

---

[31] Novick, *Conceiving Revolution*, pp 51–64.
[32] See Matthew Kelly, 'The Politics of Protestant Street Preaching in Ireland in the 1890s' in *Historical Journal*, 48, no. 1 (2005), pp 101–25.
[33] *Clonmel Chronicle*, 26 May 1915.
[34] Cf. Ernie O'Malley, *On Another Man's Wound* (Dublin, 1936, 2002), p. 31.

College Green following the deaths of Esmonde and Nannetti. Esmonde's son, hitherto of no political significance, won in Tipperary. This was a remarkable contest because the U.I.L. in the county was so weak that the normal convention system used to select candidates was abandoned, allowing three candidates professing their loyalty to Redmond to stand. Opposing Esmonde was R. P. Gill, a Tipperary agrarian, and P. J. Hoctor, the Irish parliamentary party-baiting Fenian of earlier times. Having long ago abandoned purist Fenianism, 1915 was the third time Hoctor had sought the seat – he lost the nomination twice in 1910. Other old Fenian hands, like Anthony Mackey the Castleconnell fish merchant, favoured his candidature. An amicable campaign ensued producing a remarkably close result (Esmonde 1,693, Hoctor 1,293, Gill 1,193). Hoctor, clearly a popular figure, defended himself against taunts that he was a socialist and a 'Russian anarchist', an accusation again highlighting the association of Fenianism with labour politics. Promoting himself as the champion of business interests *and* the rights of the working man, Hoctor was keen to demonstrate that his political convictions were Redmondite. In reality, he demonstrated the anachronism of his candidacy. After quoting John Dillon's famous observation that the Land League had been animated by the 'Fenian spirit', he continued:

> I have never been recreant to my obligations to Ireland, and I am prepared to follow the methods that have found recognition with the Irish people in the conduct of their political affairs, and to adopt the measures that are considered by them best calculated to serve their interests in all emergencies.

By reprising the home rule as Fenianism by other means case, now discredited by a generation of separatist polemicists and incompatible with a Redmondism purified by war, Hoctor resuscitated the politics of the 1880s and 1890s, an intimation of the generational and attitudinal divide that would devastate the I.P.P. in 1918.[35]

College Green yielded different threats. In Dublin the U.I.L. was in better shape and in convention nominated J. D. Nugent, one-time general secretary of the A.O.H. and, during the 1913 lock-out, an active opponent of the trade unions.[36] Loathed by the Irish labour movement, Nugent was opposed by Thomas Farren, the Trades Council candidate. Treasurer of the short-lived Irish Neutrality League founded in October 1914,[37] he was identified by the

---

[35] *D.I.*, 15, 19 June 1915; *Nationalist and Munster Advertiser*, 29 May, 2 June 1915; *Nenagh Guardian*, 1, 8, 15, 29 May, 5 June 1915; *Clonmel Chronicle*, 26 May 1915.

[36] Yeates, *Lockout Dublin 1913*, pp 90, 129, 278.

[37] James Connolly was president, Sean T. O'Kelly was secretary, committee members included Markiewicz, Griffith, Sean Milroy, Francis Sheehy-Skeffington, William O'Brien (the labour leader), and J. J. Scollan of the A.O.H. (Scottish Section). Arthur Mitchell, *Labour in Irish Politics, 1890–1930: The Irish Labour Movement in the Age of Revolution* (Dublin, 1974), p. 63; Greaves, *James Connolly*, p. 361.

Redmondite *Freeman's Journal* as a Larkinite and stood on an anti-recruiting platform, all of which left him vulnerable to pro-German smears. He polled very strongly, collecting 1,816 votes against Nugent's 2,445. Clearly the party could not herald the election a wild success. The optimistic home ruler might regard the vote as presaging the politics of the future home rule state, when the party would inevitably fracture along the socio-economic divides necessity had minimised. But a more realistic prognosis would admit that class tensions among Irish nationalists tended to generate divergent political aspirations. Social histories of the revolutionary period emphasise the generational shift taking place in Irish politics during the revolutionary period, with Sinn Féin benefiting from a youthful reaction against the geriatric profile of the home rule party. Recent work suggests that class tensions also strengthened Sinn Féin. In particular, some have questioned the general applicability of David Fitzpatrick's social model of the revolution based on his analysis of County Clare, which argues that home rulers reinvented themselves as Sinn Féiners. Fergus Campbell has shown that since the Land War the beneficiaries of land reform in East Galway formed a home rule elite which dominated the U.I.L. Those with little economic stake in the status quo formed alternative, semi-clandestine associations with strong I.R.B., Gaelic League, and Sinn Féin links.[38] A similar, if more tentative case, has been made for grass-roots attitudes in the A.O.H.[39] In the weeks before the polls the party was conscious of its vulnerability. J. J. Clancy M.P. warned of a possibly imminent general election, urging the reorganisation of the U.I.L.[40] It is difficult, however, to imagine the positive basis on which this could be achieved. As the collapse of the Irish National League and Irish National Federation in the 1890s suggested, popular nationalist organisations without clear political purposes soon disintegrated. Faced with surging support for Sinn Féin in 1918 – in some places promoting agrarianism, in some places not – the U.I.L. rallied but on essentially reactionary grounds. In 1915 the *Independent* appeared to embrace the fragmentation of the nationalist party, seeing few dangers where there was no unionist candidate; the *Freeman*, however, urged vigilance, rightly afraid such practices encouraged a factionalism threatening to the system that had maintained Irish nationalist unity since Parnell.[41]

While Hoctor made one last bid for significance, the authorities, empowered by the Defence of the Realm Act, began to move against the more dynamic

---

[38] David Fitzpatrick, *Politics and Irish Life 1913–1921: Provincial Experience of War and Revolution* (Cork, 1977, 1998) and his 'The Geography of Irish Nationalism 1910–1921' in *Past & Present*, no. 78 (Feb. 1978), pp 135–6; Fergus Campbell, 'The Social Dynamics of Nationalist Politics in the West of Ireland 1898–1918', *Past & Present*, no. 182 (Feb. 2004), pp 175–211.

[39] Michael Wheatley, 'Irish Party/Sinn Féin Continuity 1914–1918: The A.O.H. as a Missing Link', Irish History Seminar, Hertford College, Oxford, 9 March 2004.

[40] *F.J.*, 7, 9, 10, 14, & 21 June 1915.

[41] *F.J.*, 21 June 1915; *D.I.*, 15 June 1915.

anti-enlisters. J. L. Fawsitt was ordered to leave Cork in May and went to the U.S.A. on a lecture tour; at the end of June O'Rahilly was ordered out of Kerry and forbidden from entering Cork or Limerick; Liam Mellowes, Ernest Blythe, H. M. Pim, and Denis McCullough were ordered to leave Ireland in July. Each refused and was imprisoned by the civil courts for three to four months.[42] Sean Milroy was similarly arrested in June. T. M. Healy defended him in court – the classic means by which constitutionalist nationalists associated themselves with radicals – arguing that not only had such meetings been a regular occurrence for the previous six months but that Milroy spoke against conscription rather than recruitment in general. Milroy got three months with hard labour and it is easy to see why Healy's distinction was given little credence: 'I ask you, men of Ireland', Milroy had exclaimed, 'is there a man among you who thinks that there is any interest in Ireland to be served by a single Irishman laying down his life in the trenches in Flanders fighting the battles of England [?]'[43]

This open activity, along with Volunteer drilling and the now familiar associational culture of advanced nationalism, contrasted with the secrecy of the I.R.B. Military Council. By I.R.B. standards security was effective, but planning could not proceed in any serious way without preparing the rank-and-file. Consequently, expectations of an insurrection with German assistance were strongly encouraged. MacDermott and Clarke were in Limerick on 26 December, where they showed a cinematograph at John Daly's house to 180 Limerick Sinn Féiners. Their audience were told that Casement, the Clan na Gael, and – less plausibly – Larkin would ensure that plenty of German arms and money were forthcoming. The meeting closed, according to an informer, with the German national anthem.[44] In general, Daly was as active as ever, successfully promoting Sinn Féin and putting his weight behind the corporation's condemnation of the military authority's expulsion of men from the county under the Defence of the Realm Act.[45]

Meetings such as these left the Irish Volunteers increasingly restless and from the summer of 1915 the authorities came to regard the body as intimately associated with Sinn Féin and the I.R.B. Retrospectively, this connection seems obvious, and in some respects it had been long acknowledged, but this change in emphasis marked a greater readiness to see the Volunteers as putative rebels with serious revolutionary intentions. There is no doubt that when contrasted with the National Volunteers the Irish Volunteers were extremely dynamic and ideologically committed. In November 1914 the police had observed that the National Volunteer organisation was not effectively funnelling recruits into the army. They were 'not organised', they were

---

[42] C.O. 904/97, June & July 1915.
[43] D.I., 17 June 1915.
[44] C.O. 904/95, Dec. 1914.
[45] C.O. 904/97, July 1915.

'practically unarmed', and few members had any 'proper military training'; having been formed for a 'political purpose', that is, simply for the purposes of display, they were 'formidable only on paper'.[46] Equally striking was the slow growth of the Irish Volunteers before the surge during the winter of 1915/16, when up to a 1,000 new recruits joined each month.[47] One police estimate of December 1915 suggested a total membership of 11,393.[48] This figure seems reasonable: it was not imposing by I.N.L. or U.I.L. standards. It is hard to judge what significance, ideological or otherwise, should be attached to 5,038 included in this total who were identified as MacNeillite. If nothing else, it demonstrated his continuing influence, despite the machinations of the Military Council, and why his notorious countermanding order of Easter Sunday was effective.

Most activity was noted in County Tyrone, long associated with a lively I.R.B. culture, and the western counties, where there was a flurry of explosives thefts in January 1916 and armed Volunteers marched through recruitment meetings. Informers submitted worrying reports. 'Chalk' relayed on 16 March that medical packages and mess tins had been distributed, and a week later told of the rousing speech Thomas McDonagh gave at Fairview. McDonagh announced the general mobilisation planned for 2 April, when the Volunteers were to muster fully equipped, and warned that 'some of us may never come back.'[49] Neville Chamberlain, the R.I.C. inspector-general, commented in March that the authorities had little to fear of a military nature. But, he added darkly, these 'observations . . . [were] . . . made with reference to the provinces and not to the Dublin Metropolitan Police area, which is the centre of the movement.'[50]

The best indicator of the strength of nationalist militancy on the eve of the rising was the turn-out for St Patrick's Day 1916 (7 March) – although talk of the authorities using this as an opportunity to disarm the force kept the Cork City Volunteers at home.[51] Made about a month before Easter Monday, the police head-counts make fascinating reading, not least because they estimate the numbers of Sinn Féin supporters who were members of the National Volunteers. This time the overall Irish Volunteer total was 10,232, but to this should be added the 4,618 Sinn Féin sympathisers who were enrolled in the National Volunteer corps. A comparison with the figures given for December 1914 (see p. 233) suggests certain general trends. There had been a distinct strengthening of the Irish Volunteers in the Munster and Connaught counties

---

[46] C.O. 904/95, Nov. 1914, p. 216.
[47] Cf. Joost Augusteijn, *From Public Defiance to Guerrilla Warfare: The Experience of Ordinary Volunteers in the Irish War of Independence* (Dublin, 1996), pp 31–54.
[48] C.O. 904/120, Dec. 1915.
[49] C.O. 903/23.
[50] C.O. 904/99, Mar. 1916.
[51] C.O. 903/23.

of Cork East Riding (+367), Cork West Riding (+129), Limerick (+287), Tipperary South Riding (+233), Galway East Riding (+92), and Galway West Riding (+271). A general falling off was seen in Leinster and Ulster – Tyrone was the exception (+63) – with both provinces seeing Sinn Féin sympathisers increasingly settling for National Volunteer membership (1,515): one wonders about the lone Sinn Féin sympathiser enrolled in the National Volunteers in Monaghan. Kerry's Irish Volunteers numbers had held up (1,045: –17) and the county boasted a further 232 Sinn Féiners buried in the National Volunteers. The county's turn-out (743) on St Patrick's Day was impressive, beaten only by Cork East Riding (1,080) and Limerick (748). Kerry activity was livelier in the west of the county; things were muted in the east by concern that agitation would undermine the tourist trade. Kerry aside, the largest Sinn Féin presences in the National Volunteers were to be found in Mayo, Roscommon, and Sligo. The same broad patterns were evident in the distribution of arms. Many of the estimated total of 3,141 individual items were distributed in the most active counties. Only in Belfast and counties Cavan, Tyrone, Dublin, and Kerry was the ratio of arms to Volunteer marginally better than 1:2. Overall, these figures confirmed Chamberlain's observations. Much the greatest concentration of Irish Volunteers was to be found in Dublin (2,225), 800 of whom could be armed, and 1,400 of whom paraded on St Patrick's Day.[52]

Although separatist nationalism was often at its most innovative and advanced in Ulster, the overall weakness of advanced nationalist organisations in the province was a striking feature of this period. The three Sinn Féin by-election victories of 1917 (Roscommon North, Longford South, and East Clare) were answered by three Irish Parliamentary Party victories in 1918 (Armagh South, Waterford City, and Tyrone East). As with the by-elections of 1891, ascribing national meaning to these results invites caution owing to regional specificities. However, the home rule strip of territory in mid-Ulster does seem to reflect established patterns: where sectarian pressures were most intense nationalist solidarities held firm; elsewhere the new uncertainties left constituencies up for grabs.[53] The Waterford result was partly a sympathy vote following Redmond's death. Given the 1918 general election result it is difficult not to see those 1917 results as indicative of the overall direction of Irish nationalist opinion and those of 1918, paradoxically, as peculiar.[54]

Making sense of 'the North' had always been a problem for Irish nationalists, separatist or otherwise. The home rulers have been criticised for paying insufficient attention to the problem, for appealing over the heads of their fellow Irish to wider British public opinion and only very reluctantly talking to unionists. Robert Lynd scathingly saw the problem as equally debilitating for nationalists and unionists: 'Both are intolerant and would just as soon knock

[52] Ibid.
[53] Fitzpatrick, , 'Geography of Irish Nationalism', pp 128–30.
[54] Cf. Alvin Jackson, *Ireland 1798–1998* (Oxford, 1999), pp 200–1.

their opponents down or shout them down as convert them.'[55] Partly the problem arose because southern nationalists simply did not comprehend unionist concerns. Indeed, even southern protestants who alleged that sectarianism was not a problem in Ireland were summarily dismissed by northern unionists. For the conviction that nationalist Ireland was dominated by an expansionist Romish catholic clergy was shaped by the intimacies of northern politics, particularly the perceived influence of the A.O.H. Inspired by the example of Tone, separatists paid a little more attention to the north, but their diagnoses similarly undermined the seriousness of northern divisions, tending to argue that the sectarianism was a patina, a recent historical phenomenon that Irish historical truth would soon undermine. Lynd, as an Ulster Presbyterian separatist who had cut his teeth in the London Dungannon Clubs and whose perspective was broadened by close connections to the British liberal press, had little time for such banalities.[56] Nationalist and unionist shortcomings were well captured in his sardonic observation of 1910:

> If an impartial spectator were to go to an ordinary Green demonstration in Ireland he would come away inclined to be an Orangeman. If he were to attend an ordinary Orange demonstration he would come away feeling strangely sympathetic towards nationalism.[57]

However attractive lofty Lynd's realism was, with its echoes of O'Leary ('*No honest Irishman is the enemy of Ireland*'),[58] Herbert Moore Pim was an exponent of the more typically held view. A northern separatist, poet, and, from January 1916, founding editor of the eccentric *The Irishman: A Unique Monthly Journal*, he came to prominence by writing himself into the inner circles of advanced nationalism under the pseudonym A. Newman. At home in the Fenian mode, he escaped arrest in 1916 and seemed a possible leader of Sinn Féin until more convincing candidates were released from prison. Alongside Hobson, MacNeill, O'Rahilly, and Pearse, he contributed to the *Tracts for Our Times* series produced by the Irish Volunteers. By his reckoning there were no racial differences between Irish protestants and catholics, a significant claim given the currency of political languages of race in this period. Rather, England had nurtured Irish sectarianism to serve its own interests and a particular obstacle to progress was the effect the English public school system and Oxbridge had on the unionist leadership class. Immunised against free thought, they were left utterly deferential to English ideas and authority.[59]

---

[55] Robert Lynd, 'The Ethics of Sinn Féin', pamphlet published by the *Limerick Echo*, 1910.
[56] M. K. Sen, *Robert Lynd: Son of Eire* (New Delhi, 1992).
[57] Lynd, 'Ethics', p. 7.
[58] Ibid.
[59] A. Newman [H. M. Pim], 'What Emmet means in 1915' in *Tracts for the Times* (Dublin, 1915) and 'Ascendancy While You Wait' in *Tracts for the Times* no. 5 (Dublin, 191?).

MacNeill's 1905 *New Ireland Review* article considering the same problem was reprinted in the series. He was responding to Arthur Synon's suggestion that partition was inevitable because the protestant 'aliens' of the north could not be reconciled to Irishness. MacNeill found this absurd. Not only was partition impossible in any representative way given the complexities of population distribution in the north, but he rejected the 'alien' thesis altogether. Racial difference was a nonsense and, moreover, Germany and Hungary showed that protestants and catholics could live together in prosperity. More than this, MacNeill questioned many of the assumptions made about the entrenched nature of unionist political identity. Before 1886, he suggested, Orange sentiment was more or less limited to lower-class episcopalians and until recently Presbyterian unionism was associated with upward class mobility rather than any deep-seated political and cultural identity. Indeed, MacNeill remembered an Ulster where the very idea of a nationalist was unknown: those 'out-and-outers', retrospectively identifiable as nationalists, tended to be protestants of both creeds. Consequently, it was imperative that nationalists ignored Orange provocation.[60]

MacNeill and Hobson's opposition to the Military Council was in part tactical – Hobson believed that guerrilla warfare would prove more effective than a Fenian insurrection[61] – but it was also linked to their consciousness of the north. Like Griffith, they were playing a long game in which an Irish republic was the ultimate aim. Possibly, separatist antipathy towards insurrectionism was predicated on the half-realisation that such an abrupt intervention would intensify the sectarian divide. Home rule and its determined Irish opponents taught some separatists that Ireland's identity conflict invited no quick fixes. This separatism was part of the wider trend that included constructive unionism, revivalism, and intelligent home rule, which, regardless of divergent aspirations, recognised that a satisfactory solution to the Irish question could only be found by building cross-community co-operation and understanding. The groundwork had simply not been laid prior to the round table discussions of 1914–18; earlier initiatives by well-intentioned protestant landlords made a start but were near-irrelevant to a unionism newly rooted in popular Orangeism. Just as in Northern Ireland in the early twenty-first century, few activists a century ago were so thoroughly liberated from the nationalist and unionist mindset that they sought a future for Ireland based on social justice irrespective of the constitutional outcomes. Languages of compromise and conciliation were always underpinned by standard unionist and nationalist ends.[62] The instability created by the Ulster crisis and compounded by the

---

[60] Eoin MacNeill, 'Shall Ireland be Divided?' in *Tracts for the Times* no. 2 (Dublin, 1915?).

[61] Charles Townshend, *Political Violence in Ireland: Government and Resistance since 1848* (Oxford, 1983), pp 287–8.

[62] Today, Sinn Féin and the Democratic Unionist Party garner an ever-greater share of the total vote ostensibly because of immediate political pressures but more fundamentally

Great War undermined home rule discipline creating a sense of enlarged political possibility.

In 1915 Pim asked what lessons Emmet held for the current generation. Emmet, Pim argued,

> knew that as the martyrs have nourished and strengthened the church with their blood, so martyrs to nationality can nourish and strengthen and save from disaster the nation for which they die. Indeed, in his last moments he must have wondered whether he and the men whom he surely knew would follow him – the men of '48 and '67 and 1915 – could by their unselfish love of Ireland cause our nation to take the right road when the terrible moment of her danger came, as full surely he knew it would come.[63]

Historians have associated this sort of rhetoric most closely with Patrick Pearse and his extraordinarily powerful last speeches and writings. But as this book has shown, it had been one of the dominant modes of Irish nationalist expression since 1882, if not before. Yet, as P. J. Hoctor's late interventions threw into sharp relief, things were greatly changed. Later in the same pamphlet Pim lamented that one

> of the tragedies of greatness in Irish patriotism is that the hero becomes a victim sacrificed and re-sacrificed on the unpatriotic altars of countless West Briton debating societies. He becomes a text for men who are always spell bound at the magnificence of their own oratory![64]

Again and again advanced nationalists were angered by constitutionalist attempts to possess the separatist tradition, again and again they were frustrated by inaction, but small literary societies – rarely of a 'West British' complexion – chewing over the significance of men such as Emmet, provided the basis of the rethinking of Irish separatism during home rule's long ascendancy. Redmond, Griffith argued (according to Pim), had missed the historic opportunity the outbreak of war afforded to demand repeal of the union. Consequently, Pim suggested, historians 'fifty years hence' would see 1914 as 'the most tragic year in Ireland's history'. Parnell would have taken the right road and demanded separation. That lump of Wicklow granite in Glasnevin cemetery, its uneven surface deeply etched with the single word Parnell, powerfully symbolises how the lost leader continued to function in Irish nationalist rhetoric. His inscrutableness, ultimately that blankness, allowed all sorts of meaning to be attached to his name. For the separatists, the Parnell myth, above all, now functioned to highlight the inadequacies of Redmond.

---

because the abandoning of the centre ground is again acceptable owing to the cessation of republican and loyalist terrorism.
[63] Newman [Pim], 'What Emmet Means in 1915', p. 4.
[64] Ibid., p. 13.

All was not lost, however, for Redmond's political failure thinly disguised more significant tendencies at work in the Irish population. In the same essay, Pim asserted the 'certain fact' that in 1914 the Irish 'language and its influence saved the country from becoming completely insane'. As has been shown, the Young Ireland Societies taught that there was more to nationhood than the achievement of a particular constitutional status. According to Pim this lesson had been learnt, for cultural nationalism – the political dimension of the language movement – had protected the nation from the meretricious temptations of political compromise. Pim implied that home rule could be recognised as a step in the right direction providing the fundamental integrity of Ireland was preserved. That home rule was impossible was Ireland's tragedy, that Ireland did not accept partition was its saving grace. 'Imperialism met the Irish language activity', Pim exclaimed, 'and the Irish language won!'[65]

Since 1916 great efforts have been made to understand what made the agony of that famous Easter. Just as R. V. Comerford argued that the first generation of Fenians were 'not answering the call of any inexorable national spirit',[66] so must the same be said of the rebels of 1916. When Comerford wrote, this was not a radical historiographical claim – the literature on nationalism, the 'invention' of the nation, 'imagined communities', and so forth had done its job. Some twenty years later, this is not even a particularly radical claim to make outside of the academy, particularly in the 'new' Ireland. More than this, as part of the attempts at mutual understanding between the nationalist and unionist communities in Northern Ireland that have driven the recent peace process, historians have become readier to admit without condoning the personal bravery displayed by Irish nationalist revolutionaries and to take their ideology seriously.[67] Taking ideology seriously, as a historian, does not necessarily mean to schematise and critique as a political scientist might, though this is a valuable intellectual endeavour, but to think about how ideologies evolve in particular contexts, how they form part of popular understanding of a situation, and how these ideas form part of the constellation of factors that generate actions. Political ideologies emerge in response to the concatenation of specific circumstances and the readily available pool of political ideas; their function is to make sense of the world, and in doing so description and prescription form an organic unity. Inherently reductive, ideological thinking assumes the totality of a situation can be captured in its formulations, that, in effect, one point of view is all-seeing. And as this study has attempted to show, political ideas gain authority less through the distribution of sustained theoretical writings and more through continual popular exposure to powerful ideas and slogans. Advanced nationalist

---

[65] Ibid., pp 5–7.
[66] R. V. Comerford, *The Fenians in Context* (Dublin, 1985), p. 249.
[67] The most prominent example of this tendency is Richard English, *Armed Struggle: The History of the IRA* (London, 2003).

propaganda was effective less because it described to a particular group their lived reality than because continual exposure to these ideas came to shape how that reality was perceived.

The same effort needs to be made for the rebels of Easter 1916 – and the readiness with which very distinguished historians adopt a contemptuous tone when referring to their leadership is not helpful. The 'minority of a minority', those 900-plus individuals, embarked on an extraordinary mission. Vainglorious perhaps, but the rebels believed themselves to be acting on the authority of the nation. This nebulous authority had in Ireland been given a new substance by cultural revival leaving it seemingly more legitimate than the formal version emitting from Dublin Castle. Recognising that 1916–23 was a clash of authorities draws attention to the fact that from 1916 the Irish revolution was to a considerable extent a civil war. And although Irishmen killed Irishmen in 1916 more by accident than design, the enemy were the agents of British authority, setting the precedent for the murder of Irish catholic constabulary-men during the revolutionary war of 1918–21. To suggest that the home rulers were all Dublin Castle loyalists ('Castle catholics') is a grotesque distortion, but the logic of the revolutionary conflict ensured that constitutional nationalists had to choose between revolution, passive neutrality, or identification with the enemy.

III

A. G. Wilson's constructive unionism anticipated an Irish pantheon whose ground plan was a four-leaved shamrock. One leaf would honour those who fought English tyranny (Art McMurrough Kavanagh, the later Geraldines, Shane O'Neill, Hugh Roe O'Donnell, Somhairle Buidhe McDonnell, Lord Edward Fitzgerald), the second those lost to the British crown through English misgovernance (Sarsfield, Lally de Tollendal, Andrew Jackson, Marshall MacMahon, and the 'wild geese'), the third the Irish builders of the British empire (Nicholson, Lawrence, Dufferin, Wellington, Roberts, Hart), and the fourth the builders of Ireland (Columbille, Brian Borumhe, Dean Swift, O'Connell, Lecky, Plunkett). This was an inclusive list of a very particular stamp. It ignored virtually all the heroes of Irish separatism and those of recent constitutionalism (Fitzgerald but not Tone? O'Connell but not Parnell?) and made striking claims on behalf of Britishness and the union: economic development would solve the real problem, which was not the union but the over-mighty English. Wilson's idiosyncratic line-up was implicitly explained elsewhere in his text. Like MacNeill, he believed Irish political identities, far from immutable, were formed in the 1880s. It would take at least a generation for the self-help movement to overcome these absurd sectarian divisions. Nonetheless, he blithely asserted, Ireland had begun a 'bloodless revolution' that the north must embrace to complete:

The dreams [of young men] are concerned with a different vision – there is no dynamite in them, no Marseillaise, no bloody heads on pikes. Irish dreams are now prosaic beside those of bygone days: they are concerned with such matters as the price of tweed, the proper way of feeding cattle, the use of electricity and oil engines, the revival of music and dancing among the people, the reform of the poor law.[68]

Although it is hard to imagine a more wrong-headed, self-congratulatory analysis, it is harder still to believe that Wilson's Queen's audience bought a word of it. Around the same time, Yeats bitterly meditated on the death of 'romantic Ireland' in a poem that captured more closely the mood in Ireland.[69] But the personal agenda of both writers ensured they got things very wrong. The rights and wrongs of the Irish revolution will be debated for some time to come, but it is clear, as O'Hegarty polemicised, that idealism and brutality became entwined, twisting a traumatic pathway. It is equally clear that the radicalisation of Irish nationalism cannot be analysed simply as a dynamic internal to Irish nationalism. Irish responses to the war and the revolutionary violence that followed were in some ways typical: post-war Europe was ravaged by revolution and reaction, by population transfer, and by political violence often hard to distinguish from ethnic and sectarian murder. This period did not expose the Irish as peculiarly violent or foolish – although typicality does not make individuals any less responsible for their actions. Moreover, explanations that isolate Irish developments from unionist obstructionism and the refusal of the British government, over a forty-year period, to facilitate Irish self-determination are near-meaningless. MacNeill's argument that insurrection was 'really impelled by a sense of feebleness or despondency or fatalism or by an instinct of satisfying their own emotion or escaping from a difficult and complex and trying situation' has a great deal of psychological cogency,[70] but this does not change the fact that insurrection worked, rather as Pearse and his co-signatories hoped it would.

Ernie O'Malley's memoir of the revolution gives the most memorable account of a separatist conversion inspired by the insurrection. As he walked through Dublin in the days following Easter Monday he came to identify with the rebels. Places provoked responses: hailed from Trinity, he was attracted by the 'lark' of joining the chaps mounting a defence. A friend pointed out this meant shooting 'fellow Irishmen' and asked what Trinity could mean to him. Impressed by this quiet certainty O'Malley began to question his own lack of loyalties. Before long the bravery of the rebels produced 'faint stirrings of

---

[68] A. G. Wilson, 'Recent History of Ireland: With Special Reference to the Industrial Movement', *The Queen's University of Belfast, University Lectures*, no. 2 (April 1910), pp 28–9.

[69] W. B. Yeats, 'September 1913'.

[70] Memorandum distributed in March 1916, quoted in R. F. Foster, *Modern Ireland, 1600–1972* (London, 1988), p. 480.

sympathy'; a day later he joined a friend, a Gaelic Leaguer, on a night-time sniping mission. Their weapon? A German rifle, a trophy from the western front. James Joyce had made the meandering walk through Dublin a symbol of the city's paralysis, but O'Malley's walks traced the opposite, signposting the psychological journey that carried the young gallant, who had 'laughed and scoffed' at the Volunteers, towards conviction and action, from irony to certainty. Even a walk home had 'changed, changed utterly'. 'In the evening I was in a whirl', he remembered, 'my mind jumped from a snatch of song to a remembered page of economic history.'[71] The meaning and legacy of 1916 would embitter Irish nationalists for generations to come, purist Fenians resenting the political capital reaped by a compromising Sinn Féin. Yet Fenian song had long been conjoined with Sinn Féin ideals and even the most delicate political scalpel could not separate them.

[71] Ernie O'Malley, *On Another Man's Wound* (Dublin, 1936, 2002), pp 34–47.

Bibliography

Manuscript sources

Belfast Central Library

(F. J.) Bigger Collection (OL5)

Cork Archives Institute

(Liam) de Róiste papers (U271/A/1–16)

The National Archives, Dublin

Chief Secretary's Office Registered Papers

Dublin Metropolitan Police files 1882–1891
Each year is represented by a carton of reports.

CBS 'S' Files, Cartons 1–24, 1890–1905
Each carton contains hundreds of numbered and dated individual reports. Particular individuals and themes can be pursued with the help of a card index system, but for the purposes of this research it was necessary to work through the boxes systematically.

Reports of District Inspectors Crime Special (D.I.C.S.) on secret societies and the operation of criminal law and procedure:
3/715/1 Western division
3/715/2 South western division
3/715/3 South eastern division
3/715/4 Midland division
3/715/5 Belfast
3/715/6 Northern division

CBS Précis of reports, 6 cartons

1895–1897 1 Home Office
1898–1900 2 Home Office
1901–1905 3 Home Office
1895–1898 4 R.I.C.
1899–1905 5 R.I.C.
1895–1898 6 D.M.P.
1899–1905

Miscellaneous Police Reports 1882–1921, 5 cartons

The National Library of Ireland, Dublin

(Frederick) Allan Papers (MSS 26755–7)
(Roger) Casement Papers (MSS 13696 / 35203 / 36203 / 36210)
(Michael) Davitt Papers (MSS 913–14)
(Henry) Dixon Papers (MS 3526)
(George) Gavan Duffy Papers (MS 5581)
(Timothy) Harrington Papers (MSS 8576 / 8578 / 8583)
(Bulmer) Hobson Papers (MSS 13158 / 13165 / 13168 / 13171 / 13173–4 / 15168)
(Eoin) MacNeill Papers (MS 10882)
(Maurice) Moore Papers (MS 10561)
(Justin) McCarthy Papers (MSS 3679–714)
(Joseph) McGarrity Papers (MSS 17453 / 17457 / 17612 / 17617 / 17634)
(Leon) Ó Broin Papers (MS 31696)
(John) O'Leary Papers (MS 5927 / 8002–3)
(Francis) Sheehy Skeffington Papers (MS 21611)
Minute books of the Celtic Literary Society (MSS 200 / 19934 (i–ii))
Minute book of the Irish Transvaal Committee (MS 19933)
Minute book of the Leinster Debating Society [from Jan. 1891 Leinster Literary Society] (MS 19935)
Minute book of the Oliver Bond Club, Dublin, 1898–1899 (MS 3730)
Minute book of the Young Ireland Society, 1881–1884 (MS 16095)
Minute book of the Young Ireland Society, 1885–1886 (MS 19158)
Minutes of the editorial committee of the Irish Independent, 1896–1898 (MS 14915)

University College Dublin Archive

(Terence) MacSwiney Papers (P48b–c)

The National Archives, The Public Record Office, Kew

Colonial Office, Irish Papers, series PRO C.O. 904
/10 1882–1884 Investigations regarding secret societies and individuals
/11–14 Oct. 1907 – Aug. 1914
Précis of information and reports relating to the D.M.P. District
/15 1890–1891 Register of Foreign Associations
/16 1890–1893 Register of Home Associations
/17 1890–1898 Register of Suspects (Home A–F) Vol. I
/18 1890–1898 Register of Suspects (Home I–J) Vol. II
/19 1890–98 Register of Suspects (American)
/20 Ireland a Nation (printed extracts from speeches)
/23 Part 1: Sinn Féin Possession and Carrying of Arms 1907 – 1912
    Part 2: Sinn Féin – Volunteer Parades St Patrick's Day 17 March 1916
        Sinn Féin activities meetings etc. 1916
/28 Parts 1–2 1886–1913 Illegal importation and distribution of arms and
    reports of seizures of arms
    Part 4 1916 Arms importations and distribution corres. etc.
/29 Corres. Dec. 1914 re. Seizure of arms addressed to J.E.R. for N.V.

Divisional Commissioners' and County Inspectors' monthly confidential
    prints:
/48 Jan 1892 – June 1893

Northern division:
/49 July 1893 – Aug. 1894
/50 Sept. 1894 – Dec. 1895
/51 Jan. 1896 – June 1897
/52 July – Dec. 1897

South eastern division:
/53 Jan. 1892 – Feb. 1893
/54 Mar. 1893 – Apr. 1894
/55 May 1894 – July 1895
/56 Aug. 1895 – Oct. 1896
/57 Nov. – Dec. 1896

Western division:
/57 June 1894 – Mar. 1895
/58 Apr. 1895 – May 1896
/59 June 1896 – June 1897
/60 July – Dec. 1897

Midland division:
/60 Jan. – Oct. 1892

/61 Nov. 1892 – Oct. 1893
/62 Nov. – Dec. 1893

South western division:
/62 Jan. 1892 – Mar. 1893
/63 May 1893 – Aug. 1894
/64 Sept. 1894 – Dec. 1895
/65 Jan. 1896 – May 1897
/66 June – Dec. 1897

/67 Return of outrages reported to the Constabulary Offices (Printed), 1893–1897.

Inspector-General's and County Inspectors' monthly confidential reports:
/69 Aug. – Dec. 1898
   Jan. 1900
/70 Feb. – June 1900
/71 July – Nov. 1900
/72 Dec. 1900 – May 1901
/73 June – Oct. 1901
/74 Nov. 1901 – Mar. 1902
/75 Apr. – Aug. 1902
/76 Sept. – Dec. 1902
/77 Jan. 1909 – Apr. 1909
/78 May 1909 – Aug. 1909
/79 Sept. 1909 – Dec. 1909
/80 Jan. – Apr. 1910
/81 May – Aug. 1910
/82 Sept. – Dec. 1910
/83 Jan. – Apr. 1911
/84 Apr. – Aug. 1911
/85 Sept. – Dec. 1911
/86 Jan. – May 1912
/87 June – Aug. 1912
/88 Sept. – Dec. 1912
/89 Jan. – Apr. 1913
/90 May – Oct. 1913
/91 Nov. – Dec.1913
/92 Jan. – May 1913
[see below, C.O. 903 reports missing from sequence]
/95 Oct. – Dec. 1914
/96 Jan. – Apr. 1915
/97 May – Aug. 1915
/98 Sept. – Dec. 1915
/99 Jan. – Apr. 1916

/117 Précis of information received by the Special Branch R.I.C.
   Apr. 1905 – Sept. 1906
   Oct. – Dec. 1907
/118 Jan. 1908 – Dec. 1909
/119 Jan. 1910 – Dec. 1913
/120 Jan. 1914 – Oct. 1914

/159 1901–1913 seditious newspapers, leaflets etc. seized
/161 1906–1915 ditto

/172 police pay, appointments etc.

/173 1887–1902 Circulars to the R.I.C. – various

/174 1895–1912 Reports on value of the police in the event of an uprising or invasion and scheme of mobilisation of the R.I.C.

/182 1872–1914 reports armed meetings, agrarianism, street preaching, drilling, importation of arms

/183 1894 [*recte:* 1882] – 1891 Register of informants

/184 1899 Local government elections and notes on individuals in connection with same

/190 Dec. 1898 – *c.* Sept. 1905 Index to correspondence relating to illegal activities
/191 Mar. 1905 – Apr. 1913 ditto

/193–216 Personalities files [on movements of individual activists, primarily useful for post-1914 period]

Colonial Office, series PRO CO 903:
Intelligence Notes:
/1 1885–1892
/2 1887–1892 Misc. series 1–16
/3 1892–1894 Misc. series 1–18
/4 1894–1895 Misc. series 19–35
/5 1895–1897 B. series 1–20
/6 1897–1900 B. series 21–42
/7 1900–1905 W. series 1–10

Chief Secretary's Office – Judicial Division, Intelligence Notes:
/14 1907–1908
/15 1909
/16 1910–1911
/17 1912–1913

Inspector-General's Monthly Confidential Report together with County Inspectors' Reports for the same period:

C.O. 903/93 Apr. 1913 – June 1914
/94 July – Sept. 1914
/95 Oct. – Dec. 1914

Various relevant reports in Home Office series 144, plus H.O. 184/85 Intelligence Notes Mar. – June 1895, and Cabinet [CAB.] papers.

A. J. Balfour (PRO 30/60/1–4) and G. W. Balfour (PRO 30/60/28) Papers

Bodleian Library, Oxford

(James) Bryce Papers (MS 213)
(John) Redmond Papers (Bod. MS Film 1059: N.L.I., MS 15164).

Contemporary newspapers and periodicals

Clare Saturday Record
Cork Examiner
Cork Herald
Derry People and Donegal News
Dublin Evening Herald
Dublin Evening Telegraph
Dublin University Review
Freeman's Journal
Galway Vindicator
Irish Catholic
Irish Daily Independent
Irish Freedom
Irishman
Irish Patriot
Irish Peasant
Irish Republic
Irish Times
Irish Volunteer
Irish Weekly Independent
Kilkenny People
Limerick Echo
Limerick Leader
Munster Express
Nation
Northern Patriot
The Parnellite
Roscommon Herald
Shan Van Vocht

Sinn Féin
The Times
United Ireland
United Irishman
Waterford News
Weekly Freeman
Weekly Nation
Westmeath Guardian
Workers' Republic

Books, pamphlets, articles and theses

Primary sources

Anon., *Incipient Irish Revolution: An Exposé of Fenianism of To-day* (London, 1889).
Clancy, John J., 'The "Castle" System' in *The Irish Question*, no. 5 (London, 1886).
Davitt, Michael, *The Fall of Feudalism in Ireland* (London, 1904).
Gill, T. P., 'The Home Rule Constitutions of the British Empire' in *The Irish Question*, no. 14 (London, 1887).
Griffith, Arthur, *The Resurrection of Hungary: A Parallel for Ireland* (Dublin, 1904).
Hobson, Bulmer, *A Short History of the Irish Volunteers* (Dublin, 1918).
Hopkinson, Michael (ed.), *Frank Henderson's Easter Rising: Recollections of a Dublin Volunteer* (Cork, 1998).
Hyde, Douglas, 'Necessity for De-Anglicising Ireland' in Charles Gavan Duffy, George Sigerson and Douglas Hyde (ed.), *The Revival of Irish Literature* (London, 1894).
Joyce, James, *A Portrait of the Artist as a Young Man* (Oxford, 2000).
Joyce, James, *Dubliners* (Harmondsworth, 1968).
Joyce, James, *Occasional, Critical, and Political Writing* (Oxford, 2000).
Joyce, James, *Ulysses* (Paris, 1922, London, 1992).
Kettle, Tom, 'Would the Hungarian Policy Work?' in *New Ireland Review*, xxii, no. 6 (Feb. 1905).
Lynch, Arthur, *My Life Story* (London, 1924).
Lynd, Robert, 'The Ethics of Sinn Féin' (Limerick, 1910).
MacNeill, Eoin, 'Shall Ireland be Divided?' in *Tracts for the Times*, no. 2 (Dublin, 1915?).
MacSwiney, Terence, *Principles of Freedom* (Dublin, 1921).
Moran, D. P., *The Philosophy of Irish Ireland* (Dublin, 1905).
Nateson, G. A. (ed.), *Speeches of Gopal Krishna Gokhale* (Madras, 1920).
Newman, A. [Pim, H. M.], 'Ascendancy While You Wait' in *Tracts for the Times* (Dublin, 191?).

Newman, A. [Pim, H. M.], 'What Emmet Means in 1915' in *Tracts for the Times* (Dublin, 1915).

O'Brien, R. Barry, *Dublin Castle and the Irish People* (2nd ed., London, 1912).

O'Brien, R. Barry, *The Life of Charles Stewart Parnell* (London, 1898, 1910).

O'Brien, William, *An Olive Branch in Ireland, and its History* (London, 1910).

O'Brien, William and Ryan, Desmond (ed.), *Devoy's Postbag* (Dublin, 1948).

O'Brien, William, *The Irish Revolution and How it Came About* (Dublin, 1923).

O'Brien, William, *When We Were Boys* (London, 1890).

O'Brien, William, '"Who Fears to Speak of Ninety-Eight"' in *Contemporary Review*, lxxiii (Jan. 1898).

Ó Broin, Leon, *No Man's Man: A Biographical Memoir of Joseph Brennan – Civil Servant & First Governor of the Central Bank* (Dublin, 1982).

O'Hegarty, P. S., *Sinn Féin: An Illumination* (Dublin, 1919).

O'Hegarty, P. S., *The Victory of Sinn Féin* (Dublin, 1924).

O'Malley, Ernie, *On Another Man's Wound* (Dublin, 1936, 2002).

O'Leary, John, *Recollections of Fenians and Fenianism* (London, 1896).

O'Sullivan, J. A., 'The True Character of "Ninety-Eight"' in *New Century Review*, iv, no. 24 (Dec. 1898).

Parnell, Anna, *The Tale of a Great Sham* (Dublin, 1986).

Pearse, P. H., *Political Writings and Speeches* (Dublin, 1966).

Pearse, Patrick, 'The Separatist Idea' in *Tracts for the Times*, no. 11 (Dublin, 1916).

Pollard, H. B. C., *The Secret Societies of Ireland: Their Rise and Progress* (London 1922, Kilkenny, 1998).

Redmond, John, 'The Centenary of '98' in *Nineteenth Century*, xliii (1898).

Redmond, John, 'The Chicago Convention' in *The Irish Question*, no. 3 (London, 1886).

Redmond, John, *Historical and Political Addresses* (Dublin,1898).

Redmond, John, 'Ireland since '98' in *North American Review*, clxvi (1898).

Rooney, William, *Poems and Ballads* (Dublin, 1902).

Rooney, William, *Prose Writings* (Dublin, 1909?).

Ryan, Mark, *Fenian Memories* (Dublin, 1945).

Seymour, William Digby, *Home Rule and State Supremacy; or Nationalism Reconciled with Empire* (London, 1888).

Sigerson, George, *Political Prisoners at Home and Abroad* (London, 1890).

Stead, W. T., 'The Topic of the Month: The Centenary of 1798' in *Review of Reviews*, xviii (July 1898).

Sullivan, A. M., *Old Ireland: Reminiscences of an Irish K. C.* (London, 1927).

Sweetman, John, 'The New Spirit' in *New Ireland Review*, xxvii, no. 4 (June 1907).

Tynan, Katherine, *Twenty-five years: Reminiscences* (London, 1913).

Wilson, A. G., 'Recent History of Ireland: With Special Reference to the Industrial Movement', *The Queen's University of Belfast, University Lectures*, no. 2 (April, 1910).

Yeats, W. B., *Autobiographies* (London, 1955).
Yeats, W. B., *Representative Irish Tales* (1891, Gerrards Cross, 1991).

Secondary sources

Anderson, W. K., *James Connolly and the Irish Left* (Blackrock, 1994).
Augusteijn, Joost, *From Public Defiance to Guerrilla Warfare: The Experience of Ordinary Volunteers in the Irish War of Independence* (Dublin, 1996).
Bew, Paul, *Conflict and Conciliation in Ireland 1890–1910: Parnellites and Radical Agrarians* (Oxford, 1987).
Bew, Paul, *C. S. Parnell* (Dublin, 1980).
Bew, Paul, *Ideology and the Irish Question: Ulster Unionism and Irish Nationalism 1912–1916* (Oxford, 1994).
Bew, Paul, *John Redmond* (Dublin, 1996).
Bew, Paul. *Land and the National Question in Ireland, 1858–1882* (Dublin, 1979).
Bourke, Marcus, *John O'Leary: A Study in Irish Separatism* (Tralee, 1967).
Bourke, Richard, *Peace in Ireland: The War of Ideas* (London, 2003).
Boyce, D. George, 'A First World War Transition: State and Citizen in Ireland, 1914–19' in D. George Boyce and Alan O'Day (ed.), *Ireland in Transition, 1867–1921* (London, 2004).
Boyce, D. George, *Nationalism in Ireland* (2nd ed., London, 1991).
Boyce, D. George and O'Day, Alan, *Parnell in Perspective* (London, 1991).
Boyce, D. George (ed.), *The Revolution in Ireland, 1879–1923* (London, 1988).
Brown, Malcolm, *The Politics of Irish Literature* (Chatham, 1972).
Bruscher, J. S., *Consecrated Thunderbolt: Father Yorke of San Francisco* (Hawthorne, N. J., 1973).
Bull, Philip, 'A Fatal Disjunction, 1898–1905: Sinn Féin and the United Irish League' in Rebecca Pelan (ed.), *Irish–Australian Studies: Papers of the Seventh Irish–Australian Conference* (Sydney, 1994).
Bull, Philip, *Land, Politics and Nationalism: A Study of the Irish Land Question* (Dublin, 1996).
Bull, Philip, 'The Fall of Parnell: The Political Context of his Intransigence' in D. George Boyce (ed.), *The Revolution in Ireland, 1879–1923* (London, 1988).
Bull, Philip, 'The Formation of the United Irish League, 1898–1900: The Dynamics of Irish Agrarian Agitation' in *I.H.S.*, xxxiii, no. 132 (Nov. 2003).
Bull, Philip, 'The United Irish League and the Reunion of the Irish Parliamentary Party, 1898–1900' in *I.H.S.*, xxvi, no. 101 (May 1988).
Callanan, Frank, '"In the Name of God and of the Dead Generations": Nationalism and Republicanism in Ireland' in Richard English and Joseph Morrison Skelly (ed.), *Ideas Matter: Essays in Honour of Conor Cruise O'Brien* (Dublin, 1998).

Callanan, Frank, *T. M. Healy* (Cork, 1996).

Callanan, Frank, *The Parnell Split 1890–1* (Cork, 1992).

Campbell, Fergus, *Land and Revolution: Nationalist Politics in the West of Ireland 1891–1921* (Oxford, 2005).

Campbell, Fergus, 'The Social Dynamics of Nationalist Politics in the West of Ireland' no. in *Past & Present*, 182 (Feb. 2004).

Chatterjee, Partha, *Nationalist Thought and the Colonial World: A Derivative Discourse?* (London, 1986).

Clarke, Sam, 'The Social Composition of the Land League' in *I.H.S.*, xvii, no. 68 (Sept. 1971).

Clifford, Brendan, *James Connelly: An Adventurous Socialist* (Cork, 1984).

Comerford, R. V., 'Patriotism as Pastime: The Appeal of Fenianism in the Mid-1860s' in *I.H.S.*, xxii (1981).

Comerford, R. V., *The Fenians in Context* (Dublin, 1985).

Corfe, Tom, *The Phoenix Park Murders* (London, 1968).

Cronin, Maura, *Country, Class or Craft? The Politicisation of the Skilled Artisan in Nineteenth-Century Cork* (Cork, 1994).

Cronin, Sean, *The McGarrity Papers: Revelations of the Irish Revolutionary Movement in Ireland and America 1900–1940* (Tralee, 1972).

Crossman, Virginia, *Local Government in Nineteenth-century Ireland* (Belfast, 1994).

Curtis, L. P., *Coercion and Conciliation in Ireland, 1800–1892: A Study in Conservative Unionism* (Princeton, 1963).

Dangerfield, George, *The Strange Death of Liberal England* (1935, Stanford, 1997).

D'Arcy, Fergus A., 'Unemployment Demonstrations in Dublin, 1879–1882' in *Saothar*, 17 (1992).

Davis, Richard, *Arthur Griffith and Non-Violent Sinn Féin* (Dublin, 1974).

Denman, Terence, '"The Red Livery of Shame": The Campaign Against Army Recruitment in Ireland, 1899–1914' in *I.H.S.*, xxix, no. 114 (Nov. 1994).

Dudley Edwards, Owen, *The Mind of an Activist: James Connelly* (Dublin, 1971).

Dudley Edwards, Ruth, *Patrick Pearse: The Triumph of Failure* (Dublin, 1977, 1990).

English, Richard, *Armed Struggle: The History of the IRA* (London, 2003).

Farry, Michael, *The Aftermath of Revolution: Sligo 1921–23* (Dublin, 2000).

Fitzpatrick, David, *Harry Boland's Irish Revolution* (Cork, 2003).

Fitzpatrick, David, 'Militarism in Ireland, 1900–1922' in Thomas Bartlett and Keith Jeffery (ed.), *A Military History of Ireland* (Cambridge, 1996).

Fitzpatrick, David, *Politics and Irish Life 1913–1921: Provincial Experience of War and Revolution* (Cork, 1977, 1998).

Fitzpatrick, David, 'The Geography of Irish Nationalism 1910–1921' in *Past & Present*, no. 78 (Feb. 1978).

Fitzpatrick, David, *The Two Irelands 1912–1939* (Oxford, 1998).

Foster, R. F., *Modern Ireland, 1600–1972* (London, 1988).

Foster, R. F., *The Story of Ireland* (Oxford, 1995).

Foster, R. F., 'Thinking from Hand to Mouth: Anglo-Irish Literature, Gaelic Nationalism and Irish Politics in the 1890s' in *Paddy and Mr Punch: Connections in Irish and English History* (London, 1993).

Foster, R. F., *W. B. Yeats: A Life. I: The Apprentice Mage* (Oxford, 1997).

Gailey, Andrew, *The Death of Kindness: The Experience of Constructive Unionism, 1890–1905* (Cork, 1987).

Garvin, Tom, 'Great Hatred, Little Room: Social Background and Political Sentiment Among Revolutionary Activists in Ireland, 1890–1922' in D. George Boyce (ed.), *The Revolution in Ireland, 1879–1923* (London, 1988).

Garvin, Tom, *Nationalist Revolutionaries in Ireland, 1858–1928* (Oxford, 1987).

Garvin, Tom, *The Evolution of Irish Nationalist Politics* (Dublin, 1981).

Glandon, Victoria, *Arthur Griffith and the Advanced-Nationalist Press, 1900–1922* (New York, 1985).

Golway, Terry, *Irish Rebel: John Devoy and America's Fight for Ireland's Freedom* (New York, 1998).

Gould, Warwick, Kelly, John and Toomey, Deidre (ed.), *The Collected Letters of W. B. Yeats, Vol. II 1896–1900* (Oxford, 1997).

Greaves, C. Desmond, *Liam Mellows and the Irish Revolution* (London, 1971).

Green, E. H. H., 'The Political Economy of Empire, 1880–1914' in Andrew Porter (ed.), *Oxford History of the British Empire. Volume III: The Nineteenth Century* (Oxford, 1999).

Guinness, Selina, 'Ireland through the Stereoscope: Reading the Cultural Politics of Theosophy in the Irish Literary Revival' in Betsey Taylor Simmons and James H. Murphy (ed.), *The Irish Revival Reappraised* (Dublin, 2004).

Gwyn, Denis, *The Life of John Redmond* (London, 1932).

Gwynn, Stephen, *John Redmond's Last Years* (London, 1919).

Hart, Peter, *The IRA and Its Enemies: Violence and Community in County Cork 1916–1923* (Oxford, 1998).

Hawkins, Richard, 'Government versus Secret Societies: The Parnell Era' in T. Desmond Williams (ed.), *Secret Societies in Ireland* (Dublin, 1973).

Hobson, Bulmer, *Ireland Yesterday and Tomorrow* (Tralee, 1968).

Hoppen, K. Theodore, *Elections, Politics, and Society in Ireland 1832–1885* (Oxford, 1984).

Hutchinson, John, *The Dynamics of Cultural Nationalism: The Gaelic Revival and the Creation of the Irish Nation State* (London, 1987).

Ickringill, Steve J. S., 'Silence and Celebration in Ulster: William McKinlay and the Spanish–American War' in Sylvia L. Hilton and Steve J. S. Ickringill (ed.) *European Perceptions of the Spanish–American War of 1898* (Bern, 1999).

Jackson, Alvin, *Ireland 1798–1998* (Oxford, 1999).

Jackson, John Wyse and Costello, Peter, *John Stanislaus Joyce* (London, 1997).

Jordan, Donald, *Land and Popular Politics in Ireland: County Mayo from the Plantation to the Land War* (Cambridge, 1994).

Jordan, Donald, 'The Irish National League and the "Unwritten Law": Rural Protest and Nation-Building in Ireland 1882–1890' in *Past & Present*, no. 158 (1998).

Kee, Robert, *The Laurel and the Ivy* (London, 1993).

Kelly, John and Domville, Eric (ed.), *The Collected Letters of W. B. Yeats, Volume 1 1865–1895* (Oxford, 1986).

Kelly, Matthew, 'Dublin Fenianism in the 1880s: "The Irish Culture of the Future"?' in *Historical Journal*, 43, no. 3 (2000).

Kelly, Matthew, '"Parnell's Old Brigade": The Redmondite–Fenian Nexus in the 1890s' in *I.H.S.*, xxxiii (Nov. 2002).

Kelly, Matthew, 'The End of Parnellism and the Ideological Dilemmas of Sinn Féin' in D. George Boyce and Alan O'Day (ed.), *Ireland in Transition, 1867–1921* (London, 2004).

Kelly, Matthew, 'The Irish Volunteers: A Machiavellian Moment?', in D. George Boyce and Alan O'Day, *The Ulster Crisis* (London, 2005).

Kelly, Matthew, 'The Politics of Protestant Street Preaching in Ireland in the 1890s' in *Historical Journal*, 48, no. 1 (2005).

Kendle, John, *Ireland and the Federal Solution: The Debates Over the United Kingdom Constitution, 1870–1921* (Kingston and Montreal, 1989).

King, Carla, 'Michael Davitt, Irish Nationalism and the British Empire in the Late Nineteenth Century' in Peter Gray (ed.), *Victoria's Ireland? Irishness and Britishness, 1837–1901* (Dublin, 2004).

Laffan, Michael, 'In Search of Patrick Pearse' in Máirín Ní Dhonnchadha and Theo Dorgan (ed.), *Revising the Rising* (Derry, 1991).

Laffan, Michael, 'John Redmond (1856–1918) and Home Rule', in Brady, Ciaran (ed.), *Worsted in the Game: Losers in Irish History* (Dublin, 1989).

Laffan, Michael, *The Resurrection of Ireland* (Cambridge, 1999).

Lane, Fintan, *The Origins of Modern Irish Socialism 1881–1896* (Cork, 1997).

Larkin, Emmet, *The Fall of Parnell and the Roman Catholic Church in Ireland* (Liverpool, 1979).

Lavelle, Patricia, *James O'Mara: A Staunch Sinn-Féiner 1873–1948* (Dublin, 1961).

Leerssen, Joep, *Remembrance and Imagination* (Cork, 1996).

Le Roux, Louis N., *Tom Clarke and the Irish Freedom Movement* (Dublin, 1936).

Lynch, Diarmund, *The I.R.B. and the 1916 Rising* (Cork, 1951).

Lynch, Pat, *They Hanged John Twiss* (Tralee, 1982, 1983).

Lyons, F. S. L., *Charles Stewart Parnell* (London, 1978).

Lyons, F. S. L, *Culture and Anarchy in Ireland 1890–1939* (Oxford, 1982).

Lyons, F. S. L., *Ireland since the Famine* (London, 1971).

Lyons, F. S. L., *John Dillon* (London, 1968).

Macardle, Dorothy, *The Irish Republic* (4th ed., Dublin, 1951).

MacBride, Lawrence, *The Greening of Dublin Castle: The Transformation of Bureaucratic and Judicial Personnel in Dublin Castle in Ireland, 1892–1922* (Washington, 1991).

McConnel, James, '"The Fenians at Westminster": The Irish Parliamentary Party and the Legacy of the New Departure', *I.H.S.*, xxxiv, 133 (2004).

McConville, Seán, *Irish Political Prisoners, 1848–1922: Theatres of War* (London, 2003).

MacDonagh, Oliver, *States of Mind: A Study of Anglo-Irish Conflict, 1780–1980* (London, 1983).

McGee, Eoin, '"God save Ireland": Manchester Martyr Demonstrations in Dublin 1867–1916' in *Eire-Ireland* (Fall–Winter 2001).

McGee, Owen, 'Frederick James Allan (1861–1937): Fenian and Civil Servant' in *History Ireland*, 10, no. 1 (Spring 2002).

McKibbin, Ross, 'Why was there no Marxism in Britain?' in *Ideologies of Class: Social Relations in Britain 1880–1950* (Oxford, 1990).

Maguire, Martin, 'The Organisation and Activism of Dublin's Protestant Working Class, 1883–1935' in *I.H.S.*, xxix, no. 113 (May 1994).

Mandle, W. F, *The Gaelic Athletic Association and Irish Nationalist Politics 1884–1924* (Dublin, 1987).

Maume, Patrick, *D. P. Moran* (Dundalk, 1995).

Maume, Patrick, *Life that is Exile: Daniel Corkery and the Search for Irish Ireland* (Belfast, 1993).

Maume, Patrick, 'Parnell and the I.R.B. oath' in *I.H.S.*, xxix, no. 115 (May 1995).

Maume, Patrick, 'The Ancient Constitution: Arthur Griffith and his Intellectual Legacy to Sinn Féin' in *Irish Political Studies*, 10 (1995).

Maume, Patrick, *The Long Gestation* (Dublin, 1999).

Maume, Patrick, 'Young Ireland, Arthur Griffith, and Republican Ideology: The Question of Continuity' in *Eire–Ireland*, xxxiv, no. 2 (Summer 1999).

Maye, Brian, *Arthur Griffith* (Dublin, 1997).

Miller, Kerby A., *Emigrants and Exiles: Ireland and the Irish Exodus to North America* (Oxford, 1985).

Mitchell, Arthur, *Labour in Irish Politics, 1890–1930: The Irish Labour Movement in the Age of Revolution* (Dublin, 1974).

Moody, T. W., *Michael Davitt and Irish Revolution* (Oxford, 1981).

Moody, T. W., 'Michael Davitt and the British Labour Movement 1882–1906' in *T.R.H.S*, ser. 5, no. 3 (1953).

Moody, T. W., 'The Fenian Movement in Irish History' in *The Fenian Movement* (Cork, 1968).

Moran, Gerard, 'The Land War, Urban Destitution and Town Tenant Protest, 1879–1882' in *Saothar*, 20 (1995).

Morgan, Austen, *James Connelly: A Political Biography* (Manchester, 1988).

Murphy, James H., *Abject Loyalty: Nationalism and Monarchy in Ireland during the Reign of Queen Victoria* (Cork, 2001).

Murray, A. C., 'Nationality and Local Politics in Late Nineteenth Century Ireland: The Case of County Westmeath' in *I.H.S.*, xxv, no. 98 (Nov. 1986).

Newsinger, John, *Fenianism in Mid-Victorian Britain* (London, 1994).

Novick, Ben, *Conceiving Revolution: Irish Nationalist Propaganda during the First World War* (Dublin, 2001).

Novick, Ben, 'The Arming of Ireland: Gun-running and the Great War, 1914–16' in Adrian Gregory and Senia Pašeta (ed.) *Ireland and the Great War. 'A War to Unite Us All'?* (Manchester, 2002).

O'Brien, Conor Cruise, *Parnell and his Party, 1880–1890* (Oxford, 1957).

O'Brien, Joseph V., *'Dear Dirty Dublin': A City in Distress, 1899–1916* (Los Angeles, 1982).

O'Brien, Joseph V., *William O'Brien and the Course of Irish Politics 1881–1918* (Los Angeles, 1976).

Ó Broin, Leon, *Dublin Castle and the 1916 Rising* (Dublin, 1966).

Ó Broin, Leon, *Revolutionary Underground: The Story of the Irish Republican Brotherhood 1858–1924* (Dublin, 1976).

O'Callaghan, Margaret, *British High Politics and a Nationalist Ireland* (Cork, 1994).

O'Callaghan, Margaret, '"With the Eyes of Another Race, of a People once Hunted Themselves": Casement, Colonialism and a Remembered Past' in D. George Boyce and Alan O'Day (ed.), *Ireland in Transition, 1867–1921* (London, 2004).

Ó Catháin, Máirtín, 'Fenian Dynamite: Dissident Irish Republicans in late Nineteenth-Century Scotland' in Oonagh Walsh (ed.), *Ireland Abroad: Politics and Profession in the Nineteenth Century* (Dublin, 2003).

O'Day, Alan, *The English Face of Irish Nationalism: Parnellite Involvement in British Politics, 1880–1886* (Dublin, 1977).

Ó Duibhir, Ciarán, *Sinn Féin: The First Election 1908* (Manorhamilton, 1983).

O'Hegarty, P. S., *A History of Ireland under the Union* (London, 1952).

O'Keefe, Timothy J., 'The 1898 Efforts to Celebrate the United Irishmen: The '98 Centennial' in *Eire–Ireland*, 23 (1988).

O'Keefe, Timothy J., '"Who Fears to Speak of '98?": The Rhetoric and Rituals of the United Irishmen Centennial, 1898' in *Eire–Ireland*, 28 (1992).

O'Rahilly, Aodogán, *Winding the Clock: O'Rahilly and the 1916 Rising* (Dublin, 1991).

Pašeta, Senia, *Before the Revolution: Nationalism, Social Change and Ireland's Catholic Elite, 1879–1922* (Cork, 1999).

Pašeta, Senia, 'Ireland's Last Home Rule Generation: The Decline of Constitutional Nationalism in Ireland, 1916–30' in Mike Cronin and John M. Regan (eds), *Ireland: The Politics of Independence, 1922–49* (London, 2000).

Pašeta, Senia, 'Nationalist Responses to Two Royal Visits to Ireland, 1900 and 1903' in *I.H.S.*, xxxi, no. 124 (Nov. 1999).

Pašeta, Senia, '1798 in 1898: The Politics of Commemoration' in *Irish Review*, 22 (1998).

Pašeta, Senia, 'Thomas Kettle: "An Irish Soldier in the Army of Europe"?' in Adrian Gregory and Senia Pašeta (ed.), *Ireland and the Great War: 'A War to Unite Us All'?* (Oxford, 2002).

Phoenix, Eamon, *Northern Nationalism: Nationalist Politics, Partition and the Catholic Minority in Northern Ireland 1890–1940* (Belfast, 1994).

Porter, Bernard, *The Origins of the Vigilant State: The London Metropolitan Police Special Branch before the First World War* (London, 1987).

Ranelagh, John O'Beirne, 'The Irish Republican Brotherhood in the Revolutionary Period, 1879–1923' in D. George Boyce (ed.), *Revolution in Ireland, 1879–1923* (London, 1988).

Regan, John, *The Irish Counter-Revolution 1921–1936* (Dublin, 1999).

Robinson, Lennox, *Bryan Ricco Cooper* (Dublin, 1931).

Rolleston, C. H., *Portrait of an Irishman: A Biographical Sketch of T. W. Rolleston* (London, 1939).

Ryan, Desmond, *James Connelly: His Life Work and Writings* (Dublin, 1924).

Ryan, Desmond, *The Phoenix Flame* (London, 1937).

Sen, M. K., *Robert Lynd: Son of Eire* (New Delhi, 1992).

Sheehy, Ian, 'T. P. O'Connor and *The Star*, 1886–90' in D. George Boyce and Alan O'Day (ed.) *Ireland in Transition, 1867–1921* (London, 2004).

Short, K. R. M., *The Dynamite War* (Dublin, 1979).

Smith, Anthony D., *Nationalism in the Twentieth Century* (Oxford, 1979).

Thornley, David, *Isaac Butt and Home Rule* (London, 1964).

Tierney, Michael, 'Dr Croke, the Irish Bishops and the Parnell Crisis, 18 Nov. 1890 – 21 April 1891' in *Collectanea Hibernica*, 11 (1968).

Tierney, Michael, *Eoin MacNeill: Scholar and Man of Action, 1867–1945* (Oxford, 1980).

Toomey, Deirdre, 'Who Fears to Speak of Ninety-eight?' in Warwick Gould (ed.), *Yeats and the Nineties: Yeats Annual*, 14 (London, 2001).

Townshend, Charles, *Political Violence in Ireland: Government and Resistance since 1848* (Oxford, 1983).

Vaughan, W. E. (ed.), *A New Oxford History of Ireland VI: Ireland Under the Union II: 1870–1921* (Oxford, 1996).

Walker, Brian M., *Parliamentary Election Results in Ireland, 1801–1922* (Dublin, 1978).

Warwick-Haller, Sally, *William O'Brien and the Irish Land War* (Dublin, 1990).

Wheatley, Michael, 'John Redmond and Federalism in 1910' in *I.H.S.*, xxxii, no. 127 (May 2001).

Wheatley, Michael, *Nationalism and the Irish Party: Provincial Ireland 1910–1916* (Oxford, 2005).

Wheatley, Michael, '"These Quiet Days of Peace": Nationalist Opinion before the Home Rule Crisis, 1909–1013' in D. George Boyce and Alan O'Day (ed.), *Ireland in Transition, 1867–1921* (London, 2004).

Williams, Robin Harcourt (ed.), *Salisbury–Balfour Correspondence* (Cambridge, 1988).

Yeates, Pádraig, *Lockout Dublin 1913* (Dublin, 2000).

Unpublished theses

Anderson, David, 'The Irish Independent Printing and Publishing Company, 1891–1900', M.A., Edinburgh, 1976.

Barrett, Richard, 'The Politics and Political Character of the Parnellite Party, 1891–99', M.A., University College, Dublin, 1983.

Campbell, Fergus J. M., 'Land and Politics in Connacht, 1898–1909', Ph.D., 1996.

d'Alton, Ian, 'Southern Irish Unionism: A Study of Cork City and County Unionists, 1885–1914', M.A., University College, Cork, 1972.

Keown, Gerard, 'The Ideas and Developments of Irish Foreign Policy from the Origins of Sinn Féin to 1932', D.Phil., Oxford, 1997.

Kinsella, Anna, 'The Nineteenth Century Interpretation of 1798', M.Litt., Trinity College, Dublin, 1992.

Levitas, J. B. A., 'Irish Theatre and Cultural Nationalism, 1890–1916', D.Phil., Oxford, 1997.

McConnel, James, 'The View from the Backbench: Irish Nationalist M.P.s and their Work, 1910–1914', Ph.D., Durham, 2002.

O'Neill, Shane, 'The Politics of Culture in Ireland, 1899–1910', D.Phil., Oxford, 1982.

Index

CPSIA information can be obtained
at www.ICGtesting.com
Printed in the USA
BVHW050021210123
656721BV00008B/863